DEVELOPMENT OF
DIGITAL LIBRARIES

Recent Titles in
Contributions in Librarianship and Information Science

The Myth of the Electronic Library: Librarianship and Social Change in America
William F. Birdsall

Academic Libraries: Their Rationale and Role in American Higher Education
Gerard B. McCabe and Ruth J. Person, editors

The Closing of American Library Schools: Problems and Opportunities
Larry J. Ostler, Therrin C. Dahlin, and J. D. Willardson

Innovation and the Library: The Adoption of New Ideas in Public Libraries
Verna L. Pungitore

The Impact of Emerging Technologies on Reference Service and Bibliographic Instruction
Gary M. Pitkin, editor

Brief Tests of Collection Strength: A Methodology for All Types of Libraries
Howard D. White

Censorship and the American Library: The American Library Association's Response to Threats to Intellectual Freedom, 1939–1969
Louise S. Robbins

Librarianship and Legitimacy: The Ideology of the Public Library Inquiry
Douglas Raber

Scholarly Book Reviewing in the Social Sciences and Humanities: The Flow of Ideas Within and Among Disciplines
Ylva Lindholm-Romantschuk

Libraries, Immigrants, and the American Experience
Plummer Alston Jones, Jr.

Preparing the Information Professional: An Agenda for the Future
Sajjad ur Rehman

The Role and Impact of the Internet on Library and Information Services
Lewis-Guodo Liu, editor

DEVELOPMENT OF DIGITAL LIBRARIES

An American Perspective

Edited by Deanna B. Marcum

Foreword by Kakugyo S. Chiku

Contributions in Librarianship and
Information Science, Number 95

GREENWOOD PRESS
Westport, Connecticut • London

Library of Congress Cataloging-in-Publication Data

Development of digital libraries : an American perspective / edited by Deanna B. Marcum ; foreword by Kakugyo S. Chiku.
    p. cm.—(Contributions in librarianship and information science, ISSN 0084–9243 ; no. 95)
    Papers presented from 1994 to 1998 at the Kanazawa Institute of Technology (KIT) International Roundtable on Library and Information Science.
    Includes bibliographical references and index.
    ISBN 0–313–31478–0 (alk. paper)
    1. Digital libraries—United States—Congresses.   2. Digital libraries—Congresses.
    3. Libraries—Special collections—Electronic information resources—Congresses.
    I. Marcum, Deanna B.   II. Kanazawa Institute of Technology International Roundtable for Information and Library Science.   III. Series.
    ZA4082.U6D48   2001
    025'.00285—dc21   2001018219

British Library Cataloguing in Publication Data is available.

Library of Congress Catalog Card Number: 2001018219
ISBN: 0–313–31478–0
ISSN: 0084–9243

First published in 2001

Greenwood Press, 88 Post Road West, Westport, CT 06881
An imprint of Greenwood Publishing Group, Inc.
www.greenwood.com

Printed in the United States of America

The paper used in this book complies with the
Permanent Paper Standard issued by the National
Information Standards Organization (Z39.48–1984).

10 9 8 7 6 5 4 3 2 1

Copyright Acknowledgments

Portions of Chapter 8 originally appeared in Okerson, Ann, and James O'Donnell, eds. 1995. *Scholarly Journals at the Crossroads: A Subversive Proposal for Electronic Publishing*. An Internet Discussion About Scientific and Scholarly Journals and Their Future. Washington, D.C.: Association for Research Libraries. Available from: http://www.arl.org/scomm/subversive/. Reprinted by permission of Ann Okerson.

Portions of Chapter 19 are reprinted with permission from Wilson, Jack W. 1994. The CUPLE Physics Studio. *The Physics Teacher* 32 (December): 518. Copyright 1994, American Association of Physics Teachers.

Contents

Figures and Tables   ix

Foreword *by Kakugyo S. Chiku*   xi

Preface   xv

I. Perspectives on the Library in the Twenty-First Century   1

1. Scholarship, Information, and Libraries in the Electronic Age   3
   Stanley Chodorow

2. The Impact of Information Technologies on the Role of
   Research Libraries in Teaching and Learning in the
   United States   16
   Elaine Sloan

3. The Life of the Mind in a World Transformed by Networks
   and Digital Libraries   26
   Paul Evan Peters

4. What's Happening to the Book?   40
   Richard A. Lanham

5. The Impact of Digital Technology on Libraries: A Chaotic
   Revolution   49
   Jerry D. Campbell

6. The Future Value of Digital Information and Digital Libraries   63
   Michael Lesk

II. Meeting the Challenges of the Digital Library   83

7. The Library as Provider of Digital Resources for Teaching
    and Scholarship   85
    Ann J. Wolpert

8. Can We Afford Digital Information? Libraries? An Early
    Assessment of Economic Prospects for Digital Publications   95
    Ann B. Okerson

9. Intellectual Property Policy for an Information Society   109
    Peter Lyman

10. The Uses of Digital Libraries: Some Technological, Political,
    and Economic Considerations   127
    Donald J. Waters

11. Digital Preservation: An Update   148
    Deanna B. Marcum

12. The Impact of Digital Libraries on Library Staffing and
    Education   155
    Rachael K. Anderson

13. Government Records in a Digital World   170
    Peter B. Hirtle

14. A View on the Ecology of Information   187
    Brian L. Hawkins

**III. The Digital Library in the Service of Research and
Education: Some Experiences**   211

15. The Library of Congress's National Digital Library:
    Reaching Out to Schools and Libraries through the Internet   213
    Laura Campbell

16. Toward Libraries' Digital Future: The Canadian Digital
    Library Experience   225
    Leigh Swain and Susan Haigh

17. The Future of Libraries and Library Schools   244
    Daniel E. Atkins

18. Redefining the University through Educational and
    Information Technologies: North Carolina State
    University, Its Libraries, and Distance Education   253
    Susan K. Nutter

19. Re-engineering the Undergraduate Curriculum   272
    Jack M. Wilson

20. The Internet Public Library: Development and Future   283
    Joseph W. Janes

21. Public Libraries in the United States: Service to Business
    and Industry   304
    Beverly P. Lynch

22. Prognosis on Becoming Digital: Digital Information, Global
    Networks, and Business Education   316
    William D. Walker

Index   333

About the Contributors   345

Figures and Tables

FIGURES

5.1	Characteristics of the Current Library Environment	58
6.1	Library Economics	76
14.1	Library Buying Power, 1980–2010	190
14.2	Arithmetic versus Geometric Growth	191
14.3	Overshoot and Collapse Model	193
14.4	Overshoot and Oscillation Model	193
14.5	Sigmoid Growth Model	194
14.6	Continuous Growth Model	195
14.7	Collection Size of the Brown University Libraries	204
17.1	A Vision Space for New Knowledge and Work Environments	246
17.2	The Collaboratory Concept	250
20.1	Design Template for the Internet Public Library	297

TABLES

6.1	Information Vendors, 1993	67
6.2	Text Retrieval Market	68
6.3	Text Search Companies	69
9.1	A Model of Analog and Digital Formats	118

Foreword

This book is a collection of papers on the digital library presented from 1994 to 1998 at the Kanazawa Institute of Technology (KIT) International Roundtable on Library and Information Science. The KIT International Roundtable, initiated in 1994, has a prehistory. KIT abolished its conventional library in 1982, and the Kanazawa Institute of Technology Library Center was established. It was the first library in Japan to computerize all library management, from acquisition to circulation to information retrieval. In addition, the library was equipped with a robot system to deliver audiovisual information on demand (the first such system in the world). The library adopted other novel approaches to service, such as a system called "subject librarians," by which the faculty were mobilized to plan and develop the library's activities.

When the Technology Library Center was established, no commercial library automation systems existed; KIT had to develop its own. The computerization of the library removed various constraints on its architecture and design. The library's space became more user-friendly and the design was unique. I believe that it was one of most advanced libraries in the world at that time.

The mind behind the creation of this unique library was Yasushi Sakai, former deputy librarian of the National Diet Library and one of Japan's most distinguished librarians of all time. Throughout his brilliant career in the National Diet Library, he upheld the importance of international exchange for both Japanese and Western libraries. He was among the few people who consistently promoted such exchange and put it into action in the Japanese library arena.

In planning for the establishment of the KIT Library Center, Sakai asked for recommendations and advice from several distinguished international librarians such as Foster E. Mohrhardt, former president of the American Library Association (ALA); Warren J. Haas, former president of the Council on Library Resources; William J. Welsh, former deputy librarian of the Library of Congress; and Jay K. Lucker, former director of libraries at the Massachusetts Institute of Technology. All were his friends. Their recommendations and advice proved to be a great help for the creation of this unique library. Their counsel also convinced him that it was essential for Japanese and Western librarians to have an opportunity to exchange views on issues of common concern for improving library practice and information services.

When Sakai became the director of the newly established KIT Library Center, he decided to create an annual international conference titled "The KIT International Seminar for Library and Information Science." The International Seminar was held 11 times from 1982 to 1992, during which time 40 distinguished librarians from the United States and Europe were invited as the speakers. The International Seminar was highly regarded in Japan not only because it was the sole international conference of its kind to be held regularly in the country, but also because of its substance. The seminar stimulated the Japanese library world and greatly influenced the Western library world's understanding of Japanese libraries. In 1993, KIT published a volume of selected papers from the seminar, edited by William Welsh, entitled *Research Libraries—Yesterday, Today, and Tomorrow.*

The KIT International Seminar ended with Sakai's death in 1992. Toshio Izumiya, chairman of KIT, believed that the conference should be continued and urged the KIT Library Center to do so. Following his recommendation, we initiated the KIT International Roundtable for Information and Library Science in 1994. We set the aim of the roundtable as follows. First, the conference was to serve as a forum in which Japanese and Western librarians could exchange their views and discuss issues in the practice of library and information technology. Second, to keep the discussions from being discursive, the conference was to focus on the most current and advanced topics in library practice—that is, digital library issues. Third, for the benefit of the Japanese participants, the conference was to focus less on information technology and more on how to create aggressive information services by mobilizing current information technology. Fourth, the conference was to provide a venue for Western librarians to understand the library culture in Japan.

It goes without saying that to achieve these objectives, the most important matter is planning the agenda for each conference. Thus, a planning committee for the roundtable was formed in 1993, in Washington, D.C. Its members include Warren J. Haas, William J. Welsh, and Jay K. Lucker; Duane Webster, executive director of Association of Research Libraries; Hans-Peter Geh, honorary president of the International Federation of

Library Associations and Institutions (IFLA); Millicent D. Abell, former director of libraries at Yale University; Deanna B. Marcum, president of the Council on Library and Information Resources; Koshiro Moroya, assistant director of the KIT Library Center; and myself. This committee receives and discusses requests from the Japanese side about conference topics, sets the theme and topics of the roundtables, selects the most appropriate speakers for each topic, and settles the agenda. This international planning apparatus enables the roundtable to keep the agenda consistent, coherent, and farsighted.

The KIT International Roundtable was held six times in the 1990s. The conference has greatly influenced the establishment, practice, and implementation of the digital library in Japan. Generally speaking, the digital library is still being developed in Japan, and the ideas discussed at the roundtable will continue to influence its development. Because mutual understanding in the international library world will continue to be important, the KIT Library Center will continue to host the roundtable well into the future.

In the field of information technology, change and innovation are rapid; new ideas can quickly become outdated or obsolete. As such, some of the content in this volume may already be viewed as outdated. However, if this is the case, the papers testify to the enormous change in digital library activities since 1994, and it will be possible to say that they have gained importance in documenting the evolution of the digital library.

It is my great pleasure that, in this volume, Dr. Deanna B. Marcum has made the presentations of the recent roundtables available to Western readers. It completes the mission of the roundtable in terms of international exchange. I am most grateful to the members of the planning committee of the KIT roundtable, especially to Dr. Marcum, for leading the conference to its success.

Kakugyo S. Chiku
Director, Kanazawa Institute
of Technology Library Center

Preface

For the past 18 years, KIT has hosted seminars and roundtables that bring American (and on occasion, international) librarians and educators to meet with academic, special, and public librarians, publishers, and industry representatives across Japan, and to discuss important issues and trends that confront libraries everywhere.

The theme of this volume is the development of digital libraries. Since 1995, the KIT International Roundtable has been devoted to some aspect of this theme, beginning with the early explorations of what is meant by the term "digital library." In later sessions, there has been a greater emphasis on lessons learned from some of the early experiments in digital library development.

The essays in this volume are not in chronological order. Rather, they are grouped into three parts. Part I places digital libraries in the context of higher education and other library services; Part II addresses the challenges posed by digital libraries; and Part III documents practical experiences of major institutions as they launched digital library initiatives. Taken together, these papers, though originally prepared for a Japanese audience, chronicle the development of digital libraries in major research institutions in the United States.

The American-Japanese ties in the library community have grown strong over the last 18 years. The principals of the early seminars, Dr. Yasushi Sakai and Mr. Foster Mohrhardt, both died in 1992. Since then, Professor Kakugyo Chiku, director of the Kanazawa Institute of Technology, and Mr. Koshiro Moroya, assistant director, have proudly and ably carried on with the work the two founders began nearly two decades ago. It is my pleasure to chair the advisory committee that selects the American participants in the annual roundtable. I value both the professional connections and the personal friendships that have developed over the years.

PART I

Perspectives on the Library
in the Twenty-First Century

CHAPTER 1

Scholarship, Information, and Libraries in the Electronic Age

STANLEY CHODOROW

My purpose in this paper is to sketch the contours of a revolution in scholarship and information services that is now under way. The exact outcome of this revolution cannot yet be discerned, but its trajectory is fairly clear. We can see the general shape of new bibliographical work, of the collection of knowledge made up of paper and electronic parts, of new methods of teaching and learning, and of the dissolution of "authority" as it is understood by librarians and assumed by scholars. This paper will survey and comment on these elements of the revolution and try to look beyond them.

Only a few years ago I would not have spoken about a "revolution in scholarship and information services." I would have spoken of new scholarly resources and of changes taking place in the library. Now, I think that we must consider a revolutionary change in scholarly exchange and a complete redefinition of the library. The electronic media will change our long-established methods of presenting information and the results of research, and it will fundamentally change a major part, perhaps *the* major part, of the library's function. The place of the library in the world of information will also be fundamentally altered.

Scholarship and information services are two arcs of a circle. The way we construct and present new knowledge is largely determined by the way we get and manage existing information. Good scholarship tells us something new and places it in the context of what we already know. So, the way we establish what is already known and present it in our work depends on the organization of knowledge in library collections, which for hundreds

Paper presented at the International Roundtable for Information and Library Science, Kanazawa Institute of Technology, Library Center, Kanazawa, Japan, 1996.

of years have constituted our principal information system. The organization of knowledge in library collections rests on the formal structure of the scholarly enterprise—the disciplines and topics of research and teaching. For the purpose of this paper, it does not matter where on the circle of scholarship and information services one starts, as long as one gets all the way around the circle. I will start with scholarship.

THE FUTURE CHALLENGES OF SCHOLARSHIP

The questions we answer in our research arise from what we already know. Existing knowledge contains anomalies, gaps, and, in some fields, frontiers that produce questions. Our searches of archives, our experiments, and our theoretical speculations try to answer those questions, and our presentations of discoveries relate the newly found to what is already in hand, which is the only way we can understand and appreciate discoveries.

Contemporary scholarship is data-intensive. This is even true in fields such as the humanities, where the body of information has traditionally been relatively limited and the focus has often been on the way ideas are expressed and information organized by the human intellect. As a historian of medieval Europe (struggling with a mass of writings and records produced during more than one thousand years of the history and culture of a whole continent), I have often envied the classicists, whose entire body of source material could fit on the walls of a moderately sized study. Yet today, even the classicists are generating large bodies of data from this material, applying computer techniques to textual analysis, lexicography, archeological records, and much more. A classical scholar's footnotes no longer point only to a wall of books to which little has been added in the last hundred years. They refer to a wealth of electronically generated and stored data that is growing rapidly. All other fields of knowledge are more extreme versions of classics in this respect.

The question is not merely what kind of information scholars now cite, but also where they find it and whether they can use it. In many fields there is a rapidly growing body of information that never gets into the library. Scholars generate it and make it available on the Internet. Finding such information may be a haphazard process, because it has not been registered in any official repository of information. It is just "out there." Moreover, any particular collection of such unregistered electronic data is kept up-to-date for as long as its makers or caretakers are paying attention to it. When people cease to work on it, it rapidly deteriorates or perhaps even disappears from the electronic network.

I recently saw an article about databases on proteins that have been maintained by European scholars with the support of grants from the Swiss government. The government is now shifting its interest, and there is an urgent search for scientists and funding agencies to maintain the databases.

Nobel Prize winners and many other leading scientists are publicly calling for a savior, citing the importance of the databases for basic research. The problem is not merely that the database projects will be abandoned, to lie on a library shelf until someone picks them up and brings them up-to-date. The problem is that electronic information resources cannot be used or even found unless someone maintains them on a machine with links to the Internet. (There are also significant preservation issues that I will discuss later.)

Even when efforts to preserve important electronic sources of information are successful, the databases will often be passed from one scholar to another, so that the electronic address changes. Such migration of information sources will present difficulties for scholarship, but migration is a small problem compared to the principal characteristic of electronic information sources: they are alive.

The printed book or periodical contains information in frozen form. The electronic database changes or can change continually. Many people I have talked to about this characteristic of the new information resources have responded as if I were missing something. They point out that electronic information can be put on CD-ROMs, which are just as frozen as printed materials. That is true, but it is also treating the new information format as if it were the old one. Neither the makers nor the users of information will long resist or stand for the keeping of information in a solid state when its natural state is liquid. We lose very important aspects of the electronic revolution if we keep it in deep freeze.

In the electronic age, information will flow as it did in the age before publishers, and eventually authors, created the idea of intellectual property. In the Middle Ages, works of literature—history, theology, law, medicine, and literature in the strict sense—grew and changed from writer to writer. The great glosses on the Bible and on the foundational texts of law, medicine, theology, and philosophy were composite works put together from the works of many teachers and scholars. The glosses eventually achieved a standard, or vulgate, state but they evolved for a long period before doing so. Chroniclers, too, used earlier works and continued or enhanced them. All of these kinds of medieval works grew organically from generation to generation. What was significant about them was not who wrote them, but what they contained. Electronic works will experience the same fluid growth and alteration and the same de-emphasis of authorship. This is an age in which ownership of ideas—copyright—can create international trade crises and lead publishing houses to fight the electronic revolution with all their might.

A work of scholarship mounted on the Internet will belong to the field it serves and will be improved by many of its users. Scholar-users will add to the work, annotate it, correct it, and share it with those with whom they are working. All the really important works of scholarship, the works we commonly call "research tools," will quickly evolve into several subspecies in the hands of scholars. An example from my field will give you an idea of what I mean. We historians of medieval canon law distinguish between the French and Bolognese versions of the *Breviarium* of Bernard of Pavia, which evolved from the textbook of papal judicial opinions that Bernard produced about 1191–1192. Will we soon be able to speak of the French, Japanese, and American versions of an electronically transmitted calendar of papal letters? Or will the versions emerge within international circles representing different kinds of users of the letters—the political historians, social historians, and legal historians? The only certainty is that such works will evolve continuously once we begin to take advantage of our new medium for information.

So, how will we construct our footnotes in this brave new age? How will librarians establish the authority of information? How will the individual contributions of scholars be recognized or attributed? How will we reward or judge scholars for the purposes of promotion within the *cursus honorum* of the academy?

The future world of scholarship that I am envisioning is one in which collaboration will become the norm, even in fields that are now the province of sole practitioners. It is also one in which the information used by the teams of scholars will be in liquid form. The electronic format encourages constant change—addition, subtraction, alteration—and its organization is fundamentally different from the one used in printed materials. Right now, much of the material on the Internet is made up of digitized pictures of printed works, which can be cited by chapter, page, and paragraph. When scholars create information resources directly on the Internet, they use a variety of new organizational methods and expect the materials to grow and change constantly, perhaps even to be given a completely new organizational form if someone develops a better way to present the data. We can expect many scholars to resist such fluidity in their information resources, because it will relegate the traditional footnote—to which some of us are inordinately attached—to the dustbin. Over time, however, the tradition of citation will not be able to hinder the evolution of our methods for managing information. Some future edition of the *Chicago Manual of Style* will provide models of citation very different from the ones we use now.

One consequence of this process will be that the usefulness of scholarship will decline more rapidly than it does now. I can use many works published in the sixteenth and seventeenth centuries; they contain valuable information and insights. But occasionally I find a work that cites a source in a way that obscures its identity; such a work has nothing to teach me. The value of a work rests on the amount and accuracy of its citations of sources. In the fluid, electronic world of the future, the information base will evolve and its history will become murky. When the establishment of authority no longer becomes clear or, in some fields, possible, old publications will lose their meaning. One wonders how our successors at the end of the twenty-first century will learn the history of their scholarly disciplines.

This gloomy picture rests on the assumption that scholars will cease to use discrete publications to present their findings and interpretations. The imagined world is one in which the electronic medium has radically changed the nature of "publication." In the fluid world of the electron, the body of scholarship in a field may become a continuous stream, the later work modifying the older, and all of it available to the reader in a single database or a series of linked databases. In such a world, scholarship would progress in a perennial electronic conference or bulletin board. Contributions and debates would occur on the Internet and be continuous. The browser would become the catalog to the collection of knowledge.

This picture is exciting, but it reveals problems. First, a persistent dissenter from the way the majority of scholars are approaching an issue will remain a constant presence in the discussion, perhaps hindering its flow. Today, a dissenter publishes his or her views, which can be taken seriously or ignored as the community of scholars wishes. In the electronic environment, the community will find it difficult to ignore the gadfly. This is not an unmitigated good thing. The gadfly is usually not right, and what is interesting and stimulating in the dissenter's view is almost always absorbed by the other members of the community long before the dissenter himself is ready to move on to other issues.

Second, all fields go through periods of stagnation, and one of the ways to overcome them is to retrace the debates to find a new starting point. In the ever-changing electronic environment, the older work disappears into the newer, and the stages of scholarly thought are obscured.[1] This may be a significant defect of the electronic environment. Moreover, it is becoming clear that the preservation of electronic resources involves migration from one "platform" to another, and that implies continued use. Who will use up space and effort keeping a database alive unless it remains in use—that is, remains alive? We have not found a good storage technique for electronic sources, as we did for writings when we discovered parchment and figured out how to bind folia into codices. (More on this later.)

As you can see, this picture of the future predicts changes in the form and probably the essence of scholarly discourse. The intellectual process we have used for centuries rests both on the means of communication and on the methods of rational discourse, so a change in the former will probably alter the process as a whole in significant ways. I predict a revolution in the tools or methods of discourse. Today, the medium of exchange is the printed book or article, but the rapid growth of electronic exchanges among scholars in all fields points to the vision of the future I have sketched. If what I have imagined were to be realized, one can see the problems of collection, management, and citation of information. Who will collect the stream of scholarship presented in the electronic medium? How will it be broken up into pieces that can be cited and found with sufficient certainty?

Notwithstanding the present dominance of printed media, much of the most important information being produced by today's research activity is transmitted in the electronic medium. This trend creates great problems for scholars:

- How does a scholar cite information retrieved from the Internet? The problem is not that the resource has no address—the URL address will do—but that there are no chapters or pages in many of the resources. People are not only mounting books and articles on the Internet; they are also putting up original sources in true database format.

- How does a scholar know whether an electronic resource found on the Internet is sound—that is, contains reliable, up-to-date information?

- Assuming that the reader has the equipment and knowledge, how does he or she know whether the cited electronic source is the one to which the author referred? The address might be correct, the title or description might be fine, but the data might have been altered since its original citation. The owner or maintainer of a database may change the principles of its collection or the features of its presentation. Even the possibility of such changes would complicate both use and citation.

- How will new people enter a field, bringing new insights and related information to bear on important scientific or scholarly questions, when the sources of information "float" as they do on the Internet? I mentioned this migration problem earlier. The active participants in a field will know about the migration, but those who come afterwards, in particular those who enter the field from laboratories or academic programs that are not in the mainstream of research in the field, will have problems tracing the citations in earlier publications to the original source. There is not yet an easy-to-use reference work to track such relocations. The great, fixed classifications of the modern library are equal opportunity sources for seekers of knowledge; the Internet is not, in its current form, a stable environment that can sustain scholarship over a long time and a wide arena of scholars.

These questions are not the only ones raised by the use of new electronic resources in scholarship. The successful growth of knowledge requires a confidence in the ability of scholars to attain a nearly complete control of the existing body of information in a field. Each contributor to the field strives for completeness. Although none ever achieves this goal, the scholars in a field collectively possess the knowledge necessary for judging the significance of discoveries. Our confidence that we have mastered the relevant information in our fields has traditionally rested on our confidence in libraries and librarians. Let us then turn to the future of libraries in the new age of scholarship.

THE LIBRARY, INFORMATION, AND SCHOLARSHIP IN THE ELECTRONIC AGE

The era of great libraries—national repositories and carefully collected, preserved, and cataloged collections—has been the nineteenth and twentieth centuries. During this period, scholars have assumed that the essentially complete information they needed was present and neatly ordered on the shelves of the library. If you read the books and periodicals found there, you could lay claim to a foundation of knowledge upon which you could build your own research.

The development of electronic information resources and the Internet may end the era of great libraries. When they first appeared, electronic databases were treated as just another format in which information was gathered and made available. Libraries acquired some of these resources and provided access through the electronic network to others. The appearance of the new format merely expanded the concept of the collection that the library built and managed.

Now, the electronic resources are being created privately—by scholars or institutes or governments or companies—and the library is not collecting very many of them. Indeed, we no longer need the library to give us access to any electronic database; the most that libraries can do is lower the cost of access by purchasing site licenses for commercially produced databases.

Why is this situation different from the one that existed when printed materials were the only type of information resources we had? Libraries have never collected all of the printed books and periodicals produced; very great libraries have bought a small percentage of the total output of the world's presses. But printed works not purchased by the great research libraries generally disappeared from view and from consideration in the scholarly enterprise, because we have trusted professional librarians to choose what is significant. Few of us have understood how large a role librarians have played in shaping our body of knowledge. In fact, most of us have claimed that we were the definers of our universes of knowledge; the librarians were only the keepers, we said, of what we have created and found. Now that the librarians are losing their power to shape knowledge, because of the new technology, we can see their power and our reliance on it with an uncomfortable clarity.

Among the thousands of electronic sources of information in the new universe of information, we have equal access to those chosen and not chosen by librarians for inclusion in their collections. We can rely on librarians as we have in the past, ignoring the electronic resources that they have not flagged for us; but, now that the unflagged resources are present in our range of vision, our conceit of being the sculptors of knowledge forces us to show our craft. This conceit is driving us out to sea on the vast confusion of our information resources. We have the intellectual tools to deal with the navigational challenge. The real questions are: Do we have the time? And is the management of our information the profession we chose when we took up research?

These questions reveal what we often formally acknowledge in the prefaces of our books, when we thank librarians for their help, and informally deny, when we ignore the role librarians play in shaping the information we can find "by ourselves" in the library. Perhaps our habitual disparagement of the intellectual stature of librarians arises from our profound dependence on them. Nevertheless, the electronic revolution is quickly depriving us of their support and forcing us to do their jobs as well as ours. There is the danger that the job of information manager will drive out the job of maker of knowledge unless we work with librarians now to transform the idea of the library and of the librarian. I will devote the remainder of this paper to what I see as the first stages of such a transformation.

In the traditional library, the focus of librarianship has been on the selection, cataloging, and managing of information resources—principally books and periodicals. Library staffs have been divided into departments of collection development, cataloging, and reference or public service. The first stage of the modern revolution in the library took place in cataloging, with the development of central facilities, such as the Online Computer Library Center (OCLC) and the Research Library Information Network (RLIN), and the advent of electronic catalogs. The cataloging departments of modern libraries are vastly different from those of 30 years ago

However, these developments meant more than we expected in their early stages. The creation of the electronic catalog has already changed the context of scholarship in unexpected ways. Originally, the electronic catalog was viewed, at least by scholars, merely as a replacement for the card catalogs that had grown gargantuan, inherently complicated, and difficult to use. Every scholar of a certain age can recall days at the catalog and evenings of sore feet, sore backs, and crossed eyes. Moreover, all that backaching work in the card catalog did not satisfy the need for bibliographical work, which depended on specialized publications, such as the *Revue Ecclesiastique* and the *Bulletin of Medieval Canon Law* in my field. Such journals produced annual bibliographies that reached into the corners of scholarship, beyond where any particular librarian would look for our particular information resources.

Once the electronic catalog went on the Internet, the walls and limitations of our libraries began to crumble. It was not merely that faculty and students no longer had to go to the library to find out what was in it—and with the institution of delivery services on many campuses, they often did not even have to go to the library to get the materials themselves—but that they were no longer confined to their own libraries. Moreover, the electronic catalog is a marvelous bibliographic tool, and the scholar can now find the references, discover where—almost anywhere in the world—

an item is, and ask for it to be delivered to his or her library or office. Librarians now find themselves dealing with distant users, increasingly dealing directly with them; and parts of every library's collection are principally used by people who do not belong to the local university community. Meanwhile, local users want help in getting materials from distant collections. Librarians and collections are now serving an increasingly global public and serving it globally.

This point is important and full of irony. When I enter the Penn library, I have to show a Penn ID card. At the same moment, the librarians in the building are serving a community of users not limited by the institutional framework of the university that employs them. The advent of the electronic catalog has not only increased the demands for materials by providing better information about what is in the collection, but also created an irresistible process of dissolution of the isolation of libraries from one another. Users are driving librarians to share their collections, to create better search techniques for bibliographical work that knows no territorial limit, and to develop efficient methods for moving information from one place to another. OCLC and RLIN improved the service and performance of the cataloging departments. Now, we see that the experience with the shared facilities created a framework for the broader and more profound cooperation that users are insistently demanding.

The next great revolution in libraries will be in collection development. The change is already under way, and it can only accelerate. The Internet now has on it a great many sources of information that scholars need. It also houses a great deal of junk that could clog the arteries of scholarship. Thus, the Internet is not very different from traditional print publishing, which produces a great deal more junk than gems. The only difference, as I already noted, is that the Internet resources are easier for scholars to find than the thousands of items in the vast outpouring of printed material.

In this new information environment, the collection development staff of the library can play exactly the same role it played during the era when print was the only medium. It can "surf the net" in search of good information resources and mount their titles and addresses on the library's homepage or electronic catalog interface. Scholars who can discipline themselves can then find their information through the library just as they always have done.

However, Internet resources are maintained or owned by people outside the library. When a collection developer selects a book or periodical, it is purchased, processed, and then managed as part of the collection. In the world of print, collection development is a discreet task. In the world of the Internet, collection development must be an iterative process. The librarian must regularly check up on the resources that he or she has chosen for inclusion in the library's collection of Internet resources because the owners of those resources may let them deteriorate, or may transfer them to another owner. Thus, collection development work will change significantly, involving the collection development staff in a process of information management very different from the one it devotes most of its time to now.

I have said elsewhere and will repeat here that I think these changes in the format in which we preserve and transmit knowledge will change the nature of libraries and librarianship (Chodorow 1996a). Although we are still in the age of print, we are entering an age in which electronic information resources will be crucial, and it will not be long before these new forms are the more important ones in most intellectual fields. By the time that occurs, librarians will have had to become direct participants in scholarly endeavor. They will continue to be the guides and managers of the great collections stored in print, but the management of electronic information resources will bring them closer to their users than ever before. The kaleidoscopic nature of information in electronic form will require constant vigilance and continuous exercise of judgment to provide scholars with some certainty about what is known and what is not. The librarian will become a member of the research team in every project, in every discipline, but not as now, as an outsider brought in for the bibliographic phase. Indeed, the bibliographic phase will lose its phasic quality, because the information mined in the first few months of a project will have changed, perhaps significantly, by the time of its last few months; and the information resources of the project will need to be constantly monitored and managed.

Finally, something needs to be said about the preservation of information. Preservation does not appear to be a problem for a continuously developing information stream; the continuous reproduction of the database extends its life. But even the most extreme version of the vision I have painted must recognize that we will want to store a great deal of information left behind by scholars and scientists as they move on to other topics or questions. Just as today, the majority of our library collections preserve both the information and the interests of the past, so will the future digital library. As now, we will preserve this material both because it is a product and part of our civilization and because experience tells us that old knowledge has an important role to play in intellectual work. Many mistakes occur because people have forgotten what they once knew, and many new starts begin with the rediscovery of an old debate that appears in a new light after many years, sometimes many decades, of additional labors.

As I noted earlier, the electronic environment hides the course of debate, because continuing discussion tends to erase or blur the stages of scientific or scholarly discourse. This is one problem of preservation of electronic information resources, but the principal problem of preservation in the electronic environment is that the environment itself is evolving rapidly. The problem is not with the storage media themselves; there are some electronic storage media that have the durability of paper. The problem is that the information in current electronic formats will become unusable. If we want to keep the record of our future intellectual adventures, we will need to devise a method of preservation that involves transportation from old to new systems. Given the rapidity of technological development, this program of renewal will itself have to operate at a high velocity.

The need for this form of preservation will change the pattern of work in libraries. Just as collection development in the electronic age will be an iterative process of finding and checking, so the process of collection management will be iterative. We will need the equipment and staff to "re-shelve" our electronic collection, and as it grows, this process will become a regular and important element of the library's task.

Moreover, given the nature of electronic information resources, the task of preservation may be best done consortially or even governmentally. (One can imagine an arrangement by which the government sets up, perhaps in the Library of Congress, an agency for the preservation of electronic information resources.) It is hard to imagine a digital library composed of multiple copies of various databases; we are bound to find a way to share the materials, paying for use instead of ownership. In that arrangement we will have only so many copies of the materials as necessary for safety from fire, earthquake, breakdowns, and sabotage, and our digital collections will be the common "property" of all libraries. Whoever holds the property will certainly be charged with preserving it.

CONSEQUENCES OF THE ELECTRONIC REVOLUTION FOR LIBRARIES

It is plain to see, then, that the electronic revolution will change the whole structure of scholarship and libraries. Librarians will have to become members of scholarly or scientific teams, the information managers and specialists for each discipline or subdiscipline. This means that librarians will report within two institutional structures, the library and the research group. The first of these structures will continue to be responsible for the professional management of information; the second will continue to be the locus of intellectual progress.

In this vision, the key library staff will be distributed throughout the geography of scholarship. Today, we are consolidating libraries and their corps of librarians. One hears everywhere the argument that branch libraries are expensive, as they are, and that consolidation reduces duplication of staff and permits the shifting of fiscal resources to the acquisitions budget. Tomorrow, if my vision has any validity, the librarians in any discipline will form a universal corps—unfettered by place or institutional framework—who serve the faculty and students in the field. Libraries will not need one librarian of each major disciplinary *genus*; we are far from understanding how they will sort out their staffing needs. However, this scenario suggests that as preservation will become the task of consortia, so might library staffing. The librarian of a particular discipline might be anywhere, serving a widely spread population of scholars and students; in this scenario, the question would be, "How many groups or people can one librarian serve?" And if we need many librarians in a field, how will we distribute them among research libraries?

The library budget will also become increasingly complicated. In a pay-for-use environment, budgeting will have to be done on the basis of educated guesses about future-use patterns. In a consortial environment, budgeters will have to decide how much to put into the common pot. This decision will rest not only on an assessment of the importance of the commonly held materials, but also on the comfort local librarians have with the efficiency and service of the consortial program. The consortia will be monopolies, and no one is ever completely and permanently happy with unique sources of goods. To assure ourselves of their cost-effectiveness, we will have to work out very robust governance mechanisms for our information consortia.

These consortial environments will, of course, coexist with the traditional local administrations. Books and periodicals will continue to be published on paper for decades to come, and librarians will continue to buy, catalog, and store such publications. The traditional library tasks will be done alongside the new ones. Thus, the distribution of library staff into research groups, which I think will occur hesitantly and slowly, will not simply replace the centralized functions of today's libraries. The balancing of these environments and ways of working will be very difficult both for the budgeters and for the managers. The library is one of the largest organizations on campus, and today's university librarians are among the most skilled managers in academe. The premium on managerial ability will be even higher in the future, when the library organization will have to deal with multiple work environments and tasks.

The characteristics of our intellectual culture arise from the means of communication and the form of information. The electronic revolution is changing the nature of communication and the way we manage information, and will bring about fundamental change in our way of doing intellectual work. Elsewhere, I have argued that the electronic revolution will fundamentally change the curriculum and the way we teach and learn (Chodorow 1996b). Here, I have explored the future of scholarship, information services, and libraries. In both visions, there is much to be worried about, for significant change in a human community is always worrisome. Yet, while individuals are sometimes left behind by change, the community finds a way to preserve its basic values and objectives in the new environment. We need to be concerned about the individuals, but we need not worry about the community of scholars as a whole. As it has in the past, it will learn how to continue its historic mission of expanding knowledge in the new environment.

It is natural for a university provost to worry about people, but the general picture I have painted of the future is not a gloomy one. In it, collaboration within and across disciplines would create knowledge at a much faster pace than in the age of print. The rigidities of disciplines themselves would break down and the flow of ideas and the sharing of data would quicken. Students would have a wide-open window on the world of scholarship and could enter it much earlier than they do now. The integration of information sciences and research would be nearly complete. Can anyone fail to be stirred by such prospects? To such a future, all of us in the business of making and disseminating knowledge—the original and constant purposes of the university—can look with an expectation hardly experienced since the invention of movable type.

NOTE

1. All of us have noted the change in the meaning of "draft" in our writing on the computer. The distinct draft is now an artificial stage of composition, and often we simply do not leave a record of the development of our ideas as we rewrite and rearrange our work.

REFERENCES

Chodorow, Stanley. 1996a. Once There Was a Library Here. . . . A History of the University Library in the 21st Century. In *Scholarship in the New Information Environment*, edited by Carol Hughes. Mountain View, Calif.: Research Libraries Group.
Chodorow, Stanley. 1996b. Educators Must Take the Electronic Revolution Seriously. *Academic Medicine* 71: 221–26.

CHAPTER 2

The Impact of Information Technologies on the Role of Research Libraries in Teaching and Learning in the United States

ELAINE SLOAN

Today, I will discuss the impact of information technologies on research libraries, focusing on the role of research libraries in teaching and learning. First, I will describe the development of research universities and their libraries during the twentieth century. Next, I will examine current trends in the organization and delivery of services in research libraries. Finally, I will explore the convergence of events that creates the opportunity to use information technologies to transform teaching and learning in research universities.

Let me begin with the central theme of this talk: that is, the primary mission of the research university, as it has evolved in the United States during this century, is to advance knowledge through research. Teaching and learning, especially of undergraduates, are important but secondary objectives for research universities. As research libraries have developed during this century, they have naturally reflected the primary mission of their universities. Therefore, the primary mission of university research libraries today is the support of faculty and graduate student research. This mission is accomplished primarily by acquiring and providing access to substantial research collections in many fields. Indeed, research libraries are traditionally evaluated by the size of their collections. These libraries are staffed with highly trained professionals who have specific subject or technical skills. Even the names that these librarians choose for themselves and their organizations reflect this emphasis on research. We call ourselves "research librarians"; some of our more prominent organizations are the As-

Paper presented at the International Roundtable for Information and Library Science, Kanazawa Institute of Technology, Library Center, Kanazawa, Japan, 1994.

sociation of Research Libraries, the Research Libraries Group, and the Center for Research Libraries.

There are indications, however, that research universities are beginning to pay greater attention to undergraduate education. If this occurs—and I believe that it is happening—then research libraries, in collaboration with faculty and information technologists, will be able to use powerful digital information technologies to transform teaching and learning in research universities. Before discussing some of the changes that are taking place today, I will describe the remarkable growth of research universities and their libraries in the United States during the twentieth century.

The "university movement" in the United States is said to have begun with the founding of Johns Hopkins University in Baltimore, Maryland, in 1867. Hopkins was modeled after the universities in Germany, which were characterized by an emphasis on scholarship and graduate education. The university movement spread throughout the United States during the late nineteenth and early twentieth centuries. Frederick Rudolph (1990), in his highly regarded history of higher education, contrasted the view of Hopkins' President Gilman with the traditional colleges that existed in the United States at the time of Hopkins' founding:

The institution in Baltimore, however, saw the faculty, its need, its work, as so central to its purpose that Gilman insisted that the faculty be given only students who were sufficiently well prepared to provide the faculty with challenging and rewarding stimulation. Nothing could have been more remote from the spirit of the old time college, where the teachers were theoretically busily engaged in stimulating the student. (1990: 271)

By the early twentieth century, according to Rudolph:

This de-emphasis of the teaching role . . . introduced to American higher education at Johns Hopkins . . . was soon recognized as a necessary concomitant of the university idea. Scientific research . . . required an outlet for all the productivity that was the consequence of university purpose. University rivalry required that each university be certain that its professors were better than its "rival," and one way of making that clear was by coming in ahead in the somewhat informal annual page count in which universities indulged. (1990: 403, 404)

During the second half of the twentieth century, research universities in North America experienced extraordinary growth in size, complexity, and specialization. In less than a century, they had evolved into what Clark Kerr termed the "multiversity" (1963: 37–42). According to Kerr, "The university started as a single community—a community of masters and students. . . . Today the large American university is rather a whole series of communities held together by a common name" (1982: 91).

The development of the research university, including the emphasis on faculty research and publication, was strengthened by the funding received from federal and state agencies and private foundations for support of faculty research. Today, the overhead or indirect costs that universities receive from external funding for faculty research helps to fund faculty salaries, graduate student tuition, university administration (including facilities), and, to a lesser extent, libraries. It is important to note that in North American research universities, there exists no comparable system to reward faculty teaching, especially teaching undergraduates, either within the research universities or from external funding agencies.

As stated, the libraries of research universities developed in ways that support the research of the faculty. In fact, in the early years of the university movement, the faculty dominated the library, as they dominated all aspects of the university. Even after the 1920s, when librarianship became more professionalized, the faculty were responsible for the collections, and frequently faculty were appointed as the head librarians.

Only in the second half of the twentieth century did the library professional, frequently with the title of "bibliographer," "curator," or "selector," begin to take responsibility for the acquisitions budgets and the development of research library collections. Further, during the years of growth of research universities, many universities created centralized library administrations to manage the rapidly expanding library systems.

This is not to suggest that research librarians have ignored undergraduates. Following Harvard's opening of Lamont Library in 1949, many research universities built separate undergraduate libraries with separate staffs and collections. By the late 1980s, 28 research universities in North America had created undergraduate libraries; 21 of the undergraduate libraries were created in the 1960s and 1970s—the years of rapid growth (Undergraduate Library Institute 1986, 1987, 1988). The undergraduate library collections, which frequently duplicated materials found in the large research collections on campus, were designed to support the undergraduate curriculum and undergraduate interests. Like other specialists in research university libraries, undergraduate librarians formed their own organizations, created their own publications, and distributed statistics.

In 1987, the Association of College and Research Libraries approved a model mission statement for a university undergraduate library. The statement describes the environment of the research university library in the following way:

The quality of the library is defined in terms of the strengths of the research collection. Specialized services are often provided for those doing research. . . . The staff members . . . are selected for their ability to provide graduate-level reference services, to organize complex collections, and to select the often esoteric materials needed in a research library. In-depth subject knowledge and managerial skills are also frequently required. (ACRL 1987: 542)

The model mission statement goes on to describe the users of undergraduate libraries, especially the first-year undergraduates, as not yet having "the sophisticated research skills needed to exploit the research library's potential." The statement further characterizes first-year undergraduates as "intimidated by the complexity and size of a large library system" and "reluctant to ask for assistance." According to the model mission statement, "The undergraduate library focuses on two problems that are particularly common to undergraduates—finding the materials they need, and knowing when to ask for help and having the confidence to do so. Undergraduate libraries provide a laboratory in which to teach students how to use a library. The experience of using an undergraduate library is preparation for using all libraries" (1987: 542–543).

The distinct feature of separate undergraduate libraries in research universities is the extent to which they focus on orientation and instruction in the use of libraries. The model mission statement describes the teaching role of the undergraduate library and discusses the teaching that is performed by the undergraduate librarians in the following way: "Teaching students how to use a library is therefore a basic service provided by the staff of the undergraduate library. The teaching programs . . . are varied. They include . . . personal contact . . . preparation of printed and other materials . . . formal group instruction and informal unstructured contacts" (1987: 543).

The Bibliographic Instruction (BI) or library-use instruction movement developed the idea of the library as a center for teaching. The movement's primary goal is to teach the university community, especially undergraduates, to use libraries effectively. The movement has had a significant impact on all types of academic libraries, including those in research universities. There is substantial literature about BI, and the movement has had many successes of which it is justifiably proud. The literature, however, also reflects dissatisfaction with the extent to which librarians have succeeded in fulfilling their teaching role. Evan Farber, one of the leaders of the library instruction movement, perhaps best sums up this dissatisfaction. Farber, the long-time librarian at Earlham College, described the "university-library syndrome" (1974: 12–32), in which university libraries and librarians have caused college faculty and librarians to overlook the teaching function of college libraries. Farber describes the college faculty's view of librarians in the following way: "The librarian's role is viewed as a passive one, one devoted to housekeeping, to getting materials quickly and making them accessible with dispatch and efficiency, and with being available when needed for answering questions, compiling bibliographies, or putting materials on reserves. The result of this syndrome is so dismaying because it so effectively vitiates the potential role of the library in undergraduate education" (1974: 17).

Farber goes on to attribute the cause of the "university-library syndrome" to "the emphasis of the university on research and on graduate study rather than on teaching undergraduates" (1974: 22).

Although Farber's article was written 20 years ago, it remains relevant; for, despite the creation of separate undergraduate libraries and the development of bibliographic instruction programs in research libraries, support for the faculty in their research and scholarly activity continues to dominate research librarianship today; and librarians are making increasing use of powerful networked information systems and services.

The research libraries that grew so rapidly in the 1960s and 1970s were often among the first divisions within their research universities to apply information technologies to improve productivity and service. Circulation, cataloging, and acquisitions were the first procedures to be automated for library staff use. These early applications of automation in research libraries were designed to make the labor-intensive, manual processes more cost-effective. Later, library users were given direct access to the automated systems. By the mid-1980s, online catalogs and circulation systems were widely available to patrons in most research libraries. Similarly, online abstracting and indexing services, available from such vendors as DIALOG and BRS in the early 1970s, were first searched primarily by librarians and later searched directly by users.

With the introduction of personal computers and the development of high-speed networks in the 1980s, the landscape of university computing, and with it access to library information, began to change. No longer was use of the computer limited to a handful of knowledgeable scientists. Relatively unsophisticated humanists and social scientists began to use personal computers, not only for word processing, but also to analyze data, to access networked information, and to communicate with colleagues around the world. During the early 1990s, campus networks and campuswide information systems were developed. Library information was among the first resources to be delivered over the networks. Today, library information is being delivered to workstations in offices, dormitories, and homes. The vision of the "library without walls" is becoming a reality.

At Columbia University, for example, the campus-wide information system *ColumbiaNet* and the library information component *CLIO Plus* were developed in 1989. The menu items in *CLIO Plus* are carefully selected by a group of librarians to provide users with easy access to information most frequently requested. Only some of the information resides in computers at Columbia University. For example, the online catalog *CLIO* and *Columbia University Press Concise Columbia Encyclopedia* are stored locally. Much of the information displayed on the *CLIO Plus* menu is actually accessed over the Internet: for example, there is a menu called "Library Catalogs Outside of Columbia." The menu lists the most frequently used catalogs; however, the user can also search "Hytelnet: access to other library catalogs" if the catalog sought by the user is not linked. Further, none of the periodicals and other indexes listed on the screen reside on Columbia computers; all are accessed on the Internet.

For several years, librarians and information technologists at Columbia have been collaborating to provide users of *CLIO Plus* with easy, transparent access to local and remote information resources. The vision of the research library of the future is of a "virtual" or distributed electronic library. Information systems such as Columbia University's *CLIO Plus* are pointing the way.

Development in information technologies and the fiscal crises of the late 1980s and early 1990s stimulated a rethinking of the library as an organization, and of its relation to the university. I will comment briefly on three aspects of change in research library organizations: (1) changes in the internal organization of libraries; (2) changes in the relation of libraries and computing centers, especially academic computing centers; and (3) changes in relations between libraries and publishers.

During the late 1980s and early 1990s, when many research libraries were reducing expenditures, many libraries reorganized their operations. Librarians borrowed techniques and approaches from the corporate world, shrinking hierarchies. Middle management and supervisory positions were cut and departments were merged. Traditional distinctions between "public" and "technical" services often blurred as more cross-divisional working groups and teams were created.

At the same time, the traditional collection orientation of the research library was questioned. Fiscal constraints have caused librarians and university administrators to seek alternatives to local collection building, as the new networking and information technologies seem to offer promise to fulfill the long-held goals of resource-sharing and cooperative collection development. Consequently, more attention is being given to improving interlibrary loan and document delivery services as alternatives to acquiring materials. The occurrence of all these changes in a relatively short period has made many research librarians accept change as a stimulating constant in their activities.

As important as the continuing changes within the library organization has been the changing relationship between the library and the computing center, especially the academic computing center. The earliest relationships developed when libraries introduced automated systems during the late 1960s and 1970s. Libraries frequently hired their own systems staffs, but in most cases the systems were supported, at least to some extent, by campus computing centers.

During the 1980s, as the power of the personal computer and networking technologies developed, relations between librarians and information technologists on research university campuses became strained. In the early 1980s, the groups knew little about each other. Each group seemed wary of the other, because, although they were different in training and traditions, they appeared to claim similar turf. The topic of the relationship between the library and the computer center generated a great deal of interest during the 1980s, especially in the library literature.

It now seems that closer relationships are developing. The Coalition for Networked Information (CNI) represents a coalition of research libraries with two national higher education organizations, one that has traditionally represented academic computing, and the other, administrative computing professionals. The formation of CNI, as well as the numerous workshops and conferences that include both librarians and information technologists, is at once a stimulus to and a result of increasing collaboration between librarians and information technologists on the campuses of North American research universities.

There appears to be a trend to align these organizations more closely. Columbia University was among the first research universities to formally link libraries and computing. The title that I hold—Vice President for Information Services and University Librarian—was created more than 20 years ago and has been held by three incumbents, including me. In the early 1970s, both libraries and computing reported to the Vice President/University Librarian. From the late 1970s through the mid-1980s, only the libraries were included. Since 1986, both the libraries and academic computing have been in the organization; close advisory and reporting relations exist with administrative computing and telecommunications.

There also appears to be dual reporting in library and computing center organization charts. At Columbia, for example, the head of the library systems office reports to both the deputy university librarian and the head of academic computing. The manager of academic computing's research and development unit, who is responsible for digital library technical development, reports both to the head of academic computing and to the deputy university librarian. Furthermore, there appears to be a growing number of units in research universities that are jointly managed by the libraries and computing organizations. Again, using Columbia as the example, the Electronic Data Services, the Electronic Text Service, and the Journalism Library are currently jointly managed by librarians and academic computing staff. Whether or not it is reflected in formal organization charts, much more cooperation and collaboration is occurring between libraries and computing centers in the 1990s. This informal cooperation is the most important indicator of effective change.

Finally, I wish to comment on the recent partnerships between libraries and publishers. Most of these activities are described as "pilot projects." There has been a good deal of publicity about such projects as *Tulip* and *Red Sage*, which involve libraries and commercial publishers of scientific periodicals. There are also a number of projects between university libraries and university presses. At Columbia, we have collaborated with the Columbia University Press for some time. Johns Hopkins has recently announced its ambitious Project Muse, designed to deliver all Johns Hopkins University Press scholarly periodicals over the Internet. At present, Columbia University Libraries, like other libraries, is negotiating agreements with commercial and not-for-profit publishers to make publications available to the community in digital form over the university network.

It is too early to predict the impact of such projects on libraries or publishers. Some envision that universities will become more prominent players in the scholarly communication cycle; others envision that commercial and scholarly publishers will redefine themselves for the digital, networked environment. It seems most likely that, to some extent, both outcomes will occur. Many experiments will take place. At the very least, these experiments will strengthen the collaboration among faculty, librarians, and information technologists at research universities and will increase the understanding that publishers and librarians have of each other.

What impact have all these changes had on research libraries' role in teaching and learning? Many research libraries have created electronic classrooms and computing clusters. Many libraries collect and provide bibliographic access to instructional software and are beginning to experiment with electronic reserves. With notable exceptions, however, information technology has not been as important to advances in teaching and learning as it has been to advances in research. As noted, faculty in research universities are not rewarded financially for the quality of their teaching. It should be no surprise, therefore, that faculty are not rewarded for investing significant time in the development of instructional software or its implementation in their classes.

However, as noted earlier, there are now calls from both within and outside research universities for greater attention to undergraduate instruction. Derek Bok, distinguished former president of Harvard University, is among those who have voiced concern about the inattention to the quality of undergraduate education in research universities. In an article entitled "Regaining the Public Trust," Bok wrote: "The public has finally come to believe quite strongly that our institutions—particularly our leading universities—are not making the education of students a top priority. This is especially true of our undergraduates within the arts and sciences faculties" (1992).

Although there is yet little evidence of dramatic change in the traditional system that rewards faculty primarily for their research and publication, there have been calls for greater attention to the quality of teaching in hiring, promoting, and granting tenure to faculty in research universities.

One of my colleagues, Robert McClintock, a historian of education at Columbia University's Teachers College, is deeply involved in applying information technologies to transform primary and secondary education. He believes that the digital revolution has the potential to bring research and teaching more closely together. In McClintock's view, the divergence between research and instruction was facilitated by the Gutenberg printing press revolution. Simply put, the scholar's contributions are part of the print culture; that is, they are created and then placed on the shelf to be read, rather than becoming an active part of teaching and learning. Students are expected to read the results of scholarship outside the classroom, often in the library, rather than to be actively involved in creating and using such scholarship. As noted, librarians in research universities have tended to see as their primary function collecting and providing access to scholarly research, rather than as being actively involved with faculty in teaching and students in learning.

Now, with the digital revolution, McClintock believes that it is possible to bring into the instructional setting the products of scholarship. In essence, the library can be brought into the classroom. Students can interact with their teachers and the knowledge base in new ways; that is, teachers and students together can develop and enhance the products of scholarship. Thus, digital technologies offer opportunities to effect profound changes in the role of the teacher and to bring together the often conflicting roles of the researcher and instructor.

To follow McClintock's thesis, these information technologies provide opportunities for bringing librarians and information technologists in clear collaboration with each other, and with faculty in teaching and students in learning. When digital information is accessed at workstations located in a single place or distributed around the campus or around the world, the distinctions between the "library," the "laboratory," and the "computer cluster" may blur. This is the challenge and the opportunity that faces research libraries today.

Librarians long active in the BI movement stress the importance of the teaching role of the library. Now librarians, faculty, and information technologists can be brought together as teachers by the powerful new digital information technologies.

If they do so, librarians will move beyond the 1987 model mission statement for undergraduate libraries, which said, "direct curriculum support will be provided through reserve collections and through purchase of multiple copies of items with high demand" (ACRL 1987: 543). Rather, librarians will become active partners in developing and providing access to materials that support the curriculum.

The development of World Wide Web servers and clients such as Mosaic provide the first rich opportunity for such partnership to develop. Several initiatives now taking place at Columbia University involve cooperation among faculty members, librarians, and computing staff to develop instructional materials for the classroom.

A prime example is the Chemistry Department's *Edison Project for Communicating Chemistry*, which has as its goal the reshaping of the chemistry curriculum. The chemists state that: "Computation, visualization, and multimedia presentation hold out hope of improving the entire educational package, helping the student to learn and the instructor to teach, and demystifying the molecular universe; all in more creative and cost-effective ways" (1994: 8).

The chemists who planned the Edison Project understand the potential of such collaboration. In meetings and e-mail exchanges, they envision that library information will be included in the classroom presentations. They want students to participate with their professors in navigating through information resources; they believe that library searches will become an integral and exciting part of the teaching and learning experience. Such developments show us how the transformation of teaching and learning in research universities in the twenty-first century may occur, and the ways in which libraries and librarians may change to support teaching and learning in research universities.

If these voices calling for increased attention to teaching and learning at research universities are heeded, the research university of the twenty-first century will reward and encourage faculty teaching more than in the twentieth century; and if the research university places greater emphasis on teaching, it should be expected that the research librarian of the twenty-first century, equipped with powerful information technologies, will do the same.

REFERENCES

Association of College and Research Libraries (ACRL). 1987. The Mission of a University Undergraduate Library: Model Statement. *College & Research Libraries News* 48(9): 542–44.

Bok, Derek. 1992. Reclaiming the Public Trust. *Change* 24(4): 12–19.

Farber, Evan Ira. 1974. College Librarians and the University Library Syndrome. In *The Academic Library: Essays in Honor of Guy Lyle*, edited by Evan Ira Farber and Ruth Walling. Metuchen, N.J.: Scarecrow Press.

Kerr, Clark. 1963. The Multiversity, Are Its Several Souls Worth Saving? *Harpers* (November): 37–42.

Kerr, Clark. 1982. *The Uses of the University*, 3rd ed. Cambridge, Mass.: Harvard University Press.

Rudolph, Frederick. 1990. *The American College and University, A History*. Athens: University of Georgia Press.

The Trustees of Columbia University in The City of New York. June 6, 1994. *The Edison Project for Communicating Chemistry: A Curriculum Reform Proposal.*

Undergraduate Library Institute. Undergraduate Library Statistics for 1985/86, 1986/87, and 1988/89. In *UGLI Newsletter*, nos. 36, 39, 46.

CHAPTER 3

The Life of the Mind in a World Transformed by Networks and Digital Libraries

PAUL EVAN PETERS

For the last six months or so, I have been searching for relatively robust and long-lasting standards by which to assess the progress that libraries, computer centers, publishing houses, (and others who are intimately involved in scholarly and scientific creation, communication, and publication) can use to plan their strategies for and assess their progress in the use of networks, and the creation of networked information resources and services. My thoughts have dwelt particularly on standards that are relevant to the "life of the mind," which is to say "human behaviors that create, distribute, and use ideas."

Commentators such as Peter Drucker, Robert Reich, Walter Wriston, and John Perry Barlow (who span quite a range of experience and opinion) are encouraging us to believe that a society served by networks and digital libraries will be a society in which people who are good with words and ideas will, among other things, not only be able to create economic value in powerful new ways, but will be compensated for the economic value that they create at new and much more rewarding levels.

Libraries, computer centers, and publishing houses typify the institutions, organizations, and professions that serve the life of the mind by supporting scholarly and scientific creation, communication, and publication. So it is natural (even necessary) to try to imbed the question of the impacts of networks and digital libraries on these institutions, organizations, and professions in the question of the impacts of networks and digital libraries on the life of the mind.

Paper presented at the International Roundtable for Information and Library Science, Kanazawa Institute of Technology, Library Center, Kanazawa, Japan, 1994.

This is what I will try to do, in a suggestive rather than definitive sort of way, in this talk, using the life of the mind in higher education as my specific point of reference.

NETWORKING IS HOT

I will start by invoking the contemporary context that I believe situates and energizes this general subject in the United States. The president and vice president of the United States, Bill Clinton and Al Gore, have made networking a national priority. A lot of the heat and light that networking is now radiating can be directly attributed to the influence that presidential and vice presidential attention has on all issues and priorities in the United States. The Clinton administration has formed high-powered, productive groups, such as the Information Infrastructure Task Force inside the federal government, and the U.S. Advisory Committee on the National Information Infrastructure outside the federal government. In addition, it funded the Telecommunications and Information Infrastructure Applications Program to stimulate the development of community and other networking applications throughout the United States.

The administration has also been working with Congress on the first complete makeover of federal communications policy since the Communication Act of 1994. Legislation of this sort did not pass during the first Congress of the Clinton administration, reportedly because of disagreements between the large telephone and cable companies in the United States. Regardless, hopes are high that the next Congress will be back at work on this business in the late winter or early spring in 1995.

Another reason why networking is hot is that the concept of the "information highway" is now part of the popular culture. One not-so-serious but important sign of this development is that an increasing number of people in the United States are bluffing their ways through cocktail party conversations about the information highway. A more important sign is that the information highway and the Internet are now an assigned "beat," not only for reporters and correspondents associated with the likes of *Byte*, *PC World*, and the *Chronicle of Higher Education*, but also for those associated with national media outlets like the *New York Times*, the *Wall Street Journal*, *Newsweek*, and National Public Radio.

The good news of this development is that the Internet community no longer has to look everywhere for press coverage. The bad news is that the national media are doing about as good a job covering the Internet as they are other matters of national importance, which is to say, in my opinion, that they often do not do that good a job and that, on some occasions, they do an absolutely dreadful one.

This is another reason why networking is hot, but it is an even clearer reason why the Internet is red hot. Interest in the information highway is being rapidly converted into usage of the Internet and of Internet resources and services.

THE INTERNET IS RED HOT

The Internet Walk of August 1994 determined that 3.2 million hosts are now reachable via the Internet, an increase of 81 percent over the number that was determined to be reachable when the Walk took place in August 1993. Although the number of users who are reachable through these hosts has become a matter of dispute among Internet demographers, the host figure and its rate of growth are not in dispute. The August 1994 Walk also determined that 63 percent of the reachable Internet is located in the United States and 2 percent is located in Japan (just behind the United Kingdom and Germany at 5 percent each, and Australia and Canada at 4 percent each). It further determined that although 27 percent of the reachable hosts are located in U.S. educational institutions, 24 percent are now located in U.S. *commercial* institutions.

Another thing that is heating up the Internet is the restructuring of the U.S. region of the Internet from an NSFNet-based to a community- or market-based model. By the end of April 1995, if all goes as planned, the NSFNet backbone will be decommissioned in favor of a new, open architecture and marketplace for U.S. Internet transport services. The most visible features of these services will be predominantly privately owned and operated network service providers, and predominantly privately owned and operated network access point operators. If the hopes of the U.S. Internet community are realized, this new architecture and marketplace will allow all types of traffic to be transported (not just traffic consistent with the purposes of the research and education community, as was the case in the NSFNet-based U.S. region of the Internet). It will allow private as well as public capital to be used to expand capacity. (Private capital had generally not been used in the U.S. region of the Internet because prospective investors were concerned about asset ownership and it was difficult to determine actual costs over the extended periods of most business plans.)

The World Wide Web and its various clients (NCSA Mosaic, Cello, MacWeb, NetScape, Lynx, and the like) have been the hottest thing in the red hot Internet for almost a year now. The Web already accounts for nearly 10 percent of the traffic on the Internet. Moreover, it was recently projected that World Wide Web traffic will exceed telephone traffic in two to three years.

Web "weavers" and "dancers" have already changed the look and feel of the Internet. These developers have made it clear that it no longer takes an expert in multiple technologies to use the Internet to develop and access information resources and services that contain graphics, sounds, moving images, and other non-textual elements. They are giving real meaning to a new network metaphor, the metaphor of the network as a "Web," which says much more about how the content of the Internet is organized than it does about how the conduit of the Internet is engineered. This emphasis on the content and de-emphasis of the conduit at this basic metaphorical level is more important than has been commonly realized to date. To the degree that network users think of content first and conduit second, if at all, they will be inclined to *develop* network applications rather than *talk* about network topologies and performances. Such a change in user behavior is in the interest of imaging as well as innovating the future of networks and networked information.

HISTORICAL CONTEXT

Looking to the context for what I believe will be the future of our networks and networked information resources and services, I believe that we are deep into what is best thought of as humankind's paleo-electronic period.

Consider that our networked environment is as dangerous and forbidding as it is vast and inviting: a positive Eden of virtual delights. Our networked communities seem to be dominated by explorers, pioneers, hunters, gatherers, storytellers, and even wizards and their familiars. After all the appropriate slack has been cut, the best that can be said is that we are using crude tools with which we are having some uneven but very real success in fashioning crude but functional Internet artifacts. On the last point, I speak not only of Internet tools such as SMTP, FTP, TELNET, gopher, JPEG, HTML, and http. There is no more blunt electromagnetic tool than broadcast television and radio, and there is no more inflexible electromagnetic tool than vinyl, CD, and audio cassette.

Now, though, it seems as if we are on the threshold of what can be productively thought of as humankind's meso-electronic period. Fixed settlements are beginning to emerge in the networked environment, places that offer safe, reliable havens to folks who are much more interested in making a living and living a life than they are in discovering a resource or charting a territory. Domesticated flora (databases) and fauna (algorithms) are replacing all manner of networked things that go bump and roar in the day as well as the night. Notions of private property, and fences that enforce those notions, are beginning to appear, prompting fears that the ideals of the open range and the public good will soon be history.

To my way of thinking, we are clearly at the end of the period in which cheap stunts, brilliant hacks, and acts of ignorance or desperation were the principal ways for creating useful and affordable network resources and services. I believe that we are now at the beginning of the period in which strategic thinking, careful research and development, steady progress over time, and significant investments will drive progress in the networked environment.

This way of thinking has an important implication. Many people were originally drawn into the Internet because they had a vision of networking that the Internet roughly approximated, or because they enjoyed the challenge of proving and taming new information technologies. Most people now being drawn into the Internet are more interested in pursuing missions and seizing opportunities than they are in realizing visions and meeting challenges.

IMPACTS OF NETWORKING ON HIGHER EDUCATION

The impacts of these developments in the United States and around the world are being considered in two basic ways, and there is a growing need to add a third as soon as possible.

Most of the attention being devoted to the impacts of networking on higher education is directed toward how networks are changing and may change the ways in which scholars and scientists communicate and publish, and how the information strategies, products, and services pursued and offered by the institutions and organizations that support scholarly and scientific communication and publication may change as well. Topics commonly considered in such discussions include: production and inventory control; informal communication and collaboration; public access catalogs and databases; electronic newsletters, journals, and monographs; information resource discovery and retrieval; and knowledge management environments. These topics are already covered well in the literature and elsewhere. Because I am seeking a higher standard by which to plan networking and networked information activities and to measure the progress made by those activities, I will say no more about these topics during this talk.

The second area that has garnered attention in discussions about the impacts of networking on higher education centers on differences of opinion about whether certain facilities (such as libraries and classrooms), functions (such as cataloging and lecturing), and artifacts (such as textbooks and periodicals) will continue to be facilities, functions, and artifacts in the age of networks. I cannot resist the impulse to sketch my views on the question of whether the library is a *place* in the age of networks. "Yes, most certainly" is my answer to this question. I believe that to answer this question "no" is to mistake library collections for everything else that libraries are and do. I know that some librarians make this mistake, but non-librarians make it more often. Library collections have been and always will be but a means to an end. That end has been and always will be the enabling of access to the universe of knowledge that bears upon the thinking of the authors and readers in a given community. Since physical artifacts such as books and periodicals convey printed information, effective and efficient management of that information toward this end has required conveniently located, comprehensive, well-organized collections of these artifacts. I believe that networks and networked information will soon reduce the need for such physical collections, particularly for new materials and resources that do not exist outside of network environments. I do not, however, see anywhere close to an equal reduction in the need for the human judgments and services that organize information, that make the resulting organization known, that assist authors and readers in their respective quests to find each other, and so forth. These activities and the people, tools, and facilities that enable and support them will constitute the place of the library in the age of networks. As was the case with the first category of impacts, since impacts of this second sort are already widely discussed and since I am trying to identify a still higher standard of discussion and action, I will say no more about facilities, functions, and artifacts in this talk.

HIGHER EDUCATION MISSIONS

It has become clear that we will never be able to resolve questions about the impact of networking on communication, publication, and information strategies, products, and services; nor will we be able to do the same for questions about facilities, functions, and artifacts without getting a handle on the broader, and much more fundamental, question of what networking means to the research, teaching and learning, and community service missions of higher education institutions.

We need to derive the future of the scholarly and scientific journal and monograph from an understanding of the future of scholarship and science. We need to derive the future of classroom and library facilities from our understanding of the future geographic and social organization of learning communities. Finally, we need to derive the future of cataloging and lecturing from our understanding of what people will do on their own and what people will need help with in this future, networked information environment.

A quick assessment of what we know and do not know about this new, third category of impacts reveals that it is in the area of the research mission of higher education that the impacts of networking have been most felt. Indeed, access to network connections and networked information has become essential for attracting and retaining researchers, along with their projects and funds.

The impacts of networking and networked information on the community service mission of higher education institutions are already very real, but they are also very uneven, reflecting the wide diversity of the communities in which higher education institutions are situated. However, the higher education community in the United States takes justifiable pride in the fact that many of its institutions and people affiliated with its institutions have played important roles in establishing "civic networking" projects (such as the Cleveland Freenet and the Blacksburg Electronic Village) that offer the benefits of networking and networked information to the residents of the community in their area.

The impacts of networking are just beginning to be felt on the teaching and learning mission of higher education institutions. The most exciting research and education networking breakthroughs will likely occur over the next five years in this area.

MISSION OBJECTIVES

There are three mission objectives that people who fund and administer higher education institutions rely upon us—the people who build networks and populate those networks with users, resources, and services—to address.

The issue of costs and how to reduce them is a concern of all college and university presidents in the 1990s. These presidents, and their finance and business officers, are particularly interested in how to measure the payoffs on investments in information technology, and they are eager to learn what those measurements will show. If benefit was the handle that our presidents grasped when they first placed networked resources and services onto their tables, cost will be the handle that they will grasp when they raise networked resources and services to their next level of development. Therefore, most administrators are looking to those of us who are working on networks and networked information to increase the efficiency of higher education by using them to modernize the way that higher education institutions approach their research, teaching and learning, and community service activities.

This is not to say that these administrators are not interested in what networks and networked information can do to make higher education research, teaching and learning, and community service more effective. Many, perhaps even most, of these administrators are interested in how we will innovate the offerings of our higher education institutions using network technologies, resources, and services. They recognize that although efficiency measures will allow higher education institutions to continue to serve their current constituencies, only effectiveness measures will allow these institutions to serve the larger and more diverse constituencies that the twenty-first century will call upon higher education institutions to serve.

A small but growing number of administrators are looking to networks and networked information, and those of us who work on them, to drive the revitalization of their higher education institutions by facilitating the transformation not only of how, when, and where things get done, but also of what gets done and by whom. Changes of this magnitude are difficult to grasp at this early stage of our bringing networks and networked information to task in terms of efficiency and effectiveness; but it is not too early to begin considering how those changes will recalibrate the relationship between higher education institutions and their existing constituencies and actuate the relationship between those institutions and their potential new constituencies. Nor is it too early to consider how the changes will renew the relationship between higher education and the social goals and processes that it must serve.

MISSION OPPORTUNITIES

In reflecting upon the impacts that networking and networked information will plausibly have on the research, teaching and learning, and community service missions of higher education, I have identified three main opportunities.

First, networking and networked information enable a much-improved context of work for researchers and for their projects and programs. This new context of work will be constituted by access to and interactions among three resources that are fundamental to every researcher, research project, and research program: (1) people (e.g., theorists and empiricists, experts and novices, local and remote); (2) types of knowledge (e.g., theories, primary data, findings, commentary on theories and findings, documentation, curricular materials); and (3) formats of knowledge (e.g., text, graphics, sound, photos, animation, moving pictures). The immediate, even intimate, co-presence of types of people and types and formats of knowledge in networked communities, coupled with the rapid and frequent interactivity enabled by basic networking technologies, yields a context of work in which ideas and facts flow so widely, with such little resistance, and with such high resolution that productivity rises to much higher levels and knowledge accumulates at much faster rates than heretofore attained or even imagined.

Second, networking and networked information enable a world in which immersion and immediacy are the normal rather than the exceptional learner experience, and a world in which learning is lifelong rather than solely an activity of the young. We now have within our reach the technological means to construct learning environments that have the information density of the Library of Congress, the pedagogical skill of Socrates, and the excitement and holding power of a video game. Networked learning environments of this sort promise that every learner will be able to marshal faculty, library, laboratory, and other resources at her or his own pace according to her or his own schedule, in a setting of her or his own choosing, and in close contact and cooperation with other learners.

Third, networking and networked information enable the easy and regular flow of communications and ideas that is necessary for the identification and management of the sorts of interesting and appropriate activities and initiatives that bring higher education institutions and their communities closer together. In some cases, these activities and initiatives will arise from concerns about economic development; in other cases, they will arise from concerns about elementary and secondary education; and in still other cases, they will arise from a desire for expert knowledge to be applied to some community problem or objective. Networked communication allows ideas and proposals to be brought forward, discussed, and disposed in a much more responsive fashion than has generally been the case to date, and this responsiveness fosters the trusting, positive attitude that is essential to productive relationships.

I will now discuss each of these three opportunities in more depth.

EXPAND CONTEXT OF THOUGHT, COMMUNICATION, AND ACTION

When reflecting upon the impacts of networks and networked information on the research mission of higher education institutions, I find it useful to think in terms of three general zones of knowledge that situate each of us in our own, highly individual world of work.

Each of us is situated first within a zone of "immediately relevant knowledge" which is mostly of our own construction, although its construction is guided by our relationships with numerous authority figures throughout our lives and careers. In this zone can be found as much of the information that is directly relevant to our immediate or imminent interests (recorded on various media, conveyed by various artifacts, and embodied in the minds of various colleagues) as each of us can afford and manage on our own. This is the information that is so important to us that we simply cannot trust anyone but ourselves to deal with it.

This sort of trust and delegation of responsibility for acquiring and managing information resources is the distinctive characteristic of the second zone, in which the world of work of each of us is situated: the zone of "plausibly relevant knowledge." We populate this second zone primarily with information resources that are not presently important to us, but which we believe may become immediately relevant at any moment, or which were previously directly relevant. (This zone is also populated with information resources that we cannot afford or justify in terms of cost and which we decide to cost- and access- share with others.) We rely upon libraries and disciplinary societies, in the main, to manage the information in this zone.

The third zone of knowledge that situates our world of work can be best described as a zone about which we have only fear, uncertainty, and dread (FUD). This zone of knowledge is beyond our reach and that of our delegates. Most of us worry that there may well be something in this zone that will, sooner or later, completely change our world of work, for the better or worse (but, most likely, for the worse), and by the hand of someone other than ourselves.

I believe that networks and networked information have already begun to expand each of these zones, and that the rate and scope of expansion will increase for some time into the future. Although occupants of the inner two zones generally acknowledge the expansion of the outer, third zone, and the occupants of the inner two zones also acknowledge the expansion of the innermost zone, the occupants of the innermost zone do not generally acknowledge that the middle zone is expanding.

This is a convoluted way of saying that libraries and disciplinary societies need to do a much better job of linking their networking and networked information efforts to those of their constituents and clients, if those constituents and clients are to appreciate, let alone to participate in, those efforts.

IMPROVE RESPONSIVENESS OF PROGRAMS

It is more difficult to reflect upon the impacts of networking and networked information on the teaching and learning mission of higher education institutions than it is to reflect upon the impacts on the research mission. The impacts on teaching and learning are just now moving to the center stage of the networking community, and the picture we have of those impacts should be much clearer in three to five years than it is at present. Nonetheless, it is possible and useful to speculate about how the use of networks and networked information will change our approach to teaching in certain important ways.

For instance, it seems clear that the new approach to teaching and learning will deliver educational experiences through networks rather than through campuses. Students will access those educational experiences through courseware running on workstations while guided by teachers (who will be much more accessible through electronic mail and conferences than they have ever been in person), rather than accessing those experiences through lectures presented by teachers in classrooms. These two changes are much easier to state than they are to make, and there is certain to be a wide range of variation around each of them. Nonetheless, they are changes that will most certainly be realized in the new approach to teaching and learning that is enabled by networks and networked information.

Two other changes come quickly to mind, but they are more speculative than were the first two. First, the social interactions that will take place under the new approach to teaching and learning will be more open than has been possible under the old one. For instance, it will be possible for students who are physically dispersed, with different levels of preparation and working at very different paces, to interact with each other and with the teacher(s) at the same point or along the same sequence of points in a given educational experience. Second, progress will likely be assessed and recognized more frequently and incrementally than has been practical under the old approach. For instance, students will be able to assess their progress as often as they want the feedback that assessment provides, and they will be awarded certificates that recognize their mastery of specific sets of skills, in addition to being awarded degrees that recognize their mastery of general disciplines. Both of these changes are much more challenging and are potentially much more important than are changes to how educational experiences are delivered and accessed; but, the latter two changes have drawn most of the attention that the networking community has been devoting to the impacts of networking and networked information on the teaching and learning mission of higher education institutions. This emphasis must change in the near future if we are going to do justice to this second of the higher education missions.

STRENGTHEN PARTNERSHIP RELATIONSHIPS

Most higher education institutions are already proficient at arguing for investments in networks and networked information on the basis of the increases in research and education productivity that those investments can yield (by both decreasing the costs of and increasing the benefits of specific research and education programs and activities). However, many higher education institutions are just beginning to learn how to argue for investments in research and education networks and networked information for what those investments can do to help their communities achieve the objectives that those communities have set for *their* investments in networks and networked information. For instance, many communities are looking to networks and networked information to help develop their economies or to make the businesses in their area more productive and otherwise competitive. Other communities hope that networks and networked information will help them to improve the accessibility and accountability of their government to their citizens. Still others, particularly those who feel that they have not been well served by the mainstream media, are turning to networks and networked information to express their cultural identity, and to make their cultural heritage available to their members and known to others who are interested in their well-being and prospects.

Higher education institutions are in an excellent position to strengthen their partnerships with the communities in which they are situated by placing their expertise with networks and networked information at the disposal of the networking objectives of those communities. How to do this seems straightforward, if challenging, in the cases of economic development, government accessibility and accountability, and community and individual development; but many members of the higher education community are put off by the idea of trying to do this in the case of the most often mentioned new application for the information highway: retail and entertainment services.

RETAIL AND ENTERTAINMENT SERVICES

I believe that members of the higher education community who ignore the retail and entertainment service uses of the information highway do so at their great loss, and may do so at their great peril.

First, the financial stakes involved are enormous. In 1993, consumers in the United States spent $12 billion on video rentals, $15 billion on video games, and $55 billion on home catalog sales, for a total of $82 billion on the three applications that are destined to drive the retail and entertainment service uses of the information highway. During the same period, consumers in the United States spent $80 billion on local telephone service. When the history of the information highway in the United States is written, 1993 will undoubtedly be remembered as the year in which consumers spent more on the new than they did on the old applications of telecommunications technologies and networks.

Second, there are indications that at least some of the leaders of the retail and entertainment service industries are grappling with some of the same networking and networked information objectives and issues as the members of the higher education community. For instance, Barry Diller, CEO of QVC (the largest home shopping network in the United States and, possibly, in the world), has been quoted as saying that he believes that the winner in the new retail services marketplace of the information highway will be the firm that succeeds at "delivering expert knowledge to a point of sale, at a time of sale, in support of consumer decision-making." I find Mr. Diller's business concept to be very compatible with the "service without walls or clocks" program concept that is guiding so much of the work on networks and networked information in the higher education community. Another example comes from noted science fiction author Greg Bear, who has observed that video games look and work the way they do because the computer programmers who make them are clearly much more interested in and experienced with action, color, and sound than they are with character and story development. Mr. Bear believes that video games will soon be completely transformed by the efforts of authors like himself who are coming to believe that the technologies involved are finally getting good enough for *them* to use. He predicts that the term "works of interactive fiction" will soon replace "video games" as the term of choice for this genre of creative expression.

MISSION CHALLENGES

I also believe that networks and networked information resources and services present three basic, long-term challenges to the research, teaching and learning, and community service missions of higher education institutions.

First, networks and networked information enable effective and sustainable communication among researchers in ever-smaller research specialties. This is, of course, perceived as an opportunity by the researchers who practice those specialties. My worry is that research problems will be decomposed into progressively more esoteric research programs and projects, with the result that human knowledge will fragment to the degree that the use of research outputs and the funding of research inputs will be confounded and the whole research system will be destabilized. Higher education institutions and disciplinary societies must take the lead in devising new strategies for ensuring the relevance and coherence of research in the networked environment.

Second, networks and networked information enable parties other than existing higher education institutions to offer advanced, authoritative, even certificated, educational services to the public. The public and most politicians and government officials perceive this as an opportunity. Networks and networked information are certain to create a much more competitive marketplace for learners than higher education institutions have faced to this point, and higher education institutions will not only be competing with each other in this new marketplace. To compete successfully in this new environment, many higher education institutions will become more student-centered, less dependent on keeping students in residence, and less devoted to granting degrees. Other higher education institutions will develop the vision and the means to imbed quality instructional services in other institutions' and organizations' platforms, systems, and environments so that those services are ready for use at a point of need, at a time of need, and by the specific person or persons in need. My worry is that most higher education institutions have barely begun to realize the potential of networks and networked information to innovate their teaching and learning mission. Other organizations may beat higher education institutions to this new market, and the organizations that do will likely be very difficult to dislodge, regardless of the objective quality of the products and services that they offer.

Third, networks and networked information enable a situation in which immediate, concrete community interests could overwhelm the capacity of higher education institutions to frame and address such interests, an instance of the "insurmountable opportunity" syndrome. Community service is but one of three higher education missions, and it is important that higher education institutions pursue the other two missions in a manner that is relatively free of the immediate, concrete interests of any individual community. Higher education institutions need to find ways to use networks to improve communication with community figures and about community interests, without assuming an inappropriate stance of "general accountability" to those leaders and those interests.

MISSION STRATEGIES

In conclusion, I believe that every higher education institution needs to formulate and pursue a four-part strategy if it is to seize the opportunities created and meet the challenges presented by networks and networked information.

First, I believe that it is important to make sure that as many people as possible in a given higher education institution have the opportunity to be exposed to and to contribute to that institution's vision for networks and networked information. We simply cannot rely upon people to get and develop the "right idea" about networks and networked information on their own and without a process of testing their ideas against those of others.

Second, I believe that there is no substitute for access to networks and networked information resources and services that provides common experience and stimulates useful discussion of what an institution wants and can get from networks and networked information. Every higher education institution needs a plan, no matter how extended the time frame, to provide ubiquitous and affordable access to its faculty, students, and staff.

Third, I believe that an institution's investments in a cultivated and shared vision and in wide and easy access will be squandered if human and other resources are not made available to support faculty, students, and staff in their attempts to use networks and networked information.

Fourth and finally, I believe an institution's strategy must also address the incentives that do and do not exist for using networks and networked information. I further believe that although an institution's strategy can provide some special incentives, that strategy should dwell primarily on how to amplify the attractiveness of incentives that already exist.

CHAPTER 4

What's Happening to the Book?

RICHARD A. LANHAM

I want to illustrate today what is happening to the book as we move from the age of print to the age of digital electronic information. I say "illustrate" rather than "discuss" to make a specific point. If we are to understand the mixed-media signal, which is, in many cases, replacing the print-on-a-paper page, we have to look at the new signal, rather than simply discuss it. That is what I would like us to do together today—look at some examples of the new signal and see what changes it is bringing. After we have done this, I will reflect briefly on the implications for teaching and scholarship that follow from this new multimedia signal, for it is certain that new professional practices and structures will be built on the multimedia expressive space just as the old ones were built upon the book.

The codex book, with a protective board on front and back, and printed text between, has been with us so long that it has become a transparent window into thought itself. We no longer notice it as a means of expression. The digital multimedia signal has made that transparent window into a speaking screen, rich in moving colors. Now, we notice it as an expressive means; it has lost its transparency. In the course of doing so, it tells us much we could not before see about the traditional printed book. Thus, illustrating what has happened to the book moves us not only forward into an unknown future but backward into a past understood anew.

Let me begin with a kind of book that will be familiar to this audience, a book of scholarly argumentation written by a professor in a technological university, and one which, at least in digital form, is available here in Japan

Paper presented at the International Roundtable for Information and Library Science, Kanazawa Institute of Technology, Library Center, Kanazawa, Japan, 1996.

for use on Japanese computers. The professor is Marvin Minsky, a mathematician from the Massachusetts Institute of Technology and one of the founders of its Artificial Intelligence Laboratory. The book, *The Society of Mind*, has been published in both printed and digital form. A comparison of the two should begin to answer our central question, "What is happening to the book?"

Here is the printed book, which I have brought with me from the United States for demonstration purposes. Like many books, it contains both printed text and illustrations. It measures 8½ by 11¾ inches and weighs about 1¾ pounds. I will not again refer to it, but you should bear it in mind. Now here is the digital version, on CD-ROM, which has been published by the well-known software publisher The Voyager Company.

The substrate on which the digital version is engraved weighs about half an ounce but the information it contains has effectively no weight and no dimensions. As librarians and information systems professionals, you know how cyberspace differs from regular Newtonian space. I do not need to spell it out. Let me, then, concentrate on the electronic book that dwells in this new space.

Here is its title page. What has happened during this first step into cyberspace? First, the black-and-white world of print has turned into the world of color, in which we all live. This is no inconsequential change; all the emotional associations we have with colors, all the behavioral clues they bring with them, flood back into the expressive space. We have, of course, had color printing for a very long time, but we seldom use it in scholarly monographs. Here it comes with the expressive space, and for the words as well as for the pictures. Color is a primary ingredient of the new multimedia expressive space, obvious but very powerful.

Second, the title page has composed itself before our very eyes. It moves into place. This movement puts the title page back into time. The printed text, because it is fixed, is timeless. This change from stasis to motion is fundamental to what is happening to the book. Of all the changes that have come to the book, it is perhaps the most profound.

Third, music has been added to the expressive space. The codex book is a silent world. It has been so since, in the Middle Ages, the practice of silent reading came to replace voiced, fully performed reading. When the codex book was the universal means of conceptual expression, we did not notice this silence. But, once we have heard the music, we hear its absence well, we hear the silence. This change is irreversible. Once we are accustomed to the music, we miss it. As we are already seeing, to look forward into the digital space means also looking back into the print space, seeing new things in both.

Fourth, a small face has appeared in the lower right hand corner of the text. He is new to the title page. More about him later. Now let us start reading the book. First, I might point out the various devices that allow us to annotate an electronic book; for example, underlining, marginal marking, and notation.

We notice a symbolic cube in the left margin and begin to explore it. Press the right button and out pops a menu; make the right menu selection and out pops the author. He walks out onto the page and begins to talk to us. Here is the man who peeped up at us from the title page. The author! What do we learn from this mini-lecture by the author of the book?

First, he talks about the argument of the book, and so we gain a second authorial perspective on it. Second, we see the author in person. We learn a great deal about what kind of person he is. How does he speak? How does he dress? He is not dressed in a formal scholarly costume of suit and tie, but informally, in a way that contrasts with the formal conventions of a printed book; and, we notice, he gestures frequently. Think for a moment of what an important role gesture plays in human life. In the history of Western rhetoric, the tradition invented in classical Greece, gesture was thought a major, a fundamental part of human utterance, and public speakers were schooled in the gestures appropriate to each argument and each presentation of self. Gestures were defined, cataloged, commented upon, memorized, rehearsed. That whole immense area of human expressivity was outlawed from the printed book. The digital book allows it to flow back in. Again, when we ponder Minsky's gestures, we learn something about the book of the future and something about the printed book as well. Let's now look at another way in which the author presents himself to the digital reader.

Here, the author has been videotaped but forgot his lines! The taping session failed, but it has been included nevertheless. What do we learn from this? The author is sufficiently certain of himself, has a sufficiently robust sense of humor, to let us into a rehearsal. We not only see the film, we visit the set. We become self-conscious about the creation of the public reality that constitutes the book. The famous scholar has a sufficient sense of humor to risk losing his dignity!

Next, we leave the formal public stage of the book, the "front stage" of the scholar, and move into the "back stage," into his house, the setting of his private life. Our houses speak volumes about who we are and how we live and what we care about and what our tastes are. The author here welcomes us directly into that part of his life, into his "study," into the exterior room where he pursues the interiority of his conceptual life. In the printed book, he presents his public self; in the multimedia text, that public self remains, but the private self emerges too, and the two enter a dialogue.

Let's pause to reflect for a moment on what seems a trivial issue. What has happened to the margin of the book? Here is where the author appears to us and walks around and gestures and talks. The margin has become the three-dimensional space of ordinary life, but it is also the two-dimensional symbolic space of alphanumerical printed text. These two spaces differ fundamentally. This difference is forced upon us by the digital text, because it imposes the one on the other. We cannot exist in both a three-dimensional behavioral space and a two-dimensional symbolic space at the same time. Our intellectual focus can only oscillate from one to the other. This oscillation is fundamentally unstable and it makes the digital multimedia space a fundamentally uneasy one. More than one set of reading rules is in force at one time. We are asked to be in the public space and in the private space at the same time. We cannot, but we can, move very quickly from the one to the other. This rapid oscillation takes some getting used to. It amounts, in the terminology of classical Western rhetoric, to a new kind of decorum. We too, as readers, are asked to be two different kinds of self, one public, one private, at the same time.

As a Western visitor to Japan, perhaps I may be permitted an additional comment here. It is often said that Asian cultures emphasize the public self and the public space, while Western cultures locate the private self and space at the center of society. Doubtless, this division exaggerates both sides, but to the degree that it applies, might we not see here, in the multimedia space, a new way to relate East and West? An alternation of the two ways to conceive self and society? I myself think this is true, and will indeed be true over a wide domain of digital communications between East and West.

Returning to our focus, in a printed book, you remain securely in a symbolic public space. You know the rules and they do not change. You are asked to pay only one kind of attention. You might think of the digital space and the printed space as two different kinds of economies. The printed space is a monopolistic economy. Only one kind of signal is permitted to broadcast: black-and-white print. In the digital expressive space, several signals broadcast and they compete for attention. Especially, two different kinds of social reality, public and private, and two different kinds of self, the central self and the social self, contend with one another. The multimedia signal embodies a market economy rather than a monopolistic one.

We have now read beyond the title page two or three pages into our digital book, but already profound changes have appeared. There seem to be two authors, and the private one comments on the writings of the public one. There is a backstage author-critic of the front-stage one; the two roles of author and critic merge into one. The two authors use, too, two different stylistic registers, the one more formal, the other less so. The two authors inhabit two very different kinds of space, and we must uneasily oscillate between the two. If you add up all these differences—and they are profound, fundamental ones—you arrive at a different kind of "seriousness" for the digital book. To explain what I mean by "seriousness" I am going to digress. Twenty years ago, I wrote a book called *The Motives of Eloquence*. It was thought of sufficient interest here in Japan to be translated into Japanese. (Japanese translation by T. Saotome, Arina Publishing Co., 1995.) I argued in that book that there were really two kinds of self, the private central self and the public social self. I called these two the "philosophical self" and the "rhetorical self." The book's central thesis argued that Western literature, throughout its history, followed a central structural principle: it alternated, in one way or the other, at one frequency or the other, these two kinds of self. If this thesis is correct, then we see in the multimedia signal a new way to do something very old indeed, something that reaches back to the Greek beginnings of Western culture. We see a new statement of this old oscillation between the rhetorical self and the serious self. The printed book, in its fundamental technology, aimed to shut this oscillation down. The digital book allows it to resume. I have no space here to extend this argument, but Japanese readers may do so by reading the first chapter of *The Motives of Eloquence* in the Japanese translation. The rich but unstable "seriousness" of the multimedia world alternates the rhetorical kind of "seriousness" with the philosophical kind, and builds a new and complex "seriousness" from the oscillation.

Now, let us take our demonstration one step further. The digital edition of *The Society of Mind* deliberately imitates the layout and look of a conventional book. Its alphabetic text is fixed in two dimensions. Let's now take one step further into the world of digital expression and look at its characteristic space, which creates not two dimensions but three. Again, let me begin with something familiar to all of you, the kind of computer-graphics logo effects often found on broadcast television.

What do we notice here? First, the two spaces that we saw in the Minsky text have now become one. The text exists in a single, three-dimensional behavioral space. We can ask of the letters a question that never occurs to us in reading a conventional book. "What does the back of a letter look like?" Letters become three-dimensional objects, like the letter-blocks in Minsky's *The Society of Mind*. They have texture and color. They exist in an architectural space and, inevitably, come to resemble buildings. I have often, in my work on English prose style, had occasion to refer to the "architectonics" of a sentence. Here, one could model such a metaphor literally, conceive of a sentence as a building in a townscape of language. What happens when this three-dimensional textual space is put to use for something besides advertising display? Here is an example of what might happen. A complex alphanumeric text is projected into three-dimensional space. We can penetrate literally deeper and deeper into the text. All kinds of syntactic and argumentative subordination might be employed in such a textual space. Different levels might be provided for different kinds of readers, or the same reader looking for different kinds of information at different times.

We cannot, now, see exactly how this three-dimensional textual space will be used, but we ought not to be totally surprised by it. It has been prophesied throughout the twentieth century by the visual arts. Let me show you a quick series of examples.

Here is a lesson in explosive typography by the Italian Futurist artist and pamphleteer, Filipo Tomaso Marinetti. It is called *Scccbrannng* and comes from the year 1919. What Marinetti does is throw a hand-grenade into the conventions of Western typography. He is trying to suggest a completely new way to think about the printed letter: as an image rather than a symbol; as an animated character rather than static letter. Western typography has only in the last few years, with the work of David Carson (and the imitators he has inspired in magazines like *Wired*), come to terms with the challenge Marinetti posed here.

Here is a painting by Giacomo Balla, another Italian Futurist, called *Numbers in Love*, from 1923. It shows the explosion of numbers into the three-dimensional space, which was to become a reality only with digital

Here is a third Futurist painting, by Francesco Cangiullo, from 1914. It is called *Università*. The animated letters are walking up the steps of the university, suggesting that an animated alphabet will change the very structure of that institution, as indeed it is doing right now.

The depiction of letters as a design object became commonplace in American visual art from the Pop Art period onward. Consider Claes Oldenburg's *Soft Letters*; Ed Rushka's *Annie*; David Hockney's *Melrose Avenue*; Stuart Davis's *Owh! In San Pao*; or Jennie Holzer's 1989 Guggenheim installation, which maps an alphabetic text onto an architectural surface in just the way a computer-graphics artist would texture-map a plain surface. All these paintings were saying the same thing: something profound is happening to the alphabetic space. Watch it and watch out! Letters are not what they used to be.

When a symbolic space like the space of text becomes thoroughly mixed with a behavioral space, as in these paintings, you get animation. Let me show you what I mean. Watch what happens to the letters in this television commercial for non-alcoholic beer: the letters are walking in a straight line. This animation is just what Cangiullo's *Università* would have done if it had had the means to do so. In such a space, typography becomes choreography. Letters are animated into people. The alphabet, in such an animated world, comes to equal a society. The syntax of the language would become the constitution of such a republic and the verbal style would be something like a cityscape. The two-dimensional world of text becomes a three-dimensional world of human behavior. Would any of these equivalencies hold in the non-alphabetic written notation of Japanese? I would be interested in hearing the topic discussed.

We enter the three-dimensional multimedia space by flying into it. This "fly-through," as it has come to be called, was invented by the computer-graphics world to simulate the flight of a low-flying aircraft. It has since become the generic way to enter a multimedia expressive space, used in the same way to enter a synthesized landscape or building or textual space.

Here is a beautiful example, created here in Japan, of an architectural fly-through. This building is an imaginative re-creation of Sendai Castle, a structure long since demolished. Imagine this architectural landscape as a generalized expressive space, waiting to be assigned meaning.

Let me illustrate how this might be done in a very different area—complex quantitative information. I am going to show you a computer visualization developed by the Quantal Corporation in Berkeley, California, to display investment portfolio information in a visual way. Alphanumeric text here metamorphoses into an expressive space, which has become architecture and dance at the same time. The page of a book has become an informational landscape, a landscape that aims, above all, to teach us situational awareness within a three-dimensional space.

Anyone who works in the library or information studies field has by now absorbed the disembodiment of the book, and the implications that follow from this. In the digital universe, all the places of physical storage—libraries, publishers' warehouses, bookstores—transform into something quite different. What has been less noted is the process we just described, whereby the information itself, words and pictures themselves, change into something quite different, a symbolic informational landscape over and through which we fly into the information itself.

Once we internalize this way of "reading" the new digital "book," we survey the past in a different way. Let me show you an example of what is a very complex phenomenon, rereading the static image in dynamic digital terms. We visit an art gallery, Haxton's *Art Dream*, and each of the still images becomes animated. In this sequence, we can see a fundamental change taking place. The still image, the painting, is viewed not as self-standing but as a temporary still-frame from a film. In the multimedia expressive space, the fundamental assumption about an image has changed. Images are essentially dynamic in nature. We fly into the two-dimensional surface of an image and find ourselves in the three-dimensional informational landscape which, as we have just seen, has evolved from printed text.

Can we think of any historical precedent for this kind of interaction? Let me now reach much further back into the past to reread a page from a book. This is a famous thirteenth-century manuscript from Bologna, in Italy, of the Codex Justinianus. The Roman Emperor Justinian had this Digest of the Laws—a summary of the works of Roman jurists—compiled in the middle of the sixth century. It survives in a single manuscript, which was rediscovered in the eleventh century and became a central text for the study of law in Bologna. The Digest text is surrounded by the gloss, or comments, by Accursius (1185–1263), a thirteenth-century commentator on Roman law from the Bolognese school. His comments, in turn, are surrounded by the comment of a later professor on Accursius, and finally by a student's comments on the professor's comments!

What can we learn from this? Obviously, the world of hypertext is nothing new. Less obviously perhaps, the hunger for a rich multimedia expressive space, one that uses words, images, and sounds, is not new either. Such a manuscript as this would, of course, have been read aloud in a classroom. The text was not silent. It was also illustrated by both abstract designs and a realistic deathbed scene, which accompanies the relevant text; and of course, there are all those comments on comments on comments. As we look at them fresh from the 3-D space of multimedia text, they now look a little different, don't they? It looks as if they float in three dimensions, not two, as if the smaller texts recede into the background. Some of the letters seem to metamorphose into images in their own right. The whole page is perfused with color.

We may use this example to suggest a larger conclusion. We have always yearned for the sensory richness of the multimedia signal and created as much of it as we could contrive or afford. The digital book thus does not break utterly with the books of the past, but reaches back over the world of black-and-white print to a richer manuscript tradition. We may thus argue, for Western expression at least, that the multimedia signal does not reject the past, but strives to recover it more fully, to understand it anew, in both the literal and the metaphorical senses of the word, to animate it.

This new animation includes, to summarize what we have seen, a new sense of the author and of authorial personalities, and a new kind of reader and manner of reading. The expressive space acquires depth and motion. We enter it by flying through its space and viewing its informational landscape as both a symbolic and a naturalistic one. All this depth, motion, and color brings with it a fundamental change.

The printed page of the book aimed to be transparent and unnoticed. We were to look through the text to the meaning beneath it. It may be that logographic notation like that used in Japan works differently; it would be interesting to discuss this, but Western alphabets, ever since the Greeks modified the Phoenician alphabet, have aimed to be unnoticed. The calligraphic impulse to create an alphabetic surface, though present, was suppressed. The great Greek scholar Eric Havelock argues that the Greek alphabet worked so well because it was simple enough to learn in early childhood. It became totally internalized and unselfconscious. It created, in effect, an aesthetic of renunciation. We were not to be distracted by images, by color, by movement, by the shape or texture of the letters themselves. All this was sacrificed to the clarity of abstract thought. If we are to think clearly, Havelock argued, we cannot have an alphabet that "thinks" too.

The alphabet of the multimedia book "thinks." It brings with it an ever-changing marketplace competition for our attention, which makes it permanently self-conscious and unstable. We have hardly begun to understand this unstable surface and have as yet little idea how it will wire immature brains, although we are beginning to feel how it dazzles older ones. But that it will change what reading means, and alter the kind of thinking that books have made possible, seems certain. The new, rich multimedia signal encapsulates the past but it presents us with a truly new, expressive space as well. How that space is stored and distributed—floppy disk, CD-ROM, Internet—is less important than the signal itself. We must ponder and understand it if we are to create a genuine digital literacy.

This brings me to my conclusion, a brief reflection on scholarship and teaching in the digital age. Our scholarly disciplines and departments are based on the static world of print. People who study words constitute one cluster of disciplines; those who study sounds, another; those who study images, a third. The multimedia signal mixes words, images, and sounds in new ways, and these will require new scholarly disciplines. The digital expressive space allocates human attention in new ways, and these new "economies of attention" will require new teaching techniques. Who will teach about a text that can be considered as architecture under one and as dance under another? We must from now on be self-conscious about how we design information, about how we decide whether to express it as word, image, sound, or a shifting mixture of the three. We need both new talents and new scholars to nurture and teach them. In our search for these new patterns of teaching and scholarship, I have suggested that we ponder the multimedia texts that are beginning to surround us, and that from this platform we look not only forward into the future, but back into the past. It is from the two, taken together, that we will draw the wisdom we need to fashion the human intellect anew in the digital age.

AUTHOR'S NOTE:

This article is the edited transcript of an illustrated lecture given to a Japanese-speaking audience via simultaneous translation, but without the still and moving images which formed the heart of its argument. The argument is developed further, with illustrations, in a later essay: "What's Next for Text?" *Education, Communication and Information*, Vol. 1. No. 1, 2001; ⟨http://www.gn.apc.org/uhollands/ECi/lanham/featset2.html⟩

CHAPTER 5

The Impact of Digital Technology on Libraries: A Chaotic Revolution

JERRY D. CAMPBELL

INTRODUCTION

Because of its power and versatility, digital technology has transformed libraries like no other invention since the introduction of moveable type; and because the application of digital technology to libraries has been underway for 30 years, it has reached into almost every aspect of library operations. Indeed, if the development of digital technology ceased at this moment, so great has been its impact upon libraries that they would be forever changed. Yet, one of the most surprising aspects of the introduction of digital technology within libraries has been its unsystematic, uneven, and unpredictable character. One might suppose that a tool of such possibility would have been universally welcomed and systematically used. Yet, it has not been so.

The purpose of this essay is to explore the nature of the application of digital technology in libraries and to summarize its impact, particularly on academic libraries. It will begin by examining the context within which digital technology has emerged. Aspects of this context include the nature of the growth and development of digital technology itself, the nature of our approach to applying digital technologies within libraries, and the complex socioeconomic environment within which libraries function. The essay will continue by considering how digital technology has reshaped the library world. These considerations will include reflections on how the library as an organization has changed, and observations on how the larger library world has been transformed. The essay will conclude by describing

Paper presented at the International Roundtable for Information and Library Science, Kanazawa Institute of Technology, Library Center, Kanazawa, Japan, 1995.

the vision of libraries that is emerging from this digitally transformed environment and suggesting some of the major challenges that remain to be met.

CHARACTERISTICS OF THE APPLICATION OF TECHNOLOGY

A full generation, 30 years, has passed since digital technology entered the library environment in earnest. One of the first indications of the magnitude of the potential impact of digital technology on libraries appeared when *Library Resources and Technical Services* (9:1, Winter 1965) devoted an entire issue to the new technology. The issue contained 10 articles that were revisions of papers presented at the American Library Association's pre-conference institute held at the University of Missouri, Columbia, in June 1964. These articles bore such titles as: "Computerized Cataloging: The Computerized Catalog at Florida Atlantic University" (Jean Perreault, 20–34); "Automatic Classification and Indexing, for Libraries?" (Donald V. Black, 35–52); "Computerized Serial Records" (Don S. Culbertson, 53–58); "Computerized Circulation Work: A Case Study of the 357 Data Collection System" (Ralph E. McCoy, 59–65); "Data Processing Aids in Acquisitions Work" (Louis A. Schultheiss, 66–72); and the ominous-sounding "The Machine and the Librarian (Ralph Parker, 100–103)." Even then, many of the major functions of libraries were seen to be targets for automation; and yet, over the intervening years, its adaptation to these functions has been spotty, unsystematic, and often controversial.

Nature of the Growth and Development of Digital Technology

Three features of the nature of the growth and development of digital technology have made its adoption and application difficult over the last three decades. First, the pace at which digital technology has developed has been increasingly rapid. In recent years, the manufacturing life span of specific pieces of hardware has often been measured in months. Particular generations of digital technologies have come and gone, often before complicated applications could be completed on specific platforms. Wholesale changes in operating systems have often required well-developed applications to be entirely reworked or abandoned. This circumstance would make the application of technology difficult and expensive enough if there were only one manufacturer involved, but there are many competing manufacturers. Thus, the effect of rapid change is magnified as companies compete to introduce new advances, providing the consumer with multiple and, often, incompatible platforms from which to choose.

This environment of rapid change adds significant elements of risk to efforts to apply digital technology in any environment; many of these elements are beyond the consumer's control. They include making unfortunate platform choices, managing large, unwieldy development projects, and losing start-up capital investments to rapid obsolescence. In the resource-constrained library environment, where start-up costs cannot be easily and quickly passed on to the consumer, such risks have mitigated against early and systematic adoption.

The second feature of the nature of the growth and development of digital technology that has made its adoption and application difficult has been its tendency to stem—to spread laterally. The growth of digital technology has often been likened to that of a biological system in which rapid mutating causes multiple related, but distinctive, subspecies to appear. Thus, the application of digital technology is not simply a matter of choosing a computer, but of dealing with a growing host of offspring, digitally based devices and processes. These have included major technologies relating to data storage, printing, scanning, and networking, to name just four. They have also encompassed a dizzying array of competing software. In all cases, these offspring technologies are themselves undergoing rapid change, and often affect the relative competitiveness of particular computing platforms. Thus, the offspring technologies further complicate efforts to apply digital technology by requiring consumers to deal with a complicated matrix of interrelated decisions in an uncomfortably short time span.

The speed of change in digital technology notwithstanding, the third factor affecting rapid adoption has been the incremental process by which it has approached maturity. The capacities of computing platforms (with regard to speed, RAM and ROM, and so on) did not spring forth fully capable of supporting large library operations 30 years ago, nor did the offspring technologies fulfill the users' hopes when they were introduced. So, while the pace of development was comparatively rapid, it may also be said to have been slow enough to have placed major (and frustrating) limits on its functionality at any given moment. This, combined with the race to improve the capacity of computing platforms, created the dual problems of suboptimal performance and recurring obsolesce for the entire three decades. To make this point more simply, if the powerful computers and other digital support systems available now had been available immediately in 1965, the history of library automation might have been written more smoothly and triumphantly.

Thus, these characteristics resident in the nature of the growth and development of digital technology itself have exercised considerable influence in creating the uneven pattern in the acceptance and application of technology within libraries.

Troublesome Features in the Application of Digital Technology

The application of digital technology within libraries over the past three decades has also exhibited certain recurring features that have reinforced the unsystematic, uneven, and unpredictable elements in its growth and development. Among them, the following are notable:

Superficial Beginnings. It has been observed that digital technology is first applied to old, familiar tasks, only gradually giving birth to entirely new and better methods (Naisbitt 1982: 19). Within the library world, this phenomenon has characterized applications from the outset. The 1965 edition of *Library Resources and Technical Services,* cited previously, focused on major, familiar library functions with the purpose of automating them. The introduction of the acclaimed MARC (Machine Readable Cataloging) record format in 1968, the impact of which was tremendous, was little more than a conversion of records created, according to the *Anglo-American Cataloging Rules* (AACR) (1967), into machine-readable form.[1] These examples were typical of efforts to bring automation into libraries, and both represented efforts to "automate" existing functions rather than initiatives to reconceive processes *in toto* around the characteristics of digital technology.

The success of applications that represented superficial beginnings often slowed progress to achieve fundamental reconceptualizations. In the West, for instance, the MARC format, although criticized for its failure to rethink the basic bibliographic record (Hegerty 1985), remains the *lingua franca* of machine-readable records within libraries, even today. While the existence of the MARC record has not precluded the possibility of creative alternatives over the years, the pervasiveness of its acceptance and use has created an overwhelming obstacle. Indeed, not until recently have calls for change (Gregor and Mandel 1991), new formats for record storage, and the so-called Web information storage and retrieval technologies begun to reawaken interest in the basic record itself.

One of the first major innovative applications of digital technology was Frederick G. Kilgour's efforts, in the late 1960s and early 1970s, to lead a group of librarians in Ohio to create what we now know as OCLC,[2] the largest online bibliographic utility in the world. The innovative element for OCLC did not lie in the machine-readable records themselves (since they were basically MARC records) but in the notion of shared cataloging. This constituted the first large-scale, successful introduction of networking based on digital technology, and within a few years it began to transform the cataloging process throughout North America.

However, early success for OCLC served to reinforce the predominance of the MARC record and AACR cataloging practices. Success also slowed OCLC's innovative spirit. It was too compelling for the agency simply to spin off features from the activity that constituted its core business. Many such features were exciting and useful, but they did not represent breakthrough ideas. Not until the decade of the 1980s did OCLC again exhibit signs of serious investigation of new directions and endeavors (see, for example, Mason 1986); and while OCLC's bibliographic database remains tied to its MARC records even today, its founder and most original thinker, Dr. Kilgour (now in retirement), has moved beyond the agency in his research to push once again at the conceptual edges of library practices (Kilgour 1995).

The lessons of these examples are that our efforts to apply digital technology have been typically superficial and that such efforts, when successful, inhibited us from pursuing conceptual advances for the library functions involved. Success could be costly in more ways than one.

Unrealistic Expectations versus Unfounded Skepticism. Another troublesome feature of our efforts to apply digital technology has been the constant debate between those who expect too much too soon and those who regard the whole thing as blown out of proportion and oversold. Although most librarians occupied some reasonable ground between the extremes, the extremes always garnered considerable attention and fed an ongoing disagreement about the likely future of libraries and librarianship (Mason 1972; Avram 1972). This disagreement bred confusion and disunity in the larger library community regarding the application of digital technology.

While neither those who expressed unrealistic expectations nor the skeptics may claim absolute vindication, history has demonstrated a gradual, steady drift in the direction of an increasing role for digital technology in libraries. Not surprisingly, representatives of both extremes continue to enliven the library world.

The Lack of a Research Core. When it comes to research, the discipline of library science is something of an anomaly by comparison to other scientific or social scientific fields. In other disciplines, it is most often the faculties of universities who serve as the intellectual pioneers, pushing the conceptual boundaries of their disciplines. Most scientific disciplines advance by this model. It is not that major conceptual breakthroughs do not occur outside the science or social science faculties of universities, but, as a matter of course, faculty members are the most active individuals in pursuing such breakthroughs.

Library and information science, on the other hand, has depended almost entirely upon practitioners for advancement during the age of digital technology. The habit has been for working librarians to create projects and submit them to funding agencies. Thus, it is likely that most such "research" projects have involved single institutions. This has been troublesome in the application of digital technology because most practitioners can engage in research only in fits and starts, since libraries, unlike industries, customarily have no departments or personnel devoted entirely or even primarily to research and development.

The absence of a stable research core for library and information science has had a number of decidedly negative effects on the process of using digital technology. It has meant that there has often been no coordination of efforts among institutions (although this has been improved recently because major funding agencies have encouraged multi-institution projects). In addition, most initiatives have been short term and limited in scope because the process has depended almost entirely on grant funding, and libraries lacked the funds necessary to continue on their own. Also, often projects have been ill defined or poorly carried out because those responsible have been unaccustomed to project management, simultaneously carrying other library responsibilities and lacking deep technical proficiency.

When combined with the characteristics resident in the nature of the growth and development of digital technology, these three troublesome features in the application of digital technology have made its adoption extremely challenging. They also shed light on why it has taken the library world 30 years to achieve its current state of progress.

Culture and the Rise of Digital Technology

There is one final factor that has influenced the process by which digital technology has been incorporated in library practices and which has contributed as well to its uneven and chaotic history. This factor derives from the socioeconomic context within which libraries reside. Libraries constitute only one part of what may be described as a scholarly publishing continuum. They share the enterprise with other, major representatives, chief among which are authors, publishers, and readers. For better or worse, digital technology has implications for the entire continuum. Although each representative manages a portion of the whole, none controls the entire continuum. Unfortunately, there has been little or no coordination between the two corporate players, libraries, and publishers. To the contrary, the interests of libraries and publishers have occasionally come into conflict. This conflict has most often centered on the issues of copyright and fair use, and has grown increasingly intense because of the ease with which digital information may be reproduced. Consequently, the evolution of digital technology in libraries has been vastly different from its evolution in the publishing industry. Yet, before a digitally based knowledge environment can be perfected, the differences must be bridged.

Given the challenges in learning to use digital technology over the past 30 years, it is not surprising that it has been applied unsystematically and unevenly in libraries. Concern with digital technology has consumed great time and energy from librarians. Considering the difficulties, it is a wonder that progress has been made at all, and it seems almost miraculous when the most significant achievements are considered.

While it would take many volumes to chronicle all the ways in which digital technology has affected libraries over these three decades, several major impacts can be observed.

A RESHAPED (AND STILL CHANGING) LIBRARY WORLD

Reshaped Libraries as Organizations

In certain ways, the decade of the 1960s constituted the golden age for libraries in the West. It was, by today's measure, a comparatively wonderful time. Many libraries saw their budgets increased significantly. Scholarly publishing was healthy and growing, but still manageable in volume; and, working together, librarians from North America and Great Britain succeeded in codifying the standards for bibliographic description (the *Anglo-American Cataloging Rules*, or AACR). Even before publication, it was acclaimed as "the most complete compilation of cataloging rules that has ever been available to American libraries" (Field 1966: 421). The library community knew what it was doing. It had gotten it right. From book collecting (Dougherty 1965) to library architecture, the science of libraries was well developed in every respect. The great concerns of the time had been focused on codifying a library world that was rapidly being perfected. The basic services, procedures, management, and organizational structure of libraries were settled. Never before (or since) had libraries brought so clear a mission so close to fulfillment.

Digital technology, however, was one of the factors that ended the golden age almost before it began. It did so by facilitating the production of more published knowledge than librarians could catalog using AACR principles, by introducing vast, new (and controversial) possibilities for library functions, by introducing a totally new set of costs into the library environment, and by absorbing the attention of librarians. These, plus the increasingly rapid rate of change, placed the rigid, 1960s-style library organization under stress. Thus, while virtually all of today's libraries continue to provide access to print-on-paper resources, they are nonetheless radically different institutions than they were 30 years ago, and most of the changes have come about because of, or with the aid of, digital technology.

Reengineered Organizations. There are seven interrelated characteristics of traditional library organizations that suffered stress in the fast-paced, increasingly digital library, and that have recently begun to change: management system, organizational structure, information flow, work environment, work process, response to external stimuli, and funding model.

With few exceptions, the management system employed in libraries has been hierarchical. Top administrators typically make decisions of any importance. Library staff beneath the executive level could change work policies and procedures that pertained to their local areas only by making recommendations through channels to executive-level personnel or by service on special committees or task forces as established by executive-level personnel. To put it conversely, libraries have not used a management system that gives those who are most familiar with the work and service the power to make work and service policy, to be creative as they encounter changing needs, or to consider solutions to emerging problems.

This management system posed major difficulties at a time of significant and rapid change. It automatically excluded the creative potential of many library staff members. It conditioned most of them to expect to have no influence on decisions. In addition, the hierarchical management system did not accommodate change very quickly. It was a vertical decision tree requiring everything to rise to the top. Resolving questions and issues meant repeatedly passing information up and down the pyramid. It often took a very long time to make decisions—even about minor matters. Thus, most libraries faced the challenge of digital technology with management systems that discouraged new ideas and responded slowly.

The most common organizational structure in recent years has been consistent with the management system. Graphically represented, it was a series of boxes arranged in a pyramid. The chief librarian was represented by the box at the top. The height of a box in the pyramid signified the importance and status of the individual represented by the box. Beneath the top box, other boxes were arranged into groups, usually called departments. Most libraries had their own versions of the same departments. Within departments, the great pyramid of the whole library was reproduced by a smaller pyramid representing the "pecking order" within departments. The only connection between staff members in different departments was vertical, occurring when common supervisors were found, and this was usually at the executive level near the top of the pyramid.

Such organizations did not easily facilitate interaction among departments. Even in smaller libraries, staff members in one department often did not know those in another. In addition, this organizational structure encouraged specialization. Some librarians served entire careers within the confines of a single department. Others, despite moving among libraries, kept the same departmental focus. The organizational structure, therefore, has not encouraged developing broad knowledge and flexible perspectives among librarians. Departmental boundaries have not been easily penetrated or moved.

In these hierarchical, rigid organizations, the flow of information has tended to be vertical. Staff have often worked hard on issues and passed the results of their labors up the organization, only to be left wondering what the administration decided. In addition, it has been difficult to be well-informed about what is happening across departmental lines, and organization-wide communication has often been in the form of announcements after the fact. Such organizations have not created information-rich environments. This was a serious deficiency, since limited awareness of broad organizational issues inhibited the conceptual thinking needed to accommodate digital technology.

In recent decades, the library work environment has been centered on the individual. Librarians typically cooperated by dividing work into components and each taking a piece, and by serving on committees or task forces. Each pursued her or his own tasks in relative isolation. This was a decided disadvantage, since digital technology did not observe the existing boundaries that separated library tasks.

Most library work processes have been procedure- and service-based, with major responsibilities being to carry out instructions and assignments. For years, therefore, librarians have focused their energy on execution, and they have been evaluated and compensated on that basis. Rarely, if ever, has creative thinking been listed as a responsibility. This task orientation and focus on execution has not led naturally to the reconceptualization of library practices.

The foregoing factors have created a situation in which most individuals were divorced from decision making, restricted to their own department, ill-informed, isolated, and evaluated on how well they executed dearly defined tasks. If one added to this situation an increasing workload, the result was a staff that was harried, filled with anxiety over matters beyond its immediate control, and characterized by low morale. Staff did not take readily to the opportunity to learn a new technology.

Such an organization may be graphically depicted, as shown in Figure 5.1. At the start of the digital era, libraries' organizational characteristics tended to fall to the left end of the spectrum. Libraries did not respond well in the rapidly changing digital arena, changing slowly if at all, and they wasted the most precious resource available to them, the creativity of the staff. Conversely, libraries that could gravitate to the right end of the spectrum in most categories could create a "can do" attitude and adjust more readily to the changing environment. Digital technology, therefore, became a force to move more library organizations in this direction. As they have moved, libraries have become more flexible, nimble, and capable of accommodating change more rapidly. This movement to re-engineer libraries as organizations, like the application of digital technology, is neither uniform nor systematic among libraries, but it has begun in earnest in the decade of the 1990s.

Training, Teaming, and Tooling. Over the years, digital technology also created the need for new skills, work environments, and work methods among the library work force. The pressure to thrive in the fast-paced, economically challenged digital environment has focused attention as never before on matters of cost-effectiveness and management science. The need to lead the transformation of entire organizations requires skills and techniques not present in old-style organizations, where few librarians even espoused a specified management system.

Training has become the cornerstone of the new organization. It is both the key to learning new organizational and management systems and the

Figure 5.1
Characteristics of the Current Library Environment

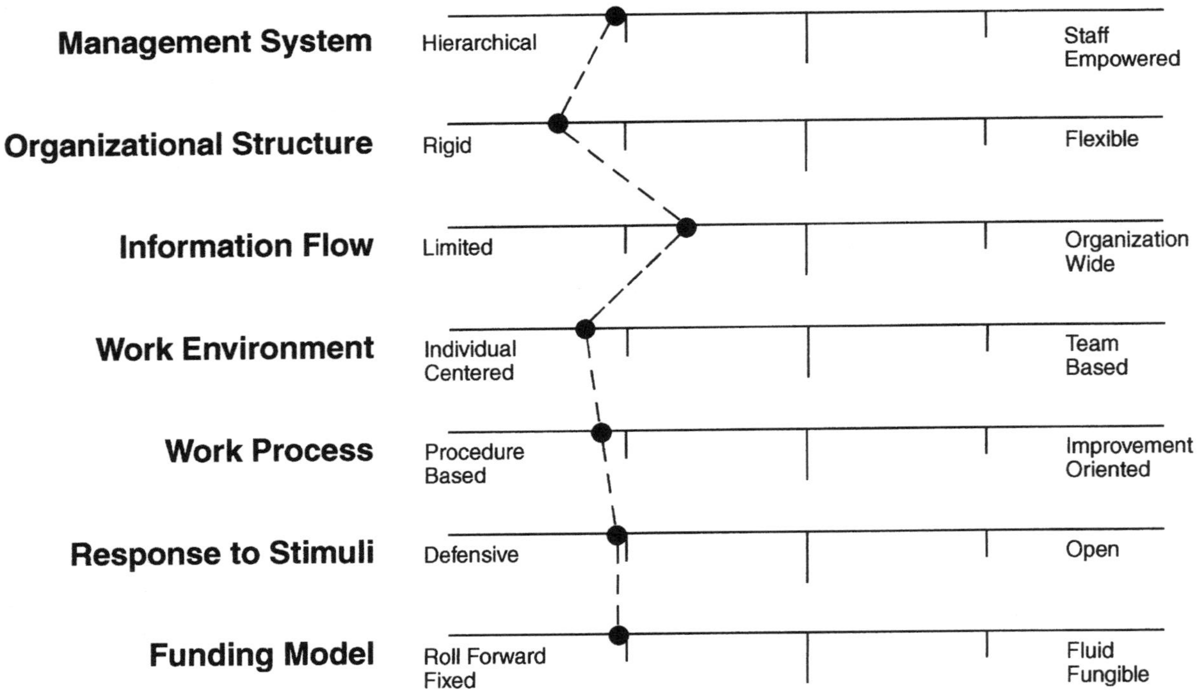

Management System	Hierarchical				Staff Empowered
Organizational Structure	Rigid				Flexible
Information Flow	Limited				Organization Wide
Work Environment	Individual Centered				Team Based
Work Process	Procedure Based				Improvement Oriented
Response to Stimuli	Defensive				Open
Funding Model	Roll Forward Fixed				Fluid Fungible

means of keeping up as technology and information continue to change. While libraries have always engaged in some staff training, the process has focused mainly on maintaining and teaching work procedures. Professional librarians have recognized the need for improving management skills and other tools for the workplace, but have often been required to pursue them on an individual basis, largely in pre-conference or workshop settings. Opportunities for such enrichment training have been unavailable to most of our staff members who are not professional librarians.

Achieving a new organizational design requires that we provide training opportunities for every staff member. For best results, these opportunities should include learning the management system of choice, improving personal skills, and acquiring the necessary technology training. Offering a continuing curriculum of training opportunities is our best guarantee that our libraries will remain viable as organizations. Large libraries should offer such training in-house or in conjunction with parent institutions. Smaller libraries may also work with parent institutions or team with other libraries or associations.

There is a reason for the corporate world's interest in a team-based approach to business. Teams are flexible; they can be more responsive to the demands of a rapidly changing market-place, and this adaptability can be the competitive edge that means survival. Teams can be focused on projects, they can be cross-functional, and they can be created quickly. Teams can provide the same benefits to libraries as they do business. Whatever management systems libraries choose, they must provide the flexibility that teams allow for in dealing with the host of problems and opportunities that arise daily. It will be increasingly difficult for our libraries to evolve toward a more digital future if they remain hierarchically organized into departments whose origins reflect the characteristics and needs of managing paper.

Sometimes human limitations arise not because of failure of attitude or effort, but because individuals have not been equipped with the tools necessary to do the job. In this sense, tools mean more than just pens, paper, and computers. They encompass the techniques necessary to plan, conduct, and follow up successful meetings, or methods for managing effective projects, such as the Joiner 7-Step Method (1990). Tools include methods to help gather data, assess it, and use it to produce informed decisions. These include flow charts, pareto charts, cause/effect diagrams, time plots, control charts, and others.

Acquiring such tools provides librarians with the means to approach work in new ways and gives them confidence in the outcome. The results are usually impressive. Such tools are essential in the evaluation of existing procedures for the purpose of improving them or in the design of new endeavors such as those necessitated by technological change. Organizations cannot be transformed without them.

Because of digital technology, training, teaming, and tooling are increasingly apparent in libraries today. They have become essential elements in the effort to move libraries toward the flexible, adaptable organizations required in this generation of rapid and fundamental change.

Changing Service Paradigm. As early as 1967, there was speculation about the implications of digital technology for library service, and it continued unabated as automation advanced (Wheeler 1967; Peck 1972). Over the years, even as libraries continued to offer traditional services, the service paradigm began to change. While this change has been multifaceted, one of its most fundamental aspects has been the exchange of face-to-face encounters for remote, electronic exchanges. As digital information proliferates, the balance of information continues to shift from print to electronic, and just as surely, the library is evolving from a warehouse operation to something more akin to a licensing agent and networked access provider. Indeed, the byword prompted by digital information has already become *access* as distinct from *ownership*.

Along with this conceptual shift to access, electronic document delivery has become a major (and growing) means by which libraries provide information. Meanwhile, the library, previously the great physical center of information, has begun to diminish in importance as a location, a building. It is as if the idea of "the library" is increasingly viewed as nothing more than a service. Within this changing notion of library is imbedded the reflection of the changing character of the larger library world.

The Emerging Common Vision

Powered by digital technology applied to the creation of knowledge, the amount of recorded knowledge has grown at an increasing rate each year. Overwhelmed by this outpouring, librarians have been forced to abandon the briefly feasible concept of the library of record—even for printed knowledge alone. It is no longer possible to try to amass all recorded knowledge in one physical location. Yet, even as digital technology rendered the concept of the library of record obsolete, it made possible the concept of a new kind of comprehensive repository: the virtual digital library.

This concept of a vast network of digital resources, available through national and international networks to the desktop of the information user, is emerging as a common vision within the library world. Like other applications of digital technology, the concept initially exceeds the capacity of technology to deliver, since in the imagination it has no limits; and it suffers from all the ills described above: rapid change, poor coordination, and disagreement. Yet, it has begun, and it is moving forward inexorably, with jerky, staggering steps, toward the possibility of the virtual library utopia.

SOME FINAL CHALLENGES

While there are no doubt thousands of challenges left in perfecting the new digital knowledge environment, a few matters stand out:

The Problem of Archival Storage. This challenge pertains both to the longevity of digital storage media and to what might be called post-catastrophic failure rights. If digital libraries are to be stable, they must be able to withstand the test of time by some affordable, dependable means. Similarly, if the concept of access is to succeed, institutions of higher learning must have some assured means of access to commercially owned data in cases of bankruptcy or other corporate disasters.

Copyright, Licenses, and Other Legal Barriers. Copyrights and licenses have become a matter of debate in the digital environment because of the value of knowledge as a commodity to be bought and sold. There are inherent dangers to the world of higher education in the commodification of knowledge, the greatest of which is that higher education will be shut away from its own heritage because of costs. It is not possible for the virtual library to become a reality until the legal issues are resolved to the satisfaction of all parties.

Unsystematic Development. The factors noted in the first part of this essay, those that prevent coordinated, systematic, and grand progress in perfecting digital technology, still hinder librarians. Indeed, Brian L. Hawkins recently proposed that incrementalism will not soon deliver the desired virtual library (1994). Yet, for reasons previously cited, incrementalism is vastly more likely than any concerted action among the plethora of interested parties. It appears, therefore, that the complex set of problems and characteristics that have accompanied digital technology for 30 years still haunt its progress.

Challenges notwithstanding, the impact of digital technology on libraries shows no sign of slowing. To the contrary, it is a young technology changing with amazing rapidity and challenging all aspects of libraries to keep pace. Thus, it is not a possibility, but a certainty, that the transformation of libraries has just begun.

NOTES

1. *Library Resources and Technical Services* 12(3) (Summer 1968) devotes an entire issue to the MARC project.

2. OCLC was incorporated on July 6, 1967, and its shared cataloging became operational on October 18, 1971. See Hopkins (1973).

REFERENCES

Anglo-American Cataloging Rules, North American Text. 1967. Chicago: American Library Association.

Avram, Henriette D. 1972. Library Automation: A Balanced View. *Library Resources and Technical Services* 16(1): 11–18.

Dougherty, Richard M. 1965. Year's Work in Acquisitions. *Library Resources and Technical Services* 9(2): 149–56.

Field, Francis Bernice. 1966. The New Catalog Code: The General Principles and the Major Changes. *Library Resources and Technical Services* 10(4): 421–36.

Gregor, Dorothy, and Carol Mandel. 1991. Cataloging Must Change! *Library Journal* 116(6): 42–47.

Hawkins, Brian L. 1994. Creating the Library of the Future: Incrementalism Won't Get Us There! *The Serials Librarian* 24(314): 17–47.

Hegerty, Kevin. 1985. Myths of Library Automation. *Library Journal* 110(16): 43–49.

Hopkins, Judith. 1973. The Ohio College Library Center. *Library Resources and Technical Services* 17(3): 308–19.

Joiner Associates. 1990. *Joiner 7-Step Method*. Madison, Wisc.: Joiner Associates.

Kilgour, Frederick G. 1995. Effectiveness of Surname-Title-Words Searches by Scholars. *Journal of the American Society for Information Science* 46(2): 146–51.

Mason, Ellsworth. 1972. Computers in Libraries. *Library Resources and Technical Services* 16(1): 5–10.

Mason, Robert M. 1986. EIDOS: Beyond Bibliographies. *Library Journal* (November 1): 46–47.

Naisbitt, John. 1982. *Megatrends: Ten New Directions Transforming Our Lives.* New York: Warner Books.

Peck, Theodore P. 1972. Reference Librarian Recast in a New Role. *RQ* 11(3): 212–13.

Wheeler, Joseph L. 1967. Bettering Reference Service. *RQ* 6(3): 99–114.

CHAPTER 6

The Future Value of Digital Information and Digital Libraries

MICHAEL LESK

Thank you for inviting me to your roundtable, and I am very flattered to be here in Kanazawa. I will talk about how I see value coming from digital information, and what kinds of changes I see coming about as a result. To summarize in advance,

1. Digital libraries are now economically efficient, and the area is booming;
2. Digital technology offers great advantages for libraries;
3. The adoption of digital information will mean changes in the role of libraries, and in how we manage them.

The most important question we must answer is how we will build a self-supporting system of digital information in a world in which libraries will need to cooperate more than they ever have in the past. In the digital world, it matters much less what libraries own and hold on their own shelves. It matters much more what they can access for their patrons. So libraries will be sharing the provision of information, and will have to trade a great many services among themselves. How will we be able to arrange things so that libraries can cooperate, rather than fight each other for patrons? How can we establish the value of librarians and library services?

WHY DIGITAL LIBRARIES ARE COMING

All libraries are under pressure as the costs of journals increase. The Mellon Foundation has prepared studies showing that between 1970 and

Paper presented at the International Roundtable for Information and Library Science, Kanazawa Institute of Technology, Library Center, Kanazawa, Japan, 1995.

2000, the typical U.S. academic research library will lose 90 percent of its purchasing power (Cummings 1992). The state of California went from more than one hundred hours of public library opening per one thousand residents to less than 50 hours from 1977 to 1993. Electronics offer several ways in which libraries can improve service while reducing cost. For example, fax machines have already made it more practical for libraries to buy copies of single articles on demand. But, digital storage carries with it even more advantages of service, and now looks as if it is about to offer cost benefits as well. Libraries may have looked the same for many centuries, but the changes under the surface are about to erupt.

In fact, the use of author-generated electronic information is growing rapidly in many areas without much, if any, involvement of libraries, thanks to the Internet. There are more than one hundred electronic journals now; one of the best known is *Psycoloquy*, edited by Steven Harnad.

Andrew Odlyzko has written an important paper arguing that traditional journals are likely to be replaced with all-electronic versions (1995). Perhaps the most dramatic example of the importance of these bulletin boards is the High-Energy Physics bulletin board run by Paul Ginsparg at Los Alamos. This is now one of the most common places for physicists to find out about new ideas. When Ginsparg found himself overwhelmed with clerical work and withdrew the service, physicists everywhere protested, and did so loudly enough to get help assigned by the Los Alamos management (Taubes 1993).

Although the instantaneous availability of online information accounts for some of its interest, one of the most important advantages of digital libraries is the ease with which they can be searched. When full-text databases are available, any word or phrase can be found immediately. As I will discuss later, this makes several kinds of tasks faster and more accurate for library users. In addition, digital storage means that items are never off-shelf; it means that a copy is as good as an original, so there is no need to worry about deteriorating physical media; and it means that a copy can be electronically delivered across campus as easily as within the library. Libraries need no longer define their patrons as people who walk in the door.

All of this has been true since libraries began to use computer storage. Now, the rapid decline in the cost of computer equipment, combined with the steady increase in the costs of buildings and staff, are about to make digital storage economical even for older materials. In the CLASS project at Cornell, scanning an old book cost a bit more than $30 (Kenney and Personius 1992). This was for material that is sufficiently fragile to require placing each page on a flatbed scanner. Paper strong enough to go through a mechanical feeder can probably be scanned for a quarter of that price. The cost of the disk space, even continuously online disk, to hold the scanned pages of the book, is less than $10. The disk drive industry will ship 15 petabytes this year, or 2.5 megabytes per person in the world! The magnetic tape industry will ship two hundred petabytes of blank tape, enough to hold the entire Library of Congress ten thousand times.

Meanwhile, the cost of building bookstacks in libraries continues to increase. Cornell has recently finished a stack that costs $20 per book. Berkeley is building one at a price of $30 per book. At the University of California San Francisco, which is building an earthquake-resistant library in a complex and cramped site, storage costs $60 per book. At the new British Library storage costs about $75 per book; at the new national library in Paris (the Bibliothèque nationale de France) it will cost about $100 per book. Admittedly, the last three prices include the construction of reading rooms and offices, and other costs—considerably more than just a bookstack. Nevertheless, we are already at a stage where a library might seriously balance building a central campus stack against scanning a few hundred thousand out-of-copyright books.

A library can save money with the "Harvard solution" of an off-site depository, built out of sight where land is cheap and architecture is unnecessary. The Harvard Depository costs perhaps $2 per book to build, but incurs both the cost of shuttling books back and forth to the users, and the service penalty of not having the books immediately available (or browsable). The shuttling cost, however, is such that Don Waters of Yale has estimated that within 10 years, digital scanning will be a cheaper solution than offsite storage. For many libraries, such as corporate libraries, off-site locations are not used, and whatever storage is used is charged at full office building rates. These libraries have even greater incentives to substitute electronic documents for paper (and are more likely to be able to do it, since they normally have more current material that is available in machine-readable form).

Returning to the preservation model, if several different libraries all need to have the same books scanned, there are additional economies. As with microfilm, doing the conversion once and then sharing the results among several libraries is a great cost saving. The Mellon Foundation is funding project JSTOR, in which 10 economics and history journals (five of each) are being scanned as a way of seeing whether a great many libraries can all save some shelf space by using the electronic copies. In another project, Cornell is scanning the world's agricultural literature up to 1950, not so much to save shelf space as to permit distribution of the literature to libraries that don't have copies. Both of the projects are careful to obtain copyright permission for every work still protected.

There are other scanning projects being done not to save money, but to improve access. Particularly valuable or particularly fragile manuscripts may be scanned to let scholars see them without risk of damage. The British Library, for example, is involved with scanning both the *Beowulf* manuscripts (stored at the University of Kentucky) and the *Canterbury Tales* manuscripts (with Oxford University). These projects demonstrate that scanning, under different kinds of illumination, can show features of the manuscripts more easily than simple visual examination in ordinary room light (Robinson 1993). On a larger scale, H3M is scanning many manuscripts from the Vatican library, and the archives of Spanish documents about the Americas held in the Archivo General de Indias in Seville. These materials will have the potential to be made available around the globe, instead of only to those who can travel to them.

Of course, the costs of scanning old material, and the disk storage, are only parts of the costs of building a digital library. There needs to be an infrastructure of terminals, networks, and people to support them (and to help users with difficulties). Fortunately, libraries are developing this infrastructure for other reasons. The switch to online catalogs has brought computers and networks to many library buildings, and the for-profit information services are expanding them. Traditionally, libraries have relied on the marketplace for most of their technology, and just as librarians find themselves wanting a way to get the infrastructure to support preservation of old material, it is arriving in the form of the businesses involved in distributing new material.

THE GROWTH OF INFORMATION AS AN INDUSTRY

The idea of information delivery as an industry is very new. It is true that there were for-a-fee lending libraries in eighteenth-century England. However, for most of the twentieth century, although books were sold, libraries normally did not charge their patrons to read them. Many librarians still view this as a principle and argue strongly that in most organizations, information should be free. There is a saying among chemical information specialists that a month in the laboratory can save you an hour in the library. Therefore, businesses should not discourage their employees from looking up information. However, as new kinds of information became available, it became common to charge for them. U.S. corporations want to treat all component operations as businesses, and, furthermore, the first text retrieval systems were so expensive that they could not realistically be made available free.

Information retrieval is now a rapidly growing industry. In the United States, the electronic information industry had revenues of about $15.6 billion in 1994, and grew 16 percent from 1993 (Hillstrom 1994). Of this, about two-thirds of the revenue is from online resources, an eighth from CD-ROM, and the rest from tape sales or other media. CD-ROM is growing fastest, doubling each year through the early 1990s. Time-Warner has estimated a U.S. market of $400 billion per year for the "information superhighway" products. Since everything being printed today passes through a computer, we can capture it for later computer distribution. Thus, there

Table 6.1
Information Vendors, 1993

Revenues	Company
$550M	Mead Data Central (Reed Elsevier)
$243M	Dialog (Knight-Ridder)
$223M	Prodigy (IBM, Sears)
$210M	Westlaw (West Publishing)
$177M	CompuServe (H&R Block)
$83M	Dow Jones News Retrieval
$43M	Genie (GE)
$40M	America Online
$36M	BRS/Orbit
$29M	Data Broadcasting
$25M	InfoAmerica
$11M	Delphi (Newscorp)

Source: Rodriguez (1995).

is now an enormous business in ASCII information distribution. In 1993, sales of paper-based information exceeded electronic by almost 10 percent. By 1994, however, sales of paper information were comparable to electronic sales, not larger. Some libraries, such as pharmaceutical libraries, are spending more than half their acquisitions funds on electronic sources.

There were 2.8 million business subscribers and 3.4 million consumer subscribers to online services in 1993, and the growth rate here is also rapid. Business subscribers grew 25 percent in 1993, while consumer subscribers increased 44 percent. About 30 percent of the sales of U.S. online services are to non-U.S. customers. The industry employs about 45,000 people in the United States. In fact, if one combines the software, data processing, and information retrieval industries, these companies employ more people than automobile manufacturing.

Most of the companies making a lot of money selling online retrieval are selling to businesses. Dun and Bradstreet's sells over $1 billion worth of online retrieval a year, and companies such as Dow Jones, TRW, and Trans-Union Credit sell hundreds of millions of dollars in financial data. In what we would consider the library world, the biggest suppliers are in the legal information business. Table 6.1 shows the largest online vendors.

Some of these companies would object to this table since they are growing particularly rapidly: CompuServe and America Online in particular. CompuServe claims revenues of $430 million in 1994, with a growth rate of 36 percent. These vendors operate enormous storage files; Mead, for

Table 6.2
Text Retrieval Market

1990	$80M
1991	$175M
1992	$232M
1993	$303M
1994	$385M
1995	$506M*
1996	$658M*

*forecast.
Source: Rodriguez (1995).

example, had 2.4 terabytes of online information in early 1994, with 1.6 terabytes of inverted file for indexing. For comparison, if all of the 20 million books in the Library of Congress were keyed, it would take only about 10 terabytes.

Text retrieval software by itself is about a $500 million business. Table 6.2 shows the growth of the business.

There are more than one hundred companies supplying text search or browser software (including Bellcore's SuperBook software). The largest companies in the business are shown in Table 6.3. Note that small companies dominate the business, with no single company having even a tenth of the business.

There is also, of course, a large free information distribution system on-line, the Internet. At present growth rates, every human will be on the Net in about 2001. The very disorganization of the Net makes it difficult to know how much information is out there. Lycos has found more than 5 million documents, but they vary enormously in size, and there might be four times as many pages inside corporations or otherwise hidden. The entire Net might contain 20 gigabytes of information, of extremely variable quality. Netnews is distributing about 140,000 articles per day containing 450 megabytes. In 1993, this number was 50 megabytes, and in 1989 it was 1 megabyte. Unfortunately, five of the six largest newsgroups are still those that feature obscene pictures. The Net in general is doubling each year, although the largest single traffic source is still FTP (file transfer). Many companies are setting up to sell Internet-based information.

Note the enormous difference between what is transmitted and what is kept. If the estimate of 20 gigabytes is correct, a mere 40 days of netnews would accumulate that much material. However, much of netnews, often called "netnoise," is of such low quality that nobody would want to save it. Although the availability of pictures and sounds on the Web means that

Table 6.3
Text Search Companies

Company	Market Product Share (percent)	Product Name
Dataware	8	BRS
Information Dimensions	7	BASIS
Fulcrum	6	(OEM supplier)
Verity	5	TOPIC
Zylab	4	ZyIndex
Intext	4	WebPak
Folio	3	
Electronic Book Technologies	3	
Excalibur	3	
CMTG	3	
Other	54	

Web pages can be as attractive or more attractive than traditionally published material, the lack of quality control on what appears often leaves searchers frustrated; and the lack of institutional responsibility means that something that is there today can be gone tomorrow. We used to say that if a million monkeys sat at a million typewriters, they would eventually write all the works of Shakespeare. The Internet has proven this is not true.

In short, a variety of modern information is being distributed digitally. Some is part of a for-profit information business; some is part of a free distribution system dependent on volunteers. Libraries are a major part of this system, and they can use much of the same infrastructure to support both the new digital content and the material they might convert from their past files.

THE ADVANTAGES OF DIGITAL STORAGE FOR USERS

Should we be encouraging the rapid substitution of computer storage for books? Some users are emotionally pleased by the feel of a book (in interviews at Cornell some chemists asked about their use of journals claimed they even liked the smell of the journals, which is only modern PVA glue). They resent the idea that more and more reading will be from screens. Certainly, paper is more portable; radio Internet links are not sufficiently common to let people connect to a library from a laptop. Some users argue that reading from paper is easier, more efficient, more accurate, or otherwise better. If reducing library storage costs was all that mattered, microfilm would have triumphed a generation ago.

A choice also has to be made between databases containing searchable ASCII, derived from the original printing process, and those containing page images, derived from scanning the pages. Some services, such as the online newspapers of Nexis and Dialog, or the various full-text encyclopedias and medical journals, are based on ASCII. Full-text searching is available, and the output can be clipped and pasted into files. On the other hand, illustrations are missing. In some cases, such as the Chadwyck-Healey English Poetry Database, there were few illustrations in the originals anyway. In others, like the Perseus CD-ROM of ancient Greek, illustrative material has been added separately. In many cases, however, as in the online publications file of McGraw-Hill publications or the journals in STN (Science and Technology Network), the illustrations are simply missing.

Other services, such as the Adonis disks of medical journals, the UMI disks of IEEE publications, or the Elsevier TULIP program, rely on scanned page images. Typically, these are distributed on CD-ROM, which solves the problem of network capacity while also making it difficult for people to make illegal copies. The full page is available with pictures; but to read the text easily requires a high-quality screen (so these services rarely distribute to the desktop) and searching is usually based on a traditional indexing service, rather than full text. Adonis relies on Medline and UMI on Inspec, while the TULIP system provides full-text searching, but it is based on OCR and is not shown to the users directly (McKnight 1993). Systems that rely on OCR cannot, today, provide the same quality of ASCII text that can be derived from production processes. Even though AT&T's Red Sage project has tried to provide such services as highlighting hits even while using OCR to get text, it will start using Postscript files as they become available (Hoffman et al. 1993).

The CORE project set out to examine the relative effectiveness of ASCII, image, and traditional paper (Lesk 1991). The full project converted approximately 300,000 pages of primary chemical journals published by the American Chemical Society (ACS), providing both scanned page images and accurate ASCII, derived from the ACS database and converted to SGML. This is one of the few projects that had both image and clean ASCII for the same material. It was a joint effort of Cornell University, the American Chemical Society, Bellcore, Chemical Abstracts Service, and OCLC. A copy of the file is at University College London, where additional experiments are run.

In our test environment, our users are chemists. They are very visually oriented; the ACS journals are about one-quarter illustrations (counting by square inches of paper). These illustrations are usually line drawings: chemical structure diagrams (schemes), spectrographic charts, and drawings of apparatus, among other things. To permit the users of the ASCII file to see the illustrations, we sort the page images into textual and non-textual material, and make the schemes and figures part of the file. We can, fortunately, obtain the tables and equations from the ACS database. These, even if clipped as "non-text" by the page analysis routines, are presented to the user in a form derived from the ASCII data, not as images.

Several different interface programs have been written to display the chemical data. In all cases, users can do a full-text search on the ASCII data; the programs differ in their search algorithms and in their screen management.

In one page image interface, Pixlook, the "browsing" mode displays a list of 20 journal names and starts by choosing a journal. The user then picks a year, and issue, and is shown a list of titles of articles in that issue. Clicking on a title will bring up the page. The largest window shows the page. In one example, the original scanning is at 300 dpi bitonal, but to get the image to fit on the screen it is reduced to 100 dpi with the introduction of grayscale to improve readability. The user can click on the "expand" window to see full resolution, but then only a small part of the page can be seen. Even with these dodges, we insisted that the participants in our trial have larger-than-normal screens on their desktop machines (800 × 600 minimum). Searching in Pixlook is by text word, with suffixing and fields (author, title, etc.). A separate window handles the searching, and then the user gets a similar display of titles. Since this is an image interface, nothing is done about highlighting hits; the user must scan the article looking for the exact place where something was matched.

SuperBook was the first of the ASCII interfaces; it emphasizes user-positioning as its main feature. Unlike hypertext systems with arbitrary jumps from one item to another, or even systems that would view documents as a collection of articles, each independent, SuperBook believes that every document collection is a linear string. Thus, the user can always view one item as before or after another, and is less likely to get lost. A table of contents, arranged hierarchically, is shown on the left side of each page, while the text is shown on the right. The table of contents is labeled with the number of hits in each section. The number of hits is shown to the left of the section titles. For example, if the user searched for "hollow cathode," he would find no hits in Macromolecular Chemistry, and only three in Organic Chemistry. As expected, these words appear most frequently (84 times) in the large section of Physical, Inorganic and Analytical Chemistry. This category is expanded in the display, and 60 hits are in the section on Inorganic Analytical Chemistry; under Apparatus an article is found with 40 hits. If the user selected that particular article, he would find the actual instances of the words shown in the text page.

One disadvantage in our context is that figures, along with footnotes, tables, and equations, are not immediately presented to the user. Instead, they are indicated with symbols in the right margin of the text, and the user must click on them to see the item. Upon such a click, the item pops up in a new window. To help the user choose what picture to view, it is shown in the margin as a thumbnail; but footnotes, tables, and equations are only icons. The searching method in SuperBook is without standard Boolean operators: the use of several words in a query automatically means "co-occurrence within a paragraph."

The Scepter interface was built by OCLC. Scepter uses Boolean searching, with fields, and uses various menus to select date ranges, which journals to search, and so on. Scepter responds to a search with a list of hits, and then the user selects an article to read. For example, if a user searches for "nitrobenzene," 50 responses are presented in the top window (which can be scrolled or enlarged to see all of them). The user can then select a particular article and Scepter displays a menu of parts of the article. The user may choose to view the text, the figures, the references, or whatever. The figure list is shown as a series of thumbnails; and, in fact, viewing the figures is the first thing users wish to do. Chemists are visually oriented, and find the pictures the most valuable part of the article. The actual text, as in SuperBook, is synthesized and reprinted, rather than shown as the page image. This makes it easier to read. The figures are viewed as bitmap images. The user preference for viewing pictures was so extreme that we joked about producing a hit list in which only the author and the pictures were shown, to be called the "comic book" version of the journals.

There is no space here to review the entire CORE project, but it may be interesting to refer to an experiment done to compare the effectiveness of paper, image, and ASCII interfaces. In this experiment, Dennis Egan and collaborators used a file of 12 issues of the *Journal of the American Chemical Society* (just over 4,000 pages or 1,000 articles) (1991). Thirty-six chemistry students from Cornell University were divided into three groups. One group had the journals on paper, with *Chemical Abstracts* for searching; the second used the journals on SuperBook; and the third group used the journals on Pixlook. Two chemistry professors created a set of tasks, of five different types, intended to represent the kinds of things that chemists do with library materials. The tasks ranged from easy (finding a fact in a known article) to quite difficult (recommending a synthetic pathway for an organic chemistry transformation). Each student spent six hours doing examples of the five tasks.

The five tasks differed in their dependence on searching. The simplest task had questions such as the following: "In the article 'Total Synthesis of Ginkgolide B' by E. J. Corey, M. Kang, M. C. Desai, A. R. Ghosh and I. N. Houpis, {in JACS} v. 110, pp. 649–51, what is reported as a medically important property of ginkgolide?" The user is supplied with the exact citation of the article to be read, and must just go off and spend the approximately five minutes required to read the article looking for this fact. Alternatively, another task had questions of the form "What is the calculated P-O bond distance in hydroxyphosphine?" in which the user must find the article.

The results show that for the tasks in which no searching is required, the electronic and paper systems are comparably effective. Most students can do the problem correctly and their times for reading are comparable. However, for the tasks involving searching, either of the electronic systems is both faster and more accurate than paper browsing. In fact, most of the students faced with searching through paper for answers to such questions gave up, unable to complete the exercise. This confirms earlier experiments, in which students asked to look for things with paper in a textbook were both 25 percent faster and 25 percent more accurate using SuperBook than using the textbook on paper. Whenever it is necessary to search for something, electronic systems are much better than paper. When it is necessary only to read, users can read material on electronic systems with large screens as quickly as they can paper documents, as previously shown by John Gould.

Thus, as libraries move to electronic information, we should expect users to do their work better. Although there will be some people who object to the change, most will probably find the migration to their benefit. There will be those who complain that they can not easily carry information home; but there will be others tickled pink to get information directly on their desktop. OPACs are probably a good model; there have been a few mournful users regretting the loss of the card catalog (including Nicholson Baker, who wrote a particularly unfortunate and error-ridden article for *The New Yorker* in 1994). However, most users have welcomed the improved searching abilities of the computerized systems. The availability of full text on computers is bringing a similar response, and it is not uncommon to see e-mail questions now requesting online sources only as answers.

NEW RESEARCH OPPORTUNITIES

Traditionally, research on information retrieval has focused on text searching. Innumerable papers have been written on ranking, probabilistic retrieval, term weighting, vector space models, and other techniques for searching for queries phrased in words. What is remarkable is that few have made it into practical systems. Many of the online systems still use Boolean searching and other technologies from decades ago; nor, if one reads the advertising for the online systems, do search algorithms seem important.

Part of the problem is that there is such a wide spread in performance over different queries and documents. Experiments often fail to show statistically significant differences between methods, because there is so much variation among queries. The best experiments, running on several gigabytes of text, are the TREC (Text Retrieval Evaluation Conference) series. In these experiments, it is still found that retrieval quality varies widely across queries. The systems that lead in performance perform better on different queries, and even among the systems leading on the same queries, they achieve their results by retrieving different documents.

With this much scatter, users fail to see reliable differences among systems. This means that it is probably time to move on from algorithms that simply count words in different ways. Instead, we must face the very large quantity of image and sound information that people wish to retrieve. It is now easy to record radio programs in digital form and create an archive that would be nice to search; it is becoming straightforward to create video archives in digital form, although still a bit expensive. However, we have little in the way of automatic techniques for searching images and sounds. Traditionally, librarians have indexed pictures by writing textual descriptions of them and then processing the descriptions as typical pictures. This is too time-consuming to do now, and as digital cameras create vast quantities of pictorial information in machine-readable form, it is not likely to become easier in the future. The Library of Congress has 9 million photographs in its collection; as they are scanned, it is not possible to imagine all of them being cataloged individually. New research is needed in this area.

For example, consider the six projects funded by the Digital Library Initiative in the United States (NSF/NASA/ARPA). Four start with more or less typical collections of paper-based information (scientific journals in Illinois, earth and space sciences in Michigan, environmental reports in Berkeley, and computer science literature at Stanford). Each project has gone on to add additional, more unusual kinds of information. Michigan, for example, includes substantial videoconference material related to worldwide geological experiments. The remaining two projects are unusual: UC Santa Barbara deals entirely with maps and images, while Carnegie-Mellon's collection is videotapes.

For example, I do some radio recording purely for personal convenience. News programs are recorded from radio stations in both the United States and the United Kingdom, transmitted to one terminal, and listened to at the user's convenience. This is easy enough that it can be set up for one person (which conveniently brings the operation within the scope of time-shifting fair use in the United States, I believe). To cite another example, maps and images captured by satellite and aerial photography can be used for marketing, urban planning, network design, and other applications, but not easily if the systems to access such data presume that everyone trying to use it is a specialist in space-based photographic information.

In the past, the problem has been that image analysis programs were very specialized. Collections of maps, of faces, of aerial photographs, of CAD (computer-aided design) drawings, and so on have all been handled with software tailored to the kind of material. Only recently, with research such as the IBM QBIC project, have we seen ways of handling images in a completely general way (Niblack et al. 1993). Additional research in techniques for handling non-standard information is needed. Griffiths' report estimates that reading in the United States, even by professionals, has declined about 10 percent in recent decades, presumably as a result of television and other media (Griffiths and King 1993). As people depend more and more on non-textual information, we need to build systems that can index it and use it.

Other techniques for finding information without a traditional text search include community recommendations. Bellcore has developed an efficient way to suggest movies (Hill et al. 1995). A group of people watch and rate movies and the computer can find, for any individual, a model in terms of the ratings of other individuals. As an example, the judgments of movies made by person A might be modeled by looking at the average judgments of B, C, and D. Then, the system can find movies that B, C, and D liked, but that A has not seen, and suggest that A will probably like them too. This turns out to be more accurate than relying on the recommendations of movie critics, since it gives individually tailored recommendations, rather than having to give only one opinion to all possible viewers.

In summary, we need ways of finding new kinds of information and new ways of finding the old kinds of information. The world is converting from text-based computer interfaces to multimedia systems. New searching modes, whether they are intelligent image understanding, fast picture-browsing, or community recommendations, can be the basis of entire industries of tomorrow. Certainly, everyone where I work noticed the initial stock offering of Netscape, which was valued at more than $2 billion despite the fact that searching and buying things on the Net is still more of an amusement than a business. Millions of viewers are drawn to the attractiveness of the new technology for viewing and reading, and we need to see that they are not disappointed by their inability to wade through the piles of material that are also accumulating.

THE FUTURE OF LIBRARIES

So far, I have explained why more information should be and will be available online. What does this mean for libraries? If all the students in a college, or all corporate employees, are going to get the information they need directly on their desks, what happens to the traditional library organization? Information vendors are thinking of bypassing libraries, for example. Will they succeed?

Figure 6.1 shows the breakdown of costs associated with putting a book into a typical U.S. university. As can be seen, little of the money that the university spends on the library goes to the author (despite the fact that most universities do not monetize space and properly account for the library buildings). Admittedly, the library is providing other services besides putting books on shelves; it may, for example, be the only quiet place on

Figure 6.1
Library Economics

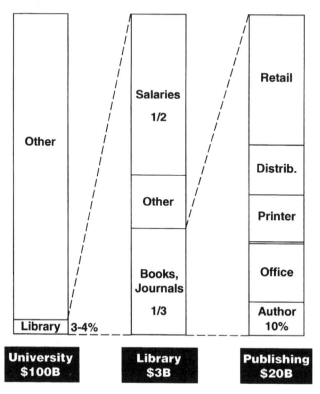

campus to study. But it is tempting for a publisher or even an author to think of providing direct access from student workstations to the source material, to eliminate a great many of the intermediate costs associated with bookstores, book wholesalers, and libraries, and collect greater revenues. Online books have other attractions for publishers; new editions would be easy to bring out, there would be no secondhand copies to sell, and so on.

This reflects the ease of transmission of digital material. The reader does not care where the original copy is stored; it could come from a local library, a bookstore system, a publisher's databank, or a distant university. Thus, there is a potential for great competition between these organizations. If, someday, a student at a small college in the United States can access any book in the Berkeley library from his or her dorm room, why does the small college need a library? The administration of the college will not allocate funds to amass books in a large building if nobody ever reads them.

Libraries were once relatively self-contained organizations. Many major research libraries in the United States had their own classification schemes, and even an interlibrary loan was slow and infrequently used. In recent decades this began to change, as organizations such as the Research Libraries Group and OCLC encouraged shared cataloging and shared purchasing of lightly used resources. Within large universities, networking of CD-ROMs has replaced (where possible) buying multiple copies. Libraries, whether university or corporate, are learning to share as a way of coping with increasing costs.

Now, libraries probably either face much more cooperation, or much more competition. Everyone views the delivery of information to the desktop as an opportunity: this includes traditional libraries and publishers, bookstores and wholesalers, telephone and computer companies, and new start-ups addressing this market. What will be the effect of the new technology on concentration in the distribution of information? Traditionally, economies of scale lead to concentration: there are more authors than publishers, more publishers than online services. Will the Internet mean that we increase or decrease diversity of authorship? This is not yet clear, and depends to some extent on how we manage the availability of servers and browsers. We need to have open protocols for server/browser connection and an economic system in which it is possible for small publishers to deal effectively with small customers.

Universities, meanwhile, must re-think the role of the library. Unfortunately, many American universities rate their libraries by counting the books they hold. The other services libraries perform, such as guiding students to information and training them in the use of information resources, are not valued appropriately. In these circumstances, as digital technology makes libraries particularly vulnerable to the idea that they could be "outsourced," we can expect to see universities urging additional budget cuts upon their libraries. Libraries can no longer value themselves either in terms of the books they own or the count of people who walk in the door, the only measures it has been easy to get in the past. Instead, they must generally take a larger role in education.

In fact, the most critical function universities can perform is to teach their students how to find information. At the rate science grows, most of what an information worker will need in his or her career will simply not have been known at the time the worker received a Ph.D. A library is not a zoo, with books in captivity and the curious looking in through the bars. Instead, a library has to be a way of finding information, and as the systems to do that become more complex, libraries have to expand their efforts to teach people how to use these systems. Also, as so much of the information has not gone through traditional publishers, people need to know how to evaluate information, not just find it.

The value of finding information is growing steadily. It is now estimated that about one-third of the workers in developed countries are "knowledge workers" (Rubin and Huber 1986). Peter Drucker has pointed out that the inputs into new industries are increasing information, not parts and labor.

The cost of an automobile, for example, is 40 percent materials and 25 percent labor, while the cost of a silicon chip is 1 percent materials, 10 percent labor, and 70 percent information. In medicine, a recent study has concluded that patients for whom MEDLINE searches are conducted promptly have significantly lower costs and shorter hospital stays (Klein et al. 1994).

The question is whether libraries will cooperate, or whether they will fight each other and the online businesses for patrons. We already see a social problem in universities as the allegiance of the faculty shifts. Once, the typical professor of (let us say) surface physics of metallic thin films at any university would have thought of his colleagues as the other physicists at that university. Now, with the many conferences, telephone calls, fax machines, and e-mail, he is likely to think of his colleagues as the other surface physicists of metallic thin films around the world. Institutional loyalty is down, with some bad consequences for long-term programs (I know one student who was on her fourth advisor by the time she got her Ph.D., the others all having left her university). Could this happen to libraries?

Libraries will find themselves in a complex world. They will still wish to keep all kinds of things that seem to have little commercial value today. On the other hand, they may find many commercial databases competing with them to deliver the current, high-value information, and they may find that many different libraries are competing to deliver information to the same students. Interlibrary loans, in an electronic world, may be a profit center rather than a nuisance. Libraries may find themselves with new opportunities. University libraries already offer to provide services to corporations; now this may be much more practical, and corporations that cannot now afford libraries (or think they can't) will be willing to buy outside services. For some low-usage information, libraries may be part of a bypass chain in which authors simply self-publish on the Net, and libraries provide the ability to find the material and the permanent copy. Since in the digital world location may be irrelevant, libraries will find that their users have far more choices than they have today. Libraries may find that there is a sorting out into "supplier" and "consumer" libraries, in which only a few large institutions supply information, and most of the rest simply access it on demand.

The likely future is that people will spend more money getting information than they do today. Partly, this will be because more information gathering is monetized, instead of being done by individuals. Partly, this will be because more information will be available, and people will substitute looking things up for doing things (as architects and civil engineers are replacing physical models of buildings with simulations). But how do we avoid the fight for this money pitting one library against another, and causing wasteful competition? For example, consider a national library's choice of subscriptions to overseas journals today. If the national library wishes to maximize the number of photocopies people buy from it, it should subscribe to the most used and most common journals. These will be exactly the ones the university and public libraries subscribe to. If the national library wishes to provide a service to its country, it should subscribe to journals no one else gets, at the cost of its own usage statistics. We do not know how to resolve such issues today, much less in the more complex future world of digital libraries.

Economically, there are many dangers. Information distribution is a business with huge economies of scale, with bad consequences for stability (Lesk 1992). Other industries with such economies of scale sometimes engage in destructive price wars in which everyone loses; consider the U.S. airline industry as an example. The communications industry, by contrast, seems to have been able to preserve some financial health and permanence, despite deregulation and competition. Libraries need to think about how they can charge for information, and how they can do this so that they remain viable organizations, able to carry on their function of preserving the world's memory.

Libraries also need to minimize administrative costs. The current way that copyright permissions are handled in the United States makes it very difficult for libraries to simplify the use of digital information. IBM prepared a CD-ROM to mark the 500th anniversary of the first Columbus voyage to America. It is said that the company spent more than $1 million on rights clearances, but only $10,000 went to rights holders, the rest disappearing in administrative and legal costs.

Perhaps the best model for information distribution is the distribution of software to corporations. Per-user, site-license-pricing permits fair charging for both large and small users, with automatic checks on how many copies are in use at any one time. In addition, individual corporations manage these contracts so that the local user deals with only one purchasing and support operation, rather than having everyone buy individual copies of everything that is needed. Similar arrangements could produce a world in which each library served as the "information buying agency" for its university or client group, making practical decisions as to whether copies should be mounted locally, bought on demand, or provided through other means. In practice, it would buy some things that its clients get from bookstores today; such materials would have a higher price and be charged back to users in some way, but would produce greater total funding for the organization. The library would retain and augment its services in training and evaluation of information, although it would probably do fewer searches for people as they learned to do their own.

Such a model might support a world in which libraries could cooperate, rather than fight for patrons (called customers). Organizations of librarians need to encourage their members to work together and turn their attention to training and education, rather than focusing on book purchases. This would also be a model for the next step in this process, in which the ready availability of university courses at remote locations causes universities to consider competing with each other for students. We will have to distinguish between ownership and access to courses, as well as to books.

In summary, it is clear that digital libraries are coming, both in free and commercial versions, and in both image and ASCII formats. This is an opportunity, not a threat. Digital information can be more effective for the users and cheaper for the librarians. Access will become more important than possession, but this must be used to encourage sharing, not competition. A library's real asset is the people it has who know how to find information and how to evaluate it. It must emphasize its skills in training, not in acquisition. If we think of information as an ocean, the job of libraries is now to provide navigation. It is no longer to provide the water.

REFERENCES

Cummings, Anthony. 1992. *University Libraries and Scholarly Communication: Study Prepared for The Andrew W. Mellon Foundation.* Washington, D.C.: Association of Research Libraries.

Egan, Dennis E., et al. 1991. Hypertext for the Electronic Library? CORE Sample Results. In *Proceedings of the Third Annual ACM Conference on Hypertext*, San Antonio, Tex. (December 15–18): 299–312. New York: Association for Computing Machinery.

Griffiths, J. M., and D. King. 1993. *Special Libraries: Increasing the Information Edge.* Washington, D.C.: Special Libraries Association.

Hill, Will, et al. 1995. Recommending and Evaluating Choices in a Virtual Community of Use. In *Conference Proceedings on Human Factors in Computing Systems*, Denver, Colo. (May 7–11): 194–201. New York: Association for Computing Machinery.

Hillstrom, Kevin, ed. 1994. *The Encyclopedia of American Industries*, vol. 2. Detroit, Mich.: Gale Research.

Hoffman, M., et al. 1993. The RightPages Service: An Image-based Electronic Library. *Journal of the American Society for Information Science* 44: 446–52.

Kenney, Anne, and Lynne Personius. 1992. *Joint Study in Digital Preservation.* Washington, D.C.: Commission on Preservation and Access.

Klein, M., et al. 1994. Effect of Online Literature Searching on Length of Stay and Patient Care Costs. *Academic Medicine* 69 (June): 489–95.

Lesk, Michael. 1991. The CORE Electronic Chemistry Library. In *Proceedings of the 14th Annual International ACM SIGIR Conference on Research and Development in Information Retrieval*, Chicago, Ill. (October 13–16): 93–112. New York: Association for Computing Machinery.

———. 1992. Pricing Electronic Information. *Serials Review* 18 (Spring–Summer): 38–40.

McKnight, Cliff. 1993. Electronic Journals—Past, Present . . . and Future? *ASLIB (Association for Special Libraries) Proceedings* 45: 7–10.

Niblack, W., et al. 1993. The QBIC Project: Querying Images by Content Using

Color, Texture, and Shape. *Proceedings of the SPIE* 1908 (February): 173–87.

Odlyzko, Andrew. 1995. Tragic Loss or Good Riddance: The Impending Demise of Traditional Scholarly Journals. *International Journal of Human-Computer Studies* 42(1): 71–122.

Robinson, Peter. 1993. *The Digitization of Primary Text Sources*. Office for Humanities Communication, Oxford University Computing Services.

Rodriguez, Karen. 1995. Searching the Internet. *Interactive Age* (July 31): 28–30.

Rubin, Michael, and Mary Huber. 1986. *The Knowledge Industry in the United States, 1960–1980*. Princeton, N.J.: Princeton University Press.

Taubes, G. 1993. E-mail Withdrawal Prompts Spasm. *Science* 262 (Octpber 8): 173–74.

PART II

Meeting the Challenges
of the Digital Library

CHAPTER 7

The Library as Provider of Digital Resources for Teaching and Scholarship

ANN J. WOLPERT

The classic academic library is at the heart of learning and scholarship in every traditional university. For centuries, scholars and students have come together around carefully selected collections of books, journals, and other scholarly materials to pursue their intellectual interests. In virtually all the world's renowned institutions of higher learning, the library is located at the physical and intellectual center of campus activity. Indeed, the library building often assumes an iconic quality, standing as an imposing and highly visible symbol of the advancement of knowledge through higher education.

Nevertheless, as we well know, some 10 years ago the academic library was widely declared to be dying. Fed by imaginative (if improbable) advertising and hyperbolical press releases, the perception across the land was that academic libraries were horse-drawn wagons on the electronic superhighway. The all-digital library was not only imaginable, but assumed to be well on the way to reality. By the turn of the century, we were told, there would be no need for books, journals, or traditional libraries.

Academic research librarians have become accustomed to sweeping prognostications about their future. Indeed, we have even made a few ourselves. I, for one, will never forget Freemont Rider's 1944 prediction that research library collections would double in size (and presumably cost) every 16 years—indefinitely. Digital library predictions, however, were a far more serious matter, based as they were on truly significant advances in information technology. Fueled by technological determinism, and reinforced by

Paper presented at the International Roundtable for Information and Library Science, Kanazawa Institute of Technology, Library Center, Kanazawa, Japan, 1998.

Moore's law, the idea of an all-digital library took higher education by storm.

Librarians had good reason to be hopeful about these predictions. In the late 1980s, both the volume and the cost of scholarly publishing were headed upward on an unsustainable trajectory. Libraries were running out of space and running low on options, and the digital library looked like an efficient and attractive alternative to traditional media. Unfortunately, even as libraries' needs were growing, colleges and universities were also scrambling for funds to computerize and network their campuses. As universities cast about for new sources of funds, the prospect of a lower-cost, all-digital library was an attractive scenario to cash-strapped administrators. Wouldn't it be nice, the thinking went, if funds could be diverted from libraries to computing with no loss in the quality and quantity of information resources?

Alas, 10 years later, the all-digital library remains an elusive ideal. The phenomenal growth of the World Wide Web has brought to our desktops all manner of popular culture, local history, and current news, not to mention some more problematic content; but an economically viable, broadly useful digital resource for serious students and scholars remains a dream. Only advertising executives still speak of the digital library as though it were imminent, and only the innocent believe it will be free. Today we have digitized collections and resources that are born digital. We have data and text and multimedia and preprint servers and Web sites. But we have yet to create an integrated entity that can approach the traditional research library for overall depth, quality, durability, affordability, and relevance.

Libraries are learning, though, and technology continues to evolve. We have moved from the infancy of the information age into middle childhood. Although the hype continues to outpace reality, there is a growing awareness of the true opportunities and diminishing technical barriers to a digital future. What have we learned in the past 10 years?

- We have learned that the true costs of digital information are additional and campus-wide, requiring extensive technical support, a robust and stable network, and a networked machine on every desktop.
- We have learned that faculty are neither uniformly nor universally in favor of the digital library, but that students (especially undergraduates) are.
- We have learned that the convenience of the Web is having a profound impact on research strategies and on information-seeking behavior on our campuses.
- We have learned that traditional library skills and traditional library organizations are not necessarily a good fit for digital content.

Perhaps the most startling revelation of the past decade has been the degree to which the management and ownership of scholarly communication has migrated into the commercial sector. It appears, increasingly, that the future of digital resources may not be decided on our campuses, nor is it even necessarily any longer under our influence. The question of who will own digital resources, how those resources will be retained over time, and what economic models will control intellectual property has become the business of big business. Never before have libraries been confronted with such powerful suppliers as the multinational media and entertainment conglomerates that now control large portions of scholarly communication. These publishers are a very different breed from the scholarly and learned societies with whom we dealt in the past, and they are not afraid to assert their point of view. They lobby aggressively for legislation and treaties that support their interests; they support their editors handsomely; nor do they fear their library customers, having recently advocated, for example, that scholarly publishers "push back" at libraries, for requesting lower prices and fair use in the digital environment.

Although many uncertainties surround the development of the digital future, I am among those librarians who believe we cannot wait passively for that future to arrive. In my experience, the process of scholarly research and communication, and the role of academic research libraries in this process, are poorly understood by nearly all the key players in the scholarly communications arena. Like the blind men describing an elephant according to the portion of the animal each man could feel, those who propose changes to the system of scholarly communication usually address only that isolated piece of the large complex system with which they are familiar. For example, research faculty tend to focus largely on the needs of today and tomorrow. It rarely occurs to them that decisions which advance today's digital future might also jeopardize the historical record of their discipline. Likewise, university presidents and provosts must be extraordinarily far-sighted to accept responsibility for future needs, when current demands clamor for attention and resources are scarce.

Digital remedies for the costs and problems of scholarly communication are neither certain nor obvious. Like all large, complex systems, scholarly communication and the processes by which it creates, records, reviews, authenticates, shares, pays for, and preserves new knowledge defy simple solutions. The former head of academic computing at MIT liked to remind us that just because something is possible doesn't mean it will happen. His favorite reality check was the story of the wires that were imbedded in the Los Angeles freeway system at considerable expense in the 1950s. Designers were utterly confident that the cars on these high-speed roads would soon be guided to their various destinations via central computers. Drivers could read, talk, watch the scenery, and relax while the computer controlled their cars. The Los Angeles freeway system of today illuminates just how great the gap can be between a technically feasible vision and the reality of human behavior.

John Diebold has said that new technology affects society in three progressive stages. In the first stage, we use the technology to do what we have always done—we just do those tasks more effectively thanks to the new technology. By way of illustrating this concept, some of you may remember, as I do, the early days of OCLC, when we were utterly delighted with the accuracy and cost-effectiveness of computer-produced paper catalog cards. We were still building card catalogs, but we were building them at lower cost and with greater consistency.

In Diebold's second stage, technology begins to change the way we actually behave and work. In offices all across America, for example, middle-aged executives have stopped giving dictation and learned to type their own e-mail. In libraries, the card catalog has now all but disappeared, replaced by a networked, online integrated library system that delivers library information directly to desktops and dorm rooms. Similarly, online databases have transformed and enlarged scholars' research strategies beyond the physical constraints of one institution's library. It is safe to say that the expanding horizons of scholars have also expanded resource sharing among libraries and, consequently, the size and importance of the interlibrary loan and borrowing operations in our libraries.

In Diebold's third stage, society itself begins to change as a result of the impact of technology. Electricity, the automobile, television, are all technologies that have profoundly changed, and continue to change, those societies in which they are deeply imbedded.

The challenge for libraries at the dawn of the digital era is that while we know change is coming, we don't yet know how sweeping or profound it will be. Scholars and students are only just beginning to experiment with new ways of behaving and working. How the scholarly and research community will ultimately deploy digital capabilities is an open question, as is the future legal and regulatory environment. At times like this it is worth remembering the predictions that surrounded some earlier technologies that we now take for granted. Radio was originally introduced as a tool for world peace. Television was to have transformed education. Both have become, instead, largely media for pop culture, advertising, and mass entertainment.

Society uses new technologies in an economic and social context, and—like radio or television or the wires in the Los Angeles freeways—reinterprets and consumes innovations in unpredictable ways. Economics, procedural complexity, or sociology can lead to unimagined outcomes. Consider libraries and microfilm. In the 1960s, microforms were cast as the salvation of libraries and scholars. Vast quantities of information could be obtained at low cost and maintained for long periods of time in small spaces. Researchers would no longer need to travel to obtain essential reports and documents. The only problem was, most scholars despised the medium and many flatly refused to use it. This wonderful technical solution failed libraries and their patrons for two very important reasons. First, microforms cannot be used without access to expensive, cumbersome machines and second, microforms are just plain difficult to read—especially through bifocals. There is a lesson in this tale.

As libraries address the challenge of providing digital resources to students and scholars, we must approach the assignment with enthusiasm for the possibilities, tempered by a firm appreciation for patron behavior. To be successful as providers of digital resources, libraries must adopt a marketing orientation. In sum, librarians must become as sophisticated about marketing strategy as are the heads of the best consumer product companies. To get the highest value from emerging digital technology, with all of its strengths and weaknesses, libraries must develop tools to assess the impact of digital resources on our patrons' research and learning behavior. We must devise techniques to compensate for digital resources' weaknesses, and develop service and operating strategies that take advantage of the tremendous convenience and flexibility of the digital environment.

There is a common misconception within library circles that "marketing" is somehow demeaning and non-professional—simply a fancy word for selling. In fact, nothing could be further from the truth. Marketing is the process by which an organization meets the current needs of its clients, and creates the tools and resources to assess and meet future client needs.

Marketing obliges us to decide who our clients are, to determine (not just assume) what their current needs are, to track behavior and options in order to anticipate future needs, and to create cost-effective services for today and tomorrow. The marketing process forces the focus of attention away from our collections and buildings, and toward the current and future needs of our patrons. This is not to say that our collections and buildings are not important, but rather that patron requirements are important, also, and less well understood. While our buildings represent the historical strength of our roots and educational values, our future lies in the ongoing behavior, choices, and expectations of students, researchers, and scholars.

In recent years, for example, many academic libraries have learned to build their undergraduate bibliographic instruction program around the World Wide Web; not because the Web is superior to libraries, but because so many students arrive on campus more familiar with the Web than with a traditional research library. This strategy accepts the reality of the Internet as an easy and convenient source of information for undergraduates, then uses it as a device to teach them how to search the Web efficiently, how to evaluate sources and use search engines wisely, and what to do when the Web fails them, as it inevitably will. Undergraduate students learn far more about the value of research libraries through this strategy than they did before librarians learned to use students' established behavior to our mutual advantage. A marketing orientation is not rocket science, nor is it non-professional. In fact, libraries can easily learn and benefit from some standard marketing techniques. Here are a few.

Identify the library's key market segments. Librarians must get beyond the notion that the needs of all elements of our community are identical, especially in the digital environment, or that those needs can be adequately managed with one service model. A great advantage of digital resources is that libraries can create customized service modules for different sectors of the user community. Each module can reflect the needs and interests of the specific client community; for example:

- Help screens and finding aids can be tailored for the novice or infrequent visitor;
- Minimal click-to-content may be provided for the frequent user who needs little or no help;
- Hot links to related sites can be provided for the curious who wish to explore;

and so on.

Become highly familiar with existing library usage patterns. Gather data and track usage over time. Survey the information-seeking behaviors of the market segments within your communities. Learn to think of your front-line staff as ambassadors, client contact representatives, and market information gatherers. Only through an accurate, fact-based assessment of needs and behaviors can the library justify and provide relevant, affordable digital resources. This marketing technique may, at first, be alien to some librarians, as we have historically prided ourselves on our ability to predict and provide for our patrons. In fact, deliberate data gathering and analysis simply extend this traditional value while acknowledging the need for quantitative data in times of rapid change.

Strengthen and protect the library's brand identity. A high-quality library provides both distinction and comparative advantage to a university. The digital environment can weaken the link between the library and its clients, because personal contact between librarian and client is lost. Products and services delivered digitally must clearly identify the library's role, and alternative forms of contact with students and faculty must be established. Consistent packaging is one time-honored technique to increase and sustain market visibility. If a library's digital presence looks and feels drastically different from its traditional library products, library patrons may not realize that digital resources are a service of the library.

Lastly, look for opportunities to develop strategic partnerships. Just as high-technology businesses often find strategic alliances preferable to developing in-house expertise, so too must libraries seek appropriate alliances and partnerships. Such partnerships might be financial, resource related, technological, or service based. They might involve faculty, students, other libraries, purchasing consortia, or vendors. Just as the contemporary business cannot run without a robust and reliable distribution system for its products and services, neither can the academic library provide digital resources without a robust and reliable network, responsive help desks, set-up and training teams, and electronic classrooms. Likewise, communities of interest can speed communication concerning the availability of new digital resources, and give feedback on the value of these new resources.

However, none of this speaks to the fundamental question of the library as actual provider of digital resources for teaching and scholarship. Marketing techniques may describe how the library can achieve success in this new role, but marketing does not address what the library must do. It is increasingly clear that libraries play four separate and distinct roles with regard to digital resources.

First, libraries create digital resources. The online catalog is perhaps the most obvious example of a digital resource created by the library, but it is only one type of many. Resources such as archival finding aids, electronic reserve reading, images of unique resources owned by the library or the institution, student theses and dissertations, and faculty working papers are increasingly common digitized library resources. Then there are the digital publications created by library staff for publication on the World Wide Web. For example, many librarians are actively exploring the Web as a tool for bibliographic instruction and the teaching of information competency. Others use the Web to inform patrons regarding everything from binding schedules to frequently asked questions, to hours of operation, to library policies and procedures.

Second, libraries add value to others' digital resources by lowering barriers to use. We design uniform, easy-to-use interfaces, we build hot links into our online catalogs, we create information buttons and Web forms to invite users' questions. The Web is also used extensively as a tool to package selected digital resources for distance learners.

Third, libraries become suppliers of digital resources when they distribute products across the campus. Libraries instruct students and faculty in choosing the right digital resource for the problem at hand, and in utilizing the system software to achieve optimal results. Vendors of digital resources are well aware of the importance of this role libraries play in higher education. Vendors generally believe that library support reflects positively on their products, and builds future commercial demand for their content.

Fourth, libraries attempt to collect the digital output of their faculty, and their communities. Libraries archive the digital journals of their academic departments and university presses, purchase the digital textbooks of their faculty, and struggle with requests to host and/or archive specialized Web sites. Libraries whose responsibilities include the institution's archives also know full well the impact of e-mail and word processing on archival practice.

Obviously, the skills and organizational structure needed to perform these four separate roles are distinct and variable. While there may be analogs in the traditional print environment, the work in the digital environment is actually very different.

- Building a high-quality, reliable database is similar to editing and publishing, but requires specific technical skills.
- Adding value to others' digital resources is more like software design and development than like traditional library services.
- Teaching the campus community to use distributed digital products is an unusual educational challenge. No company would expect one person to possess all these competencies, yet libraries often expect existing staff to perform this full range of new and different tasks. Nor is the traditional organizational structure of a discipline-oriented library a good management system to support this new work. Much of the new work cuts across disciplines and falls outside traditional library functional areas. Clearly, the sustainability of digital service will require both new skills and new organizational structures.

Library schools are working hard to develop educational programs that will prepare the librarians of tomorrow for the work we must do today. Meanwhile, we are all conducting real-time experiments that might best be described as field education. Seminars, continuing education, workshops, and pre-conference educational opportunities are flourishing as libraries retool. New positions spring up daily, bearing such titles as Digital Instruction Librarian, Intellectual Property Librarian, Digital Resources Acquisitions Librarian, Web Librarian, Electronic Journals Librarian. This is not a good time to be without a supportive human resources department and a substantial training budget.

Organizational structures are also in flux. In some institutions, the library and the information systems department are being merged with no clear pattern as to who absorbs whom. Sometimes the two organizations simply persist as oil and water under one management. In a few large systems, digital resources are being consolidated into what could best be described as a separate and distinct digital library. This solution brings economies of scale but leaves the digital library service isolated from other library functions, and disconnected from the traditional library customer base.

Those libraries that have entered digital publishing in a substantial way have additionally had to deal with institutional accounting systems that reflect an older era. For example, traditional library buildings are capital expenses, incurred by the institution and amortized over a 15- to 25-year schedule. Shelving space for print resources was typically "free" to the library as a result. Computer expenses and digital storage, on the other hand, are generally handled as annual operating expenses of the business unit. This means that digital resources are not only not free, but the storage cost must come at the expense of some other annual operating activity.

One final topic remains. This is the challenge of integrating digital resources into our larger library collections. Before the advent of the integrated online catalog, libraries had few tools to provide an integrated view of the rich array of resources available in our collections. Today, new library standards for describing non-book library resources, together with ambitious, retrospective conversion projects, have made visible to scholars a dazzling array of print collections and archival resources. We sorely need comparable visibility and integration for digital resources. Much interesting and productive work, such as the Dublin Core, is under way. For this we can thank the Council on Library and Information Resources, the Coalition for Networked Information, and OCLC, among others.

Resource integration also requires a rational and affordable model of digital publishing, if we are to predict the continued availability of digitally formatted products. So-called "bundling" of titles is a fine economic model for publishers, but generally obliges the library to purchase more than it wants and can often can afford. Tying digital access to historical print subscriptions ensures that the publication has an enduring physical presence, but ignores the natural evolution of research and education within the academy. CD-ROMs have an uncertain shelf life, from both physical and platform perspectives. An abiding responsibility of research libraries is to ensure that advances in knowledge persist beyond one generation. Until a sustainable and affordable model of digital publication is developed, libraries will continue to tread gingerly among the various alternatives offered.

The thoughts presented here have focused primarily on the marketing challenge libraries face in providing digital resources for teaching and scholarship. Libraries still face a variety of challenges and needs in the digital environment. Together, libraries must work collectively and internationally for solutions to these important and compelling issues.

First, we need new metrics to characterize library excellence in the digital resource environment. Traditional measures of success assume a walk-in clientele, and collections you could touch. We count items added to the collection, items circulated, number of in-person visits. In the networked environment of digital resources, such numbers are largely irrelevant. Libraries need different measures of value and utility. System failures or system response time, number of successful connections, or number of times a resource selection was an effective choice might be better activities to count as success measures for digital resources. We must work with vendors and our own systems operations to create new measures of library excellence and to build the tools to collect these measures.

Second, we need new economic models for the digital environment. At a recent meeting of the Scholarly Publishing Division of the Association of American Publishers, the agenda was thick with programs on digital object identifiers. There should be no doubt in any librarian's mind that one possible scenario for publishers is that they will own scholarly works in perpetuity, and will expect to sell that content to academia one reader at a time. This economic model would be a radical departure from the current financial model of fixed price, unlimited access that academic research libraries currently enjoy. Without an adequate analysis of the cost to higher education of such a model, libraries will be flying blindly into the future. We must do that analysis and then develop and promote economic models that work for higher education.

Finally, on behalf of the students and scholars of 2050, we need new strategies for capturing scholarly communication in its emerging forms. The gray literature of conferences, meetings, and symposia is moving inexorably onto the Web. Preprint servers host working papers. New forms of literature and new pedagogical tools are springing up in every discipline. Articles in today's journals routinely refer readers to an author's home page for the supporting data to an article. Will that data be there five years from now? Fifty years from now? Scholars have always depended on research libraries to capture and preserve the important works of their disciplines and their times, and we face the prospect that a generation of work, and the richness in our collections—whatever form they take—will be lost to future scholars if we do not solve this problem.

This discussion began with a reference to library buildings, and their literal and symbolic importance to higher education. Although the noted architect and author Jane Jacobs never wrote about the challenges of providing digital resources to students and scholars, she could well have. In her classic work *Death and Life of Great American Cities*, she speaks to those of us who will breath new life into great libraries in the years to come. "Old ideas can sometimes use new buildings," she wrote. "New ideas must come from old buildings." Let us find the new ideas we need, within the values of our institutions, and the traditions of our splendid, richly symbolic, and continuously relevant library buildings.

CHAPTER 8

Can We Afford Digital Information? Libraries? An Early Assessment of Economic Prospects for Digital Publications

ANN B. OKERSON

INTRODUCTION

The theme of this roundtable is "The Prospect of the Digital Library" and my assignment is to review prospective digitization of the publications, such as books and journals, that will be the content in the Digital Library. Rather than discuss the important projects and progress in this area, I have chosen to concentrate on a critical subset: the economic issues. There is no question that the future of information will be dominated by electronic means of authoring, publishing, storage, distribution, and retrieval, but whether and how this revolution affects the formal and rigorous communication that now takes place among scholars and scientists through print publication is a question with no sure answers. My approach today is to leave aside all technical questions. I think experts would agree that there are no *serious* technical problems that hinder any current ambition for electronic scholarly publishing. There are interesting questions to be resolved, but it is clear that the technology is sufficient to the task. (Electronic information technology will be strained to the limit in other areas, but not this one, for the near future, at any rate.)

However, the highly evolved, formal, and rigorous standards of performance that guide scholars and scientists in their research and writing create a set of social and economic parameters within which the system of scholarly communication will continue to evolve. Social and economic parameters are closely related, for economics may be understood as a particularly rigorous and quantitative way of describing social behavior.

Paper presented at the International Roundtable for Information and Library Science, Kanazawa Institute of Technology, Library Center, Kanazawa, Japan, 1995.

To solve the economic problem requires us to address the social issues in a realistic, responsible, and imaginative way. I hope that this contribution will be of use in attempting to think about how best to engage in that kind of activity.

Discussions about costs of formal scholarly publishing on the Internet have been flourishing throughout the 1990s on the Internet, and in meetings of librarians, publishers, and scholars. As recently as the early 1990s, the Internet was predominantly a carrier of scientific and academic electronic mail, data, and software. Then, the first peer-reviewed Internet journals were started for the new medium by scholars and researchers in academia, and shared freely with other colleagues who were able to connect to electronic networks and read e-mail. The desire of many researchers and academics was that the new communications medium would enable the distribution of scholarly research more rapidly and cheaply than ever. Costs of computers and of network connections would be borne by universities and research institutes, enabling their communities to share information widely and at no cost. Scholarly information—and thus scholars and libraries—would be liberated from the crippling yoke of upwardly spiraling prices that are damaging institutional budgets.

With the start-up of the first academic peer-reviewed Internet serials (there were nine by the end of 1990), primitive in their ASCII appearance but powerful in their outreach, there began a dialogue that engaged representatives from scholarly publishing houses (those who produce journal publications in particular and earn much of their income from such journals). Publishers had varied responses to the idea of widely accessible networked digital information. Some were quick to break down their current costs of publication into editorial, printing, and distribution categories and to show that the print-related costs of their journals and books were a tiny fraction of overall production costs and therefore of prices to customers. Thus, they maintained, the maximum savings that could be achieved through digital distribution were small and would be offset by the costs of using new technologies: equipment, training, or retraining editorial staff, developing new subscription or licensing agreements suitable for the new medium, keeping current with hardware and software as it upgrades.

In this paper, I will describe both of these lines of reasoning and reference the few cost studies of digital publishing or digital libraries that have been attempted. I will then take an agnostic position: we do not know at this time what the costs of scholarly publishing and distribution in digital format will be, and it is probably too early to make accurate assessments. At the same time, I will express some hopes and speculate briefly on what might come of this new digital information field.

THE SCIENTISTS SPEAK: A SUBVERSIVE PROPOSAL

In mid-1994, Stevan Harnad, a cognitive psychologist at the University of Southampton in England, editor of the prestigious paper journal *Behavioral and Brain Sciences* (Cambridge University Press), and editor of the first peer-reviewed scientific journal on the Internet, *Psycoloquy*, incited a wide-ranging debate on several North American–based Internet discussion lists. By the fall of 1994, it had abated, but it never died down among a small circle of friends, of whom I was one. It resurfaced again in spring 1995 in Europe, after the *Times* (London) *Higher Education Supplement* carried an editorial debate between Harnad and Steve Fuller (Professor of Sociology and Social Policy, University of Durham) presenting opposing views on Internet publishing. The former saw digital scholarship as a solution to current publishing dilemmas, and the latter found that view a mirage or fantasy (Harnad and Fuller 1995: vi–vii).

Harnad had titled his opening gambit on the Internet "The Subversive Proposal." He wrote:

We have heard many sanguine predictions about the demise of paper publishing, but life is short and the inevitable day still seems a long way off. This is a subversive proposal that could radically hasten that day. It is applicable to ESOTERIC (non-trade, no-market) scientific and scholarly publication (but that is the lion's share of the academic corpus anyway), namely, that body of work for which the author does not and never has expected to sell the words. The scholarly author wants only to PUBLISH them, that is, to reach the eyes and minds of peers, fellow scientists and scholars the world over, so that they can build on one another's contributions in that cumulative, collaborative enterprise called learned inquiry. For centuries, it was only out of reluctant necessity that authors of such publications entered into the Faustian bargain of allowing a price-tag to be erected as a barrier between their work and its relatively small, specialized readership, for that was the only way they could make their work public at all during the age when paper publication (and its substantial real expenses) was their only option.

If scholarly authors in the world this very day established a globally accessible World Wide Web, Gopher, or FTP archives for their scholarly writing, the transition from paper publication to purely electronic publication (of esoteric research) would follow suit almost immediately. The two factors standing in the way of this outcome at this moment are (1) quality control (i.e., peer review and editing), which today still happens to be implemented almost exclusively by paper publishers, and (2) the reputation and prestige of paper publishing, which results from this locus of quality control. If scholars' preprints were universally available to all scholars online, these scholars could, quite naturally, and at the appropriate time (that is, after peer review has been done, and then on a continuing basis) substitute refereed articles for the unrefereed preprint.

When this scenario or some variant of it comes to pass, as it likely will, then current publishers will either restructure themselves (with the cooperation of the scholarly community) so as to arrange for the much-reduced electronic-only page costs (which I estimate to be less than 25 percent of paper-page costs, contrary to the 75 percent figure that appears in most current publishers' estimates) to be paid out of advance subsidies (from authors' page charges, learned society dues, university publication budgets and/or governmental publication subsidies) or they will have to watch as the peer community spawns a brand new generation of electronic-only publishers who will.

The subversion will be complete, because the (esoteric—no-market) peer reviewed literature will have taken to the airwaves, where it always belonged, and those airwaves will be cheap or seemingly free (to the benefit of all) because their true minimal expenses will be covered the optimal way for the unimpeded flow of esoteric knowledge to all. (Okerson and O'Donnell 1995: 11–12)

REACTIONS BY OTHER SCIENTISTS AND SCHOLARS

The science researchers who contributed to those Internet discussions during the summer of 1994 sided wholeheartedly with the Subversive Proposal. Paul Ginsparg, a distinguished high-energy physicist at the Los Alamos National Laboratories (LANL), endorsed the Subversive concepts and its cost estimates. In 1991, Ginsparg had started the High-Energy Physics preprint server at LANL. The new model, he affirmed, is already happening in the high-energy physics (HEP) community with its 20,000 users worldwide and 35,000 "hits" on HEP per day, as well as in several dozen related science disciplines in which his software has been cloned. He wrote, "these systems have entirely supplanted recognized journals as the primary disseminators of research information in certain fields."[1] He continued:

the driving force will not only be economics but the enhanced functionality of the electronic medium. there are many things that the new medium supports including the overall fluid nature (online annotations, continuously graded refereeing, automated hyperlinks to distributed resources including non-text based applications, etc., etc.) that simply has no analog in print.

. . . formerly we were at [the publishers'] mercy because we needed their production and distribution facilities. now we can outdo them on both counts, at dramatically reduced cost. at the same time, we expose how little intellectual added value they provide in general (I mean the validation and identification of significant research which can only come from within the community). sure they could remain in the game if they were willing to scale down to the more efficient operation enabled by the fully electronic medium, but the bottom line will not be there for them and they will have little ability to compete with a streamlined operation organized by researchers in alliance with their research libraries (and perhaps non-profit professional societies). (Okerson and O'Donnell 1995: 159)

Andrew Odlyzko, a mathematical researcher at AT&T Bell Laboratories, echoed these views. "Traditional scholarly journals," he speculated, "will likely disappear within ten to twenty years." On the basis of articles abstracted in *Zentralblatt Fuer Mathematik* and *Mathematical Reviews*, the principal sources of information and reviews of mathematical literature, Odlyzko made some calculations about the size and growth of mathematical literature, important because no one else has offered this sort of data for any other field:

- The current number of mathematics papers published per year is about 50,000.
- The number of papers doubles every 10 years.
- On this basis, about 1 million mathematical papers have been published, half of them in the last 10 years.
- If the rate of publication were to stay at 50,000 papers per year, the size of the mathematical literature would double in another 20 years.

He then analyzed changes in the costs of electronic storage and suggested that:

- It is possible to store all the current mathematical publications at an annual cost that is much less than the subscription to a single journal.
- The 1 million papers published previously, if converted to electronic format at all, are likely to be converted simply as bitmaps or page images. Compressed to current fax standards, these papers will require less than 1,000 gigabytes of storage.
- This is large, but still less than 150 current large optical disks.
- Within a decade personal computers, not to mention university departments, would be able to store all this mathematical literature—a development that alone could have startling implications for the way mathematicians work and libraries operate.
- The rapid improvement in communications networks and the impending entry of the entertainment industry, with video and film on demand at consumer-affordable prices, suggests that if a movie to one's home cost $10, then sending much less capacious scientific research papers over the Internet will cost pennies.

His analysis concluded:

Two centuries ago there was a huge gap between what a scholar could do and what the publishers provided. A printed paper was far superior in legibility to hand-written copies of the preprint, and it was cheaper to produce than hiring scribes to make hundreds of copies. Today the cost advantage of publishers is gone, as it is far cheaper to send out electronic versions of a paper than to have it printed in a journal. The quality advantage of journals still exists, but it is rapidly eroding. (Okerson and O'Donnell 1995: 64–67)

REACTIONS BY PUBLISHERS

Several publishers offered economic visions, approaching the issues from a different direction and coming up with a different set of answers altogether. Lorrin Garson of the American Chemical Society, publisher of the indispensable *Chemical Abstracts* and a number of primary journals in chemistry, noted, "Approximately 80–85 percent of our costs are for creating this [electronic chemistry] database and 15–20 percent for printing. The majority [of our incurred cost] is for peer review, processing manuscripts (50 percent are now done electronically; this will probably reach 60–80 percent by the end of 1995), editing, copy-editing, proofreading, etc."

Introducing the notion of different cost structures for different types of journals, Garson made the following significant point about differences in costs and presentation between different disciplines:

In fact, chemistry may be the most challenging of the sciences with much information in complex tables, display math, graphics—including chemical structures and other line art, half tones and color. Tables, math, and artwork are labor intensive (expensive) to handle whether for print or electronic products. Also, in the sciences, there are many special characters and multilevel positioning which must be handled; we have over 500 special characters for our journals and seven levels of super- and subscripts (on line, 3 levels above and 3 levels below) . . . even with undergraduate text books, there is a marked difference in manufacturing costs because of the difference in complexity of material. . . .

I would like to suggest that publishing electronic journals is in fact going to be more expensive than printing. For example, I believe most of the data we currently publish in journals today will in the future be acquired as coherent, digital data. This is starting now in the field of x-ray crystallography and will likely spread to other areas of structure such as spectroscopy (IR, UV, MS, NMR, etc.), biological data, in vitro testing, etc. The journal *Protein Science* (published by Cambridge University Press for the Protein Society) now publishes with each issue a floppy disk that contains protein/enzyme structure data that can be visualized with a program called Kinemage, which is also provided with the journal. The Protein Society plans to make these data also available on CD-ROM and via the Internet. The collection, maintenance (including indexing and cataloging), and dissemination of these data will, I believe, be more costly than printing, but the information will be much more valuable to the scientific community. Of course, when we get to this point we won't be publishing journals; the output will be called something else. (Okerson and O'Donnell 1995: 64–67)

Janet Fisher, Associate Director of Publishing at the Massachusetts Institute of Technology (MIT) Press, chimed in that electronic journals will have staffing and structures, which account for many of the costs of a journal, regardless of format.

Most of our editors have at least a half-time assistant to handle the clerical parts of the editorial tasks (acknowledging manuscripts, contacting potential reviewers, sending manuscripts out for review, dogging reviewers, writing authors, etc.), and if the assistant is a "managing editor type" and also does copy-editing, this is more likely a full-time position. These costs can be anywhere from $12,000 to $30,000 per year just for that staff position. (Not including equipment, phone, fax, postage, office space, university overhead . . . Editorial board members are usually not paid, but this doesn't mean that Editors are not . . . I would also argue that there will still be some "typesetting" cost with electronic journals. I do not believe that authors—even in the most highly sophisticated fields—will ever do all the formatting required to take manuscripts directly without some intervention. "Typesetting" will really become formatting, I guess, but there are costs associated with this. (Okerson and O'Donnell 1995: 133–34)

THE LIBRARIANS' ANALYSIS

Librarians in the Great Debate have tended to take a realistic if not a cynical view of prospects that Internet-distributed information will reduce costs, at least to their libraries in their lifetime. In extended postings, Bernard Naylor, university librarian at the University of Southampton, chided optimists that the publishing industry is a large one with many players (publishers of all kinds) and many satellite industries, such as secondary publishers, vendors, document delivery providers. Such large, generally profitable industries, not to mention the entire systems of which they are a part, do not change rapidly. Scholarly communication has several unique characteristics, including the pressure on scholars to publish, the lack of a clear distinction between "esoteric" and trade publications, the continued growth of academic publishing counter to logical arguments that this growth should and must subside for various reasons, and the vexing problem publishers will have in figuring out electronic pricing models at all during a long transitional period. When sheer size is coupled with these characteristics, Naylor and others argue that there will be no easy solutions—and possibly no solutions at all—to today's library quandary of trying to supply more information to users in a time of shrinking financial resources (Okerson and O'Donnell 1995: 140–44).

Hard data from librarians about the costs of servicing and storing digital information is hard to come by in these experimental days. While there are large numbers of networked delivery experiments between individual libraries or library systems and single or multiple publishers, the prototypes are in research and development (R&D) rather than in routine production mode. In an R&D mode, funding for projects is allocated through special, often one-time or time-bounded grants and staff reallocations. Project teams are far more focused on whether systems will work and how to achieve functionality than on economics. Fortunately for us all, one organization in the United States, The Andrew W. Mellon Foundation, is generously funding developmental projects in electronic publishing with an emphasis on economics. Within a couple of years, the Mellon-funded projects, at least, will begin to generate good information about the costs and economics of digital information.

That said, two recent papers offer some useful starting points. *Preserving Digital Information: Report of the Task Force on Archiving of Digital Information* (1996) makes a start on one aspect of electronic information, the cost of digital archives, which the Task Force characterized as "exceedingly complex." Reasoning that there are a variety of cost factors to understand, for a wide assortment of digital information types, at a time when we still know too little, the report presents a possible model for bitmapped monographs developed from Yale University's Project Open Book, a collection of 2,000 digital texts as black-and-white TIFF images. Projecting a 10-year scenario for this type of information stored in this way, compared to traditional paper storage costs, the data suggest that after about five years, unit costs for the digital archive fall to half of the unit costs of the paper collection. Nonetheless, total costs over 10 years in this model are calculated as being higher for the digital archive, defying widely held assumptions that digital will be necessarily cheaper.

The model, however, is wrapped in appropriate caveats: (1) It may be that the assumed rate of decline in technology-based costs is too conservative; and (2) It may be that current thinking about electronic models is papyrocentric rather than electronic. Altering the electronic model from a highly self-contained, multi-institutional one (much like current library paper collections) and entertaining a viable but very different construction of digital storage and access (for example, distributed networked archives shared widely by many organizations through contractual arrangements), the picture for electronic network-based resources becomes financially more attractive and begins to compete with the costs of storing and servicing paper toward the end of a 10-year period.

In June 1995, Charles Lowry, university librarian at Carnegie Mellon University (CMU) in Pittsburgh, Pennsylvania, presented a paper (with Denise Troll) about the experiences of CMU libraries, whose economic findings, they felt, should dispel some of the "cockeyed optimism" about how readily institutions can afford digital collections (1996). The CMU analysis was based on experiments with two electronic journal producers: University Microfilms International (UMI) and Elsevier Science Publishers. Characterizing today's institutional buying power as almost a zero-sum game (that is, there is little room in library budgets to afford digital media in addition to current printed publications), the authors do not see much incentive for publishers to develop digital publications. If such publications, specifically journals, *increase* publisher costs and do not add much new income, then there will be no way for information producers to make a profit to stay in business. The entire industry will have to be reconfigured to work with new technologies and processes, and information producers will not be able to drop print formats any more quickly than purchasers worldwide can receive new electronic formats. Four tables in the paper calculate that the costs for both storage and building maintenance at CMU are now substantially higher than for print. In a somewhat pessimistic conclusion ("The current publishing environment *and* the cost analysis of the work at Carnegie Mellon does not support the notion that digital libraries are about to happen"), the authors nonetheless ameliorate their pessimism: "It seems certain that within two decades we will reach a state of development in which electronic-networked access to scholarly information is the norm."

CURRENT PRICING FOR ELECTRONIC JOURNALS

Today's digitally available journals (there is not much in the form of electronic networked books, for nearly all the development in networked academic publishing has been for journals) can be categorized in one of two ways:

1. Journals distributed out of universities and laboratories. There are at least 200 peer-reviewed journal titles now available and they are growing; there are hundreds of unrefereed electronic networked serials and thousands of electronic seminars or discussion groups on every conceivable academic subject area (Okerson 1995). For all of these digital resources, the costs are borne "up front" through university connections and workstations and delivered to worldwide readers free, provided those readers also have computers and connectivity.

2. Journals distributed digitally via networks by today's print-on-paper publishers. Again, most of this distribution is experimental and, with a few exceptions (such as the journals distributed by the library utility OCLC), the distribution happens as a time-defined experiment in which the institution receives the content without charge to mount a collaborative, learning experiment with one or more journal publishers. Because only a handful of conventional publishers have started brand new *electronic-only* titles, it is not possible to discern any kind of pricing pattern or compare them with equivalent paper publications. Springer-Verlag, for example, has offered a couple of brand new Internet serial titles free for the first year to test market readiness. Subscription fees will be established after a suitable period of assessment. For 1996, a few publishers will make their heretofore print journals available via digital licenses to institutional subscribers. An early participant in this innovation is Elsevier, whose recently announced policy is a surcharge of 35 percent over the cost of the print titles. This practice of charging more for the electronic format follows established industry practice for Indexing and Abstracting services. As long as the demand for digital versions is comparatively small and restricted to large research in-

stitutions, we may expect such pricing to continue—and it will not hasten the days of digital libraries.

WHAT WILL COME TO PASS?

So, the early economic signals are not clear; analysis by people in different parts of the scholarly communication system is so different that sometimes one wonders if they are talking about the same thing at all. What do we make of such discrepancies?

Publication and publishing present many faces, held together in the mind's eye by the common technologies of printing and binding. Comic books, phone books, popular novels, and scientific texts all find their audiences through one facet or another of an industry whose business decisions are made on certain common grounds: costs of acquiring the content and preparing it for publication, costs of mechanical reproduction, and costs of distributing it effectively to the target audience. Those costs are recovered in many ways. If a publication is to be judged successful and to continue, then profits must be made, although such profits may come from many sources and directions. For example, the purchasers of popular fiction pay for the costs of best-sellers and advertisers pay most of the cost of newspapers. University, government, or research institute budgets pay for much scientific literature by funding the initial research, by contributing "page charges" toward the publication of certain articles, and by paying subscription fees for the journals in which such articles are published.

Not every branch of publishing is equally healthy in the late twentieth century. The murder mystery genre is wildly successful, but the scientific journal and the scholarly monograph are threatened by rising costs, rising output, and constrained academic budgets, many of which have been well documented in library writings (Association of Research Libraries 1994b).

The most painful paradox is that in the interests of scholarship, the law of the marketplace generally does not function well and probably *cannot* be allowed to function in any pure sense of the word. An item with a tiny market may yet be the indispensable link in a chain of research that leads to a result of high social value. What makes it more difficult for a real market to function in scientific and scholarly publishing is that the societal value may be—at the moment of production of the small market item—years or even decades away. The research libraries of the world have the unenviable task of seeking in common to acquire the totality of scientific and academic discourse for researchers to use, even as that totality explodes in size and cost and its functionality may not be assured.

Accordingly, it is impossible to say with any confidence what the introduction and widespread use of networked electronic technology will do to digital publications and distribution. All the stakeholders (authors, editors, publishers, vendors, libraries) profess to have the good of the higher educational and scientific mission in mind, but it cannot be denied that everyone seeks a future in which not only that mission but also their own economic and professional future is assured. Researchers, librarians, and commercial publishers have all emerged with distinct points of view. The discussions are far from empty of practical consequences, for strong ideas well expressed are the basis for the confidence people will place in electronic publishing experiments and future projects that go beyond the experimental to bring a vision of electronic publishing for the scientific and academic community to reality.

CAN SCHOLARLY PUBLISHING TAKE ADVANTAGE OF INTERNET ECONOMICS?

The simplest answer is that the matter is not technical, but sociological. Ideas and technologies can change the world. Yet, the uncertainties are many. The model that Paul Ginsparg has brought to life for physics is one that clearly can work, at least under specific conditions. Where a well-defined group of users, all acclimated to the same kind of discourse and familiar with standard software packages that transmit well by network, concentrate on producing rigorously analytical material, the relatively unobtrusive preprint server can be a powerful tool. Does it scale up to digital libraries? When the group gets larger or more diverse, when research interests start crossing disciplinary boundaries, when fundamental disagreements of method and style are a substantive part of the field itself—does this kind of communication bog down? Are third parties needed to organize, control, and referee the conversations?

One reason that economics of scholarly information are so vexing is the economic immunity of the professorate. The "serials crisis" and the problems that publishers have marketing monographs have not yet had an appreciable impact on the authoring public of academe. It is not palpably difficult to "get published": rejection of a given article is taken as a personal, not an institutional, problem, and most articles in which their authors believe find homes eventually. The insulation of scholars and scientists from the economic burdens of the publications in their disciplines means that they can remain content with the print system as it is. A natural tendency to prefer the familiar, usually expressing itself as a concern about whether e-publication will be accepted by promotion and tenure committees, exerts its staying hand as well. In addition, the economy of academic publishing has been constructed so that whatever money changes hands, virtually none ever reaches the authors of the works. They receive their compensation indirectly, from employers who value their research output. Thus, it is fair to say that the researcher looking at the published article wants more than anything for it to reach as wide an audience as possible, with as few barriers as possible. In this case, traditional publishers cannot defend the need to recover costs from the end-user by appealing to their need to reimburse authors. That is a real economic change whose ultimate purport we can now only surmise.

Economic pressures are, of course, being felt not by faculty but by publishers and by librarians; but publishers have no desire to reposition themselves too rapidly into a market that may not be widely accepted and in which they are not sure they can recover costs of production. This leaves the librarians, guardians of the integrity of the system of scholarly communication as a whole. It is, in fact, from the library community that some of the most venturesome and pragmatic proposals have come forth. In 1992, The Andrew W. Mellon Foundation published a study of the state of library budgets, noting the declining share of university budgets that libraries have had the last 20 years. The study pointed to electronic publishing as a possible source of amelioration, a recommendation they are studying and supporting. The series of symposia conducted by the Association of Research Libraries (ARL) since 1992 has given stakeholders on all sides a place to express concerns and inform themselves. The Association of American Universities, that is to say the presidents of the leading research institutions, teamed with ARL in 1994 to write strong reports pointing a way forward through judicious use of electronic publication.

Confounding the economic questions is the fact that we also do not know how much technology and support scholars will need. It is now easy to say that the traditional article will take up little or no bandwidth and so place a minimal strain on the network; but what if a scientist begins to believe she needs to give you full motion video, from six different angles, of a crucial experiment? Or if a report on an experiment conducted on the space shuttle feels it *must* be accompanied by gigabytes of the raw telemetry data sent back to earth? In principle, such full presentations of data are possible and desirable; this is the power of the medium. In practice, however, they may begin to add unanticipated costs, such as formatting the video in a standard way for transmission to all platforms. The best current economic analysis of the cost of using the Internet superhighway itself is about a dollar a year per user: Hal Varian and Jeff MacKie Mason studied this topic in ARL's *Filling the Pipeline and Paying the Piper* (1995: 77–85).

Despite these concerns, it is impossible not to have at least some guarded optimism about the digital future. We need not imagine substitution or totalitarian takeover by any of the players on the cyberspace frontier. What needs to be foreseen, instead, is the shift in the mixture of kinds of information available on what terms. There is already a lot of *free* information in the world (that is, information given away at no direct cost to end-users): the phone book or all the information in bookstores that browsers consume but do not necessarily buy. On the other hand, some information, such as stock tips from qualified advisors, we pay for at a high price.

There are many examples of cooperative, affordable, and sometimes even seemingly for-free publications on the Internet that encourage us to dream large dreams about the ready flow of information in the future; but even if those dreams fall short of realization, it must be considered likely that the *proportion* of the total information economy that will be occupied by this liberal digital exchange will be larger than is now the case for print libraries. What this will mean, none can say, but it will influence the market for purchase and sale of information in many ways.

The responsible course for universities and research institutions concerned about the future is to press the claims of that sector, to experiment responsibly and venture bravely, to see if those lines can be drawn in a way that favors the widest and most generous flow of information of a scholarly and scientific nature. The way to find the answers to these questions is, wherever possible, to begin substantial projects of the kind that some academic preprint and e-journal editors in the research sector have already undertaken. The "hard sciences" are the obvious place to begin, for theirs is the academic culture most dependent on the journal form (to the near exclusion of the monograph) and on wide and timely distribution of the results of their investigations; but there are areas of the social sciences and even the humanities where similar enterprises can reasonably expect to succeed.

In his *Four Quartets*, T. S. Eliot described the poet's mission as "to purify the dialect of the tribe." In a sense, science and poetry work to that goal from different directions, seeking by their discourse to enhance the quality of society's common discourse, by rooting out error and imprecision and finding new and true things to say and ways to say them.

NOTE

1. Dr. Ginsparg does not begin his sentences with capital letters.

REFERENCES

Association of Research Libraries (ARL). 1994a. Graphs from the 1993–94 and Earlier ARL Statistics. (ARL Statistical Information on prices and trend lines for monographs and journals purchased by North American research libraries.) Available from http://viva.lib.virginia.edu:80/arlstats/1994/graphs.html.

———. 1994b. *Reports of the AAU Task Forces*. Washington, D.C.: Association of Research Libraries. Available from http://arl.cni.org/aau/frontmatter.html.

Cummings, Anthony M., et al. 1992. *University Libraries and Scholarly Communication: A Study Prepared for The Andrew W. Mellon Foundation*. Washington, D.C.: Association for Research Libraries. Available from http://www.lib.virginia.edu/mellon/mellon.html.

Harnad, Stevan, and Steve Fuller. 1995. "Post-Gutenberg Galaxy." *Times Higher Education Supplement*, May 12.

Lowry, Charles B., and Denise A. Troll. 1995. CMU/UMI Virtual Library Project:

If We Build It, Will They Come? Paper presented at the North American Serials Interest Group Conference, Duke University, Durham, N.C.

Okerson, Ann, ed. 1995. *Directory of Electronic Journals, Newsletters, and Academic Discussion Lists.* Washington, D.C.: Association of Research Libraries.

Okerson, Ann, and James O'Donnell, eds. 1995. *Scholarly Journals at the Crossroads: A Subversive Proposal for Electronic Publishing.* An Internet Discussion About Scientific and Scholarly Journals and Their Future. Washington, D.C.: Association for Research Libraries. Available from: http://www.arl.org/scomm/subversive/.

Task Force on Archiving of Digital Information. 1996. *Preserving Digital Information: Report of the Task Force on Archiving of Digital Information.* Washington, D.C.: Commission on Preservation and Access. Also available from www.rlg.org/ArchTF/.

Varian, Hal R., and Jeffrey K. MacKie Mason. 1995. Some FAQs about Usage-Based Pricing. In *Scholarly Publishing on the Electronic Networks: Filling the Pipeline and Paying the Piper.* Washington, D.C.: Association of Research Libraries.

CHAPTER 9

Intellectual Property Policy for an Information Society

PETER LYMAN

In each period of history the concept of intellectual property reflects the way information technologies shape the relationship between knowledge and wealth. Thus the evolution of intellectual property from the print to the digital age will reflect both the way that technology shapes how knowledge is created and used, and the resulting new roles of knowledge in the economy.

In the United States, the political debate about the future of intellectual property is now dominated by an attempt to adapt and extend existing law to manage the products of new information technologies. Yet, although the principles of copyright and patent policy are of great value because they reflect generations of thoughtful debate and compromise, old laws do not always fit new technologies neatly.

Copyright protects intellectual property in printed texts, but depends upon two of the physical characteristics of print and printing technologies. First, the printing press is a technology for mechanical reproduction of texts; thus, printed expressions of ideas are protected by focusing upon the right to make copies ("copy-right"). Second, texts are physical objects, so copyright also focuses upon the right to distribute protected works. These two strategies are typical of the property rights that protect ownership to other economic commodities in industrial societies, even though the value of intellectual property is in the ideas expressed rather than the physical commodity itself. However, information networks are not mechanical technologies for copying, and digital documents are not physical commodities.

This is a revised version of a paper presented at the International Roundtable for Information and Library Science, Kanazawa Institute of Technology, Library Center, Kanazawa, Japan, 1995.

As a consequence, old laws do not apply neatly, and it is even possible that entirely new principles will have to be invented. New intellectual property policy will need to balance the need for continuity and stability with economic incentives for innovation and change, but most of all they must be grounded in research upon the nature and value of digital documents, and the product of thoughtful political dialogue.

Patent law protects intellectual property in new inventions, which must be novel and represent an unexpected advance in the state of the art. Software is the most important invention of our time, along with new genetic technologies, but is software a mechanical innovation (which would be protected by patents) or a new kind of writing (which would be protected by copyright)? (Samuelson 1990). This question cannot be answered by looking at the physical characteristic of the innovation, for software may be packaged either as a text ("code") or instantiated within chips. Rather, this debate about what are called "process patents" turns upon a philosophical debate, the terms of which originated in the Medieval university: is software part of the "liberal arts," because it rests upon mathematical algorithms that reflect basic laws of nature, or part of the "useful arts," because it is a technology for transforming nature into useful products? Many people think that neither traditional patent rules nor this philosophical debate will resolve the issue; rather, it may require entirely new intellectual property rules.

But the process of change may go beyond reconsideration of the rules that govern new kinds of digital documents; new economic realities may also change the way that traditional printed documents are treated as intellectual property. Since the copyright mechanism for the regulation of intellectual property rights directly reflects the history of print technology, it would seem logical to assume that the legal and market mechanisms which govern printed knowledge in a digital age will not change fundamentally. Yet, changes in the economic role of knowledge may change even traditional copyright. Coinciding with the birth of the computer revolution and the development of an information economy, the price of printed information has begun to increase dramatically, reflecting the increased commercial value of scientific, technical, and medical knowledge. Changes in the economic value of information have created economic incentives for the development of new hybrid print/digital formats: new businesses like document delivery use digitized images of printed documents delivered worldwide on computer networks. The copyright mechanism will still provide adequate protection for intellectual property in traditional print formats, including commodities like books and journals, but it is distinctly possible that copyright will not be adequate to regulate networked modes of distribution for printed commodities that have been digitized. These hybrid documents are the primary focus of current legislative interest in extending traditional copyright law.

Yet beyond digitized print, the information revolution has begun to create entirely new forms of knowledge which are "born digital," such as:

- *Hypertext*, in which the reader rather than the author or publisher creates the final narrative structure of the document;
- *Scientific visualization*, such as three-dimensional interactive models of information with which the reader can interact in ways far beyond the traditional meaning of the verb "to read";
- *Virtual communities*, such as scientific collaboratories, within which researchers scattered around the globe can work together to create and analyze scientific data;
- *Multimedia*, which enables the reader to choose different modes of representation for information;
- *Interactive publications*, such as databases or electronic journals that are continuously edited by scholars around the world to provide the most current research findings, as well as real-time scientific debate.

In each case, intellectual property will have to take forms far more complex than those protecting print commodities.

There are fascinating unanswered questions: (1) copyright rests upon being able to identify an "author" who created a new expression of an idea: Who is the "author" when "reading" consists of a technical performance by a large group of people? (Biagioli 1998; Powell 1998); (2) how can we define who owns an expression of an idea when many different kinds of intellectual rights may be layered and mixed in a single act of reading, including hardware patents, software copyrights and patents, network protocols, standards and transmission rights, user interface designs, and bits of information, pictures, and music assembled from all over the world? Established rules and procedures are important in thinking about the answers to these questions, but we must return to two fundamental principles that underlie any intellectual property regime.

First, the American Constitution defines the political purpose of copyright, which is "progress in the useful Arts and Sciences." This is very important, for copyright is not simply a private property right like any other; it is a property right that serves a public purpose. Thus, before we invent new intellectual property rules for digital documents, we must understand how the rules will serve the public interest in scientific and technical progress, not just how they will help to develop new markets.

Second, we must understand when and why digital documents should be managed by intellectual property rules, and when they should be governed by other principles. At one end of the spectrum, the First Amendment links freedom of speech to print, thus we must ask when digital documents should be treated as forms of free speech which serve democratic and educational goals, and when they should be treated as property. This is sometimes ambiguous in the case of printed documents, and equally so in the case of digital documents on the Net. At the other end of the spectrum, we must ask when digital documents should be managed by the same contract law that governs markets in other economic commodities, for it is clear that digital documents have great economic value, which must be protected. Intellectual property law is complex precisely because it must balance the political principle of free speech with the economic principle of private property.

To conclude this introduction, it is most appropriate at this Kanazawa Roundtable for Library and Information Science to acknowledge that the same forces changing intellectual property are changing libraries, and for the same reasons. Inevitably, libraries are changing because information technology is changing the way knowledge is created, distributed, and used. The issues confronting the library as an institution are exactly parallel to those facing intellectual property law. Libraries are based upon the assumption that the principles guiding access to information must balance marketplace forces with democratic principles. Communities, whether corporations or colleges or neighborhoods, are defined by their shared knowledge and modes of learning. Libraries are one of the most important ways that communities organize themselves, by collecting, preserving, and circulating shared knowledge. Although my topic is not the future of the library in a digital age, any exploration of intellectual property rights in the digital age must consider the fate of the library. Thus, the purpose of this paper is not so much to provide lasting answers to questions—any answer would quickly become outdated by technological progress—but rather, to define the political and philosophical debates surrounding intellectual property, debates in which libraries and librarians must participate.

CAN IDEAS BE PROPERTY?

Three ideas have been fundamental to the intellectual property policy as it has developed around print culture over the past centuries:

- Although ideas are really human activities, contained within thinking and speaking, it is useful to treat the *expression* of ideas as property;
- It is in the *public interest* to treat the expression of ideas as property, because economic wealth is created by the production and distribution of knowledge, but the creators and distributors of knowledge must have an economic incentive to invest in production and distribution;
- Yet, third, there are limits to this economic right, such as the First Amendment, which supports democracy, and the public interest in education, which leads to innovation and the production of new ideas.

Let us briefly consider each of these ideas in turn.

Only the Expression of Ideas May Be Property

It is fundamental to the concept of intellectual property that only original and tangible expressions of ideas may be treated as private property. Even so, there is an obvious philosophical contradiction in the very idea of *intellectual* property. Ideas are thoughts or speech which are inherent in human communication, and thus by definition are in the public domain. For this reason, ideas themselves cannot be copyrighted, but only specific and original *expressions* of ideas.

Moreover, this formulation refers to printed ideas, for print is a tangible thing that may be treated as a commodity (Strong 1995). This second criterion is important for our subject, for many digital expressions are signals, not tangible things, or may exist as both an intangible communication and as a commodity that has economic value at the same time.

Knowledge Creates Progress, Therefore Wealth

Why are the expressions of ideas alienable, treated as commodities that can be bought and sold? It has been a fundamental assumption of market society that progress in human discovery is greatly accelerated if knowledge is treated as property. This reflects the dependence of industrial economies upon innovation, which is reflected in the belief in progress that underlies liberal political regimes. This assumption is illustrated in the clause of the Constitution that establishes copyright as a means to promoting progress in the useful arts, which is what the eighteenth century called technology, and science. In Japan's copyright law, the fair exploitation of cultural products is intended to contribute to the development of culture (Doi 1980: 202). If ideas are treated as property, the argument goes, inventors and thinkers will have an incentive to be innovative; and underlying this, in turn, is the assumption that technological progress is the means to a public good, the growth of the economy and social wealth.

But Some Intellectual Property Rights Are Inalienable

These principles are part of a utilitarian theory of intellectual property, but even in industrial societies there are limits, for not every human relationship is governed by the market. Many exchanges of knowledge are gift exchanges made for the sake of improving the quality of social relationships, not market exchanges made for the sake of profit. As mentioned above, libraries often have a special status in copyright law because they represent the need of communities to share knowledge as a common good. Thus, intellectual property law frequently recognizes two limits on the marketplace of ideas.

First, education is as fundamental a public good as wealth because it develops the human capacity to develop new ideas and inventions; thus education is the foundation of cultural and economic progress. Thus, the doctrine of "fair use" evolved as a limited exemption from copyright, a right to copy for one's personal educational use. Although some conceive of fair use as a social subsidy for education or as a right to education, others argue that in law it is only an affirmative defense against a copyright infringement.

Second, in Europe and Japan there is a principle of the author's moral rights, which limits the alienability of intellectual property. Although an author may sell intellectual property rights in the marketplace, the integrity of that expression may not be compromised with the author's permission. These moral rights protect the reputation of an author. Moral rights, however, are not recognized in the United States.

These three principles are the basic structure of a utilitarian philosophical justification for copyright as a legal mechanism for defining intellectual property rights within industrial society. Because these principles limit property rights, there is a strong counterargument based upon natural right philosophy. In this argument the author's right to ownership is absolute because it was the author's genius which created new economic value; by extension, this absolute right extends to those who buy the expression of ideas from authors. The natural right argument is often made by large corporations whose key assets are intellectual property, such as entertainment companies. Recently, it has become very influential in attacks upon the concept of fair use, and leads to an argument that contract law should replace copyright law as the regime governing intellectual property.

Still, it is the political and cultural power of ideas that has dominated most of the thinking about intellectual property. Sociologists describe medieval communities as resting upon a sense of moral community; the invention of the printing press created a new kind of society based upon printed records, the rule of law, and objective decision making. In Europe, the turning point between these two systems might well have been the use of the printing press by Martin Luther to copy and distribute ideas that questioned the moral community. Thus, the first intellectual property laws concerned the control of printing technology itself, to protect the divine right of kings and religious consensus. Only later, with the Statute of Anne in England, did intellectual property in the modern sense develop, establishing the idea of copyright to regulate printed commodities, such as books and newspapers. The printing press was the first innovation that made it possible to mass-produce intellectual property; books, in fact, were one of the first manufactured commodities which were traded in early international markets. Thus, the right to copy, copy-right, was intended not to regulate the content of ideas, like earlier rules, but to establish a marketplace for ideas.

The invention of methods to mass-produce paper and print copies, and the creation of a marketplace for ideas led to the establishment of science, the first international intellectual community (Febvre and Martin 1976: 10). Printed letters, then science journals, made it possible for discoveries to be communicated, and thus be applied to solve practical social and economic problems. Thus, technology and science began to be linked to social progress, through the production of ideas, as in the political philosophy of Francis Bacon in England. This is still a powerful ideology today, as many nations are now striving to define national information policies to promote internal investment in developing intellectual capital, and to prepare to compete with other nations in the international marketplace.

WHAT IS THE KNOWLEDGE ECONOMY?

The key question is this: will the institutions and legal arrangements that characterized industrial society continue to hold true in the digital age? In an industrial society it was assumed that knowledge led to progress, and wealth was conceived as industrial capital, usually in the form of machinery. In contrast, consider this description of wealth in the digital age as described by Walter Wriston, former president of Citibank: "Intellectual capital is becoming relatively more important than physical capital. Indeed, the new source of wealth is not material, it is information, knowledge applied to work to create value. The pursuit of wealth is now largely the pursuit of information, and the application of information to the means of production" (Wriston 1992: xii).

This statement has two profound implications for intellectual property policy: that knowledge is the primary source of wealth in the digital age; and that the world economy has replaced the nation-state as the manager of wealth. Let us consider each in turn.

Intellectual Capital Will Be the Origin of Wealth

At the birth of the industrial age, in *The Wealth of Nations*, Adam Smith described the source of national wealth as the technical division of labor in manufacturing, which required workers to act as if they were machines. Today, at the birth of the information age, Shoshana Zuboff describes the origin of wealth as the ability of workers to use information in a skilled way. Digital technologies are what she calls "an informating technology," that is, technologies that continuously create new knowledge which workers must understand in order to manage the production process. She says,

An informating technology challenges the organization to recognize the skill demands associated with computer mediation and the redistribution of knowledge that intellective skill development implies. . . . Obedience has been the axial principle of imperative control. When tasks require intellective effort, obedience can be dysfunctional and can impede the exploitation of information. Under such conditions, internal commitment and motivation replace obedience as the primary bond between the individual and the task. As the work that people do becomes more abstract, the need for positive motivation and internal commitment becomes all the more crucial. (Zuboff 1988: 291)

Since these words were written, management theory has developed a corresponding strategy called "knowledge management," which places central focus upon developing the worker's intellectual capacities in order to increase productivity (Nonaka and Konno 1998). Similarly, the theory of the corporation no longer distinguishes manual and mental labor, for in an "informated" environment, the ability to make intellectual judgments becomes the key to productivity.

Informating technologies replace mass production with customized production, by allowing the worker to adjust the industrial process to create specialized products that are cost-effective even in relatively small numbers. Zuboff's point is that because digital technologies continuously produce information, the worker becomes both a reader and a creator of new knowledge.

By analogy, just as machinery freezes work into one discipline pattern, so print freezes knowledge into one pattern. In each case there is a benefit, because a human activity becomes predictable and can be treated as a thing, a commodity, and as property; but this is not necessarily true of digital knowledge, which is dynamic, and requires the reader to be as creative as the author. In a digital age the human/tool relationship is more like that of a musician playing a musical instrument than the repetitive, disciplined work described by Adam Smith.

The World Economy

Second, Wriston argues that "the old political boundaries of nation-states are being made obsolete by an alliance of commerce and technology" (1992: 11). Wriston argues that no nation-state can control the value of its currency in a global market; thus, in a real sense, global information systems are the new currency, because they have the power to define the value of money and credit in the world market. If this point about fiscal points is valid, and can be generalized to other markets as well, the emergence of the global economy will make the nation-state less and less able to control its domestic economy. Thus, Manuel Castells has pointed out that capitalism has always been international, creating an international division of labor in which some nations provided raw materials and others refined them into products (Castells 1989, 1996). Because of the rise of information networks, he argues, a global system in which production can be coordinated worldwide in real time has replaced the international market system. This results in a fundamental difference between intellectual property rights in an industrial age in which nation-states were dominant, and in the coming digital age. In industrial nation-states, intellectual property has been defined, regulated, and enforced by national legislation and litigation. In the digital age, intellectual property will be the primary content of world trade, and will be regulated by international treaties.

This is illustrated by the creation of the World Trade Organization (WTO), and specifically by the emergence of the World Intellectual Property Organization (WIPO), which created a treaty that is to serve as the model which nation-states are to adapt in national legal systems. This uniformity of intellectual property laws is necessary if production is to be coordinated worldwide in real time. Thus, national differences in intellectual property policy will increasingly be seen as constraints on free trade. For example, the Database Privacy Directive of the European Union (EU), which the EU sees as a human rights provision, is seen as a restraint of trade by the United States (Swire and Litan 1998). Unfortunately, the implementation of the WIPO treaty in the United States, called the Digital Millennium Copyright Act (DMCA), is widely regarded as hostile to fair use and to libraries, for it places central emphasis upon the development of the digital economy.

In summary, each of Wriston's points might be illustrated by examples from the library world. First, the historic price rise in the cost of serials publications in science, technology, and medicine (STM) reflects the commercialization of knowledge; since 1950, for-profit publishers have replaced non-profit publishers, and since 1990 multinational corporations have begun to control STM publishing. Second, the cost of library collections now reflects the relative value of a national currency in the global monetary markets; and third, the economic value of STM information is reflected in the increasing specialization of knowledge, and the resulting proliferation of the number of STM journals.

WHAT IS A DIGITAL DOCUMENT?

This new mode of information has been called a "digital document," which has been defined as any information represented in bits, but particularly those "born digital," which exist "at the interface of content, format, use and technology" (*Documents in the Digital Culture* 1995). This unusual definition includes two important implications for intellectual property theory. First, digital documents are created by a performance of the reader as much as the expression of ideas shaped by an author. For example, a reader may access or "pull" information off the network, might choose to read it within a specific software package, may combine it with other information in a novel way, and might send a copy to someone else to work on. Intellectual property rights have always begun with an author, but with

Table 9.1
A Model of Analog and Digital Formats

Analog	Digital
Physical medium	Signal
Representation	Simulation
Author centric	Reader centric
Broadcast push	Interactive pull

digital documents it is unclear who the author is. Second, by definition every digital document might contain bundles of intellectual property rights, each linked to the specific content, format, and technology which is used.

Thus, digital documents have a dynamic quality, and in contrast to print may be a signal that has no necessary physical substance. The implications of this are well described by Geoffrey Nunberg:

Two features set electronic technologies apart from the technologies of mechanical reproduction that have shaped the cultural role of the book. The first is the versatility of the technology. Unlike mechanical antecedents like the printing press, the typewriter, or the telegraph, the computer isn't restricted to a single role in production or diffusion. In fact, the technology tends to erase distinctions between the separate processes of creation, reproduction, and distribution that characterize the classical industrial model of print commodities. (Nunberg 1993: 21)

Before computers it was relatively easy to control the reproduction and distribution of print because the production process itself separated the various stages which are vital to the management of intellectual property—creation from reproduction and from distribution. Moreover, the immateriality and malleability of digital documents deprives intellectual property law of its primary mode of rights control and management, control of reproduction and distribution of a physical thing which could be regulated as part of the commerce system.

One way to conceptualize the differences between printed and digital documents is to place these distinctions within a broader model of the difference between analog and digital information formats (see Table 9.1). Let us consider each of these differences in turn.

Medium versus Signal

Analog formats store information within distinct and fixed media, whether paper or electronic wave. Digital formats are contained into a binary signal that in principle can be transformed into any analog medium.

Representation versus Simulation

Analog media create representations of the real, but digital signals are based upon simulations of the real. According to the artist Frank Popper, "what is simulated is no longer the territory, an original substance or being, but a model of the real. . . . From now on it is the map that precedes, and thus generates, the territory" (Popper 1993).

Author versus Reader

The owner of intellectual property controls the design and content of analog media, while the design and content of digital signals is interactive. Interactivity means that while content and form are initially determined by the author or publisher, the final document is designed by the reader, who may then copy and distribute the new design.

Push versus Pull

Analog media are centrally reproduced and distributed, and thus the reproduction of intellectual property is controlled, whether by a publisher or broadcaster. But digital signals are "pulled in," or chosen by the reader, who then shapes the signal by interacting with it, choosing its specific analog form—for example, printing it, listening to it.

The difference between print and digital information flows from the fact that print takes the form of a material commodity, but digital signals are immaterial, which reduces the cost and difficulty of copying and distribution. Geoff Nunberg describes the implications of this difference.

One important consequence . . . is that with electronic reproduction, the user has a much greater role in the process of reproduction. A mass produced book is both bound and bounded in a way that's replicated for all of its instances; each copy contains the same text in the same order. But the computational representations of texts can be divided and reassembled in an indefinitely large number of documents, with the final form left to the decision of the individual user. (Nunberg 1993: 22)

Just as the worker described by Zuboff adds value to manufacture by customizing the product, the "user" adds value to information through the performance of reading.

The mechanisms for the enforcement of intellectual property are dependent upon the characteristics of analog media: they take a material form, and they are centrally reproduced and distributed, both characteristics that can be regulated easily. In print, the reproduction and distribution of knowledge was regulated by controlling the technology of copying, the printing press. In the early stages of printing, printers had to obtain a government license; in more recent times, printing technology became very common, and enforcement took the form of ex post facto penalties for unauthorized use of intellectual property.

Networked digital information raises new problems for copyright; thus the owners of digital information have adopted two strategies. First, they have tried to create markets for digital formats that take material form, such as CD-ROM, which are commodities just like other commodities. Second, they have encouraged the DMCA legislation, which not only encrypts information so only authorized users can read it, but prohibits the development or use of technologies to break encryption. While encrypted information is still a signal, access to the signal has been made technically difficult.

WHAT ADDS ECONOMIC VALUE TO INFORMATION?

As we have seen, Walter Wriston argued that the origin of wealth in the digital age results from "knowledge applied to work to create new value." Ultimately, intellectual property is created whenever value is added to information, but it appears that the value of networked information may be very different from the value of printed information in important respects. These differences reflect both the intrinsic characteristics of each format, but also some of the characteristics of the emerging information economy.

Understanding an appropriate intellectual property regime for digital documents requires understanding how they differ from the value chain for printed documents. How is economic value added to digital and networked information in ways which might justify added intellectual property rights?

The essential elements of the value chain for printed works are familiar, and include things like the creative activity of the original author; the quality control provided by the publisher (including editorial control, design and manufacture, marketing and distribution); and, finally, those who provide access to printed information, such as distributors and bookstores. Also, let us not leave out the library, which adds value by creating information inventory management tools, such as published indices and bibliographic control technologies; by archiving and preserving knowledge; and by providing public access.

We do not yet have enough knowledge of the value chain surrounding networked and digital documents, because digital commerce business models are still evolving rapidly; but let us begin by considering the value chain of the World Wide Web.

Infrastructure

Value is created by the network infrastructure itself, the high-capacity optical fiber networks, switches, and routers, conforming to the TCP/IP standard. Each of these industries has significantly different views of intellectual property policy; patent and copyright protection is not as urgent as one might expect in a market in which technology changes so rapidly that being first to market and establishing a brand name is often given higher priority. Indeed, many of these industries promote "open standards," and oppose the high-protection intellectual property policies promoted by the entertainment industry.

Distribution

HyperText Markup Language (HTML), although a limited subset of the Standard Generalized Markup Language (SGML), is far more significant, for it transformed "the Network" into "the Web." Before the Web, the Internet was defined as a "network of networks," by virtue of the shared TCP/IP standard; TCP/IP also supported three important information management tools—e-mail, FTP, and Telnet. But the essential structure of "the Net" was a technical infrastructure of circuits. With HTML, the essential infrastructure of the "Web" is knowledge, hypertext links between bits of information which may be located anywhere in the world. Together they are a fundamentally new invention: if the Net is the paper of the information revolution, the Web is the printing press.

Quality Control

In the past, information was valuable because it was scarce. Today there is too much information on the Web, and value is created through selectivity, whether that is accomplished through artificial intelligence, search engines, agents, portals, or collaborative filtering. Thus, filtering and quality control, which were provided for print through the editorial control process of publishers and collection development by librarians, has as yet no parallel in the digital world.

Virtual Communities

The print model assumes that the reader is an individual, but networked information is more likely to be created and consumed by groups. Communities are defined by shared knowledge, shared cultures of learning, and collaborative choices about what kinds of knowledge ought to be preserved. On the network entirely new kinds of social groups have evolved, called virtual communities or communities of practice, based precisely upon these kinds of shared knowledge cultures (Furlong 1989; Virnoche and Marx 1997; Wellman and Gulia 1999; and Lave and Wenger 1991).

In sum, this brief discussion of the Web is only intended to be an example of how one might think about the new value chain of the information revolution. Because technology is changing so quickly, it is too soon to offer more than an example of how the question might be posed. For librarians, however, it is not too soon to think about the role of the library in the new value chain. For example, while search engine companies are using Library of Congress subject headings to catalog the Web, what is the role of the reference librarian? As yet there is no archive or preservation strategy for the Web, and digital signals are as ephemeral as broadcast signals. Or, how would the library change if we conceive of the user as a virtual community?

WHAT IS THE FUTURE OF INTELLECTUAL PROPERTY?

There is a second way that the new kinds of economic value created by digital networks might be explored, by examining some of the specific characteristics of networked information that may provide new kinds of *intellectual* value for innovation and education. Electronic journals are a good example of the invention of new kinds of information value that take advantage of the network to communicate in ways that printed journals cannot. What are the *unique* characteristics of networked information that add value to information in digital formats, which could lead to the creation of new kinds of intellectual property rights?

Timeliness

In highly competitive markets, such as science and technology, the value of information is related to its scarcity and timeliness: the older the information, the less value it possesses. Thus, a new subject of intellectual property law may be *timeliness*, the ability of the network to deliver information while it is still on the leading edge. Historically, those in closest geographical proximity to the publisher have paid the least time penalty in accessing information, but with a global network, access to information will be close to instantaneous.

Multimedia

Although thus far the Web is largely filled with texts and numbers, the digital signal can represent information in any analog medium, and even more importantly, can juxtapose the same information in different modes of representation. For example, scientific data can be simultaneously represented numerically, as text, as photography, and as graphics. Thus, a new subject of intellectual property rights might be (and has been) the "look and feel" of a user interface, the way different representations of information are linked to each other (Lyman 1996).

Customization

As we have seen in the discussion of the changing roles of the author and reader, interactive digital environments allow the reader to customize information to precisely the form required. By extension, from the point of view of intellectual property, a new source of value is the ability of the publisher to customize information for the individual reader, which will transform mass media into personal media.

Genre

We read for different purposes, and over centuries of use a number of genres to optimize different kinds of reading have evolved for printed texts—journal articles, newspapers, novels, textbooks, and so forth. However, thus far digital genres have tended to imitate printed genres. The design of information will become a source of value, and perhaps a new kind of intellectual property. For example, Bellcore studied how well readers understood the text of a statistics textbook when organized in three different formats—print, an ASCII text file, and hypertext (Egan et al. 1989). It turned out that readers understood the print version better than the ASCII version scrolling by, but the hypertext version better than the print. Readers preferred hypertext to print because they could more efficiently search the next to find answers to their questions. This kind of reading resembles the way we use a reference work, like a dictionary or encyclopaedia, and yet hypertext is also being experimentally used for other genres, such as novels.

Preservation

How will digital information on the Net be preserved? The very intangibility of the digital signal creates a problem for preservation, but far more serious is the rapid evolution of technical standards, which makes information unusable because it is technically obsolete.

Standards

Technical standards for the management and creation of digital information are evolving rapidly, and might well become a source of intellectual property value. Here enters the debate between proprietary standards, such as Microsoft Windows, and open standards, such as TCP/IP. Proprietary standards are now protected by intellectual property regimes—patent, copyright, trade secrets—but in the past have raised public interest questions when they assumed a monopoly position, causing government regulation. Open standards are an alternative business model by which a company tries to make its standard ubiquitous by making it free or easily licensed, in order to establish a brand name position.

Filtering

As we have seen, an important source of value will be innovations which allow the user to search the Net and find the most appropriate, high-quality and cost-effective information.

CONCLUSION

The historic function of intellectual property policy has been to provide incentives to promote the development and distribution of innovations, and thereby to promote social wealth and, thereby, the public good. Thus far, the problem of intellectual property in the digital age has been focused on the question of protecting the future of printed documents in networked environments, and insufficiently focused on the broader question of innovation, and so it fails the public interest test. This is not an unusual pattern of diffusion of a new technology, for established economic interests generally dominate the political process in the early stages, and often attempt to suppress or change them. In the case of the Web, however, the economic advantages of global communication and coordination are rapidly creating new kinds of markets that will lead to continuous legal and political innovation.

We often imagine technology to be the cause of social change, to which the political and legal systems respond, but political and legal decisions also shape or reshape technology in ways that are more consistent with the established order. For example, encryption is necessary to provide security to information, which is a precondition to the development of digital commerce. When the United States prohibited the export of advanced encryption technology, American software companies had to develop different security systems for products sold overseas, creating a competitive disadvantage for them in international markets.

The problem is, in reconstructing the design of digital documents in order to optimize for the protection of intellectual property, the process of innovation is frozen at one stage in order to protect the established economic order. The DMCA, for example, gives optimal protection to the entertainment industry, which is a major American export product, but in doing so may result in relative disadvantages for other information industries. If digital communication is made to fit the needs of analog communications corporations, the advantages of new technologies are sacrificed in order to conform to the legal and social structures of the past. The printing press itself was used for over a century to produce imitations of hand-illuminated manuscripts (Eisenstein 1980). We will only know if the DMCA and process patents are good information policy when we are able to look at their consequences for the innovation process and the public good in the long run.

If current legislation is designed to create strong market incentives to invest in the digital economy, one might well ask how the economic interest in intellectual property should be balanced with an adequate definition of the public interest. Several problems have already arisen in this area. The Clinton administration's information policy initially placed emphasis upon "universal access" to the network, adapting the concept of "universal service," which was developed in the 1930s to justify a subsidy for local telephone service. The local telephone subsidy was paid for by higher long distance rates, on the theory that the rich made more long distance calls. However, the "E-rate" which was to subsidize network access by public libraries and schools is not hidden; it is printed on the telephone bill as a visible tax, which has led to extensive protest. Moreover, a recent Commerce Department report called "Falling through the Net: Defining the Digital Divide" raises the question whether the market approach to distributing access does not make access to information a class privilege even as we move into a knowledge economy (U.S. Department of Commerce 1999).

As librarians, we must be aware that there is a direct link between the technologies of information and the institutions that organize the use of knowledge, including the library. Libraries have been made possible by copyright law, and serve as a boundary institution that must balance the needs of the marketplace with the needs of their user communities. As intellectual property laws change, the library will change. Thus, this essay has described intellectual property as a political process of governing economic and technological change, rather than as a technical legal process which is best left to lawyers. By virtue of standing on the boundary between markets and communities, librarians have a unique perspective on the future of intellectual property, and must enter the debate even as they struggle to manage the process of change within the library itself.

REFERENCES

Biagioli, Bario. 1998. The Instability of Authorship: Credit and Responsibility in Contemporary Biomedicine. *FASEB Journal* 12: 3–16.

Castells, Manuel. 1989. *The Informational City*. Oxford: Blackwell.

———. 1996. *The Rise of the Network Society*. London: Blackwell.

Documents in the Digital Culture: Shaping the Future. A Report on a Workshop held at the Hawaii International Conference on System Sciences, January 1995.

Doi, Teruo. 1980. *The Intellectual Property Law of Japan*. Alphen aan den Rijn, The Netherlands: Sijthoff & Noordhoff.

Egan, D., et al. 1989. Behavioral Evaluation and Analysis of a Hypertext Browser. *ACM CHI 1989 Proceedings* (May).

Eisenstein, Elizabeth L. 1980. *The Printing Press as an Agent of Change: Communications and Cultural Transformations in Early-Modern Europe*. New York: Cambridge University Press.

Febvre, Lucien, and H-J. Martin. 1976. *The Coming of the Book: The Impact of Printing 1450–1800*. Translated by David Gerard. London: Verso Editions.

Furlong, Mary S. 1989. An Electronic Community for Older Adults: The SeniorNet Network. *The Journal of Communication* 39: 145–53.

Lave, Jean, and Etienne Wenger. 1991. *Situated Learning: Legitimate Peripheral Participation*. New York: Cambridge University Press.

Lyman, Peter. 1996. How is the Medium the Message? Notes on the Design of Network Communication. In *Computer Networking and Scholarship in the 21st Century University*, edited by T. Harrison and T. Stephen. Albany, N.Y.: SUNY Press.

Nonaka, Ikujiro, and Noboru Konno. 1998. The Concept of "Ba": Building a Foundation for Knowledge Creation. *The California Management Review* 40(3): 40–54.

Nunberg, Geoffrey. 1993. The Places of Books in the Age of Electronic Reproduction. *Representations* 42: 13–37.

Popper, Frank. 1993. *The Art of the Electronic Age*. New York: Harry Abrams Publishers.

Powell, Walter W. 1998. Learning from Collaboration: Knowledge and Networks in the Biotechnology and Pharmaceutical Industries. *California Management Review* 40(3): 228–40.

Samuelson, Pamela. 1990. Benson Revisited: The Case Against Patent Protection for Algorithms and Other Computer Program-Related Inventions. *Emory Law Journal* 39: 1025.

Strong, William S. 1995. *The Copyright Book*. Cambridge, Mass.: MIT Press.

Swire, Peter P., and Robert E. Litan. 1998. *None of Your Business: World Data Flows, Electronic Commerce, and the European Privacy Directive*. Washington, D.C.: The Brookings Institution Press.

U.S. Department of Commerce. 1999. Falling through the Net: Defining the Digital Divide. Washington, D.C.: Author. Also available from http://www.ntia. doc.gov/ntiahome/fttn99/contents.html.

Virnoche, Mary E., and Gary T. Marx. 1997. "Only connect"—E.M. Forster in an Age of Electronic Communication: Computer-Mediated Association and Community Networks. *Sociological Inquiry* 67(1): 85–100.

Wellman, Barry, and Milena Gulia. 1999. Net Surfers Don't Ride Alone: Virtual Communities as Communities. In *Communities in Cyberspace*, edited by Peter Kollock and Marc Smith. Berkeley: The University of California Press. Also available from http://www.chass.utoronto.ca/~wellman/links/index. html.

Wriston, Walter. 1992. *The Twilight of Sovereignty*. New York: Charles Scribner's Sons.

Zuboff, Shoshana. 1988. *In the Age of the Smart Machine*. New York: Basic Books.

CHAPTER 10

The Uses of Digital Libraries: Some Technological, Political, and Economic Considerations

DONALD J. WATERS

THE REARRANGING EFFECT

The use of technologies, including the use of those that underlie emerging digital libraries, are subject to what historian Edward Tenner calls a rearranging effect. Malcolm Gladwell called attention to the phenomenon in a recent commentary in *The New Yorker*. He observed that "anyone standing on a city subway platform on a hot summer day" experiences a rearranging effect.

> Subway platforms seem as if they ought to be cool places, since they are underground and are shielded from the sun. Actually, they're anything but. Come summer, they can be as much as ten degrees hotter than the street above, in part because the air-conditioners inside subway cars pump out so much hot air that they turn the rest of the subway system into an oven. In other words, we need air-conditioners on subway cars because air-conditioners on subway cars have made stations so hot that subway cars need to be air-conditioned. It's a bit like the definition the Viennese writer Karl Kraus famously gave of psychoanalysis: "the disease of which it purports to be the cure."
>
> Not all technological advances result in this kind of problem, of course. But it happens often enough so that when someone comes along making spectacular claims in behalf of a new technology . . . it's worth asking whether that technology really solves the problem or simply rearranges the hot air from the car to the platform. (Gladwell 1997: 7)

And so it is with digital library technologies. Popular rhetoric attributes considerable transforming effects to them. Yet, digital information and the

Paper presented at the International Roundtable for Information and Library Science, Kanazawa Institute of Technology, Library Center, Kanazawa, Japan, 1997.

technologies on which they depend are extremely fragile. Their fragility makes it highly uncertain that digital libraries can endure over time, and it makes one wonder about the durability of their supposed benefits. Does the emergence of digital libraries, rather than helping to transform research, learning, and other forms of scholarly communication, promise merely to rearrange the hot air from car to platform, shifting the balance of information services from enduring to immediate access? If such a rearranging effect is indeed at work, then systems of scholarly communication will have to pay dearly to compensate for the loss of the information that they generate and on which the quality of future scholarship depends. At a time when higher education is already under fire for, among other things, its soaring costs, we must avoid such a perilous outcome. But how?

To develop an understanding of how we can avoid the rearranging effect in digital libraries, I ask you to please join me in thinking through the following chain of reasoning. First, the pressures to transform systems of scholarly communication do not arise solely, or even primarily, from technological imperatives. Rather, new digital technologies give us tools with which to respond to profound political and social impulses in the emerging knowledge economy. Our success in responding to these impulses depends on how astute we are in identifying and understanding the key organizing principles of the knowledge economy and then in designing appropriate means of applying the technologies as part of its overall development.

Second, among the key organizing principles of the knowledge economy is that libraries play an essential, preservation role in the pursuit of knowledge. What libraries of all kinds, including digital libraries, preserve is the integrity of information objects. In doing so, they ensure that knowledge is available reliably and economically to the specific communities they serve for use and reuse in the creation of new knowledge through research, in learning environments, and in publication.

Third, because of the fragility of digital information, the challenge of the digital environment is for communities of common interest to ensure that the information crucial to their pursuits of knowledge endures. The challenge is one of economic development, of setting in motion the political, technical, and other conditions for digital libraries to thrive as agents of preservation, as pervasive and trusted foundations for cultural discourse. And in the community of interest with which I am most familiar, namely, the research universities in the United States, the political, economic, and other conditions that shape the use of digital information are giving rise, before our eyes, to new and distinctive kinds of library organizations.

THE EMERGING KNOWLEDGE ECONOMY

In his 1993 book entitled *Post-Capitalist Society*, Peter Drucker identifies a worldwide transition that is now well under way. He characterizes the transition as a shift from a society founded on a capitalist economy to one founded on a knowledge economy. "The traditional 'factors of production'—the land (i.e., natural resources), labor, and capital—have not disappeared, but they have become secondary." Instead, the distinctive source of value in the emerging economy is the pursuit of knowledge as its own end. In the workplace, according to Drucker, "knowledge is now being applied to knowledge." It is "being applied systematically and purposefully to define what *new* knowledge is needed, whether it is feasible, and what has to be done to make knowledge effective"(Drucker 1993: 42; emphasis in original).

Writing at about the same time as Drucker, Richard Lanham, a distinguished professor of English at the University of California at Los Angeles, describes the distinctive features of the new knowledge economy from his vantage point within the academy. In *The Electronic Word*, among other recent publications, Lanham (1993) argues that the scarce commodity in the knowledge economy is not information. We are glutted with information. Rather, the scarce commodity is the human attention, which gives information its structure, its usefulness, and its value as knowledge. In Lanham's scheme, human attention is labor, information technology is the means by which the labor is applied, and attention-structures designed to capture the interest of consumers, including students and other scholars, are the products of the labor and technology.

At its core, Lanham's theory is an application of the labor theory of value to the knowledge economy. His unique contribution to the theory is his further argument that the discipline of rhetoric provides the framework for systematically describing and evaluating the end products of this knowledge work, the attention-structures. Note, however, that Lanham agrees with Drucker about the distinctive source of value in the knowledge economy: as attention-structures, or works of knowledge, capture attention, they beget further attention-structures. Knowledge begets knowledge: knowledge is its own end.

Drucker and Lanham also agree that the developing nature of the knowledge economy is palpable and is propelled not only, or even primarily, by technological forces, but by a complex mix of political, economic, and social forces. Drucker traces the changes in the organizational entities responsible for economic decisions and the international and regional political forces that shape the development of new, knowledge-based business organizations. Compared to the global sweep of Drucker's analysis, Lanham's argument is more focused but reaches the same conclusion as Drucker's does. The knowledge economy touches us all, in large part, because one of its fundamental characteristics is the force of democratizing the value of knowledge as its own end.

Lanham marshals considerable evidence that the rapid expansion of the division of labor around digital technologies—what George Gilder (1995;

see also Bronson [1996]) in other contexts calls the technologies of sand (for silicon chips), glass (for optical networks), and air (for wireless networks)—has democratized the cultures it touches. The products of the knowledge economy—the attention-structures—are easier to generate and to use. They make knowledge more accessible. The markets for them continue to expand, demanding more knowledge workers and creating more knowledge consumers who are broadly educated in the arts and sciences and are also masters of specialized knowledge that they can marshal in the solution of specific problems in the workplace.

In the United States and elsewhere, the pressure of these democratizing forces on the educational system, particularly the system of higher education, has been extraordinary and at least fourfold. First, the system must serve a growing number of students who by conventional standards need remedial training to advance through the curriculum. This pressure is, in part, an expression of the distinction between the *haves* and the *have-nots*. Second, the broader range of constituents in higher education, whether they need remedial training or not, presses for different approaches to the curriculum. The expression of this pressure appears, in part, in the form of debates over the place of multiculturalism on our campuses and in our curricula. It also appears in the strong demand for various forms of distance learning. Third, the division of labor in the knowledge economy has resulted in both increasing specialization within disciplines *and* the rapid growth of interdisciplinary study. Fourth, the system can only serve the broader range of constituents and interests by drastically lowering the costs of education to affordable levels.

Note, as Lanham does, that the dynamic described here represents a profound impulse to achieve the pre-eminent goal of education in a democracy (Lanham 1993: 23). That is, insofar as knowledge is both the source and outcome of human labor in this rapidly growing segment of the economy, literate citizens will prevail who value the lifelong pursuit of knowledge as its own end, as both the source and outcome of their labor and livelihood. Yet, ironically, just as this democratic goal has come into plain view, and enthusiasm abounds for the application of digital information and digital technologies to extend the reach of higher education (to improve its quality and to lower its costs), there intrudes what the psychologist Donald Norman calls the "psychopathology of everyday things" (1988: 1–33). Despite the declining costs and increasing power of information technologies, long-promised productivity gains remain elusive, especially in higher education. Following Norman, I submit that the solution to the productivity paradox is a matter of the careful design and development of information products and services in response to the larger, "democratizing" forces shaping the emerging knowledge economy. Astute design, however, requires not only sensitivity to these larger forces; it also demands an understanding of the inner dynamics of the knowledge economy itself (see Lynch 1995).

THE VALUE OF PRESERVING KNOWLEDGE

If the knowledge economy is shaped in the modern world by a confluence of technical, social, and political forces and is defined by the expanding role of the pursuit of knowledge for its own sake, then what is the internal structure of this economy? In *The Idea of the University: A Reexamination* (1992), Jaroslav Pelikan, the distinguished religious historian at Yale University, has produced one of the most eloquent and detailed theories of the inner workings of the knowledge economy. He focuses on the university, in which the principle of knowledge as its own end has long provided the central operating concept.

According to Pelikan, the principle of knowledge as its own end is merely one of a more comprehensive set of first principles that he calls the "intellectual virtues." These virtues are essential for the development of knowledge, and include principles of free inquiry and intellectual honesty, an obligation to convey the results of research, and an affirmation of the continuity of the intellectual life, upon which each generation builds and to which it contributes in turn (1992: 3–6). Building on this set of first principles, Pelikan argues that the advancement of knowledge through research, the transmission of knowledge through teaching, the diffusion of knowledge through publishing, and the preservation of knowledge in scholarly collections are the four legs supporting any table made for the pursuit of knowledge; they particularly support the table that has come to be known as the research university (pp. 16–17, 78–133).

Invoking the nineteenth-century phrasing of John Henry Newman, Pelikan goes on to suggest that support for teaching, research, and publication constitutes the "endowment of living [genius]," while efforts to preserve knowledge by organizations like libraries, museums, and archives represent "the embalming of dead genius" (p. 110). Lest the connotations of these archaic phrases give you pause, note that Pelikan is careful to distinguish embalming from entombing and his use of "embalming" is a colorful synonym for preservation, which he takes to include all of the means necessary to make knowledge accessible to present and future generations.

Moreover, Pelikan vigorously argues that "new knowledge has repeatedly come through confronting the old, in the process of which both old and new have been transformed" (p. 120). Memory is not a warehouse, but an active process of recategorizing based on previous categorizations. In the province of the knowledge economy that we know as the research university, the two motives at work—embalming and endowment of genius, the looking backward in preservation and the looking forward in research, teaching, and publication—thus are inextricably linked and flow from the principle that the pursuit of knowledge is its own end. Preserved work from past generations is a necessary foundation for present and future work, which in turn defines the accessibility of the preserved work.

Although derived from reflection on the internal dynamics of the modern university, the logic of Pelikan's argument extends straightforwardly to the knowledge economy, which now reaches well beyond the traditional walls of the academy. Because the pursuit of knowledge requires, as its basis, preservation of the record of knowledge, it follows that an expansion of the knowledge economy, particularly through the application of digital information and digital technologies, requires a corresponding expansion of the preservation function. To take Pelikan's logic one step further: the natural agents for the expansion of the preservation function are digital libraries.

THE CHALLENGE OF PRESERVING DIGITAL INFORMATION

Libraries can, of course, take a variety of organizational forms, including those that individuals manage for their own personal use, as well as more elaborate entities such as public, corporate, academic, and research libraries. The time frame over which libraries preserve works of knowledge can also vary from the relatively short span of an individual's personal library to the centuries covered by a large national or university research library. Regardless of their particular form or the time frame of their preservation objective, what libraries preserve is the integrity of the works they contain so that these works are readily available to the individuals or communities whose pursuits of knowledge they support. Depending on their scale, libraries preserve the use and usability of works of knowledge through the more or less elaborate management of a set of operating features, such as the selection of particular works for the collection, as well as their acquisition, cataloging, storage, and circulation.

As a new and special variant of the form, digital libraries manage collections of works in digital form and, like libraries of other kinds, must organize themselves to preserve the integrity of works they contain for use over time by individuals or communities that they support in the overall knowledge economy. However, rapid changes in the means of recording information, in formats for storage, in operating systems, and in application technologies threaten to make the life of information in the digital age much like life in Hobbes' state of nature: "nasty, brutish, and short." The fragile nature of digital information thus gives special shape to the essential preservation function of digital libraries and to the core features of their operations. Unfortunately, with rare exceptions, published discussions of digital libraries have routinely failed to account for the preservation function of digital libraries and its implications. The following analysis draws heavily on one of the exceptions, the report of the Task Force on Archiving of Digital Information, on which the present writer served as co-chair and principal author (Task Force 1996; for two other exceptions, see Graham 1995 and Lehman 1996).

The Integrity of Digital Information

The central goal of preservation in digital libraries, as in other libraries, must be to preserve the integrity of the objects in their care. Knowing how to preserve a digital information object depends on being able to define and preserve the features that give it a distinct identity and define it as a whole and singular work. In the digital environment, the features that determine information integrity and which deserve special attention for preservation purposes include content, fixity, reference, provenance, and context.

Choices about preserving the content of digital information objects range over a continuum. At one end of the spectrum, preserving content simply means preserving a collection of bits. An archival choice at this level often means preserving the hardware and software that may be uniquely capable of interpreting the bits associated with a particular information object. Preserving content may also refer to preserving the composition of ideas in a particular structure and form. Encoding characters in ASCII or UNICODE provides varying ability to represent multiple languages, formulas, and equations. Markup languages, such as TeX, Standard Generalized Markup Language (SGML), and HyperText Markup Language (HTML), offer both advantages and disadvantages in representing layout and document structure compared with the use of proprietary word processing systems and interchange formats. In the realm of digital images, consideration of resolution, color, and compression often pits the quality of content representation against storage efficiency and loss of content. At the other end of the continuum, preserving content may refer to preserving the knowledge and ideas embodied in an object in a way that abstracts the ideas in the work from the limits of the hardware and software needed to read bits or to render the information for use in a specific format or structural representation.

Preserving the fixity of information objects is especially troublesome in the digital world, where objects are frequently subject to change or withdrawal. Outside the digital arena, there are various methods of fixing information in objects: business records contain evidence of transactions, the acts of production and broadcast record specific radio and television programs, and publishers generate specific versions of editions of works. In the digital environment, however, the use of cryptography and other techniques is still maturing to support digital libraries in establishing trusted channels of distribution, and to help them discriminate among multiple versions and to identify canonical versions. Moreover, some digital information objects are better modeled as continuously updated databases for which the preservation choice is whether to compile a complete record of changes, or to capture snapshots of the database as the means of preserving information integrity.

Systems of citation, description, and classification provide the necessary means of reference for consistent discovery, identification, and retrieval of information objects over time. Preserving reference is therefore an essential means of preserving the integrity of digital information, but it is problematic for several reasons. Self-referential information in digital objects seldom meets conventional citation quality. Moreover, consistently resolving names and locations of digital objects is, given the current state of the art, either difficult or unreliable. Finally, conventional reference mechanisms, such as online catalogs, do not easily accommodate certain kinds of reference data, such as information about the terms and conditions of licenses for intellectual property, which increasingly govern the use and cost of culturally significant information objects in the digital world.

Provenance is another essential feature of information integrity, and refers to the origin and chain of custody through individuals, organizations, and instrumentation, including within the archive itself. By documenting provenance, libraries create the presumption that an information object is authentic. Compared to conventionally published objects, which employ well-known techniques for establishing their origin that are usually shown on a title page or its verso, the means of establishing the provenance of information published digitally are not yet well established. In addition, there are special problems in the digital world, as in other arenas, for establishing the provenance and authenticity of individual records, such as mail, diaries, and personal databases, and of corporate records, the understanding of which depends fundamentally on an appreciation of their origins in policies, procedures, and organizational roles an responsibilities. Of special note are the integrity problems associated with digital information objects produced by digital instrumentation in scientific experiments, clinical services, and remote sensing. Establishing the provenance of these objects—and thus their integrity—requires a detailed understanding of the calibration, units of measure, sampling rate, recording conditions, and other features of the instrumentation that generated the information (see National Research Council 1995a, 1995b).

The fifth attribute of information integrity that bears on the preservation of digital information objects is their context, the ways in which they interact with elements in the wider digital world. Among the various dimensions of interaction, there is a technical dimension, in which digital objects depend for their existence on specific hardware and software. There is also a dimension of linkages to other objects. In the World Wide Web, the integrity of many objects resides in the network of linkages. To preserve both the objects and the linkages is a daunting challenge, for which there exists no good solution today other than to take periodic snapshots of the network of objects. A communications dimension of information context defines the effects of the medium of transmission, such as CD-ROM or networks of varying bandwidth, on the types and characteristics of digital information objects. Finally, a social dimension, in which government policies, role relationships, and other political and organizational factors shape the creation and use of digital objects, also affects information integrity and the ability of archives economically to preserve it.

Organizing for Preservation in Digital Libraries

The digital environment today is so fragile that those who disseminate, use, re-use, re-create, and re-disseminate various kinds of digital information can easily, even inadvertently, destroy valuable information, corrupt the cultural record, and ultimately thwart the common pursuit of knowledge. Digital libraries need to build and maintain reliable collections of well-defined digital information objects and to preserve the features—content, fixity, reference, provenance, and context—that give those objects their integrity and enduring value. They must do so operationally, by managing costs and finances within an environment that has a core set of features, including the means of migrating digital information to maintain its vitality as hardware and software environments change.

Among the core set of features in the operating environment of digital libraries is a selection and appraisal process. Digital libraries cannot save everything. To identify the most valuable objects for preservation, archives must appraise the content of the object—its subject and discipline—in relation to the collection goals of the library; the quality and uniqueness of the object; its accessibility in terms of available hardware, software, and legal status; its present value; and its likely future value. Once an object is selected for inclusion, it needs to be accessioned—that is, prepared for the library. Accessioning involves describing and cataloging selected objects, including their provenance to authenticate them, and securing them for storage and access. Storage, depending on expected use and the kind of performance needed in retrieval, may be online in magnetic media, near-line in optical or tape media in a jukebox retrieval system, or off-line in media that require manual intervention to retrieve. Access systems must facilitate discovery, retrieval, and use, including the management of intellectual property rights as appropriate, in a distributed, presumably networked, environment. Finally, digital libraries need a high level of systems engineering skills to manage the interlocking requirements of media, data formats, and hardware and software, and to help determine when objects should migrate to new systems or system components.

Migration is the periodic transfer of digital materials from one hardware/

software configuration to another, or from one generation of computer technology to a subsequent generation. As the Task Force defined it, "the purpose of migration is to preserve the integrity of digital objects and to retain the ability for clients to retrieve, display and otherwise use them in the face of constantly changing technology" (Task Force 1996: 5). Digital libraries have various migration strategies available to them. Internally, they can build hardware or software emulators to preserve the technical operating environments of the information objects, they can change, or "refresh," the media on which the objects are stored as storage technology evolves, or they can reformat the objects to accommodate changing technology. In addition, they can work externally with creators so that digital information incorporates standards that simplify the migration issues. They can work with systems designers to engineer cost-effective migration paths into the hardware and software on which information objects depend. Finally, they can use processing centers that develop best practices and achieve economies of scale in certain kinds of migration techniques.

DEVELOPING AN ECONOMY FOR DIGITAL ARCHIVING

It is one thing to identify, as I have just done, the features of information integrity that digital libraries must preserve and the organizational processes they must ideally embrace to accomplish that essential goal and ensure the vitality and continued growth of the emerging knowledge economy. It is quite another thing to set these factors in motion, to stimulate the various stakeholders with interests in the creation, management, dissemination, and use of various kinds of digital information objects—text, images, numeric data, sound, video, simulations, geographic information systems, hypermedia, and so on—to recognize and act on their common interests in preserving digital information. Because digital information is not only a product but also a source of knowledge, it will remain difficult and costly to use as long as its design makes it difficult or costly to maintain use, especially over time. Economy in the use of digital information, in other words, means that real economies are necessary and must emerge in the preservation of digital information for the knowledge economy truly to flourish.

Posed in this way as a problem of design and development, those of us in the business of managing the record of knowledge for posterity can easily succumb to terror in the face of the explosion of digital information. I identify my own feelings with those of the woman so clearly captured in one of James Thurber's wonderful cartoons. She sits before a bow-tied, pince-nezed, and long-eared doctor to whom she has come for help. He looks just like a rabbit and he observes: "You said a moment ago that everyone you look at seems to be a rabbit. Now just what do you mean by that, Mrs. Sprague?" (Grauer 1995: 148). Everywhere we look, there is digital information. How do we put ourselves as a culture in the position of identifying and giving sufficient attention to the digital material that is worth saving?

My central argument, following the Report of the Task Force on Digital Archiving, is that "the problem of preserving digital information for the future is not only—or even primarily—a problem of fine-tuning a narrow set of technical variables. . . . Rather, it is a problem of organizing ourselves over time and as a society to maneuver effectively in a digital landscape. It is a problem of building—almost from scratch—the various systematic supports, or deep infrastructure, that will enable us to tame our anxieties and move our cultural records naturally and confidently into the future" (Task Force 1996: 6). Although the task overall may be daunting, we are not helpless and without places to start.

In the complex mix of factors by which digital libraries must operate to preserve the integrity of digital information objects, there is much room for the play of specialization, division of labor, and competition that will not raise costs, but drive the economy of preservation vigorously to lower them. Division of labor and specialization are already evident in the development of key technical parts of the common infrastructure. For example, some important services, such as rights management and network charging facilities, are emerging generally in the marketplace and will undoubtedly serve the interest of digital preservation as well as other segments of the knowledge economy. The developments of other services, such as durable naming conventions and expanded metadata facilities, are well under way. Still other kinds of specialized preservation services—those, for example, that require the complex weaving of information holdings in particular disciplines from among a variety of providers and custodians—will require time and a commitment to a complex iteration and reiteration of exploration, development, and solution as the relevant issues emerge and become clearer and more tractable.

The process by which digital libraries engage in these more difficult aspects of designing how to preserve the use and usability of digital information is essentially a coming to terms about the centrality of preservation—the embalming of dead genius—in the pursuit of knowledge. It is a setting in motion of the conditions for digital libraries to thrive as part of a pervasive and trusted foundation for cultural discourse in an electronic age. The process occurs, however, only in the actual understandings and agreements that digital libraries reach with their formal partners, informal allies, competitors, and users as they create or re-create communities of interest in the pursuit of knowledge. Just as one can make sense of the apparent chaos of the World Wide Web by focusing on the various, and sometimes interlocked, communities of interest that have found a home there (see, for example, Hagel and Armstrong 1997 and Hof 1997), so too, one can chart the building of the "deep infrastructure" needed to preserve the use and usability of digital information in the emerging knowledge economy by distinguishing and tracking the development of the various communities of interest in the pursuit of knowledge.

These communities differ, of course, and are even changing, in the nature and subjects of their common interests, in their uses of digital information, and in the corresponding development of their digital libraries. I focus here on the uses of digital libraries in the community I know best, namely, the community of research universities. To illustrate how the "deep infrastructure" for the enduring use of digital libraries is developing in and affecting that community, I focus on three specific issues: the distributed organization of repositories of digital information; the dependence on contract, rather than copyright law, as the basis for using these repositories; and the evolution of integrated systems of discovery and retrieval.

Distributed Repositories

It is worth observing that the real intellectual action for some scholarly disciplines, mostly in the biological and physical sciences, no longer occurs in the conventional publication stream, but elsewhere: in online databases, online exchanges of preprints, listservs, and so on. Conventional publication in these disciplines adds little value to the work that has already been disseminated in these other channels; rather, it is a redundant process, undertaken to generate, in effect, a certified archival record of the work. Because the audience paying attention to the field has already seen and absorbed the work in online versions, the printed publication channel grows increasingly narrow and consists primarily of libraries who serve as the archival institutions. Given such a narrow market for the material, unit costs and prices rise on the supply side. On the demand side, libraries respond by cutting titles from their collections.

There is clearly little logic or economy in a process whereby scholars use printed publications to establish an archival record only to find that the institutions responsible for ensuring that the record endures cannot afford to purchase the publications. Framed in this way, the problems in the scholarly communication process that appear as a spiral of escalating prices and journal cancellations are, at least in large part, problems of ensuring the durability of the electronic record of knowledge. As such, they give research libraries, publishers, scholars, and universities substantial economic motive to save money and streamline the process (see Waters 1996).

In increasing numbers, scholarly societies, such as those in high-energy physics, astrophysics, engineering, and computing, are recognizing the diseconomies of the present system, and have accepted responsibility for setting up and maintaining electronic channels of communication for their disciplines. Conventional publishers, such as Elsevier, Springer-Verlag, and Academic Press, are also opening electronic channels for disseminating their publications. Colleges and universities, usually through the agency of the library, or through consortiums of libraries acting as buying clubs, ensure that the information in these newly opened channels reaches the researchers and students in their institutions.

The dynamics of this shift from conventional printed publication to the electronic medium raise a number of intriguing issues. My colleague from Yale, Ann Okerson, identified several of the more notable economic issues of the transition in her presentation at the 1995 KIT Roundtable (see Okerson 1995). Not only is the transition incomplete, but it is uneven across disciplines, meaning that the scholarly community is today experiencing significant transition costs. Stakeholders maintain both print and electronic streams of publication as they decide when to shift permanently to the electronic medium. The unevenness of the transition, however, is also a positive signal, at least in this case, because there is tremendous competitive pressure to take advantage of the benefits of the electronic medium. The differences in skill and products among the scholarly societies and publishers provide an intense learning environment which, under substantial competitive pressure, generates a highly productive "leap-frog" effect. Each new investment builds on known solutions, but also advances the field by offering competitive solutions to remaining problems. The cumulative result is a rapid, sometimes disorienting, advance in the quality of reliability of the electronic systems.

Despite the rapidity of the changes under way, the dust may not settle for some time on the transition from print-based to electronic scholarly communication. Still, the transition is far enough along in many disciplines to discern that there is little economic benefit for libraries each to manage the costly logistics of disk storage, software compatibility, and forward migration of scholarly works that publishers distribute to them in electronic form (see, for example, Task Force 1996: 29–35). Instead, economies of scale in the electronic medium favor a model for the management of the scholarly record over time that is network-based and centers on responsibility, at lease initially, with creators, providers, and publishers. Thus, scholarly societies and publishers are today creating and will presumably manage over time—either by themselves or by an outsourced repository management agent—their own electronic repositories of scholarly works. From these repositories, they distribute virtual copies to users over networks using standard browser software.

Organizing repositories in this way, closer to the point of the creation of electronic works than to the point of their use, vests long-term care of the works with those who, at least initially, care most about them. Such an organization also opens numerous possibilities for redesigning the scholarly publication process so that labor in tasks that are currently bundled in the process may be divided, the quality of work in these tasks improved, and the overall costs of the process reduced. Imagine, for example, as Paul

Ginsparg has done from his considerable experience managing the preprint archives in high-energy physics, a network of discipline-based repositories for which scholarly societies are responsible and into which scholars deposit their works as they complete them. The repositories could help simplify at least two separate components of the complex publication process. Editors could manage the certification of quality through peer review by simply pointing reviewers to works rather than physically distributing them. Similarly, they could simplify the publication process itself by compiling pointers to the network of repositories for the works that they wish to disseminate to the targeted audiences they serve, rather than repackaging those works (Ginsparg 1997). Further development of these processes might even suggest that certification of the quality of scholarly works would be more effectively and efficiently managed separately from, rather than as part of, the publication stream that leads to the dissemination of works to targeted audiences.

Organizing repositories close to the point of the creation of scholarly works has significant implications not only for the publication process, but also for the development of digital libraries. Some libraries might position themselves to serve as mirror sites for the electronic repositories of publishers. Others might contract with scholarly societies, as Stanford University's Hire Wire Press has done, to provide repository and other publication services. Still others might follow the lead of The Andrew W. Mellon Foundation's JSTOR and position themselves to serve as a fail-safe repository for back issue works that publishers themselves no longer wish to manage. Generally, however, economies of scale in the storage and accessibility of digital works means that the challenge of collection management in digital libraries will be to preserve the use and usability of works that are stored not locally and under the direct control of the digital library, but remotely and under the control of various and widely distributed agents. In the community of research universities, libraries are meeting that challenge on two major fronts: by developing licenses for digital works and by redesigning systems of discovery and retrieval.

Dependence on Contract

The common means today for libraries to acquire the rights to use scholarly works in digital form is to execute a detailed contract, or license. For owners and providers, the general protections that copyright law affords in the sale of intellectual property seem completely inadequate in the digital realm. There, copying is technically so easy that it seems to put at great risk of loss the rights that owners have in their property. Thus, in the application of contract law, they seek directly from users the greater protections they feel they need.

Libraries, on the other hand, have regarded the resort to licensing suspiciously. They have viewed it as an attempt to subvert or sidestep the general protections, such as fair use, which copyright law affords to users of intellectual property in the interest of promoting "the progress of science and the useful arts." Indeed, in the worst case, licensing may actually constrain the rights of users in substantial ways. For example, if libraries terminate a license and the provider withdraws previously licensed information, the prior investment becomes worthless and the user experiences a loss of the record of knowledge. Licenses may also extend the liability of users in the case of misuse, while limiting penalties for the provider if the information products fail to endure over time or otherwise to perform as advertised (see Okerson 1996a: 6–9).

Although licenses for the use of digital works appear to put libraries and their users at a disadvantage, growing experience of both providers and libraries in creating them suggests that contracts are not only appropriate to present circumstances in the digital arena, but can actually benefit both parties. Contracts provide the means for divergent interests to meet in times of uncertainty, high risk, and great promise. By engaging in the negotiation of content licenses, publishers and libraries are not just forging agreements, they are crafting the durable and trustworthy relationships that are so necessary to sustain the electronic information products they both need. In their contract-making, publishers and libraries are, in the words of Ann Okerson, "making [their] own peace, thoughtfully and responsibly, one step at a time" (Okerson 1996b).

When publishers and libraries are as unsure of one another as they are today in the digital environment, one way that licenses enable them to "make peace" is to define formally and legally who the parties to the agreement are. Licenses also enable the parties to specify their mutual responsibilities and provide for ways to settle disputes, should they arise. A growing trend in the creation of content licenses is for libraries joined by regional affiliation or other common features to define themselves as a consortium or buying club in relation to a publisher, for the purpose of acquiring a license to use a digital work or set of works. Such an arrangement benefits publishers because it reduces the overhead of marketing products separately to each institution. For the libraries, the benefits include discounts on the purchase price, or inclusion in the purchase of more works for all the institutions than any institution acting separately could have afforded. Perhaps more importantly, licenses that define groups of libraries as buying clubs are beneficial because they serve to align library interests where previously there was disunity. Such an alignment is especially critical in an environment in which repositories of digital information are widely distributed and under external control. To assert any influence over the information products, libraries must be able to act in concert with themselves and the publishers. Buying clubs provide libraries an identity, defined by contract, for such concerted action.

Content licenses also provide a way for libraries and publishers to "make peace" with one another when the stakes are high. The retooling necessary to traffic in electronic, rather than print, publications is expensive for both parties. Publishers suddenly need to invest in systems engineering of processes that have been relatively stable for years, and they have to provide annual budgets for R&D where previously they had little or none. Research libraries, which generally have had systems engineers on staff for years, regard with concern the relative naiveté of publishers. Libraries worry about the 5 to 10 percent of their collection budgets that they currently have at risk in electronic information.

Publishers seek to limit their risk under contract by defining and limiting the community of users who can use the electronic information they provide to libraries. The categories of authorized users generally tend to exclude alumni and corporate partners in the research university community, the very categories to which these institutions are looking to extend their services. Libraries, however, focus in the development of content licenses on what authorized categories of users can do. Can they make copies? On what terms can they make copies for colleagues or readers who do not have a license to this particular resource? How can the resource be used in the rapidly evolving world of classroom access? Libraries are finding that, within the defined categories of users, the answers to these questions lead both parties back to the provisions of fair use and other rights generally afforded under copyright (Okerson 1996b).

Finally, when the need and promise is as great as it is in the emerging knowledge economy, content licenses afford a way for libraries and publishers together to create and develop new markets and ways of conducting business. They provide a space to experiment and explore, affording a pragmatic way to achieve change and to build the necessary infrastructure for improving the quality, lowering the cost, and expanding the reach of education in research universities. One of the areas most in need of such attention is how new electronic information products integrate into the large mix of resources that digital libraries provide their users. In the present jargon, the question is, how do electronic systems of discovery and retrieval "interoperate?"

Systems of Discovery and Retrieval

The information that digital libraries in research universities are licensing for use from various and distributed repositories is composed of works that have diverse document and data structures and depend on various search engines and vocabularies for access. The heterogeneity of the information in structure and form significantly challenges users in their ability to identify, retrieve, and discern the quality of needed information. Designing and constructing systems that lower the barriers for discovery and retrieval of these heterogeneous materials is essential for the enduring use of digital libraries and is, as more and more materials become available to members of the research university communities, an increasingly urgent task.

To reliably stimulate the attention of users over time, information from a distributed set of repositories must integrate into the information space of a digital library. Such a space typically consists of four areas: a catalog of the works selected for the library or set of libraries; a series of index structures that describe works in greater detail than the catalog, or in ways that the catalog does not permit; the works themselves; and tools with which to use or analyze the works.

The library catalog describes and organizes, at the item or collection level, much of the material selected for a library and judged to be most pertinent to the community of users it serves. MARC is the standard interchange format in which catalog records are represented electronically. Concern about the complexity of the MARC record and its inability to represent complex hierarchical and certain other kinds of relationships among source works has led in recent years to the development of the so-called "core" record and the exploration of alternatives such as the Dublin Core and the use of SGML for tagging fields. MARC has proved remarkably durable, however. The development of the 856 field in the MARC record (which links to related objects in digital form), the Z39.5 protocol, and World Wide Web interfaces to the protocol have made it possible for MARC-based library catalogs to integrate seamlessly into a networked environment.

Although crucial, library catalogs simply are not sufficient for digital libraries to provide intellectual access to the world of knowledge. Traditional abstract and index files have long been available electronically to provide detailed information about the contents of journals, and providers are moving quickly to place them in the networked environment. Significant recent work on the Encoded Archival Description (EAD) has produced a standard method for detailed, online descriptions of archival collections. Similarly, work is progressing under the auspices of the Inter-university Consortium for Political and Social Research (ICPSR) for a standard means of encoding the data dictionaries, or codebooks, for data files. Less advanced, but now moving rapidly, are efforts to organize the methods for describing and classifying visual resources, such as photographs and works of art. Finally, inverted indices for full-text documents and the means of searching them are also figuring prominently in the digital landscape.

As catalogs and index structures for various types of works—books, serials, archives, data files, and visual resources—all appear online in a distributed networked environment, so too are the sources, or digitized surrogates of them, also appearing there in great quantities. In some cases, the library may have licensed the sources; in other cases, it may own and hold them locally. In addition, tools for online textual, data, and image analysis and manipulation also exist online and have become increasingly sophisticated in function.

Given the short span of time since the invention of the World Wide Web, it is almost miraculous that so many of these components—catalogs, index structures, sources, and tools—now live on the Web, and that together they comprise a fully navigable information space for discovery, retrieval, and use. One can, for example, search a catalog, find a record, and link from it through the Web directly to the source book. One can also search, find a catalog record for an archival collection, link to the EAD for collection, traverse the finding aid, and then link again to a surrogate of a photograph contained in the collection. Alternatively, one could skip the catalog search and start directly by searching an EAD or collection of them. Perhaps more complex is the example of a student searching the catalog, finding a data file of survey results, linking to the relevant online codebook, and using it to extract a subset of data for analysis using a favorite statistics program.

Experiencing for the first time an integrated online information space for discovery, retrieval, and use in these ways can leave one breathless with excitement. However, it is mostly an excitement of anticipating a promising future rather than of having it realized. As publishers deploy repositories into this online space, they are learning about weaknesses in design and how to correct them. For example, some publishers provide journal titles that are directly addressable from a catalog or other index structure. Many, however, do not, and this deficiency in effect cripples the navigation mechanism for the reader who cannot move from a catalog record or journal index directly to the title. Publishers, such as Academic Press, have designed their system to force the reader, upon entry to it, to initiate another search to find the title, regardless of the information the reader brings to the repository from other searches elsewhere.

A design problem like this one clearly prevents a body of work from being well integrated into prevailing information space, and the appropriate solutions are not always obvious. The development of supporting mechanisms, such as standard protocols for repository access and facilities for searching across a multitude of index structures, would facilitate such integration, and is presently the subject of sustained research on agent architectures at the University of Michigan and at Stanford University under the auspices of the National Science Foundation's Digital Library Initiative. In the end, however, the success of such research and of its eventual implementation cannot be measured solely by how well or poorly it supports integrated systems of discovery and retrieval. Rather, the measure is against a higher standard: does it lower, rather than raise, the barriers to effective use of digital libraries by those in the communities they serve? And does it thereby fulfill the essential library goal of preserving for future members of those communities the use and usability of the record of knowledge?

CONCLUSION

Will Rogers once said that a revolution is like one cocktail—it just gets you organized for the next. The unfolding of the knowledge economy in what Peter Drucker calls post-capitalist society is not the first revolution in the organization of knowledge. How well did those earlier cocktails organize us for this one? Are we just drunk now with hype about the significance of current developments? To return to the questions with which I opened: Are we simply moving hot air from car to platform?

The development of the digital library in all its aspects—technical, economic, political, and social—amounts to nothing if it does not generate literate citizens capable of engaging sensibly and productively in the discourse of the world in which they live. The literate citizen in the emerging knowledge economy is smart about how to use information and has it ready at hand or, in the current jargon, at one's desktop. Allow me now to close by offering a description of such a desktop.

With this desk a man absolutely has no excuse for slovenly habits in the disposal of his numerous papers, and the man of method may here realize that pleasure and comfort which is only to be attained in the verification of the maxim: a place for everything and everything in its place. The operator, having arranged and classified his books, papers, et cetera, seats himself for business at the writing table and realizes at once that he is master of the situation. Every portion of his desk is accessible without change of position and all immediately before the eye. Here he discovers that perfect system and order can be attained; confusion avoided; time saved and vexation spared; dispatch in the transaction of business facilitated and peace of mind promoted in the daily routine of business. (quoted in Cooper 1983)

Don't you want one of these? This advertisement appeared in 1880 and describes the Wooton Patent Desk. The desk is a lovely piece of furniture but, as Donald Norman points out, in *Things That Make Us Smart*, it proved, for a variety of reasons, to be relatively useless (Norman 1993: 158–59). It did not spare vexations. It created more and worse ones.

As we aspire to the high purpose of preserving the use and usability of the record of knowledge in digital form, and as our technical, political, economic, and social strategies for doing so lead us to create and maintain digital libraries, let us resolve at least to learn from one past drunken mistake and avoid the fabrication of more Wooton Patent Desks.

REFERENCES

Bronson, Po. 1996. George Gilder. *Wired* 4.03 (March): 122–26, 186–95.
Cooper, Deborah. 1983. Evolution of Wooton Patent Desks. In *Wooton Patent Desks: A Place for Everything and Everything in its Place*, edited by J. Ca-

mille Showalter and Janice Driesbach. Indianapolis and Oakland: Indiana State Museum and the Oakland Museum.

Drucker, Peter. 1993. *Post-Capitalist Society*. New York: HarperBusiness.

Gilder, George. 1995. Telecosm Angst and Awe on the Internet. *Forbes ASAP* (December 4): 112–32.

Ginsparg, Paul. 1997. Winners and Losers in the Global Research Village. Paper presented at the International Conference of the Academia Europaea on *The Impact of Electronic Publishing on the Academic Community*, Stockholm, Sweden, April 16–20.

Gladwell, Malcolm. 1997. Chip Thrills. *The New Yorker* (January 20): 7–8.

Graham, Peter. 1995. Requirements for the Digital Research Library. *College and Research Libraries* 56(4): 331–39.

Grauer, Neil. 1995. *Remember Laughter: A Life of James Thurber*. Lincoln: University of Nebraska Press.

Hagel, John, and Arthur Armstrong. 1997. *Net Gain: Expanding Markets Through Virtual Communities*. Cambridge, Mass.: Harvard Business School Press.

Hof, Robert. 1997. Internet Communities. *Business Week* (May 5): 64–80.

Lanham, Richard A. 1993. *The Electronic Word: Democracy, Technology and the Arts*. Chicago: University of Chicago Press.

Lehmann, Klaus-Dieter. 1996. Making the Transitory Permanent: The Intellectual Heritage in a Digitized World of Knowledge. *Daedalus* 125(4): 307–29.

Lynch, Clifford A. 1995. The Technological Framework for Library Planning in the Next Decade. In *Information Technology and the Remaking of the University Library*, edited by Beverly P. Lynch. *New Directions for Higher Education* 90 (Summer). San Francisco: Jossey-Bass.

National Research Council. 1995a. *Preserving Scientific Data on Our Physical Universe: A New Strategy for Archiving the Nation's Scientific Information Resources*. Washington, D.C.: National Academy Press.

———. 1995b. *Study on the Long-Term Retention of Selected Scientific and Technical Records of the Federal Government: Working Papers*. Washington, D.C.: National Academy Press.

Norman, Donald. 1988. *The Psychology of Everyday Things*. New York: Basic Books.

———. 1993. *Things That Make Us Smart: Defending Human Attributes in the Age of the Machine*. Reading, Mass.: Addison-Wesley.

Okerson, Ann. 1995. Can We Afford Digital Information? Libraries? An Early Assessment of Economic Prospects for Digital Publications. In *The Prospect of Digital Library*, KIT International Roundtable for Library and Information Science (November 9–10). The Japan Foundation: Library Center, Kanazawa Institute of Technology.

———. 1996a. Licensing Perspectives: The Library View. Paper presented at the ARL/CNI Licensing Symposium, San Francisco, December 8. Available from http://www.library.yale.edu/~okerson/cni-license.html.

———. 1996b. Buy or Lease? Two Models for Scholarly Information at the End (or the Beginning) of an Era. *Daedalus* 125(4): 55–76.

Pelikan, Jarislov. 1992. *The Idea of the University: A Reexamination*. New Haven, Conn.: Yale University Press.

Task Force on Archiving of Digital Information. 1996. *Preserving Digital Infor-*

mation. Report of the Task Force on Archiving of Digital Information. Washington, D.C: Commission on Preservation and Access. Also available from http://www.rlg.org/ArchTF/.

Waters, Donald J. 1996. Realizing Benefits from Inter-Institutional Agreements: The Implications of the Draft Report of the Task Force on Archiving of Digital Information. Washington, D.C.: The Commission on Preservation and Access. Also available from http://arl.cni.org/arl/proceedings/127/waters.html.

CHAPTER 11

Digital Preservation: An Update

DEANNA B. MARCUM

When I last addressed the roundtable audience, I described in some detail the work of the Task Force on Archiving of Digital Information. The report received a great deal of attention but, in all candor, the problem seems as serious today as it seemed two years ago. Today, I am going to describe the work that has been done in the United States and elsewhere to advance our understanding of digital preservation.

When the final report, *Preserving Digital Information*, was published in May 1996, it prompted a great deal of discussion in the library and archival communities. Professional associations planned meetings that focused on the themes of digital preservation, and the U.S. bibliographic utilities began to consider the roles they might play in developing digital repositories for member libraries. National libraries in many different countries have begun to discuss what their role should be in assuring the long-term preservation of digital information.

THE ASSOCIATION OF RESEARCH LIBRARIES

The Association of Research Libraries (ARL), a membership organization of some 120, mostly large, U.S. and Canadian university libraries, devoted its entire membership meeting in 1997 to the digital archiving issue. Individuals who are known to have thought most about the problem and possible strategies for solving it were invited to present their ideas to the directors of these prestigious libraries. To prepare for the meeting, ARL

Paper presented at the International Roundtable for Information and Library Science, Kanazawa Institute of Technology, Library Center, Kanazawa, Japan, 1998.

commissioned George Soete to conduct a review of digital archiving projects of various related organizations. The review revealed that several groups were experimenting with migration strategies, but there were no reports of organizations that believed they had the answer to digital archiving.

THE GETTY CENTER

In February 1998, the Getty Center of Los Angeles, in collaboration with the Long Now Foundation, hosted a meeting of digital theorists to discuss the current state of digital archives and their future. The meeting focused not so much on the technical issues as on the sociocultural and economic implications of both the problems and solutions for long-term digital cultural preservation.

Peter Lyman and Howard Besser of the University of California, Berkeley, developed a background paper for the conference, entitled "Time and Bits: Managing Digital Continuity" (1998). The authors developed a checklist of the types of preservation approaches that have been applied to digital information. These include:

Save Everything. The Internet Archive, managed by Brewster Kahle, attempts to save most of what is on the public Web in time slices governed by how long it takes its Web-crawlers to copy everything they are seeking (currently, approximately two full slices per month). Most computer scientists agree that while this is an interesting prospect, it is not, in the end, feasible. There are several long-term questions: How well will this scale as the Internet continues its explosive growth? What strategies will ensure that these extensive backups will persist over time by evolving copyright regimes and liabilities? Will decisions that have been made about what not to save have long-term implications?

Refreshing Strategies. Any organization that maintains large databases or large quantities of data understands the process of moving bits from one storage medium to another. Most large organizations with mainframe computers understand the technical and economic issues involved in periodic movement of data to new physical strata, and in storage of these strata over time; but this strategy does not take into account the problem that the file formats that are continuously refreshed may not be readable by future applications.

Migration Strategies. The process of refreshing data, while at the same time moving to new, more accessible file formats, is called migration. Most libraries are now attempting to gain experience with migration, but there is a great need to understand the technical issues and costs involved in migration strategies.

"Exercising" Strategies. The idea that continual community use of a digital object will make it persist over time is a powerful one. It is easy to

imagine that members of the public will continuously convert popular works into forms viewable in newer environments, but little is known about how this will affect the integrity of these works, nor of how this strategy will affect less popular works. It is a strategy that leaves cultural legacy in the hands of popular tastes.

Life-Cycle Management. Innovators within the archives and record management community have begun stressing "life cycle management"—information professionals becoming involved with documents as early as possible in the document's life to best ensure that document will persist over time. This paradigm has been applied particularly to collections of electronic records.

This list of possible strategies provides a checklist of work that needs to be done in the future if we are to solve the digital preservation problem, but as research proceeds, information in digital form is vanishing. What can be done? Lyman and Besser noted that in the long run, both print and digital preservation strategies are best sustained by the definition of technical standards; but standards evolve from best practices. They offered the following advice to follow while research proceeds.

1. Save in the most common file formats. The more files that exist in a given format, the more likely that file converters or emulators will be written for that format (because of economies of scale). Conversely, files stored in less common formats will face more obstacles being viewed in future environments.

2. Avoid compression where possible. The viewing equipment of the future will not necessarily know how to decompress current compression formats. When compression is necessary, use the most common compression formats. Whenever possible, avoid lossy compression, as the full implications of that loss on future viewing environments are not adequately understood.

3. For image capture, use color bars and scales. Color bars within an image can be effective in rebalancing color for future viewing environments. Scales can provide users with an idea of object size, and could potentially be used to develop online measurement tools.

4. Keep a log of processes and changes to the digital object. Many seemingly innocuous things we do to a digital object may have significance for future viewing of that object. For example, the color palette of a scanner or attempts to match screen color to the color of an original object may severely affect the use of color management systems in future viewing environments. Keeping a record of processes and changes made to an object should help future environments adjust for artifacts digitized today.

5. The Rosetta Stone strategy: save as much metadata as possible. When a digital object is created or altered, the librarian and technicians usually have much greater access to information about that object than at any other point in its life cycle. Because so little is known about future viewing en-

vironments, seemingly innocuous bits of metadata may later prove important to those environments. The more information that can be saved, the more likely we will be able to provide future generations with a "key" for unlocking the contents of whole classes of lost data.

ARTS AND HUMANITIES DATA SERVICE

An equally important study of digital archiving policies has been carried out in England. In May 1998, the Arts and Humanities Data Service issued a report entitled *Digital Collections: A Strategic Policy Framework for Creating and Preserving Digital Resources*, following a workshop on the long-term preservation of electronic materials held in Warwick in November 1995. The workshop had called for the development of a policy framework for addressing many of the problems that had been identified. It established a working group to draft this report, which is now being reviewed and commented upon by a broad international community.

Digital Collections is especially helpful in its analysis of the prospects for and the costs of preserving digital resources. The group concluded that over the longer term, prospects for digital preservation rest heavily upon decisions made about those resources at different stages of their life cycle. Decisions made in the design and creation of a digital resource, and those made when a digital resource is accessioned into a collection, are particularly influential.

The study also suggests that documents are viewed differently as creators, publishers, and distributors become involved with data resources at different stages. Indeed, few organizations or individuals that become involved with the development or management of digital resources have influence over (or even interest in) those resources throughout their entire life cycle. Data creators, for example, have substantial control over how and why digital resources are created, but very few creators extend that interest to how those resources are managed over the longer term. In some cases they cannot, particularly where resources are not available or allocated for this task. Organizations with a responsibility for long-term preservation, on the other hand, acquire digital resources to preserve them and encourage their re-use, but often have little direct influence over how they are created.

Although each participant in the information chain has a clear understanding of his or her own involvement with and interest in digital resources, each has less understanding of the involvement and interests of others. Further, the participants have little or no understanding of how their own involvement influences the total system or awareness of the current challenges in ensuring the long-term preservation of the cultural and intellectual heritage in digital form.

The Digital Archiving Working Group emphasized the necessity of applying standards throughout the life cycle of digital resources. It concluded that costs could be minimized only if standards are rigorously followed. They also observed that standards offer the greatest assurance that digital materials can later be moved across platforms.

One of the most interesting aspects of the British study is its analysis of the influence of the funding agencies that invest in the creation of digital resources. Since those who invest in the expensive digitization projects are likely to take greater interest in the preservation of the results, the Working Group believed that it would be beneficial to acquaint the funders with the current problems associated with digital archiving. The group also hoped that funders, after they understood the risks, would build in requirements of the grantees to follow certain practices and standards in creating digital collections.

The Working Group went on to issue several observations and recommendations, which are described below.

1. Long-Term Digital Preservation

a. To increase the prospects for digital preservation and reduce its cost, all groups associated with the process must become more aware of the implications of their own involvement with a digital resource across its life cycle.

b. Data creators may attach little or no value to the long-term preservation of the data resources they create, and are unlikely to adopt standards and practices that will facilitate their preservation. This is particularly true if standards and practices are costly to implement. Therefore, raising the awareness of data creators must be done in a way that appeals to their interests.

c. Certain best practices appropriate for digital preservation can be automated for data creators through the application software they use, especially data documentation and metadata. The development of such software and tools may play a key role in digital preservation.

d. Several stakeholders are involved in managing data over the longer term, including data banks, institutional archives, and academic data archives. Further research and development initiatives are apparent in the library and cultural heritage sectors, though particularly in the former. Despite their different aims, and the different business, funding, and legal environments in which they work, these agencies share a great deal in common. Particular attention should be paid to the experience of the data banks and the institutional archives—experience that is often overlooked in other current research and development activities.

e. The nature and scale of long-term digital preservation will encourage cooperative activity among organizations. No single agency is likely to be able to preserve all digital materials within its purview, or do the necessary research and development in this field, and cooperative agreements and consortia will be required. These agreements and consortia will need to address a wide range of issues, including, for example, the division of responsibility for different subject areas or materials; the degree of redundancy that may be desirable for preservation, or multiple locations for access; funding; and different national or regional needs.

2. Standards

a. Information about standards is currently documented by organizations that identify, document, and promote them. Relatively little information is available about how a constellation of standards and methods may be applied effectively to a digital resource at various stages of its life cycle to achieve specific and clearly articulated aims. This study recommends that such "best practices" be identified and, where necessary, documented, and that integrated access to them be provided in a meaningful way.

3. The Policy Framework

a. To implement the framework, stakeholders are urged to assess the issues pertaining to their own situation, but also to understand how their approach to those issues may affect the data resources that come under their remit and how it may affect other stakeholders who have been or may become involved with the resources at other stages of their life cycle.

CONCLUSION

The ongoing work of the initiatives I have just described will be important contributions to the digital archiving agenda, and the Council on Library and Information Resources (CLIR) will report regularly on developments through its newsletter. In addition, CLIR has commissioned the film *Into the Future*, which identifies the problem of digital longevity, and was broadcast on public television in the United States earlier this year. CLIR also has undertaken a number of awareness-raising efforts to place this issue on the public agenda for action. We have consulted widely with the public policy staff to alert them to the fragility of government information. We have published a brochure and a discussion guide to help libraries and archivists use the film more effectively in their local institutions.

Jeff Rothenberg, of the Rand Corporation, has been commissioned to develop a research agenda for studying emulation techniques, and Cornell University has been provided funds to develop the actual procedures for moving different formats of material from one system to another. There remains much to be done, and it is now left to all of us to work on solutions to the problem.

REFERENCE

Lyman, Peter, and Howard Besser. 1998. Time and Bits: Managing Digital Continuity. Available from www.longnow.com/10Klibrary/TimeBitsDisc/tbpaper.html. The paper also appears in the published proceedings under the same name, edited by Margaret MacLean and Ben H. Davis. 1999. Los Angeles: Getty Research Institute.

CHAPTER 12

The Impact of Digital Libraries
on Library Staffing and Education

RACHAEL K. ANDERSON

Librarianship is undergoing an identity crisis of sorts, and there is a growing recognition of the need for major redefinition of librarians' roles, their
education, and of the field's relationships to other information professions.
Librarianship is gripped by a serious professional angst, not only in assim-
ilating rapidly changing technologies to develop future information programs, but also in assuring that librarians actually have a place in that
future.

Given the expanding range of networked information accessible on the
Web that enables users to transcend international boundaries and bypass
the resources in a local or regional library, some legitimately question
whether there will even be a place for librarians in a future populated with
digital libraries. As navigators such as Mosaic and Netscape make the Web
easier to use, as users become ever more proficient, as more substantive
knowledge resources come online, what will librarians do? When "virtual
libraries" become ubiquitous, will there still be a recognized need to maintain or develop local libraries as we know them, and will there be a role
for librarians?

Today, at a time when information is being recognized as a critical component of society and of international infrastructure—when information
management, information access, and information systems command significant attention in academia, industry, and even in the media—library
schools, including several of great renown in the United States, have been
closed. Why? Can it be that, in general, the connection is not made between

Paper presented at the International Roundtable for Information and Library Science, Kanazawa Institute of Technology, Library Center, Kanazawa, Japan, 1996.

librarians and information? Librarians are strongly associated with the place, the library, and with the volumes on the shelves, rather than with the information within these containers or with information functions. However, a library is, and has essentially always been, a function, not merely a place. That function is providing access to information—bringing constituents and the information they need together; constructing information access infrastructures; developing systems that will enable educators, scholars, business managers, physicians, researchers, students, and others to get the information they need, when they need it and where they need it; and then teaching them how to use these systems most effectively. The library room, building, and volumes are just some of the tools in our armamentarium, which has been considerably enlarged by technology in the last two decades, and is growing at what appears to be an ever-increasing velocity. The environment is changing and the tools are changing, but the essential, underlying functions of libraries and librarians continue. However, in order to thrive in the digital environment library, practice must also change and be transformed in ways it has not before, with concomitant changes in education that are more substantial than just teaching new skills.

The automated systems currently in use in libraries have already led to significant deprofessionalization in staffing of the technical services departments of even the largest research libraries. While fewer librarians will be needed for acquisitions and cataloging operations, their work will not be oriented to files and procedures but to planning and managing databases not limited to the traditional bibliographic components. Likewise, libraries of all types are beginning to implement tiered reference services that use more support staff and students to provide routine information services and, thereby, afford the opportunity for librarians to function as information consultants and collaborators.

Contrary to common apprehension that librarianship is a vanishing field, I perceive a growing demand for librarians—not necessarily for greater numbers of librarians—but for librarians who are well prepared to exercise a more expansive view of their roles and responsibilities. While fewer librarians will be needed, they will assume responsibilities that are more complex and that require better preparation and broader skills. A medical informatics colleague, a physician, recently predicted that the age of digital information resources would witness "the second ascendancy of the librarian" (Masys 1996).

Experience in developing integrated information systems points up the need for librarians to apply proficiencies in thesaurus building and in authorities work beyond the traditional creation of catalog records, applying these to the construction and management of databases and to collaborative research on natural-language processing and knowledge representation. It has been noted in the health care area that "librarians have valuable information organization and retrieval skills which, until recently, were undervalued and ignored. It was not until clinicians and information systems designers began to develop online patient record databases that the complexity of reliably indexing, organizing, and retrieving information from those records was appreciated. Thus dawned their recognition that thesaurus construction, indexing, and database design were exceedingly valuable skills and the discovery that it was librarians who possessed them" (Anderson and Fuller 1992: 209).

Librarians have skills that are, in effect, generic; that is, they are applicable beyond library, where we have traditionally exclusively practiced them. Those who are trained to interview others about their information needs and who can look at systems from the user's perspective can be valuable for computer-user services. Librarians possess information management and retrieval skills that are transferable beyond bibliographic databases, and they understand how students, scholars, and others use information.

THE NEED FOR LIBRARIANS' SKILLS IN THE DIGITAL ENVIRONMENT

In digital information environments, librarians can fulfill active roles that build on current areas of library responsibility. These areas include collection development, organization and management of information resources, reference and information service, training and education, interface design, and preservation. Several examples follow.

Collection Development

Selecting electronic resources and evaluating their quality. Even enthusiastic Web users today complain about the amount of time they waste on the Internet pursuing sites that are of dubious quality or that are outdated.

Blending access to print and electronic resources so they are mutually complementary, and relating digital libraries to existing library materials to form an integrated information resource rather than several disparate entities. In addition to the issues of large legacy collections, we face the prospect that print on paper will continue to be the medium of choice for the foreseeable future for some subject areas and types of publications, as well as for the various purposes and circumstances in which it is faster and easier to use.

Organization and Management of Information Resources

Developing expeditious and effective locator tools to make the complex web of resources more readily accessible to both sophisticated and naïve users.

Bringing value-added components and indexing to the morass of resources, which will continue to proliferate since anyone can now, in effect, publish on the Web.

Applying experience with bibliographic standards to the development of "best practices," to which all can subscribe for formatting, content, and exchange of electronic information. While many current discussions of digital libraries assume that all systems under development will connect, such interoperability is not yet a reality. Each system that is being developed for a limited group of users will not necessarily be interoperable with others when they are scaled up for access by the broad base of users with whom the library community is accustomed to working.

Reference and Information Services

Delivering information services where librarians are not merely the passive catalysts who direct inquiries to relevant sources, but provide the information that users actually seek—analyzed, evaluated, synthesized, and transferred in its most useful form.

Developing mechanisms for providing digital library access to large segments of the population who do not have computers readily available. Librarians can take the lead in trying to avert a future in which a nation's citizenry is composed of information "haves" and "have-nots." One possible method is by setting up networks of public kiosks that can serve as successors to today's public libraries.

Training and Education

Teaching novices how to find resources. It is unlikely that all electronic libraries will use the same approach to organizing and describing digital collections. Given the variations in users' backgrounds and information needs, "the prospects for creating a single, all-purpose method of helping everyone with maximum efficiency" appears "remote" (Jacobson 1995: A19). In their expanded roles as educators, librarians can also teach specialists how to locate relevant resources outside their own disciplines and even within their own fields, since computer proficiency levels and information skills vary substantially, even among scholars who work in the same area.

Teaching critical evaluation skills, which include assessing the authenticity and quality of what is found and determining whether an identified document is worth downloading.

Interface Design

Functioning as a "bridge" between systems designers and users. Those charged with the design of systems and who have the requisite extensive technical and programming expertise are not necessarily familiar with what users need. Librarians can be a "multilingual" link, speaking the language of both the programmer and the user. By having sufficient credibility with programmers and by understanding users' needs, librarians can serve as the user's advocate with the system designer while also interpreting to the user what may or may not be technically feasible.

Preservation

Deciding on the disposition of records, as many do not need to remain, or should not remain, online indefinitely.

Determining what is preserved or archived, and how. Web sites are notoriously ephemeral. As journal articles increasingly cite references to Universal Resource Locators (URLs) on the Web, how will access to and authenticity of these sources be assured as URLs or electronic information may change or disappear? (Weingarten 1996: 16)

IDENTIFYING AREAS FOR CURRICULAR CHANGE

To enable librarians to recast their responsibilities, meaningful changes are needed in their education and training, as well as in recruitment to the profession. The library community in the United States has begun to address these issues through planning and defining educational goals. My major experience in the last decade has been in health sciences libraries, where this has been a major concern. Work being done in the medical library area has also generated interest in the broader library community because of the recognition that these issues are not parochial, but are relevant to the profession as a whole. I would like to share some of this experience with you.

The Medical Library Association (MLA) has long had an active, continuing education program and has periodically tried to grapple with identifying the educational needs of its membership and developing programs to address them. In 1989, the MLA appointed a Task Force on Knowledge and Skills, which was charged with developing an educational policy statement to share with the American Library Association's Committee on Accreditation. The Task Force developed a roster of the knowledge and skills it determined were needed for effective professional performance now, and in the future. These were discussed with the membership and with various experts, including library educators and the directors of academic libraries, who noted the relevance of the content to their own settings and to general research libraries outside biomedicine. The MLA published the resulting document, called *Platform for Change*, in 1992. The MLA is now committed to undertaking programs that will bring about a professional "sea change," in other words—a radical remodeling—maintaining that if we are to continue as a vital profession, librarians must evidence initiative and risk-taking commensurate with rapidly changing circumstances. To achieve this into the twenty-first century, the MLA advocates a "continuum of learning" which "moves from the didactic to the self-directed" throughout an individual's career. In this continuing learning process, each individual assumes the primary responsibility for directing his or her own lifelong education (MLA 1992: 7–8).

Demographic data from both the Association of Research Libraries (ARL) and the MLA show that the librarians in their member populations are preponderantly middle-aged. According to recent ARL data, the age distribution of academic librarians in North America is "anomalous because of its under-representation of young people and over-representation of individuals aged 45 to 49" (Wilder 1996: 1). Likewise, MLA survey data show that the typical health sciences librarian is in her forties (Roper and Mayfield 1993: 404). Conclusions drawn from these demographics highlight the ever-increasing need for continuing education.

Since librarians who are already employed in academic and health sciences libraries are likely to still be working there well into the twenty-first century, high-quality continuing education can be as important as upgraded initial professional degree education in assuring that librarians are adequately prepared to meet future challenges, including those posed by digital libraries.

In examining librarians' education programs, it is vital that we not advocate changes that merely provide training for today's technology and job tasks. Instead, we must focus on recruiting people with the requisite attributes and on preparing them to be librarians who can take the initiative in dealing with rapidly changing technologies and shifting organizational priorities. Almost a generation ago, Estelle Brodman, of Washington University, clearly articulated this current issue when she said, "We must educate for the problems of a generation hence, not for the problems of today . . . librarians must be imbued with the psychological ability to handle change and to live with ambiguity. Without this they will be performing tomorrow's tasks with yesterday's concepts" (Brodman 1979: viii).

Since librarianship has a strong service component, education programs also need to maintain a healthy balance between, on the one hand, course work that emphasizes broad theories and methodologies and, on the other, the hands-on experience called for in the service setting. The great diversity required in education programs for librarians, whether initial or continuing, will also lead to drawing on courses and training from many fields and schools outside library and information science.

Here I will briefly note several training areas that merit serious attention. Please keep in mind that my perspective in this discussion is that of a practitioner who is calling attention to directions for change. I leave it to the professional educators to design the curricula that can address identified needs.

Technical Knowledge and Skills

Some library staff will need high levels of technical proficiency in computers and in telecommunications to oversee installation and management of networks and other infrastructure. However, all librarians will need to be sufficiently adept and knowledgeable about hardware, software, and networks so they can function, and be recognized, as sophisticated users of the technology.

Organization of Knowledge

Instead of teaching cataloging per se or just the organization of bibliographic information, the emphasis should be on the theory of organization of knowledge, which can be applied generally. The future of library technical services departments is far broader than traditional acquisitions and cataloging, as even in the near term it will involve managing the contents of an integrated information infrastructure, including remote and non-bibliographic resources. A major objective will be to develop the means for users to find the information they need by moving seamlessly among the multiple media, both print and online, whether available gratis or from commercial sources. Robert Braude has cogently argued that bibliography, the systematic description of sources of information, will still be needed in the digital world. It will, however, require a different approach than that currently used for print, audiovisual, and other physical items. He contends that the "task is not to rigidly apply the cataloging or bibliographic schema developed for print literature; neither is it to abandon the principles of bibliography that have stood for so long as a useful paradigm for knowledge organization. Rather, it is to apply [to digital literature] the same rigorous intellectual approach to the organization of information that librarianship has always brought to the process of scholarly communication" (Braude et al. 1995: 290).

The construction of thesauri and vocabulary is important for projects linking concepts from the several vocabularies used in diverse, machine-readable sources. For example, current work in the health care arena aims to provide access to external information sources, such as scientific literature, from within clinical patient records. This knowledge could also be used to develop user interfaces that translate queries from the searcher's vocabulary into the vocabulary of specialized information resources.

It will be increasingly important to understand database structure and design—the concepts that underpin the building of databases. It will not suffice for librarians to just learn how to search specific information retrieval systems effectively. If they understand the underlying theories and principles of those databases, they will be in a better position to use and plan different information systems in other subject domains.

Teaching Skills

Effective teaching depends on expertise in designing and delivering instruction as well as on content knowledge. With many disciplines now recognizing the importance of information literacy, librarians are collaborating with subject domain faculty to incorporate it into the courses of various schools, and are developing library-sponsored, stand-alone curricula. This expanding role as educator calls for training in curriculum design, needs assessment, teaching methodologies, and the evaluation of learning outcomes.

Subject Domain Expertise

In addition to gaining expert knowledge of the information resources, librarians will need sufficient background in the actual subject areas in which they work. Whether it be in music, architecture, business, engineering, history, or molecular biology, greater depth of knowledge than has generally heretofore been required will be necessary for librarians to evaluate the quality of information sources, to communicate and build effective links with scholars, and to collaborate with them in the design and delivery of instruction that incorporates digital resources.

Research Methods

We need a critical mass of librarians who are well trained in research methodologies and committed to pursuing significant questions, both alone and in collaboration with researchers from other disciplines. Incorporating new findings and advances in technical and theoretical underpinnings are as necessary for maintaining the vitality of this field as they are for any other. Strong theoretical foundations are essential to tackle the broad, fundamental issues facing librarianship. Three years ago, Warren Haas, former president of the Council on Library Resources, noted that "the overall importance and quality of library science research and its perceived pertinence to broad university objectives has been questioned." He deplored this state of research as one in which "the intellectual foundation of professional education has narrowed and become derivative at a time when expansive thinking and intellectual rigor are called for" (Haas 1994).

While all librarians may not actually perform basic research, all should be able to comprehend and to knowledgeably evaluate its outcomes. Librarians also need to understand and incorporate in their work advances in relevant technical applications and tools, whether that research emanates from library science or from other disciplines.

Librarians in practice should be prepared to contribute to the profession's research base by conducting applied research on issues such as how information is used, defining the information needs of various constituencies, evaluating the efficacy of particular information systems and methods, and demonstrating the usefulness and worth of current information to practice outcomes in fields such as health care.

In the last few years, most of the professional library associations in the United States—including the American Library Association, the American Association of Law Libraries, the Special Libraries Association, and the MLA—have issued research statements or incorporated research agendas into their strategic plans. The MLA's approach "goes beyond a statement of need for research as an adjunct to professional practice. . . . The MLA document views research knowledge as the basis for responsible information practice now and in the future." According to Joanne Marshall of the University of Toronto's Faculty of Information Studies, "such evidence-based practice will set library and information science professionals apart from their competitors in the expanding world of information service providers" (Marshall 1995: 1–2).

Knowledge of Management Theory, Economics, and Law

Knowledge of management theory, and of relevant economics and law, will be useful in dealing with the increasing complexities of funding, licensing, and copyright. In-depth economic and legal background can be brought to bear in planning various aspects of the inevitable reconceptualization of the information infrastructure in a global, distributed digital environment including the resolution of ownership and copyright issues and the related problems of fee structures, payment mechanisms, and licensing agreements. The issues associated with intellectual property are difficult, and their ramifications in the emerging electronic arena are fraught with further complications as publishers and vendors seek greater compensation while librarians try to promote broad and easy access.

The problems related to the rapidly escalating costs of journals, especially scientific and technical journals, are not likely to vanish in the digital environment, even as the current financial model is breaking down. New models that are likely to emerge will be more complex, as they will encompass diversified modes of delivery of electronic information. Some resources may be accessible at no cost, some will be supported by advertising, some licenses will be negotiated, and some would entail transaction-based fees.

Integrating policies and funding of expanding access to electronic resources, while also developing and maintaining print collections, is not a trivial issue. Richard De Gennaro points out that "for a long, long time we'll have to maintain the traditional library. . . . At the same time we have to work at developing the digital library and do it at a time of limited, even shrinking resources." He predicts a "long period of the transitional library, with the gradual building of the electronic library," which will be "very expensive and will not be a replacement" (Berry 1995: 31).

In some institutions, librarians have already become significant players in the overall strategic planning for their campuses and for institution-wide information policies. For this level of participation to become more prevalent, librarians need to be knowledgeable about the policy, politics, and financial issues with which the institution or organization is grappling and which influence planning endeavors that extend far beyond the library per se. To maintain a strong position in the institution's future information environment, we would be well-advised to turn library services and resources into strategic assets for the parent institution in the context of cost containment and quality improvement programs.

Socialization and Acculturation

We must learn to think and plan globally rather than parochially. A recent report from the ARL notes that "information technologies afford an unprecedented opportunity to rethink the ways research libraries manage global resources and to fashion cooperative strategies for ensuring the success of the aggregate holdings." Technological advances and the Internet will "now make it possible to leverage existing investments in technology and library materials to provide ubiquitous access to global research resources through the creation of a distributed networked program" (Reed-Scott 1996: 2–3).

We must also learn to function effectively in administrations that are less hierarchical than the traditional library, as organizations place greater emphasis on collaboration than on top-down decisions.

Institution-wide information system planning must be regarded as integral to one's job. The primary responsibility of the librarian is not to run the library. Rather, it is to meet the information needs of our constituencies. The functioning library is a means to that end. The focus must be on the utility of information resources to the mission and purpose of the users, not on the mechanics of library operations and processes. To this end, librarians need to perceive that one of their main functions is collaborating with people from other disciplines and departments in their institution and sitting with them at the table as a peer, and even as a leader, to plan and manage institutional information systems and services.

As part of their professional socialization, library students and practicing librarians must become, if they are not already, risk-takers. Recognizing that perpetual ambiguity is likely to be a permanent characteristic of our working environments, librarians must be both willing and comfortable with being change-agents in "going out on a limb" with new endeavors and services, rather than waiting for total agreement on procedures and processes. In this rapidly changing environment, I believe that if we wait until all details are defined, our options may well be pre-empted by others, and librarians would then miss valuable opportunities to be pivotal participants in digital information development and services.

One further, and basic, reorientation will entail abolishing the automatic association of the librarian with the library. Librarians will not necessarily be institution-based. Growing electronic resources will provide even greater impetus for librarians to undertake freelance and other entrepreneurial enterprises.

TRAINING LIBRARIANS FOR THE FUTURE: SEVERAL PROJECTS

Three years ago, the National Library of Medicine (NLM), under Dr. Donald Lindberg's direction, convened a planning panel on the education and training of health sciences librarians. It comprised a diverse membership of librarians (both medical and academic), educators, medical informaticians, clinicians, and association executives. The purpose of this panel was to analyze what the NLM and others might do over the next 10 years to assure that our society benefits from the skills of health science librarians. It also wanted to assure that people who choose medical librarianship will be properly educated and trained, and that they have an opportunity to engage in the most important work concerning information and health care. At its meetings, several groups of outside experts from a variety of fields joined the panel. The ensuing report (NLM 1995) presents goals and recommendations under four headings: evolving roles for the health sciences librarian, professional educational programs, lifelong learning programs, and broadening recruitment. The recommendations focus on the health sciences arena, but it was clear from the planning panel's discussions that many of the needs and issues identified are equally pertinent across a broad spectrum of librarianship, especially for academic, research, and other special libraries. In 1995, the NLM responded with the announcement of challenge grants, soliciting proposals for innovative and collaborative program initiatives that address the planning panel's recommendations.

The NLM awarded funding to seven universities, five of which include library schools. At four of those five universities, the library schools are leading the program initiatives. At the fifth, the university's vice-chancellor for health sciences heads the initiative. The other two funded proposals are at universities that do not have library schools, and at these institutions the medical libraries are leading the programs.

While several of these projects aim to enhance existing graduate degree programs, each also will test new technical or organizational innovations that are likely to be adaptable by other institutions or collaborative teams. I would like to briefly describe the site and major focus of each of these projects:

The University of South Carolina's College of Library and Information Science's project aims to "create a lifelong learning community" via technologies used by its distance education program. They foresee a virtual campus through which information professionals will participate in various continuing education opportunities. The program is a collaboration among three organizations: the college, a consortium of library and information science programs that is already providing distance education, and the MLA. The project's major objective is to transmit programs throughout the country using cameras, satellites, telephone systems, and fiber optics, and to complement these with listserv discussions, other online resources, e-mail, and fax.

The University of North Carolina at Chapel Hill School of Information and Library Science received a grant to work with the medical school's program in medical informatics and with the university's Health Sciences Library to conduct feasibility and marketing studies as a basis for developing five alternative educational approaches, including two new models. One new program would be an Executive Certificate of Advanced Study, modeled on executive training programs offered by many business schools which provide advanced training to those in mid-career who cannot leave their jobs and families to relocate and enroll as full-time students. The other would be an Advanced Internship Program of several months' duration that would provide either experienced or newly degreed librarians a customized program combining hands-on experience in using the latest technologies with academic coursework chosen from the curricula of various schools at the university, and that will also develop the intern's research capabilities.

The School of Library and Informational Science at the University of Missouri is developing a model curriculum that includes alternative means of delivering both graduate and continuing education for those who cannot relocate to the school. They will test the effectiveness of three delivery modes: satellite broadcast, World Wide Web, and intensive seminars.

The proposal from the *University of Illinois at Urbana-Champaign Graduate School of Library and Information Science* entails an interdisciplinary, multi-institutional collaboration among two library schools and two medical schools. The three other participants are the Indiana University library school and the medical schools at Washington University, St. Louis, and the University of Illinois at Chicago. This project includes expanding opportunities for research and fostering collaborative research by library school faculty and graduate students with informatics researchers at the medical schools who are actually building hospital and other clinical information systems.

While the program at the *University of Pittsburgh* is being led by the vice-chancellor, its key participants include the library school, the health sciences library system, and the various schools that the medical center comprises. This project will explore the opportunity to bring library school students and interns together with medical students in a joint teaching and learning experience in information management through the medical school's problem-based curriculum.

At *Vanderbilt University*, the project goal is to create a model post-graduate and post-doctorate training program. According to Vanderbilt's proposal, "the program will provide pathways to retrain practicing . . . librarians. The underlying hypothesis is that the focus of . . . librarianship is shifting from managing the containers of information to information management within the broader context of the institution." This program will include internships in which librarians will work closely with health care teams at the Medical Center. They will also strengthen their educational skills by participating in planning and teaching courses to medical and nursing students. Recognizing that "much of the research published in . . . librarianship concentrates on factors that are intrinsic to the field itself rather than attempting to build bridges to the mainstream of biomedical research," this project aims to provide opportunities for librarians to participate on existing clinical and biomedical research teams.

The project funded at the *Welch Medical Library of Johns Hopkins University* concentrates on continuing education. In an attempt to counter the various drawbacks associated with traditional forms of face-to-face continuing education (including travel and its attendant expenses, job demands, limited capacities of classrooms, and the preference some people have for self-directed study), its program consists of four complementary and interconnected activities: an on-site course, a tele-course, an online course, and electronic proceedings. Its goal is to learn how to "transform traditional lifelong learning activities . . . to networked-based mechanisms of the future."

CONCLUSION

As digital information resources proliferate, librarians can make important contributions by broadly interpreting their established mandates and by expanding their current work. The librarian will continue to function at the point of inquiry and at the point of service. Increasingly, this point may not be the comfortable and familiar one in a room or a building labeled "the library," but on a network, at the end of a fiber-optic cable, or, for the medical librarian, at the point of delivery of tele-medical care.

As we look at our library education and training programs, as we recruit new librarians, and as we examine curricula and criteria for student admission, we need to keep in mind that the rapid changes in our field call for people who are problem-solvers. They cannot simply be what one of my colleagues has referred to as "camera-ready" librarians prepared to function as-is. Although certain skills are critical, librarians must also be equipped with the recognition that their expertise and knowledge are not task-specific, format-specific, or site-specific, but that they also have generic value. In addition, they should be endowed with the self-confidence to apply these in unconventional ways and in new settings.

NOTE

All information and quotations describing the seven projects are taken from the proposals submitted to the National Library of Medicine by the grantee institutions in response to RFP number LM–95–002.

REFERENCES

Anderson, R. K., and S. S. Fuller. 1992. Librarians as Members of Integrated Institutional Information Programs: Management and Organizational Issues. *Library Trends* 41(2): 198–213.

Berry, J. 1995. Departing Shots from Richard De Gennaro. *Library Journal* 120(19): 30–31.

Braude, R. M., et al. 1995. The Organization of the Digital Library. *Academic Medicine* 70(4): 286–91.

Brodman, E. 1979. Keynote Address: Pragmatism and Intellection in Medical Library Education. In *Allerton Invitational Conference on Education for Health Sciences Librarianship*. Proceedings of a conference held in Monticello, Ill., April 2–4, 1979. Chicago: Medical Library Association.

Haas, W. J. 1994. America's Libraries: Distinguished Past, Difficult Future. *ARL* 172: suppl.

Jacobson, R. L. 1995. Researchers Temper Their Ambitions for Digital Libraries. *Chronicle of Higher Education* (November 24): A19.

Marshall, J. 1995. MLA Research Policy Statement Stresses the Role of Research in Information Science. *Hypothesis*: the newsletter of the Library Research Section of MLA (Fall): 1–2.

Masys, D. R. 1996. Presentation given at "Internet-able Health Care, a Technology Awareness/Transfer Conference," co-sponsored by the Pacific Southwest Regional Medical Library and the Medical Library Group of Southern California and Arizona, San Diego, Calif., April 11.

Medical Library Association (MLA). 1992. *Platform for Change*. Chicago: Medical Library Association.

National Library of Medicine (NLM). Planning Panel of the Education and Training of Health Sciences Librarians. 1995. The Education and Training of Health Sciences Librarians. Bethesda, Md.: National Institutes of Health.

Reed-Scott, J. 1996. Scholarship, Research Libraries, and Global Publishing. *ARL* 184 (February): 1–3.

Roper, F. W., and M. K. Mayfield. 1993. Surveying Knowledge and Skills in the

Health Sciences: Results and Implications. *Bulletin of the Medical Library Association* 81(4): 396–407.

Weingarten, F. W. 1996. Superhighway Speed Limit Abolished; Information Policy Swerves. *American Libraries* 27(1): 16–17.

Wilder, S. 1996. The Age Demographics of Academic Librarians. *ARL* 185 (April): 1–3.

CHAPTER 13

Government Records in a Digital World

PETER B. HIRTLE

What happens if one searches for government information on the World Wide Web? What may one find, and what are the implications for libraries and archives as they become evermore digital? I would like to begin my talk this afternoon by showing you some sites found on the World Wide Web that contain information produced by an agency of the federal government. Because I know the U.S. government the best, I have chosen examples from the United States, though I believe much of what I say would apply to other countries in the process of creating digital libraries and archives. The major themes of my talk are very simple. First, I want to stress the difference between government *information* and government *records*. Second, I will suggest that digital libraries will need to adopt some of the principles of archives and, in particular, pay attention to the integrity, authenticity, completeness, and usability of digital information, to function effectively in the digital realm.

To illustrate the difference between government information and government records, we will use the example of the Farm Security Administration, a unit of the U.S. Department of Agriculture. Investigation into what is currently available from the Farm Security Administration on the World Wide Web, and where it is located, can provide a useful context for the discussion of government records in the digital library.

First, a little background on the Farm Security Administration. In the 1930s, farms in the United States were ravaged by two reinforcing disasters that made farm life perilous at best. The first challenge facing the farmer

Paper presented at the International Roundtable for Information and Library Science, Kanazawa Institute of Technology, Library Center, Kanazawa, Japan, 1998.

was the Great Depression and the worldwide collapse of markets for the products of the farm. The second was a multi-year drought that destroyed many a farm in the semi-arid portions of the United States and led to the need to relocate many farmers. The government responded by creating several New Deal agencies to address the problems of farm life; one of them was the Farm Security Administration. The Farm Security Administration was only in existence for a brief time, from 1937 to 1942, but during that time it had several major, enduring accomplishments. One of them was to hire some of the best photographers in the United States to document the nature of farm life during the Great Depression. The photographs that they took bear witness to the nature of everyday life and are, in many cases, works of art in their own right.

Records of the Farm Security Administration can be found in several places on the World Wide Web. We will consider four examples.

The first example comes, as one might suspect, from the National Archives and Records Administration. The National Archives is the agency of the federal government charged by law with preserving and making available to citizens the permanently valuable records of the U.S. government. The National Archives' new electronic catalog of its holdings contains a record for a photograph taken by the noted photographer Dorothea Lange. The photograph is of a migrant labor camp near Modesto, California, in 1940. The photograph is found in the records of the Bureau of Agricultural Economics, a unit of the Department of Agriculture, and is intended to help document the work of the Farm Security Administration.

The second Web site to consider is from the Library of Congress, the premier research library in the United States. While a unit of the federal government, the Library of Congress has no legal responsibility for the records of government agencies. Nevertheless, in the American Memory portion of the Library of Congress's Web site one can find a collection devoted to photographs of the Farm Security Administration. In this case, the photographs are in color.

One photograph in the collection is of migrant labor housing created by the Farm Security Administration in Texas. As with the photograph at the National Archives, the photographs found at the Library of Congress were produced by government photographers as part of their official duties. The photographer of this picture, Arthur Rothstein, was a colleague of Dorothea Lange, the photographer of the first picture.

The third Web site is from the University of California at Berkeley's Bancroft Library. It, too, has a collection of photographs produced by the Farm Security Administration, and on its Web site has a sample of photographs from the collection. Among them is a photograph of migrant workers and their housing in the Imperial Valley of California, taken by Dorothea Lange as part of her government employment.

The final example comes from a project devoted to the history of the

New Deal, the government's attempt to deal with the social dislocations caused by the Great Depression. The "New Deal Network" has developed a research and teaching resource on the World Wide Web devoted to the public works and arts projects of the New Deal. At the core of New Deal Network's Web site is a database of photographs, political cartoons, and texts including speeches, letters, and other historic documents from the New Deal period. The "Library" portion of the Web site contains items pertaining to the Farm Security Administration, including a photograph from Dorothea Lange of the covered wagon of a migrant farm worker near Holtville, California.

If one looked further on the Web, other collections of Farm Security Administration photographs could be found. There are collections at the University of Indiana and the University of Minnesota, for example. The purpose of this paper, however, is not to discuss the extent to which the history of photography in the federal government in the 1930s and early 1940s is reflected on the Web. Instead, these four Web sites have been chosen to illustrate a very simple point: on the Web sites of the National Archives, the de facto national library, a major university, and a private organization one can find documents from the same federal agency. For a researcher interested in Farm Security Administration photographs, it may be immaterial whether the original photographs are located in a university library or in an archives; on the Web the photographs exist in a virtual archives, to be found and used interchangeably.

Does this mean that in a digital environment libraries and archives are becoming the same? Certainly, the general belief in the need to "archive" information, including library information, to ensure its long-term access seems to be spreading. Brewster Kahle, the founder of the WAIS search engine, for example, has created what he calls the "Internet Archive" intended to capture all of the World Wide Web for the future. The Commission on Preservation and Access, in conjunction with the Research Libraries Group, funded a task force (of which I was a member) on the problem of digital archiving in libraries; and, recently, I received an e-mail message in which the sender, in his signature block, referred to "archivists" such as DejaNews and Yahoo. Both of these are Web-indexing services. The fact that government information can be found on the Web sites of an archives, two different kinds of libraries, and a private organization does suggest that in the digital world archives and libraries may become synonymous.

Yet, while there may be similarities in the content of the four Web sites, there are also fundamental differences in their approaches to government information. The bulk of this paper will be spent exploring what those differences are, and what the implication for digital libraries and archives may be. The digital environment makes possible, more than ever before, the convergence of libraries and archives in ways that will benefit the library user and the citizen. The government archival records can be integrated into the emerging digital library in ways that have never been considered in the past. In order to make government records an integral of the emerging digital information infrastructure, digital librarians will need to understand the similarities and differences in the ways libraries and archives approach government information.

WHY GOVERNMENT INFORMATION EXISTS IN LIBRARIES

Before we begin exploring how archives differ from libraries in their approach to information, it would be useful to explore why, in the first place, government information exists outside of the legal repository for government records. After all, if *all* the Farm Security Administration photographs were in the National Archives, and not found at the Library of Congress or in a major university research library, there would be no need to address the different ways they approach the same information.

Part of the reason for the presence of government records in research libraries is historical. Government-sponsored and -administered archives are a relatively late development in the United States. No state government had an archives until Alabama established the first state archives in 1901. New York was the last state to establish an archives for its official records; the New York State archives was authorized and funded only in 1978. Even the National Archives, which houses the records of the federal government (but not the state governments) is a relatively recent creation, having been established only in 1934.

For almost 150 years, therefore, between the founding of the United States and the creation of the National Archives, there was no organized agency responsible for the records of government. Some federal agencies maintained their own records, a few others passed important records to the State Department, and many others either gave their old records away or destroyed them. In the absence of a central federal or state agency responsible for the appraisal, preservation, and use of government records, it is little wonder that many federal and state records found their way into the emerging research libraries. Many important documents pre-dating 1934 are found in the Library of Congress and other research libraries simply because there was no other home for them.

Other government documents are found in libraries because of the conscious effort on behalf of the government to make them available to citizens. The Government Depository Library program, in particular, is the product of a conscious effort to distribute the information gathered by the government. Under the program, copies of government publications, congressional reports, and other documents prepared for distribution by the federal government are sent to designated libraries around the country. The cost of printing the extra copies is usually borne by the agency that publishes the document. The libraries that receive the publications agree to make the copy available to the public. In this way people across the country have access to the information their government thinks they should receive.

More recently, the Government Printing Office (GPO) started the GPO Access program. GPO Access can deliver online versions of many current government publications, bills in the legislature, regulations, and other federal documents. The rationale behind GPO Access is to increase even more the availability of government information to the public.

THE BLURRING OF DISTINCTIONS BETWEEN LIBRARIES AND ARCHIVES?

For reasons both historical and programmatic, therefore, American citizens have had access to a wide range of government information, primarily in printed format through their libraries. To gain access to a large percentage of the printed information produced by their government, citizens did not have to rely on the government's own archives; they could use libraries instead.

In the digital environment, the lines between libraries and the traditional repository for government records (archives) are blurring even more. The presence of Farm Security Administration photographs in a variety of repositories is one example of how government information is not restricted to government-controlled distribution mechanisms. There are other examples of creative partnerships between libraries and government agencies.

Two interesting government and university partnerships are at Cornell University. The "USDA Economics and Statistics System" is a product of Cornell's Library for Agriculture, the Albert R. Mann Library. The Mann Library has agreed to publish on the World Wide Web some of the reports and datasets from three agencies in the U.S. Department of Agriculture. Information from the Economic Research Service, the National Agricultural Statistics Service, and the World Agricultural Outlook Board is included in the system. Currently, the system contains nearly three hundred reports and datasets on U.S. and international agriculture and related topics. Construction of the Web site was funded by a grant from the Department of Agriculture. Thanks to this collaborative partnership, information from the three agencies that might have languished in the agencies is now being made available via the World Wide Web.

A similar cooperative venture between Cornell's Martin P. Catherwood Library of the School of Industrial and Labor Relations and several agencies within the U.S. Department of Labor has resulted in the creation of the Catherwood Electronic Archive (www.ilr.cornell.edu/library/e_archive/). The Catherwood Library, in a move designed to make U.S. government reports more accessible to a wider population, including scholars and businesses overseas, is collecting, transmitting, and archiving selected federal reports, with special emphasis on employer/employee relationship. Documents are available within 24 hours after the Department of Labor releases them.

A third collaborative effort between a university and the federal government is Oregon State University's Information Sharing Project. The project is administered by the Oregon State University Libraries and is designed to provide remote users access, via the World Wide Web, to government information published on CD-ROM. Currently, the site makes available eleven major databases from the Bureau of the Census and the Bureau of Economic Analysis, both part of the Department of Commerce, and the National Center for Education Statistics (Miller 1996).

Clearly, universities are finding new opportunities as distributors of government information. They are being assisted in the effort to make more government information readily available to the public by government initiatives, such as GPO Access, designed to broaden the availability of government information.

At the same time that initiatives in the universities and the government are moving forward to increase the accessibility of government information, archives, as well, are striving to make their holdings more accessible. The National Archives and Records Administration, for example, has taken as its new mission providing to the citizens of the United States "ready access to essential evidence." As part of this mission it has committed to building "a nationwide, integrated online information-delivery system." Information that once may only have been available in an archival facility or, at best, through the government depository library, may soon become available directly from an archival agency.

One might well ask whether, in this new digital environment, where it is relatively easy to provide access to information in holdings, if it will still be necessary to have government agencies, the Government Printing Office, collaborating universities, and the National Archives and Records Administration all providing access to government information. At a recent conference on digital libraries, William Arms, the vice president of the Corporation for National Research Initiatives and a leading theoretician of the digital library, identified many of our assumptions about how technology will develop in the future, and if those assumptions are warranted (1997). Among the difficult questions he asked are, "Will the old disappear?" and "Which organizations will die?" He noted, for example, that "with cuts in government expenditures and the development of government Web sites, do we need the Government Printing Office?" He might well have asked whether, with the explosion of government information on agency and library Web sites, we really need to draw a distinction between libraries and archives. Can government records exist in the digital library, removed from their office of origin and not under the control of even a "virtual" archive?

INFORMATION VERSUS RECORD

For many users of government information, the answer would be yes. For them it makes little difference whether, for example, the copy of a report on family and medical leave in the workplace comes from the Department of Labor, GPO Access, Cornell University's Catherwood Library's electronic archive, or the National Archives and Records Administration. These users are concerned only with the informational content of the report and the ease with which they can get a copy. Modern librarianship has made improving the use, organization, and dissemination of information, including government information, one of its highest priorities, precisely in order to address the perceived information needs of this type of user.

Archivists, however, take a radically different approach toward the products of government. Archivists deal not in information, but in records. For users interested in government records, as opposed to government information, the source of the government record is of paramount importance. The remainder of this paper will consider briefly how government information differs from government records. In addition, it will consider the kinds of requirements that are needed to make government information from a virtual archive comparable to the government records found in a traditional archive. Finally, we will consider the implications of these distinctions for other sorts of resources found in the emerging digital library.

WHAT IS A RECORD?

Exactly one hundred years ago, three Dutch archivists, Samuel Muller, Johan Feith, and Robert Fruin, published their famous *Manual for the Arrangement and Description of Archives*. In the manual, they codified existing German and French archival theory and developed a definition of archives and the records within them that has been adopted in one form or another by most of Western society. According to them, archives are "the whole of the written documents, drawings and printed matter, officially received or produced by an administrative body or one of its officials." In this definition of archives are found the key concepts of the modern archive. First, archives consist of documents. For Muller et al. these documents had to be written or printed, but modern archivists have extended the definition to include multimedia records, including sound recordings and motion pictures. More recently, archivists have added electronic records to the definition of documents. There is currently a court case in the state of Tennessee in the United States that is arguing that "cookies," the small transactional file created by many Web browsers when surfing the Internet, may also be government records when found on a computer used by a government official. In short, archives consist of documents, regardless of their form (Muller et al. 1968).[1]

Second, in addition to noting that archives consist of documents, Muller et al. also noted that these documents had to be officially produced or received by an administrative body. Documents that are produced or received by an administrative body become records. According to the most recent glossary of archival terms, published by the Society of American Archivists, a record is a "document created or received and maintained by an agency, organization, or individual in pursuance of legal obligations or in the transaction of business" (Bellardo and Bellardo 1992: 28). When you request a visa to visit the United States, or when Americans report their income for tax purposes, or when President Clinton issues a proclamation, records are created because each agency or official involved in each transaction is fulfilling its legal obligation.

It is important to note that the definition of a record does not consider the perceived utility of the record. A record does not have to be interesting or important or even something that anyone would ever want to consult again to be a record. Pure archival interest in records depends not on the informational content of the record, but on the evidence it provides of government or business activity. As the Australian archivist Glenda Acland recently noted, the "pivot of archival science is evidence not information" (1992: 58). Records as evidence provide internal accountability for an agency, making it possible for the agency to be able to determine what it has done in the past. More importantly, archives, when they contain records that can serve as evidence, are essential in any democracy where leaders and institutions are required to account to the people for their actions. Finally, archives, when they contain evidence of the actions of government, can ensure that the rights of individual citizens are protected. Both of these themes—the ability of archives to hold public officials accountable and to protect the rights of individual citizens—form the basis of the new mission statement for the National Archives and Records Administration. Its mission is "to ensure ready access to essential evidence [note the emphasis on *evidence*] . . . that documents the rights of American citizens, [and] the actions of federal officials."

Of course, records preserved as evidence may also be interesting because of their informational content. Census records, for example, retained in an archive because of the evidence they provide about the activity of the Census Bureau, may be of great interest to genealogists because of the information they contain about families. To archivists, however, the fact that census returns are created by the Census Bureau in the course of conducting the agency's legally mandated business is of paramount importance—not the information contained in the record.[2]

For a time, the essence of records as evidence slipped from the center of the archival vision. Ironically, the challenges inherent in dealing with the most modern of records—electronic records—forced creative archivists to reinvestigate basic archival principles. Most notable, perhaps, has been David Bearman in many of his publications on electronic records, but especially in his collection of essays on *Electronic Evidence: Strategies for Managing Records in Contemporary Organizations.* Similar analysis has been conducted by the Australians Sue McKemmish, Frank Upward, and Glenda Acland, and by the archival educators Luciana Duranti in Canada and Margaret Hedstrom in the United States. All have concluded, to some extent, that one can deal effectively with electronic records only if one returns to the first principles of archival theory, including the importance of records as evidence (Bearman 1994).

An archival record, therefore, and especially an electronic archival record, is defined by the circumstances of its creation, as a product of legal or business requirements. The archival definition of a record stresses the *context* of the record's creation rather than the informational content of the record. A record exists only within the context of legal or business transactions, or both, as evidence of those transactions.

For a record to be able to ensure and protect the rights of citizens and to provide accountability for government actions, more is required. Records found in archives must have integrity, completeness, accuracy, and usability. Only by respecting all four can archives ensure that the records in their custody are authentic evidence of government actions. Archivists have developed mechanisms for guaranteeing the integrity, completeness, accuracy, and usability of records in paper form. The leading archival theorists are working on translating these concepts to the virtual archives of the future. We assume that the virtual archives of the future will consist of primarily electronic records stored in a variety of virtual locations. The problem facing archivists, therefore, is how to maintain the same degree of integrity, completeness, accuracy, and usability as is found in paper archives.[3]

Digital librarians would do well to consider the archival approach to each of these concepts as a way of distinguishing digital library information from other information found on the Web. Libraries are acquiring more and more material in electronic form. Furthermore, many libraries are converting many of their existing paper holdings into a digital form, either through scanning or encoding. In time, it will become harder and harder to distinguish the information from libraries from other information sources on the World Wide Web, possibly threatening the very existence of libraries. Yet, as Peter Graham recently noted, "For information to be available for any meaningful length of time, someone has to select it and take responsibility for it, which has been—and remains—the role of the library. Libraries continue in the paradigm learned in library school of acquiring (or linking to) information, organizing it, making it available, and preserving it" (1998: 234–35).

The work of managing digital libraries will be made easier if libraries pay attention to the core concepts of integrity, completeness, accuracy, and usability that underlie archival practice.

INTEGRITY

The first archival concept that must be maintained in the digital environment is the importance of the continued integrity of records. Maintaining the integrity of the records is the most important factor in ensuring the value of archives as evidence of governmental activity. Archivists need to be able to assert, often in court, that the records in their custody were actually created in the agency specified. In the physical world, this has been accomplished by legal and physical transfer of the documents from the agency to the archives. Archives truly exist only when there is an unbroken chain of custody from the creating agency to the archives. Furthermore, the transfer of custody is best accomplished as a matter of law. As Margaret Cross Norton, a pioneer theorist of American archives, noted: "We must disabuse ourselves of the concept that the acquisition by the state historical society of a few historical records . . . automatically transforms the curator of manuscripts into an archivist. . . . An archives department is the government agency charged with the duty of planning and supervising the preservation of all those records of the business transactions of its government required by law or other legal implication to be preserved indefinitely" (Mitchell 1975: 13).

The ease with which records can be created, transferred, and modified when in electronic form only heightens the importance of maintaining the integrity of records. Several different ways have been proposed to ensure that their integrity is preserved. Legal transfer of the electronic versions to a repository charged by law with maintaining the records may be sufficient. Continuous legal custody and transfer at least allows for the presumption that the integrity of an object has been preserved, that it is what it purports to be, and that its content, however defined, has not been manipulated, altered, or falsified. Some archivists have, in addition, encouraged other archivists to be involved in the design and implementation of software systems so that checks can be designed in the system from the start to ensure the integrity of the records (Duranti 1995).

The integrity of digital information is also of paramount importance to the emerging digital library. As the recent seminal report by the Task Force on Archiving of Digital Information, organized by the Commission on Preservation and Access and the Research Libraries Group, noted: "To preserve the integrity of an information object, digital archives must preserve a record of its origin and chain of custody." The report then describes several different channels of information distribution, and the need to establish the chain of custody and control in each channel, to ensure the integrity of the digital library object. Formal publication may be one means of trusted distribution; one may assume that a digital file received from a publisher is complete, but other kinds of documents, including the records of individuals, organizations, and scientific projects may not have as clear a chain of authority. The report encourages the development of metadata standards to document both the source of digital files and any changes to the files that have taken place during software or hardware migration (1996).

COMPLETENESS

A concept related to the integrity of archival documents is their completeness. Only records that are complete can ensure accountability and protect personal rights. As soon as records become incomplete, the authority of the records is called into question. For example, when information is missing in a record, we do not know if it is because the information was never created in the first place (perhaps to the detriment of a citizen or to the disgrace of an official), or was merely discarded at a later date. Hence, individual records must be complete; they must contain all the informational content they had when they were created. They must also maintain their structure and the context in which they were created.

In addition to each individual record being complete, it is also necessary that the record series in which the record is created is complete. Because records gain meaning from their context, it is important to know the nature of other records. Take the example of a case file. A case file is a record relating to one person as he or she interacts with a government agency. It might be an application for food stamps, or an assessment of someone's eligibility for veteran's benefits, or a request for a reproduction of a photograph in an archives. By itself, the case file can tell you much, but it cannot tell you if the citizen was treated differently than other people in the same situation. To understand the one record in context, one needs the whole series. There may be references from the case file to other records in the same series. Whenever possible, therefore, archivists seek to preserve entire series, in order to ensure the completeness of the record.

This does not mean that archivists never throw anything away. On the contrary, the normal archival principle is to save only 2 to 4 percent of an organization's records. What archivists try to avoid, however, is assessing individual records or parts of records. One keeps either the entire record, or discards the entire record. Similarly, the normal presumption is that one keeps either the entire series of similar records, or discards the entire series (though there may be times when the bulk of the records makes this impossible).

ACCURACY

Everyone wants information to be accurate, but in an archival context this can have special meaning. A librarian may be willing to update an online file to reflect new or corrected information. An archivist would realize that updating the file would destroy its value as evidence. As the Pittsburgh records project has noted, "No data within a record may be deleted, altered, or lost once the transaction which generated it has occurred." Accuracy, therefore, must be maintained not by modifying the original record, but by creating additional records. No one today would think that one could correct the "misspellings" in the first Folio of Shakespeare and still have an equivalent to the original volume. A similar sensibility must be at the root of the digital library and archive.

Accuracy may be especially at risk as digital information ages. The Report on Digital Archiving noted the fragility of digital information, and suggested that long-term access to digital information will depend on the constant migration of digital information to new storage media and new software and hardware environments. There is the real risk that as information is moved from platform to platform, the representation of the digital surrogate may change. The depiction of colors, fonts, and relationships all may be subtly altered by the changing technological platform. If changes in the nature of the record cannot be avoided, archivists at a minimum will need to be able to describe the changes that have taken place, in the hope that in the future people may at least reconstruct a semblance of the original appearance.

Archival interest in preserving an accurate representation of a document as it exists today differs somewhat from contemporary digital library practice. Current emphasis is on the immediate utility of documents, and librarians seem quite willing to change documents to address current interests. Peter Graham, one of the more thoughtful theoreticians of the digital library, identified early on the need to ensure that the document delivered 20 years from now is the same as the document delivered today. He proposed that digital libraries be built using a combination of digital hashmark technologies and public keys, but few other digital librarians have picked up his call.

USABILITY

Finally, digital archival records must be usable. But here again, archivists mean something different than their colleagues in libraries. Of course, the records must be readable, just as they must be for librarians. However, archivists are also concerned about the usability of the records over time. Ideally, the same functionality will be present in systems as the records migrate into new systems and new environments so that the record will display or be rendered as it appeared in its original environment. Records must always contain within themselves not just the content, but also the structure of the record and the context in which it fits. Most of all, records must have all the characteristics that would allow them to be used as evidence.

The need to develop digital archiving systems that maintain records as evidence by preserving the integrity, completeness, accuracy, and usability of the records is a daunting task. Fortunately, archivists are far from alone in seeking to define and implement environments that ensure the integrity and manageability of electronic information. In a number of business areas, including health care, manufacturing, research and development, and document management systems, managers are seeking to define standards for data interchange that ensure that electronic communication and exchange is adequate for business purposes. As part of its research project, the University of Pittsburgh team has reviewed much of the ongoing work in these areas and has developed a set of 13 functional requirements for a record-keeping system that can meet legal, regulatory, and business requirements—what they have dubbed "business acceptable communication." The Pittsburgh project envisions attaching to each electronic record an "encapsulated metadata object" containing the necessary information needed to ensure that the record continues to function as "business acceptable communication." Pilot projects are currently under way, most notably in the city of Philadelphia, to test whether this model can be translated into actual practice (see Bearman 1996).

ARE EXISTING WEB SITES VIRTUAL ARCHIVES?

Virtual electronic archives, as we have seen, must be designed with respect for the integrity, completeness, accuracy, and usability of the records so that the records found in the virtual archives may be used as evidence. If we reconsider the four Farm Security Administration Web sites described at the beginning of this paper, would any of them fulfill our definition of a virtual archive?

The entry from the National Archives and Records Administration may come closest to representing a true virtual archives. The catalog entry includes a link to the context of the photography, the "Series Description." The "Series Description" contains much information on the history of the photographs, and describes links to related record series. One assumes that in the related series are records that provide additional context for the photograph. The records may, for example, specify whether Dorothea Lange, the photographer, was directed to specific subjects by her supervisors or was given freedom to photograph what she wanted. The related records may also specify if a certain political or ideological point of view was supposed to be present in each of the photographs. The supplementary records may also detail the agency's reactions to her photographs. Did the photographs meet with approval, or were they relegated to the back filing cabinets and storage drawers, only to re-emerge when transferred to the National Archives? Unfortunately, none of this contextual information is as yet online, though it would exist in the paper records of the National Archives.

Furthermore, the record provides hints as to the integrity of the photograph. The "agency history record" referred to in the "Series Description" provides details on various successor agencies to the Farm Security Administration within the Department of Agriculture, and suggests how the records may have been transferred internally within the Department. At some point, the records were transferred to the National Archives, one assumes in accordance with the relevant laws, although the date of and authority for the transfer are not spelled out in the record. Still, the contextual and custodial history of the records as they exist at the National Archives is fairly clear.

It is harder to assess the integrity, accuracy, and completeness of the online version of the photograph. While the "Series Description" tells us that the photographs in the series are either black-and-white prints or negatives, we cannot tell from the record whether the online version was made from a print or a negative. Nor are the original dimensions of the photograph given. If the original was a negative, it could be 4×5, 5×7, or 8×10 inches in size. There is also no indication given as to the method of scanning or the fidelity of the image to the original (although there is elsewhere on the Web site a grayscale bar which does allow one to make rudimentary adjustments to a monitor to better reflect the original).

Because the online catalog of the National Archives and Records Administration lacks information needed to establish the integrity, authenticity, completeness, and usability of the Lange photograph, its value as evidence is limited. The Lange photograph serves primarily informational and illustrative, and not evidential, purposes.

The library Web sites with Farm Security Administration photographs found at the Library of Congress and the University of California are even less of a digital archive than the National Archives and Records Administration Web site. The Library of Congress Web site provides no information on the source of the Farm Security Information photographs in its custody. It is unlikely that, in either case, the photographs were received as part of a legal transfer, a requirement for a formal archive. We do not know, therefore, whether there were other photographs that the collecting repositories or the donors considered inappropriate for the collection and hence removed. The integrity of both collections must be called into question. Both collections lack information about the context of the photographs: why the photographs were taken, under whose authority, for what purpose, and with what results. In addition, the two Web sites lack even the grayscale bar and other information found on the National Archives site intended to help people judge the fidelity of the images to the original.

The Web site of the New Deal Network, the fourth example shown earlier, is, from the perspective of a digital archive, the least useful Web site of all. A code in the "Agency" field of the record indicates that the image comes from the "FSA"; we are forced to assume that this means Farm Security Administration. The "Owner" of the image is identified as "FDRL." It would take a learned researcher to know that this stood for the Franklin D. Roosevelt Library. We might assume that the Dorothea Lange photograph is actually a copy of the photograph found at the Roosevelt Library, but there is no direct confirmation of this. Furthermore, there is no indication of why the Roosevelt Library has this photograph. The Roosevelt Library is a component unit of the National Archives and Records Administration, but it has no direct legal authority for the custody of Farm Security Administration photographs. All of the context in which this photograph was created has been lost. We have no way of knowing if the photograph is typical of the other photographs taken by Dorothea Lange, or is an anomaly, the sole such photograph in a series of thousands. We cannot even say with any certainty that the photograph by Lange is a Farm Security Administration photograph; we must trust the attribution provided by the Web site. At best, the photograph exists as evidence of the interests of the creator of the Web site. It tells us nothing about the Farm Security Administration, however.

Analyses similar to the one we just conducted on these Web sites could also be applied to other sources of government information found in libraries. One could well ask, for example, whether GPO Access, the online publishing arm of the Government Printing Office, obviates the need for an electronic virtual archive. With some effort, one can find on the GPO Access site the legislation that created GPO Access and which mandates the creation of an "archival" server for the information published by GPO Access. There is to some extent, therefore, a legal mandate for the maintenance of the electronic files. There is no indication, however, of GPO policy toward the "archives" under its purview. How long, for example, will GPO Access keep copies of the electronic publications? Will they maintain the integrity of the files as they are published, or are they willing to replace published files with "improved" or "corrected" versions? Will they be able to attest to the integrity, completeness, accuracy, and usability of the digital files under their control?

CONCLUSION

By now, I hope you can see that government records are different from government information. There is no reason why digital libraries cannot provide with their digital files the assurances of integrity, accuracy, completeness, and usability that allow archival records to serve as evidence. Digital libraries, if they are to distinguish themselves from the mass of undifferentiated information accessible via the World Wide Web, will have to establish new paradigms for the organization, management, description, and preservation of digital resources. Recognizing that digital resources can serve as evidence as well as information will make the design and organization of digital libraries easier, and lead to an age when libraries and archives can truly support each other.

NOTES

1. Of course, the question of what constitutes a document can be problematic, as noted in Buckland 1997.

2. While most archivists would agree with the definition of a record as presented in this paper, there are strong differences about what criteria should be used in the appraisal of records for retention or possible destruction. Some archivists argue that only the evidentiary value of the records should be taken into account, whereas others argue that sociocultural requirements, including the need to establish memory, should be taken into account. For a majesterial survey of archival thinking on this topic, see Cook (1997) and Cox (1994, 1996).

3. While I cite four primary factors that distinguish an archival record, the University of Pittsburgh Recordkeeping Functional Requirements Project has identified 12 functional requirements for documents to endure as evidence within a recordkeeping system. These are detailed in the project's home page at http://www.lis.pitt.edu/~nhprc/.

REFERENCES

Acland, Glenda. 1992. Managing the Record Rather than the Relic. *Archives and Manuscripts* 20(1): 57–63.

Arms, William Y. 1997. Relaxing Assumptions about the Future of Digital Libraries: The Hare and the Tortoise. *D-Lib Magazine* (April). Available from http://www.dlib.org/dlib/april97/04arms.html.

Bearman, David. 1994. *Electronic Evidence: Strategies for Managing Records in Contemporary Organizations*. Pittsburgh: Archives and Museum Informatics.

———. 1996. Virtual Archives. Paper presented at the International Congress of Archives meeting, Beijing, China, September. Available from http://www.lis.pitt.edu/~nhprc/prog6.html.

Bellardo, Lewis J., and Lynn Lady Bellardo, comps. 1992. *A Glossary for Archivists, Manuscript Curators, and Records Managers*. Chicago: Society of American Archivists.

Buckland, Michael. 1997. What is a "Document"? *Journal of the American Society for Information Science* 48(9): 804–9.

Cook, Terry. 1997. What Is Past Is Prologue: A History of Archival Ideas Since 1898, and the Future Paradigm Shift. *Archivaria* 43 (Spring): 17–63.

Cox, Richard. 1994. The Record: Is it Evolving? *Records and Retrieval Report* 10(3): 1–16.

———. 1996. The Record in the Information Age: A Progress Report on Research. *Records and Retrieval Report* 12(1): 1–16.

Duranti, Luciana. 1995. Reliability and Authenticity: The Concepts and Their Implications. *Archivaria* 39 (Spring): 5–10.

———. 1989. Diplomatics: New Uses for an Old Science. *Archivaria* 28 (Summer): 7–27.

Graham, Peter. 1998. Special Collections on the Network. *College and Research Libraries* 59(3): 234–35.

McKemmish, Sue, and Frank Upward, eds. 1993. *Archival Documents: Providing Accountability through Recordkeeping*. Melbourne: Ancora Press.

Miller, Jacquelyn. 1996. Oregon State University's Government Information Sharing Project. *D-Lib Magazine* (March). Available from http://www.dlib.org/dlib/march96/briefings/03oregon.html.

Mitchell, Thornton W. 1975. *Norton on Archives: The Writings of Margaret Cross Norton on Archival and Records Management*. Carbondale, Ill.: Southern Illinois University Press.

Muller, S., et al. [1898] 1968. *Manual for the Arrangement and Description of Archives*. Translated by Arthur H. Leavitt. New York: H. W. Wilson Co.

Task Force on Archiving of Digital Information. 1996. *Preserving Digital Information: Report of the Task Force on Archiving of Digital Information*. Washington, D.C.: Commission on Preservation and Access.

CHAPTER 14

A View on the Ecology of Information

BRIAN L. HAWKINS

Population, when unchecked, increases in a geometrical ratio. Subsistence increases only in an arithmetical ratio. A slight acquaintance with numbers will show the immensity of the first power in comparison of the second.

—Thomas Robert Malthus, *An Essay on the Principle of Population* (1798)

Our society faces enormous challenges in education as our population is expanding and our university faculties are shrinking. We are encountering the stresses faced by applying teaching and learning methods that have essentially not changed since the University of Bologna was established in the thirteenth century. The instructional model of placing a professor in a classroom in front of a group of students is an inefficient approach. The demography of our society projects enormous increases in the total number of students to be served, and the current model does not scale in a cost-effective manner, thus putting education out of the reach of many people. At the same time, we are in the midst of one of the most rapidly changing periods of innovation ever seen on the face of the globe. The new technologies of computers, networks, and worldwide electronic communication, however, have not yet created any radical transformation in the manner in which we instruct our students, although significant changes have occurred in the nature of scholarship. The integration of this new technology, in combination with a broad base of available information and

Paper presented at the International Roundtable for Information and Library Science, Kanazawa Institute of Technology, Library Center, Kanazawa, Japan, 1994.

new paradigms of teaching and learning, is essential if higher education is to adapt to the changing environment. *The problem, however, is that a transformation of education cannot occur without a prior (or at least concurrent) transformation of the information environment.* We cannot create exciting multimedia learning environments because we do not have access to basic information, and much of what is available requires us to address copyright issues. There are no currently available electronic archives of media materials, and the existing archives of print material are in serious jeopardy of being sustained as we have known them. While there is much excitement and talk about new educational opportunities, these dreams are based upon an extremely fragile and precarious foundation of information. If we are to see such a set of transformations, we must begin with the library!

The university is a complex institution which has multiple missions, including instruction, research, and the diffusion of new information through scholarly communication. All of these functions are dependent upon the library and the resources that it houses. Over a century and a half ago, Thomas Carlyle suggested that "the true University of these days is a Collection of Books" (1920: 147). While the library of today is far more than books, the interdependency of the primary functions of the university and these information sources is just as true today.

In a recent paper, Robert Heterick discusses these difficulties and compares the problem to that of population growth and the work of Thomas Malthus. He states:

We must find ways to use our computer and communication technology to deliver materials that facilitate learning—whether or not the learner is located on a college campus or even in a specifically constructed learning environment. We need to find ways for our faculty members to use their expertise to design learning venues for the nontraditional, as well as the traditional learner. And we need to find ways for our populace to learn—ways that are considerably less expensive than conventional residential instruction. Only then can we escape the Malthusian trap. (Heterick 1993)

While Heterick's discussion focused largely on the economics of higher education, he raises an interesting metaphor that is worth pursuing. This analysis seems to be on target, but what it glosses over is that the "materials" for learning that would be delivered are also facing a Malthusian dilemma. An analysis of library acquisitions found that from 1981 to 1991, the library acquisition budgets of 89 of the nation's finest schools more than doubled; in real dollars, they increased by an average of 51 percent when normalized based upon the Consumer Price Index (ARL 1981, 1991). Although these increases are significant, the average library in this elite group of libraries lost 27 percent of its buying power during this period (see Figure 14.1). Also during this period, the inflation rate for acquisitions was consistently in the mid-teens. Although the cost of books and monographs did not rise at quite this fast a rate, the cost of some serials (especially those in the sciences) increased by more than 20 percent per year. Brown University, which ranks fifth among this group in the percent of total university budget committed to the library, lost 40 percent of its library buying power from 1980 to 1994.

Although this cost problem is extremely significant, it should be viewed less as a financial problem than a problem of long-term access to information, and the extent to which the scholarly record is being lost. Money and buying power are merely metrics that reflect the severity of the problem and the extent to which we are no longer capable of capturing the scholarly advances that are being made and preserving them for generations to come. One should not be fooled into thinking that "all information" has ever been preserved. The rule of thumb is that libraries collect about 6 percent of all information that is published. The point is that even this amount of preservation is in serious jeopardy and this level or baseline is not capable of being sustained.

Unless something dramatic is done quickly, we have the potential of losing our society's ability to capture the information that chronicles and documents our civilization. If these same trends continue, by the year 2035, the acquisitions budgets of our finest libraries will only have 10 percent of the buying power they had in 1990. It should be noted that even this dire outcome assumes the unlikely probability that universities will be able to afford to continue to fund libraries at more than twice the general rate of inflation.

The issues of library acquisitions that are described here, as dramatic as they are, only touch on the total cost of supporting a library in this period of exploding information. To truly understand the problem, one has to understand the associated support costs necessary to assure access, and one needs to consider the cost of space to house these ever-growing collections. These issues will be dealt with in greater detail later in this paper, but it is important to recognize from the onset that it is essential to consider total costs of a library, and not get too narrowly focused just on acquisitions. Second, it is important to once again emphasize that these discussions—while looking at costs as an indicator—must keep the more fundamental issues clearly in focus, namely, access to information, and the implications of that access for the broad community of scholars.

This problem of libraries should be of paramount concern, because if adequate source material is not freely available, then the supposed revolution using technology to enhance the educational process will never come about. While multimedia tools for education have exciting potential, their reality will depend upon legal access to textual documents, slides, video clips, and sound recordings, and that legal access (in any affordable man-

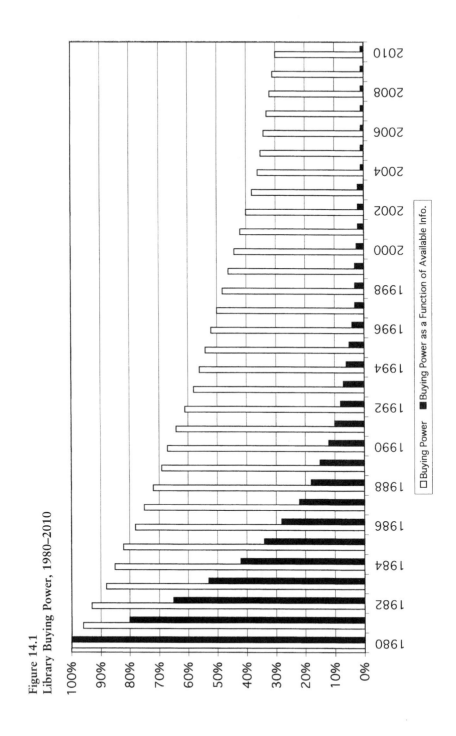

Figure 14.1
Library Buying Power, 1980–2010

Figure 14.2
Arithmetic versus Geometric Growth

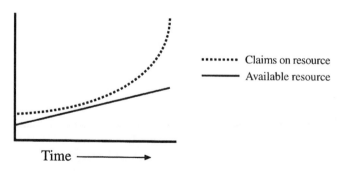

ner) is not presently available. Furthermore, the advancement of scholarship depends on being able to draw upon the record of previous scholarship in a complete and comprehensive manner, and libraries are losing their ability to provide this access. The irony here is that as we enter an "age of information," we may lose our ability as a society to preserve the record that is so essential for the educational missions of our colleges and universities. The problem that is being faced is directly related to the explosion of information, and that problem is Malthusian in nature. It might, therefore, be useful to see what Malthus and the broader literature in ecology have to tell us about dealing with these geometric claims on resources.

MALTHUS AND THE CONCEPT OF OVERSHOOT

Malthus looked at the issues of population growth and the agricultural capability of society as he knew it, in concert with the number of available farmers. He observed that the population was growing in an exponential manner, while the agricultural capacity was growing in an arithmetical function, and he concluded that the result of these two different growth patterns would be devastating to the human race. Thus began the call for population control. As can be seen in Figure 14.2, when the available resource is either flat or growing only in a linear fashion, while the demand on the resource is growing exponentially, the intersection bodes poorly for the long-term outcome.

While the predicted outcome is certainly not desirable, the critical observer should ask the obvious question: "Why should we be concerned, Malthus was obviously wrong?!" Malthus was wrong . . . at least thus far. But it is worth examining why he was wrong, and what these moderating factors can tell us about the library dilemma in which we find ourselves. In retrospect, and simplifying the problem greatly, one could suggest that Malthus was wrong because of three reasons: (1) he extrapolated his conclusion from the trends of available data; (2) he didn't adequately predict innovation; and (3) he used a "snapshot" versus a kinetic model.

These factors are highly related and they can be viewed, logically, as somewhat spurious. It is oxymoronic to suggest that he did not adequately predict innovation; if he could have used the innovations in his prediction, by definition they would not have been innovations. Indeed, his prediction would have been different if he could have predicated his outcome based upon these innovative practices. The implication is that one should not automatically panic when one considers doomsday prophecies such as the ecological apocalypse associated with population control, deforestation, global warming, or depletion of the ozone layer. This same caution is appropriate when one hears of the erosion and ultimate demise of libraries. The reasons are twofold; first, innovations changed the assumptions about agricultural production and thus enlarged the available resource. Second, society often has time to react and adapt to the negative feedback provided within the system.

In terms of innovation, the industrial revolution introduced technology that allowed for an exponential increase in food production; consequently, the available resources were able to keep ahead of the demand. Other innovations, such as genetic advances to produce more and better crops, pesticides to reduce crop depletion, and various other technologies all have contributed to making Malthus wrong—thus far.

To fully appreciate the complexity of interacting systems, it is imperative that any examination be done over time, and that the kinetics of systems as they interact be explored (Miller 1978). Again drawing from the ecology literature, there are predictable modes of reaction related to the "carrying capacity" or "available resource" in a system. These modes suggest the kinetic reaction of systems after the "demand" overshoots the available capacity. This notion of "overshoot" means to go beyond a limit, specifically going beyond the available resource. What happens after a demand has overshot its resources? Two reactions to this overshoot phenomenon are possible (Meadows et al. 1992).

The first reaction is overshoot and collapse, as illustrated in Figure 14.3. In this scenario, the demand is so great that the entire system fails, as in the case in which a predator eliminates its food source and the result is the extinction of both predator and prey. While this is theoretically possible, the more likely scenario is one in which the excess demand causes a reduction in supply, which in turn causes less demand, and so on. Such would be the case in which a predator overfeeds, causing a lack of prey, which results in starvation of the predator, then an oversupply of prey, and so on, as there is an oscillation around some mean level. This is the reaction, referred to as "overshoot and oscillation," shown in Figure 14.4.

If we try to relate these two models to the world of libraries and information, it is unlikely that the "overshoot and collapse" model is applicable.

Figure 14.3
Overshoot and Collapse Model

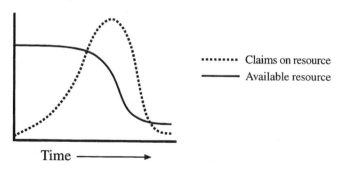

Time ──────▶

.... Claims on resource
──────── Available resource

Figure 14.4
Overshoot and Oscillation Model

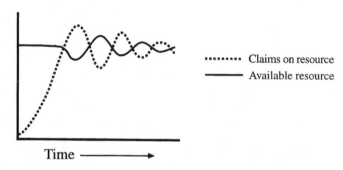

Time ──────▶

.... Claims on resource
──────── Available resource

It is doubtful that our inability to collect information will result in a new period of "the dark ages" from which our society will never recover. Instead, we will see the oscillation model, as we are not able to provide adequate information in an area, thus resulting in some sort of system failure, thus calling for the recreation of this information which was not collected, thus repeating this oscillatory cycle. This obviously has great cost to the total system, as these cycling periods are costly and wasteful. This pattern is perhaps seen today in our experience with collections, in that we cut back in subscriptions and other acquisitions to meet budget restrictions, only to have to rebuild collections later as a function of demand for a new or enhanced program. This rebuilding of a collection is quite costly and often not possible at all, since some information will be lost forever.

While this author and others have identified a potential system collapse in libraries, it is unlikely to be of the "overshoot and collapse" variety, but rather it is likely to be of the oscillation variety. The learning point of this comparison, however, is that a system in an overshoot condition is ex-

Figure 14.5
Sigmoid Growth Model

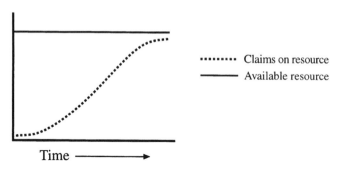

tremely precarious, and the consequences are likely to be significant and costly. The second point that needs to be drawn from this analysis is that, while it is unlikely we will be able to completely avoid the condition of overshoot, we must try to mitigate the damage and keep whatever oscillation occurs around as highly sloped a line as possible. This premise will be dealt with in detail in the next section of this paper. While it is unlikely that we will be able to completely cope with the current avalanche of information, it is important to explore ways in which some coping is possible.

The ecology literature identifies two models of coping with carrying capacity or demand. One of these is a "sigmoid growth model" in which the demand is scaled back to meet the constraint and becomes asymptotic with the supply, as feedback makes it clear that continued exponential growth is not possible (see Figure 14.5). In the case of population, one observes efforts to control birth rates, therefore avoiding overshoot situations associated with overpopulation. In the library world, we would find this applicable in that we buy and collect materials only up to the level of our appropriated budgets. The accountants of the world may be pleased that library expenditures level off at the budgeted amounts, as this solution may keep the budget from overshooting. While the budgetary and accounting systems have avoided overshoot in this example, user demand has not leveled off, and the broader information system is not considered. Realistically, staying within the budgetary system inhibits the actual ability of the information system to collect information in a coherent fashion. This lack of collected information may, in fact, cause other systems to overshoot because of a lack of technically "available" information.

The final model of carrying capacity is a continuous growth model (illustrated in Figure 14.6), in which the available resources are allowed to grow exponentially as well, thus paralleling the demand and thus never reaching a point of overshoot. Usually, this model is an artifact of time, in that the available resources are not really growing, but rather are just so

Figure 14.6
Continuous Growth Model

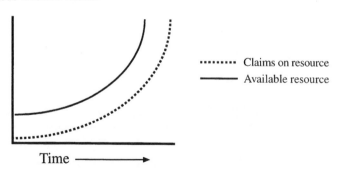

········ Claims on resource
———— Available resource

Time ——————→

abundant that overshoot is far away and not yet at that point on the time axis that any constraining forces or feedback are being encountered. This was the type of situation that reflected growth in the United States in the nineteenth and early twentieth centuries, when virtually unlimited land, physical resources, and human resources allowed periods of enormous expansion and growth. It is not that there were no limits, it is just that they were not in sight. Thus, a continuous growth model was reflected during that period.

While this pattern would be the ideal toward which we would strive in our attempts to cope with the growth of information and the role of the library in supporting the collection and codification of information, it is not a model that is found in the physical world. One must therefore question whether the limits of the physical world are applicable when dealing with information.

Harlan Cleveland would emphasize this last point, as he states that "Information (in its generic sense) is not like other resources; neither, as some would have it, is it merely another form of energy. It is not subject to the laws of thermodynamics, and efforts to explain the new information environment by using metaphors from physics will just get in our way" (1985).

Although he is correct that information itself is different, we should not confuse the dynamic quality of information with the materials that are collected in libraries, which may contain information. This distinction is made vivid as Barlow suggests that information is a relationship, having unique qualities that are not physical in nature. He states: "Information is an action which occupies time rather than a state of being that occupies physical space, as is the case with hard goods. It is the pitch, not the baseball, the dance, not the dancer" (1994: 89).

In fact, libraries store the baseballs, the records of the dancers, and other physical manifestations that are clearly physical. The process of information management—the business of libraries—is very much bound by the laws of physics, because of two major issues:

1. The copyright laws that treat information as property and therefore impose the laws of physics upon information; and
2. The physical nature of the media for the information (e.g., paper or other medium, bindings for that paper, or shelves to store that paper).

Cleveland suggests that information is the key resource in a post-industrial society, and he suggests whole new sets of possibilities for society based upon the unconstrained flow of information. While some of these opportunities may well come about, the real challenge is to avoid the restrictions on information that force information to work under the laws of physics and which will inevitably result in the outcomes associated with overshoot phenomena. Thus, in an idealistic world, information and food are not analogous, and continuous growth is possible; but, in reality, the physical constraints that librarians face prohibit this possibility. Our libraries are in an overshoot condition, and we have received the necessary feedback and signals informing us of the impending collapse. So, what will we do with this feedback information?

While there may be physical limits to deal with, our goal should be to strive for a model of exponential growth in collecting and making information accessible. Relating this back to the overshoot and oscillation model, if we cannot truly achieve an exponential increase in our use of available resources, it is essential that everything possible is done to make this line as highly sloped as can be achieved. If we fail to do so, it is almost certain that the lack of needed and potentially available information will result in overshoot problems in other areas of society, such as education, medicine, and the environment. Trying to slow the growth of information to stay within a physical constraint of a budget contradicts the need for information in dealing with society's problems, and yet that is precisely what characterizes the present efforts.

It is unlikely that we will see any reduction in the growth rate of information, thus alleviating the pressures on our libraries. If we look at the contributors to the growth rate of information and demand for library information, we find at least four factors. First, there are more people generating information. Second, computer technologies and other electronic tools are allowing for ever-increasing generation and processing of information. Third, the demand for information is outgrowing pre-existing parameters, as seen with the need for college-level collections to cover materials on an expanded set of cultures and in more languages as the internationalization of all of our curricula continues. Finally, the "publish or perish" pressures in academia are resulting in unnecessary material (not necessarily to be confused with information) being generated. Colleges and universities have a modest degree of control over this last factor, and they should keep this in mind as they review tenure and promotion policies, which potentially encourage the production of some of this unnecessary material. While this last factor should and perhaps will be moderated in the years to come, it is unrealistic to expect any reduction in the other factors. More realistically, technological advances are likely to increase the rate of data that is available to be collected. The "demand" in the form of new information being generated is not going to subside, and if we accept the premise that information is essential to our society, we must instead redefine the model in terms of available resources, or, more precisely, the manner in which we use our resources. We must change the way in which we do business!

Returning to the ecological metaphor, Meadows et al. identify three responses to the signals that a system is growing beyond sustainable limits. These are as follows:

1. To disguise, deny, or confuse the signals.
2. To alleviate the pressures from limits by technical or economic fixes without changing their underlying causes.
3. To step back and acknowledge that the current system is unmanageable, has overshot its limits, and is headed for collapse; therefore, to *change the structure of the system* (1992: 190–91).

If we are to adequately collect and make available this ever-increasing amount of information, a new paradigm—a new structure of the system— is essential. When this prediction of system failure within the next 30 years or so was presented to a group of librarians at a recent conference, one participant commented that he agreed with the statement of the problem, but he suggested the solution was to "educate the administrators of our colleges and universities so that they fund libraries like we used to." This solution is the modern-day equivalent to Marie Antoinette's response to the hungry of Paris when she said "let them eat cake!" and clearly reflects the denial response that Meadows et al. identified. For years, academic libraries have served a broad societal role, and the funding for this function has been subsidized by student tuition. Using the current models for libraries will inevitably lead to the overshoot calamities already described. Trying to "buy time," or even to mitigate these information system problems, by creating greater dependency on educational funding will only drive tuition rates up faster, eliminate educational opportunity for many, and exacerbate the overshoot problem presently being seen in our instructional systems of education. Instead, we need to change the paradigm and figure out ways to realistically increase the efficient use of available resources, if this Malthusian disaster of information is to be avoided.

INCREASING THE EFFICIENCY OF AVAILABLE RESOURCES

If we return to the basic premise of the arguments put forth by Malthus, the problem is one of geometric versus arithmetic growth. The mathematics is quite clear. The formula for an arithmetic line is as follows,

$$y = ax + b$$

while the formula for a geometric growth curve is found below.

$$y = (ax + b)n$$

The only way to have continuous growth in our access to information (or anything approximating this) is for us to develop cost solutions that bring about an exponential change in the way we do business. Returning to the previous arguments as to why Malthus was wrong, it was because the technological advances had an exponential impact on the production of food. What, then, are the factors that contribute to the problems that libraries are experiencing, and what factors can create the exponential outcomes necessary to maximize the efficiency of the available resources associated with library acquisitions? Before continuing, it should be emphasized that any efforts that are taken will not save money! Moving to an electronic solution, or to any other strategies that can be identified, may help make available resources keep pace with the demand, but will not reduce the total expenditure. In fact, the total set of expenditures to support information-related functions is more likely to increase. Instead, the focus must be on how to leverage existing resources to assure access to information. Such leveraging may permit the achievement of something resembling the continuous growth model. We should be reminded that the problem is access to information, and cost is only an indicator.

As mentioned earlier, there appear to be three basic contributors to the "total cost" of the library; that is, purchase costs, support costs, and space costs. Therefore, it is appropriate to examine each of these factors independently to see what kinds of exponential or leveraged opportunities are possible.

Purchase Costs

Clearly, the cost of purchasing information is the factor that has been most closely examined by librarians and others concerned about the library collections in colleges and universities. The extraordinary impact of inflationary increases in the last decade, especially on scientific, technical, and medical journals, has been well documented. The impact of cost increases was shown in the earlier graph related to library buying power. If the solution is not to add money to the acquisitions budgets of our institutions at an exponential rate, then what can change this geometry?

Several possible solutions may contribute to a continuous growth model. The first is to encourage scholars to publish their own scholarly communication. At present, our colleges and universities subsidize and pay for the costs of research, and the faculty give this intellectual property away to professional organizations and profit-making publishers, only to have the colleges and universities buy this material back at ever-increasing prices. Over time, if continued, this model will devastate the scholarly publication paradigm. The solution is to have professional organizations and other non-profit organizations become their own publishers and distribute their materials electronically over the network.

Distribution of information over the network is one of the keys to cost reduction and more cost-efficient distribution of information. The work done so far suggests that the savings in avoiding paper, binding, mail distribution, and so on do not appear to be as great as one imagines. There are still labor-intensive processes, such as editorial review and peer review, copyediting, and production preparation that are imbedded in the process as we know it today. While some advocates suggest that some of these functions can be reduced or eliminated in an electronic world, clearly the quality of scholarly publication would change, and professionals in those fields would need to be the judge as to whether these changes would be deleterious. The added value of these processes will certainly come under greater scrutiny given the pressures that are being encountered in the cost of scholarly publication. Current work suggests that the cost savings might only be about 35 percent, but these analyses fail to consider the "downstream" costs of support and storage, which will be discussed shortly.

If scholars essentially become their own publishers, and if these materials are contributed to a "commons," then the economies of this model more clearly approximate an exponential change (Okerson 1992). The most fundamental change that must occur is in the manner in which rights are given to publishers for the academic information that is generated within the higher education community. This basic premise is not new, but it has become of greater importance in the last few years, and is well summarized by Anthony Cummings et al. in a report to The Andrew W. Mellon Foundation:

Alternatives to current copyright management can be imagined. For example, universities could claim joint ownership of scholarly writings with the faculty they pay to produce them, then prohibit unconditional assignment to third parties, thus becoming important players in the publishing business themselves. Or universities could request that faculty members first submit manuscripts to publishers whose pricing policies are more consonant with larger educational objectives. Another possibility is that university-negotiated licenses grant unlimited copying to libraries and individual scholars and specify said permission in the copyright statement. All these proposals are extensions of the broader idea under current discussion, that universities should reclaim some responsibility for disseminating the results of faculty scholarship. (Cummings et al. 1992)

The authors of the Mellon report go further to suggest that in an electronic world, at least some of the functions of publishers may be obviated, as the faculty editorial and review efforts can become part of the "circle of gifts" that may fuel such an enterprise. An effort must be mounted to stop our current practices of giving away exclusive rights to the developments that come from our institutions of higher education.

Further changes in copyright law as it applies to the electronic world need to be explored. There are many aspects of information in an electronic world that need review, including the concept of fair use, the contributions and availability of information in the public domain, and the need to balance personal gain and societal cost. As national and global information infrastructures are being established, it is imperative that public policy issues be carefully discussed, assuring that the laws, regulations, and other restrictions that are created keep the public interest and the availability of general information clearly in focus.

Distributing information over the network fundamentally changes the library model. In the model that has been operative since Alexandria, we have had scholars go to the library, as that was the only feasible solution, even though it limited the use of these resources to those who could get to these facilities. In the new library, the library is brought to the scholar, and the only limits are who has access to the network. This more egalitarian access has the strong potential of increasing the volume of information (or at least the volume of scholarly "products") being generated in a scholarly publishing environment not limited by "page" costs.

The final approach in creating any kind of exponential change in the acquisition of materials has to do with the distributed versus centralized model of acquiring information. How does one define a collection policy in an electronic environment? Historically, a college or university defined its collections as a function of the academic programs that it offered. In this non-duplicative world, a new business model needs to be found that looks at information from a broader and more centralized approach, if anything approximating an exponential solution is to be found. Such a model is described in some detail elsewhere (Hawkins 1994), and this or some other more centralized and less fractionated solution is critical.

Overhead and Support Costs

Much of the current worry about the costs of acquisitions is focused on the initial purchase of materials. As already discussed, this is a significant problem. However, there are other imbedded costs that may not be readily apparent, and which are often hidden in some other budget. One of these sets of costs is the overhead support of the library, while the other is the cost of space. The overhead and support costs for a library include catalogers, reference librarians, and so on. The costs associated with these support and service functions are substantial, averaging about twice the annual cost of acquisitions in the typical research library in the United States, not counting the costs of the space for storing materials, or the maintenance of that space.

Strides have been made to develop cooperative and sharing arrangements to keep support costs down, and such solutions should continue to be pursued. However, it should be recognized that none of these approaches has provided the requisite exponential changes. While it is necessary to further collaborate and cooperate in leveraging specialist talents, such as catalogers, all of these efforts are arithmetic in nature. The two-to-one nature of support costs to actual acquisitions reflects the labor-intensive nature of libraries, which have long been known for their commitments to service and support of students and faculty. Pelikan, in describing the role of the library in meeting the broad missions of the university, suggests that "As the volume of scholarly helps increases, the need for professional guidance in the use of such helps increases with it; and that professional guidance can come only from subject bibliographers who are sensitive and thoroughly trained and whom research scholars recognize as their peers and colleagues in the raising up of future scholars" (Pelikan 1992: 115).

The importance of the service that reference librarians provide is unmistakable. However, it is unlikely that the employment of such professionals will increase in any proportion to the growth in the total number of patrons and students that we are likely to encounter, much less with the growth of information. In looking at ARL data from 1981 and 1993, it is found that the percentage of the budget spent on acquisitions increased from an average of 32 percent of the typical library budget to nearly 36 percent. This reflects the need to try to keep up with the inflationary spiral of costs associated with acquisitions, but the last five years of this period were characterized by significant budget reductions in university budgets and the support staffs of libraries were not exempted from these reductions. While information was growing, and attempts to re-engineer the support structures of our universities were under way, the ratios changed only slightly. While the trend is in the "right" direction in leveraging the available resources, Pelikan and others would argue it is in the wrong direction in support of scholarship. As the information explosion continues, and as more and more information is available, everyone will need to have more help in finding, sorting, and filtering the available materials in order to solve problems. It is unreasonable to expect that this assistance will be as available or as capable of supporting users with the traditional model. The number of users, the amount of information, and the costs of a labor-intensive model clearly make the current model unfeasible and unscalable, even though this support function will be more critical than ever. If one breaks these support categories into the two categories of technical and public services, while there may well be means to share resources and to leverage the technical services, the likelihood that public services can gain any exponential level of efficiency is not as evident. Although there will certainly be some gains as a "virtual reference librarian" supporting many users on the network would gain some leverage, the combination of numbers of users and lack of current means of supporting these professionals is not something that can be anticipated in the short term.

It is unreasonable to expect any significant transformation in the near future in assisting users to sort and select information, since the issues of "filtering" become greater as the amount of available information increases. Some place high hope in the work that is going on in using "agents" or "knowbots" to electronically filter through the increasing mass of available information, selecting the information that matches a person's personal profile of information interests and preferences. While dreams of these "digital aliens" provide intriguing possibilities, a prudent planner would more likely expect increases in the human capital needed to help people navigate the network, rather than any exponential decrease in the near future. In this environment of increased access and availability of networked information, the challenge will be more on the process of eliminating unnecessary and irrelevant information than on finding information.

Space Costs

While the problems associated with the acquisition of new information are extremely alarming, focusing on this set of costs alone masks the magnitude of the real problem. If we proceed with the library model as we have known it, the costs of storing and archiving the information will bankrupt our institutions of higher education. While this problem was clearly identified nearly 15 years ago, our institutions have failed to heed these warnings and act accordingly (Gore 1976). If one assumes that new building costs are approximately $170 per square foot, then the cost of physically housing a single volume approaches $20. This would correspond with the $10–$12 cost identified in 1982 (Leighton and Weber 1986: 124), when inflation is factored in. In addition to the physical cost of constructing this space, at Brown University, on average it costs about one dollar per volume per year for maintenance of the library building, including heat, light, custodial service, and so on. Looking at the experience at this university, building construction in the last three decades would be more than $40 million in today's currency value. In addition, the maintenance costs of library facilities at Brown exceed $2 million per year. Often, these associated costs of housing and maintaining our library collections are ignored because space costs are often not reflected in line items in the library budget. However, regardless of where the costs are reflected in an institutional budget, these annual costs, plus the capital costs of new construction, need to be clearly understood if one is to fully appreciate the level of crisis associated with continuing our current library traditions. If we look at library construction, in combination with the size of the total library collection, the exponential problem is clearly seen. In Figure 14.7 each bar on this graph reflects the size of the Brown University library collection at the time of construction of a new library, or opening a new dedicated facility. The exponential growth curve is quite evident.

The three libraries built at Brown since 1961 reflect an addition of more than two hundred thousand square feet of space and a very large proportion of all new construction that occurred at the university in the past three decades. With the information explosion occurring in the exponential fashion already described, the space costs of physically housing these materials will become astronomical, especially when one considers that this problem is duplicated to some greater or lesser degree on each campus in the United States, as well as on campuses around the world. This problem becomes especially disturbing when one factors in the recognition that about 80 percent of the materials in a research library are never checked out. Clearly, circulation does not directly correlate with use or with the value that access to these materials might have. Access to information, no matter how often it circulates, is a strongly held value that is part of the fundamental mission of a library—especially a research library. However, the old model of access cannot be sustained, and need not be duplicated by scores of other institutions. In keeping with the "efficiency" value of the corporate world of the past decade, libraries have been criticized for not adopting a "just-in-time" model of information (vis-à-vis the industrial manufacturing model), but instead maintaining a "just-in-case" philosophy. While this parallel phraseology is perhaps clever in the criticism of the failure to achieve efficiency, what is missed is that the archival and stewardship roles of the library are essential to the enhancement of knowledge and cannot be judged solely by a criterion of efficiency. Certainly, the efficiency of the archival function can—and should—be enhanced. However, the archiving of important information is extremely important to scholarship and to our society, "just-in-case" it might be needed by scholars and practitioners in years to come, and so as not to "lose" critical information that has been discovered in our own era.

With the dramatic decrease in the price performance curve of electronic information storage, the desired exponential reductions in cost of storing information could be achieved if electronic storage were the accepted medium for archiving scholarly information. Not only would electronic storage be far cheaper, it would also eliminate the present duplication.

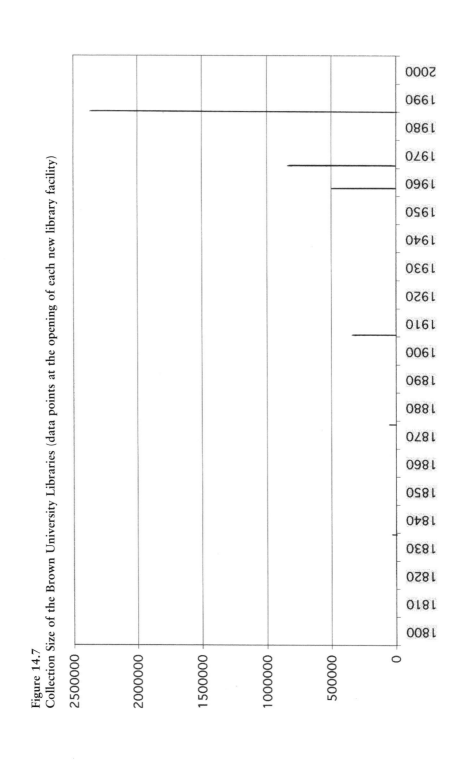

Figure 14.7
Collection Size of the Brown University Libraries (data points at the opening of each new library facility)

Information could be available in a very few defined locations on the network, and yet accessible to users internationally, at all times and places that the network was available. This aspect of the cost of scholarly information is the most easily dealt with, drawing upon a solution that requires no innovation, and which attains the exponential levels of efficiency that are needed.

It is important to note that moving toward a cooperative strategy of electronic storage will not only reduce problems associated with physical space, but will simultaneously address the critical problems of preservation of print materials that our society is facing. The decaying materials, which are being destroyed by the acid-based paper upon which they were printed, must be either treated, copied, or stored on an alternative medium if these intellectual contributions are to be saved. Thus, movement of many of our library resources to an electronic medium would solve multiple problems.

If the overshoot that we are experiencing (and which we expect to experience) is to be avoided, some combination of these or other innovations must be introduced to provide the exponential growth of the base of available resources necessary to maintain the intellectual record. Understanding the specific contributors to the problem helps to set priorities and strategies for effectively adapting to new circumstances.

CONCLUSION

Any good scholar knows that there are logical dangers inherent in arguments based upon metaphorical comparisons. However, having gone this far, it would seem appropriate to draw some implications from the ecological literature. The ecological comparison is useful because it is clear that if we proceed on the present course, we are destined for (if we have not already experienced) an overshoot condition. If we draw conclusions from the ecology literature, in all likelihood, an outcome of overshoot and oscillation will occur. It is incumbent on all of us to assure that everything possible is done to make the curve that reflects available resources as close to parallel as possible, trying to approximate the geometric curve that is shown in the continuous growth model (Figure 14.6). A number of strategies have been identified to try and leverage existing resources for acquisition, support, and space costs, so that the efficiency of these resources can be maximized, thus reflecting a more exponential growth of available resources than is now the case. While these strategies are essential, there are several other conclusions that can be drawn directly from the literature on systems and ecology. Three overriding principles that apply to systems and the management of systems need to be kept in mind as we try to more fully understand and cope with the ecology of information.

The Current Unit-of-Analysis Is Inappropriate

First, we are looking at a complex, interdependent system, and when a system is endangered, one should look for solutions at a larger system level, in which the subsystem exists. It is clear that the current unit of analysis—the campus library—cannot survive in the existing environment. The leveraged resources of larger system levels are called for, with the best solution being at the highest level possible. While associations of campuses, consortia, and other groupings will alleviate the problem, the best solution is found when no system or national boundaries are limiting factors, but where information is maximally available. This principle is already shown to be the case in one of the few present examples of information that is available across virtually all boundaries.

"For the sake of science, the knowledge base of molecular biology should be a public, international electronic library, supported by all for the benefit of all. No one organization or nation should control this type of information for public gain. Another reason for public ownership, especially of scientific knowledge, is that database and knowledge management is of such magnitude that individuals and their organizations cannot be expected to bear this burden as they have in the past" (Matheson 1988).

This example illustrates the intellectual advantages for using a broader system perspective, as well as the economic advantages. While there may be a sense of nostalgia for the desirability of the self-contained library on our campus, this sense of convenience and ownership is a luxury that is no longer affordable on economic or intellectual bases.

A Change in Values Is Needed

In examining the needed changes in the ecological systems of the world, Meadows et al. (1992) suggest that any solution to the population growth problem—and for that matter, any overshoot problem—requires more than technological change: it requires that the values within a system change. In addressing the ecological challenges facing us, these value changes have to do with the number of children per family, the values of consumption and waste, and so on. In looking at the library and the challenges that are facing our society, three fundamental values must be confronted and changed if the future of our intellectual heritage is to be maintained: (1) collaboration across all boundaries must be achieved, (2) the defining characteristic of "bigger is better" should be tossed out, and (3) the encouragement of generating unnecessary information should stop.

The first of these values relates strongly to the concluding statement that was just developed. It is fine to suggest that the solution to the problems of the library rest in looking across system boundaries but, currently, the competitive instincts of our campus cultures mitigate against this type of solution. Status is conferred upon an academic institution for having more volumes in its library than does another competing institution. We rank the "best" libraries as a function of the total number of holdings, rather than the appropriateness of the collection in service of curricula, the quality of services, or other qualitative measures. Part of the reason higher education finds itself in this difficult situation, with respect to libraries, is a long and fairly unproductive history of competition rather than coopera- tion. The new electronic library would be a major step in reversing these tendencies and overcoming some of the inherent difficulties identified by Patricia Battin several years ago.

Commitment to new cooperative inter-institutional mechanisms for sharing infra- structure costs—such as networks, print collections, and database development and access—in the recognition that continuing to view information technologies and services as a bargaining chip in the competition for students and faculty, is in the end, a counterproductive strategy for higher education. If the scholarly world is to maintain control of and access to its knowledge, both new and old, new cooperative ventures must be organized for the management of knowledge itself, rather than the ownership of formats. (Battin 1989: 382)

Part of the pressure that keeps us focused on the smaller unit of analysis of the campus is the tendency of our institutions to use the size of the campus library as a competitive factor, falling into the trap of "bigger is better." As long as we continue to rank libraries on the basis of the total number of holdings, we reinforce the suboptimization of information re- sources. It is only when the available access to information is ubiquitous that we can gain the economies of scale, and the intellectual opportunities for everyone that are necessary. "Bigger is better" is not particularly mean- ingful in an electronic age, and is an entirely relative statement when the unit-of-analysis is that of a given institution or set of institutions. We can no longer afford this competitive stance, as such competitiveness is not only not cost-effective, it is ultimately destructive.

The economic problems that have been ascribed to libraries in this paper apply equally well—and perhaps more importantly—to the basic structures of our educational institutions. The old models are breaking down, and trying to "go it alone" and to emphasize independence rather than inter- dependence with our sister institutions are not principles that will succeed or endure much longer.

Broad System Interdependencies Need to Be Recognized

Without pushing the metaphor of ecology too far, one final comparison seems appropriate. In his classic treatise on "The Idea of the University," John Henry Newman suggested that the library is the embalming of dead genius, while he suggested that teaching was "the endowment of living (genius)" (1976). In his re-examination of Newman's work, Jaroslav Pelikan emphasizes the interdependence between teaching, learning, and the essential role that libraries play in facilitating these educational functions: "A university that would, in its enthusiasm for 'living genius' or in its eagerness for 'development' and 'looking forward,' neglect its vocation as a repository for 'the oracles of the world's wisdom' and for the tradition would lose not only the past but the present and the future as well" (Pelikan 1992: 112).

This living layer of teaching is built upon the top of past genius, just as in a coral reef, one finds a delicate, vital, living layer of coral polyps, grounded on the top of the calcium-based remnants of millions of previously living animals. To destroy or allow the erosion of the foundation of these stone-like structures will in turn cause the demise of the living reef. So, too, the destruction or erosion of our libraries has a vital relationship to teaching and learning, which in itself, is the very basis of the vitality of society.

A reef provides a marvelous example of the previously defined problem of looking at the right unit of analysis. When examining the ecosystem of the reef, it makes little sense to study a given cell, a particular coral polyp, or even a marvelous coral head. While each of these subunits may be of special interest, or particularly beautiful, these subunits cannot survive in isolation if the ecosystem is under attack. It is the entire reef structure and ecosystem working together that provides the necessary structure, protection, nutrient base, and latticework that supports a much grander set of life forms. There is a richness of life on a coral reef, teaming with plant and animal life, all intermeshed with, supported by, and dependent on the dead remnants of centuries of previous generations of coral which preceded that current thin living layer. These other animal and plant habitats depend on the coral structure of the past, and its destruction would in turn result in the system collapse of many of these interdependent life forms. If we look at the idea of the university, with its multiple functions, we cannot have the "living genius" of teaching in isolation, if we allow the "embalmed" genius of the library—this stone-like structure that reflects the accumulated information of the centuries—to be destroyed. Not only will the educational system be irreparably harmed, the impact on related systems and other dependent systems will also result. As Pelikan states, "The dynamic interrelation of research with teaching, and of both with the acquisition, preservation, and circulation of documents and artifacts, applies to galleries, museums, and above all to libraries" (1992: 113).

As we enter an age of information, we must be vigilant in the preservation of the "embalmed genius" of the past in order to allow for the exciting "living genius" of the teaching and research that are possible in a new electronic world. However, preserving the "embalmed genius" is also essential if our society is to prevent the ecological collapse of related and dependent systems. We are presently in an "overshoot" mode, and the responses that the ecology and systems literature would tell us will result in an unacceptable set of outcomes. The feedback is there for us to interpret—our success in saving the concept of the library will depend upon how quickly, thoroughly, and responsively we decide to react.

REFERENCES

Association of Research Libraries (ARL). 1981. *ARL Statistics 1979–80*. Washington, D.C.: Association of Research Libraries.

———. 1991. *ARL Statistics 1989–90*. Washington, D.C.: Association of Research Libraries.

Barlow, John Perry. 1994. The Economy of Ideas: A Framework for Rethinking Patents and Copyrights in the Digital Age. *Wired* (March): 89.

Battin, Patricia. 1989. New Ways of Thinking about Financing Information Services. In *Organizing and Managing Information Resources on Campus*, edited by Brian L. Hawkins. McKinney, Tex.: Academic Computing Publications.

Carlyle, Thomas. 1920. *Lectures on Heroes, Hero-Worship, and the Heroic in History*. Edited by P. C. Parr. Oxford: Clarendon.

Cleveland, Harlan. 1985. *The Knowledge Executive: Leadership in an Information Society*. New York: Truman Talley Books.

Cummings, Anthony M., et al. 1992. *University Libraries and Scholarly Communication*. Washington, D.C.: Association of Research Libraries for The Andrew W. Mellon Foundation.

Gore, Daniel. 1976. *Farewell to Alexandria: Solutions to Space, Growth, and Performance Problems of Libraries*. Westport, Conn.: Greenwood Press.

Hawkins, Brian L. 1994. Creating the Library of the Future: Incrementalism Won't Get Us There! *The Serials Librarian* 24(3–4): 17–47.

Heterick, Robert C. 1993. A Malthusian Solution? *EDUCOM Review* 28(5): 64.

Leighton, Philip D., and David C. Weber. 1986. *Planning Academic and Research Library Buildings*. Chicago: American Library Association.

Matheson, Nina W. 1988. Strategic Management Knowledge as a National Resource. Paper presented at the Medical Librarians Association Annual Meeting, New Orleans, Louisiana (May).

Meadows, Donella H., et al. 1992. *Beyond the Limits: Confronting Global Collapse, Envisioning a Sustainable Future*. Post Mills, Vt.: Chelsea Green Publishing Co.

Miller, James G. 1978. *Living Systems*. New York: McGraw-Hill.

Newman, John Henry. 1976. *The Idea of the University Defined and Illustrated*: I. In Nine Discourses Delivered to the Catholics of Dublin (1852); II. In Occasional Lectures and Essays Addressed to the Members of the Catholic University (1858). Edited with introduction and notes by L. T. Ker. Oxford: Clarendon.

Okerson, Ann. 1992. The Missing Model: A "Circle of Gifts." *Serials Review* 18(1–2): 92–96.

Pelikan, Jaroslav. 1992. *The Idea of the University: A Reexamination*. New Haven, Conn.: Yale University Press.

PART III

The Digital Library in the Service of Research and Education: Some Experiences

CHAPTER 15

The Library of Congress's National Digital Library: Reaching Out to Schools and Libraries through the Internet

LAURA CAMPBELL

THE NEW WORLD OF DIGITAL LIBRARIES

Libraries will undergo radical transformation as they become digital. Every component of traditional work will change: acquisition, cataloging, delivery, archiving, and preservation. But at the same time that we are inventing a new kind of librarianship, most of us in major libraries will continue to provide traditional library services conducted in traditional modes. This dual mode existence poses challenges for all of us.

Major responsibilities of the new digital library lie under new, broad headings. One is the duty to "acquire," catalog, deliver, archive, and preserve the mass of information and artistic expression that already exists in digital form—indeed, items that now often exist *only* in digital form. Second is the duty to "convert" our existing collections to digital form.

There are two types of digital information with which libraries are concerned. The first type is physical artifacts with digital content. An example is a CD-ROM. Such digital materials pose few problems for libraries. CD-ROMs can, in many ways, be treated like traditional library materials. They can be bought or licensed, cataloged as an unchanging artifactual library holding, physically stored in book stacks and delivered to a reading room, and subjected to preservation by the library that owns them.

By contrast, the other type of digital information, online information, is typically outside the control of a user library. It can be accessed but not, in the traditional sense, acquired. It can be cataloged and indexed, but only on very different terms from traditional cataloging. It must also be delivered

Paper presented at the International Roundtable for Information and Library Science, Kanazawa Institute of Technology, Library Center, Kanazawa, Japan, 1997.

to our patrons quite differently. The problems of archiving and preserving this ephemeral body of important information are among the most pressing in modern librarianship. Will these problems result in modern society's losing its memory in the twenty-first century?

Converting existing collections to digital form and making these artifacts accessible poses its own set of challenges, including what to convert and for what audience.

We are fortunate to be present at the creation of this medium, which brings with it such extraordinary potential for stimulating progress. Libraries can and should be a powerful force for an international renaissance made possible by this technological revolution.

OVERVIEW OF DIGITAL PROJECTS AT THE LIBRARY OF CONGRESS

The Library of Congress is embracing the online world through a set of programs delivered on the World Wide Web. The new age of access to the Library of Congress began with the American Memory pilot program in 1990–1994, to make historical collections available electronically. We now provide over the Web more than 40 million records, including the Library's bibliographic data; summaries and status of federal legislation; copyright registration records; and abstracts and citation to foreign laws—in addition to hundreds of thousands of historical collection materials.

Highlights of some of our new services include the following:

THOMAS

In January of 1995, at the request of the U.S. Congress, the Library implemented a new online legislative system called THOMAS, named after Thomas Jefferson, the father of the Library of Congress.

THOMAS is a service that provides American citizens with online access to information about the work of their Congress—the full text of bills, the *Congressional Record*, and Bill Summaries are now all available for searching. This online index of legislative activity is updated daily and is available for anyone in the world to search freely. Rather than waiting for the postal delivery of the *Congressional Record* and manually collating information, anyone with Internet access can search the *Record* online for the 103rd or 104th Congresses, 1993 to date.

THOMAS also provides associated materials, such as the full text of legislative bills, which the system displays by the day of their introduction. This is a major change in the quality and timeliness of legislative information available to the citizenry of the United States. From January 1995, when it was introduced, through September 1995, THOMAS transactions exceeded 9 million. THOMAS transactions now average more than 270,000 per day and more than 8 million per month.

We are confident that the legislative process is more open to the people today than it was even two years ago.

GLIN

We are beginning to make foreign legal information searchable online. Since 1994, a number of governing bodies throughout the world have been contributing legislative information to our Global Legal Information Network (GLIN) database. GLIN is a cooperative international network in which participating nations contribute the full text of laws and regulations in their country's language and share access to the resulting database, which is hosted by the Law Library of Congress. This database, which includes abstracts in English, assists the Law Library's foreign law specialists in providing timely answers to congressional requests.

Copyright Recordation and Deposit System (CORDS)

There is an abundance of other work at the Library of Congress that contributes to our digital library effort. For example, the Copyright Office, which is a branch of the Library of Congress, is conducting the CORDS project, which will result in the Office's use of the Internet for digital copyright registration and for digital deposit of copyrighted material. On February 27, 1996, we received our first digital submission.

Online Exhibits and Access to Curatorial Divisions

Since 1995, each of our library exhibits has been mounted online so that people unable to come to Washington may view the exhibit. In addition, each of our curatorial divisions has mounted its own home page with useful information about the holdings. This includes the Asian Division and the Japan Documentation Center, in addition to eight other Library divisions.

The Library's National Digital Library Program: American Memory

American Memory is the cornerstone of the Library's digital library efforts, called the National Digital Library (NDL) Program.

Of the Library of Congress's 111 million items, 80 million are in special, or non-book, collections. While the Library collects in many languages from many countries, its collections are especially rich in the documentation of American history and creativity. We have the papers of the U.S. presidents; all the commercial sound recordings of Duke Ellington; the scores of such famous composers as Leonard Bernstein, George and Ira Gershwin, and Irving Berlin; a vast collection of early films; and millions of other rare and unique items.

These unique treasures, many in fragile condition, were previously available to visitors to Washington only on a restricted basis. Now, digital versions make it possible for citizens anywhere to see this record of the American experience. We have targeted the American historical and cultural material as the first stage of our NDL effort. This program had its beginnings in a five-year pilot effort to convert materials in different formats—pamphlets, photographs, movies, manuscripts, sound, and graphic arts. The pilot was intended to test the process of converting materials and making them available.

An evaluation of these digital collections was conducted at sites across the country, revealing a much broader audience than we originally thought. These primary source materials, unembellished and in their raw state, supported teachers and librarians. Educators use the electronic materials to teach the historical thinking skills, and school librarians use the materials to introduce research methods. The test included libraries in 16 schools beneath the college level and in 18 colleges and universities. The evaluation showed that American Memory's multimedia primary-source material supported the educational reforms previously mentioned: increased emphasis on primary-source materials and multidisciplinary coursework.

The end-user evaluation showed that American Memory collections permitted teachers to reduce their reliance on textbooks and encouraged independent thinking by students. The multimedia resources stirred curiosity and engaged the student in learning. American Memory primary-source materials were often the springboard for further inquiry, that is, sending the student back to the library to carry out research in books and other sources.

During the evaluation, the Library received many letters from schools and from college and university libraries requesting access to American Memory in the future. We also learned that libraries wanted more pictorial materials and local or regional history materials.

The pilot ended in 1995 and we were challenged to find the funding to continue and expand the effort. In late 1995, we established a strategic plan and a fund-raising campaign to build the program to support a large core of digital content of high educational value. The expanded program differs from the previous pilot in its scope and ambitions.

The Library and its advisers have identified two hundred collections from the holdings of the Library for digitization: unique documents, photographs, sound recordings, printed matter, sheet music, maps, and motion pictures that truly represent the nation's memory. By the year 2000, the Library of Congress, in collaboration with other repositories, aims to digitize and make publicly available 5 million items of historical significance.

We intend to reach all 15,000 school districts and some 15,000 public libraries across the United States.

THE EXPANDED AMERICAN MEMORY DIGITAL ARCHIVE

In the newly expanded NDL Program, the Library of Congress creates a complete version of each digitized subject collection and assembles these as broad, heterogeneous "plain vanilla" *source editions*—selections from the American Memory digital archive are available on the Web at http:// lcweb.loc.gov. Containing a minimum of explanatory and interpretive information, this body of content documents the history and culture of the American people. The material is neither encrypted nor inextricably imbedded in proprietary software; the only special controls protect intellectual property rights in the materials. This open access permits interested parties to develop tools for re-presenting the collections.

Online or on disk, each collection allows the user to search for, study, and print material, or electronically copy selections onto a floppy disk for further study or incorporation into the researcher's own report or document. We now have 20 collections online. Each collection has its own home page from which one can search and browse the collection items.

The educational audience figures prominently in the development of the NDL Program. The findings of our American Memory pilot endorsed the value and importance of making the materials available to the K–12 community. Providing electronic access to collections previously unavailable to students offers a compelling argument for reaching out to schools. We feel a responsibility to help teachers and school librarians know how to use these materials. With funding from the Kellogg Foundation we have been able to develop an educational program that:

- shapes selected Library of Congress historical collections for schools;
- produces descriptive guides to help teachers and students use the collections;
- explores CD-ROM, Internet, and cable television distribution channels to schools;
- helps teachers learn about using primary sources; and
- engages in a distance learning initiative.

The services currently available to schools through the Web home page are only the beginning of what will be necessary to meet the objectives of educational outreach to schools. It will be most important to draw on the expertise of teachers, school librarians, and media specialists to ensure that the services we provide meet their needs.

For the last two years, we have worked with educational consultants to help us learn more about this new audience. We have conducted focus groups to learn how educators want to use primary sources. We have engaged teachers in developing pathfinders through the collections as well as sample lesson plans for use in the classroom. We are not in the business of delivering curriculum, but rather in making exciting primary sources usable.

AMERICAN MEMORY'S LEARNING PAGE

In 1996, we launched a page on the Library's Web site just for educators, called the Learning Page. Its goal is to provide help in finding and using the Library's primary sources. For instance, educators new to our site may want help finding materials to match the curriculum. From the Learning Page, one might go to Search Guides, in which one finds Pathfinder indexes organized around subjects familiar to K–12, Events, People, Places, Time, and Topics. For example, if you are searching for presidents, under the People Pathfinder, you will find that the Library of Congress offers 11 collections and exhibits that feature presidents, such as the Civil War photographs of Abraham Lincoln.

Educators have limited preparation time and primary-source materials require additional planning. Other online Learning Page activities include special topics and features, such as a special on the presidential inauguration; sample lesson plans; activities for students (e.g., searching for history clues or answering a history quiz); and a new offering, "Today in History," with facts about events of the past on this day in history. Together, these tools create a convenient method for teachers to search across collections organized in a fashion most useful to them.

WHAT IS THE LIBRARY'S OVERALL STRATEGY?

The United States is building a national information infrastructure, the so-called information superhighway. For this highway to deliver the information so badly needed by a democratic society, and indeed a democratizing world, library holdings—both historical and current—must be brought online. The Library of Congress views American Memory as a first stage in its contribution to the Global Digital Library of the twenty-first century.

Presenting historical collections to a large and far-flung community of users represents a significant expansion of the service provided by the Library of Congress. An essential element in the expansion concerns what is offered. The Library has always played the role of custodian of collections and has, for nearly a century, distributed its *cataloging* information. Only now will it begin the wholesale dissemination of the content of its collections

Working with the U.S. Congress, foundations, and the private sector, we hope to build a national digitizing program producing millions of items by the year 2000. The result will be a core of historical content and a program that may serve as a model for the parallel delivery of material in other subject areas.

HOW ARE WE SUPPORTING THE PROGRAM?

This expansion of service carries an increased cost to the Library. The American Memory pilot received nearly $6 million in appropriations and gifts. The cost of creating additional American Memory collections and building a more robust program, which can scale to handling millions of digital objects over the next five years, is estimated to be $60 million.

The overall funding strategy is to support the costs of the program through a public-private partnership. The U.S. Congress is supplying $15 million over the next five years and the private/philanthropic sector is contributing $45 million. Gifts to date total $28 million.

The Library has assembled a team of 80 technical and library specialists to build the NDL Program. There are about a dozen functions performed by this group, from describing and organizing materials to raising funds to support the conversion costs.

HOW IS THE LIBRARY CREATING 5 MILLION DIGITAL ITEMS?

Program management involves the following elements.

Program coordination entails working closely with an editorial board and Library experts in the selection of collections. After collections have been selected, the administrative headquarters coordinates activities with the Library's custodial divisions, which process materials to prepare them for digitization.

Processing consists of organizing materials, ensuring that they receive preservation treatment, creating a catalog or finding aid, and carrying out a variety of quality reviews.

Digitization involves scanning images, converting texts to searchable form, and digitizing audio and video. This work is carried out largely by specialist contractors, who come to the Library to handle rare and fragile original items under the watch of Library custodians.

Creation of the national source edition begins with the assembly of collections. In assembly, the cataloging or finding aids provided by the Library's special collections divisions are combined with the digital reproduction delivered by contractors. After quality review has been completed, security copies of the digital information are properly archived. Some materials included in the source edition will be protected by copyright. The preparation and handling of these materials includes obtaining permission to reproduce them and for ensuring that any required royalties or license fees are paid. The entire source edition is then made accessible on the Web or a similar computer network. Some individual collections are also available on CD-ROM.

Maintaining public/private sector relationships entails developing relationships with partners, overseeing the copyright permission process, and performing a variety of bookkeeping functions.

COLLABORATION WITH OTHER ARCHIVES

The Library's NDL Program is being developed in collaboration with other libraries and archives with important historical content. In 1995, the Library of Congress, the Council on Library Resources, and officials from 14 other research libraries signed the National Digital Library Federation Agreement. This group is working to bring together digitized content for students, scholars, faculty, and citizens. In addition to providing content, the Federation is charged with addressing issues related to economic models, intellectual property rights, and interoperability among content repositories.

This spring, the Library announced grants to 10 other libraries across the country in a national competition funded by the Ameritech Foundation. These grants are for digitizing American history content that will be included as part of the core National Digital Library. For example, Denver Public Library will contribute 6,000 photographs from the western United States, and New York Public Library will digitize 11,000 stereoscopic views of the New York region from 1870 to 1930. These grants will be extended to between 16 and 20 additional libraries over the next three years, creating a rich and diverse digital archive. One of the most important aspects of this collaboration is the opportunity to test some of the technical challenges of interoperability so that users will be able to easily search across many collections no matter where they are located.

Other collaborative efforts include working with our sister cultural institutions in Washington to produce content; and, in 1997, we will begin working with the National Science Foundation on the next phase of its digital library research initiatives.

FUTURE CONSIDERATIONS

The NDL Program's planners envision a library "without walls" that provides easy access to cataloging and finding-aid data and to electronic surrogates of the full content of collections. This virtual library will be available in many academic offices, student dormitories, and private homes, but its existence will not eliminate the need for the library "with walls." Many users will rely upon physical libraries and living librarians for access to electronic information. More important, readers will continue to request books and other items "in the flesh," either because this is the best way to use them or because available surrogates will never answer every question a researcher may ask. Some advanced researchers will always have to look at that original George Washington letter, no matter how good the copy.

We believe that the future electronic library will include a catalog and finding aids. We respect the efforts of those who seek new ways to find needed information—neural networks, hyperlinks, and the like—and the NDL Program will make use of such features. But many of us believe that users will always find additional value in a central, organized point of access that (among other things) employs structured thesauri of subject terms, possibly enriched by keywords drawn from the items themselves. Of course, we hope that improved software will streamline the work of assembling the catalog as well as ease the task of searching.

We will prepare American Memory collections for computer equipment of the type likely to be found in a school library or public library today. Images, audio files, or large bodies of data will not work on the least-sophisticated machines, but will work on microcomputers at the middle of current price ranges. We design our collections for use on this middle range of equipment.

Audience

We expect that the audience for the NDL will change as the program proceeds. Over time, after enough collections have been produced to make the NDL an extensive and well-rounded resource, the program's audience will resemble the diverse patrons of a large public library: a mix of young people, college students, and adults. In the short term, however, we have to mount a special effort to connect users to available content. The connection between potential users and available content can be accomplished in educational settings and, for the first few years, the NDL Program will emphasize content that can be used in schools, including colleges and universities.

Selecting Collections

Selecting collections for the NDL is a lengthy process. Recently, the voices of educators have begun to counter the voices of curators and experts inside the Library. Some have spoken from the user evaluation sites, others from focus groups, and others through e-mail on the World Wide Web. Everyone (and we took heart from this) has vigorously asked for more, in the broadest possible sense.

Starting our conversion projects has been time-consuming. The time required to convert a collection is long and the cost high. Our predicament may be compared to an encyclopedia publisher who has only produced the volume *Aardvark to Amphibious*. Even after five years of effort, the American Memory Project and NDL Program have converted to digital form fewer than 1 percent of the Library's 111 million items. How can we make just a few collections—even if they comprise hundreds of thousands of items—as useful as possible as we digitize more? Our answer is to try to assemble a set with as much coherence as possible and thus create a synergy among collections.

Selection means compromise. Here are some of the considerations that we have tried to balance as have drawn up our list of 200 collections as candidates for conversion.

1. Value and interest to Library patrons, students, and educators;
2. Variety of formats (e.g., manuscripts, recorded sound, books, and photographs);
3. Limitations of present technology;
4. Assembly of groups of collections within time periods;
5. Few legal restrictions;
6. Unique Americana content;
7. Costs and time.

Cost of Conversion to Electronic Form: An Example

As indicated, the costs of conversion to electronic form are high. The contract we awarded (based on competitive proposals from vendors) to convert the double-spaced, typed manuscripts in an oral history collection from the Great Depression era of the 1930s requires an accuracy rate of 99.95 percent. This text was encoded with a subset of the Standard Generalized Mark-up Language (SGML). The SGML coding will indicate such features as underlined passages, footnote or illustration locations, page breaks, and titles. The Library of Congress pays nearly three dollars per page to create this machine-readable text. That price excludes the cost of preservation work, cataloging, and placement in a retrieval system

We believe that conversion costs will be significantly reduced in the future as technology advances.

ADDITIONAL CHALLENGES

Preservation: the greatest challenge in digitizing historical collections is finding appropriate ways to handle rare manuscripts, glass plate negatives, bound books, and other fragile originals. Specialist contractors must bring their equipment to the Library and digitize the physical artifacts under the watchful eyes of Library staff members.

Rights and restrictions: copyright issues are widely known, but other legal issues are also frequent and challenging in archival collections. In the case of a group of folk music recordings, for example, the team faced not only the question of identifying composers, but also accommodating the rights of the song collector and the folk performers. (This complex investigation is still under way.) Meanwhile, privacy and publicity rights emerged in the case of photographs. The pilot team has begun to establish procedures for cases like these, but many details remain unresolved.

Institutionalizing the effort: the American Memory pilot provided a model for digital access to historical collections. It also demonstrated that achieving this goal required the contribution of many Library units or, put another way, that the work of digitization must be dispersed broadly within the institution

Networking with other libraries: technical architecture and interoperability must be considered if libraries are to share and manage digital content. Decisions about the handling of digital objects, metadata, protocols, and other workable standards are critical to the success of networked digital libraries.

CONCLUSION

The Library's digital library program rests on a foundation that has been constructed carefully over the past seven years. The program rests on nine layers.

1. Support from the head of our organization, the Librarian of Congress;
2. Support from America's presidential administration and the U.S. Congress;
3. Collections of unique and important materials to digitize;
4. A successful pilot (American Memory) that demonstrated the value of the product;
5. A solid technology infrastructure that includes years of experience with MARC records, complex databases, and the American Memory pilot;
6. Talented and interested staff at all levels to act as agents of change;
7. A successful record of production under pressure;
8. A program of institutional fund-raising; and
9. Support from crucial constituencies, including end-users and technology labs.

This is our experience to date. We know we will be refining our program as we learn from those who have experience in the electronic world. We hope that our digital venture can serve as a stimulus and guide to other organizations beginning similar efforts.

We look forward to joining our efforts with many partners toward the end of providing to students, researchers, and citizens everywhere ready access to the core riches of the world's libraries. It is the collective vision of many that is creating just such an international shared database of history, culture, and change. This database will present the very real possibility of assembling a comprehensive picture of a global society from fragments of the past impossible to bring together before the digital era. The Library of Congress is grateful to be present at the creation of this electronic world. We at the Library of Congress are excited about the enormous opportunities and challenges that lie before us, and we pledge our continuing best efforts as we all move forward together to make our joint vision a reality.

CHAPTER 16

Toward Libraries' Digital Future:
The Canadian Digital Library Experience

LEIGH SWAIN AND SUSAN HAIGH

INTRODUCTION

There is not one single, "right" definition of what a digital library is, and likewise there is not one single, "right" approach to building a national digital library. In Canada, we are not now building a single, monolithic digital library or collection. Rather, in a typical, loosely federated Canadian fashion, a range of activities on several fronts has been under way. Taken together, these provide impetus, coordination, content, and infrastructure support to a national—or more accurately, nationwide—digital library effort.

THE ENVIRONMENT

The advent of the Internet, and in particular the World Wide Web, has affected the ways in which we expect to find information. In some disciplines, electronic resources have become information seekers' first and best choice, outstripping print resources in currency, availability, low cost, and plenitude. Increasingly, people seek to find the information they need instantly from their offices or home desktops.

In Canada, as in much of the world, libraries have been eager to establish an Internet presence, and many have developed their own Web sites. An increasing number are now ready, or have already begun, to mount some of their local resources for the benefit of their connected clientele and the broader Internet public.

Paper presented at the International Roundtable for Information and Library Science, Kanazawa Institute of Technology, Library Center, Kanazawa, Japan, 1998.

However, the Canadian context is not an easy one in which to sharpen diverse, homegrown energies into a cohesive, nationwide effort. One reason is our geography. With an area of almost 10 million square kilometers, we cannot easily travel by train or car to drive to a meeting in some central location. Our Trans-Canada Highway runs 7,604 kilometers from east to west, the longest national highway in the world. Domestic flights are also costly and even a plane trip from St. John's, Newfoundland, to Victoria, British Columbia, would take 10.5 hours of elapsed time.

We are also a relatively sparsely populated country, with 33.3 million residents in 1997. Canada's population density is three residents per square kilometer, as compared with 332 in Japan, 239 in the United Kingdom, or 28 in the United States. Because of the harsh northern climate and terrain, most of us reside within a few hundred kilometers of the southern border in a long, thin band stretching between the Atlantic and the Pacific and bordering (for 8,892 kilometers!) on the United States.

Culturally, Canadians are a linguistically and ethnically diverse people. In the 1996 census, 16.9 million cited English as a mother tongue, French accounted for 6.6 million, and the remaining 5 million or so cited a plethora of other languages. Canada is officially a bilingual country, meaning that all federal government services and publications must be available in both English and French. One province (New Brunswick) is also bilingual, and the rest are officially English except Quebec, whose government functions in French.

Politically, Canada is a federation of provinces, and governance is split between federal and provincial parliaments. In Canada, the responsibilities of the central, or federal, Parliament include national defense, interprovincial and international trade and commerce, immigration, the banking and monetary system, criminal law, and fisheries. The courts have also awarded to the federal Parliament such powers as aeronautics, shipping, railways, telecommunications, and atomic energy. The provincial legislatures are responsible for schooling and higher education, health, property, and civil rights, the administration of justice, natural resources within their borders, social security, and municipal institutions.

Responsibility for culture and heritage—libraries, archives museums, parks—is to some extent borne at both levels of government. There is no single, central institution (not the National Library, not a federal government ministry) that is mandated to undertake, oversee, or fund Canadian libraries as a whole. Public, school, academic, and provincial libraries are all overseen and funded at the provincial level, and the ten provinces and two territories that make up Canada each undertake this quite differently.

So what does all that mean for the development of a national digital library? It means, in a nutshell, that we have a lot of obstacles to overcome, and that we take a decentralized approach to overcoming them. I will talk about our approach more in a moment. Let's first step back and review the broader issues of digital library development.

THE ISSUES

Librarians, as information professionals, can list many reasons for concern about the new electronic information age. We recognize that much of the information on the Internet is not timely or reliable, nor, in many cases, is it easily found. We know that it can be difficult to separate the "wheat from the chaff"; that the search engines, while powerful, all have idiosyncrasies and limitations; and that result sets are often too large to be useful. On one hand, we worry that much good Web information is not being fully exploited and, on the other hand, that there is not yet as much good information as users require and expect. We are all too aware that there is a need for more organization of Web resources, for more rigorous description of resources, for more substantive content.

While we know that libraries in some sectors are being used more than ever, we can see a potential for libraries to be avoided or ignored. We might reassure ourselves that the Internet's resources cannot replace leisure reading of good books, but we also realize that the main business of libraries—organizing and storing information and helping clients to use it—is challenged.

The issues that libraries face in confronting the digital age have been widely documented and discussed within the community over the past few years. Some of the more enduring and confounding include the following.

1. *Definition.* In the information technology industry, a "digital library" could mean software repository or a particular set of hardware products. However, to most librarians it is likely to mean traditional library functions—acquiring, organizing, describing, preserving, and supporting use of information—applied to electronic resources. While this definition provides a useful framework, it begs a wealth of questions. How feasible or necessary is it to "acquire" digital resources in the traditional sense? Are there electronic services, products, or collections that go beyond the traditional and that might assure libraries' continued relevance? How can we best contribute to the organization of such a vast array of essentially unstable and widely distributed information resources? What new criteria are needed to clarify our access, organization, or preservation choices?

2. *Knowledge and skills.* Many librarians are excited by the possibilities of digital libraries. However, few can keep abreast of the broad issues and rapid developments in the digital information field. Gaining the necessary skills for library personnel is a transformative process, requiring time, money, and reconsideration of traditional hiring criteria.

3. *Rapid technological obsolescence.* Even libraries that are sufficiently "with it" to want to undertake ambitious digitization projects are worried

(with good reason) about the long-term viability of their choices of hardware, operating platforms, software applications, markup languages, and document formats.

4. *Standards.* Standards have been an area of much activity and—for standards—relatively rapid evolution in the digital library/Internet sphere. Constant and unpredictable technological change, coupled with a staggering number of new and proposed standards and an increase in the number of stakeholders in the standards and user communities have created something of a standards crisis in the informatics community. A recent glossary of digital library standards, protocols, and formats produced by the National Library of Canada listed more than 90 relevant standards, and the list was in no way comprehensive (Haigh 1998). Given the plethora of standards from which to choose, it is difficult to determine which are the "best."

5. *Costs.* There can be no doubt that digital library activities—whether resource digitization, data migration, Web site management, licensing, maintaining a sound technical infrastructure, or staff skills development—carry a high price tag. Cost recovery through charging is, in most cases, not an option, while measuring and defending a non-monetary return on investment, such as usage, can be difficult. Some libraries are able to shift a few resources from traditional to electronic functions but, so far, many have found no reduction in user demand for traditional materials or in the rate of print publishing.

6. *Ownership, custodianship, and preservation.* Intellectual property rights can impede or even nullify libraries' ability to transform print resources to electronic. Licensing access to remote or tangible (CD-ROM) electronic resources also transforms libraries' traditional custodial role from owning materials to owning equipment that offers access to materials, and the right to provide that access. Libraries are not necessarily prepared to undertake costly digital preservation activities such as conversion and migration if they only, in effect, rent the resource. How much information loss owing to technical obsolescence and resource obscurity is inevitable, how much is acceptable, and how much is preventable by libraries and archives?

7. *Connectivity and transmission issues.* Some libraries are confronting insupportable costs (e.g., long distance charges) for connectivity. The network backbone in Canada is strong, but "last mile" connections directly to the institution or home through service providers are lagging. Slow response time can affect users' willingness to find and exploit Web resources.

8. *User needs and capabilities.* Many digital library projects have been undertaken to increase user access to resources that were viewed by the library as potentially valuable—basically, a "build it and they will come" approach. Study is needed to better establish what Internet users most need

and want from digital libraries, and to augment what is already known in terms of Canadians' connectivity, technical configurations, and Web usage.

9. *Leadership and coordination.* Libraries tend to look for ways to share information or costs, which is one reason why there are numerous Canadian library associations and consortia. However, as other countries were setting up centralized, structured digital library programs, in Canada there was little overarching coordination to sharpen the focus and thrust of our digital library efforts.

CANADIAN INITIATIVE ON DIGITAL LIBRARIES

All these issues, together with Canada's unique geographic and political makeup, furnish the context in which, in 1997, it was decided to form the Canadian Initiative on Digital Libraries. This non-profit alliance aims to support communication and collaboration among Canadian libraries to meet the new challenges of the digital information age. The basic premise of the Initiative was that entering into the realm of digital libraries is fraught with challenges, and all libraries can benefit by sharing useful knowledge and experience as they become engaged in the field.

In Canada and internationally, many groups are active and projects are proceeding in diverse efforts to chip away at digital library questions and problems. There are some promising developments in several areas. For example, the Resource Description Framework, especially the Dublin Core metadata vocabulary, holds some promise in the area of resource description. Extensible Markup Language (XML) is emerging as a possible structured, encoding option that is "lighter" to implement than Standard Generalized Markup Language (SGML). Technologies are emerging to support user authentication and e-commerce. The implementation of a much faster, high-capacity network infrastructure with CA*Net 2, and the promise of a future Optical Internet will address congestion problems on the main Canadian network backbone.

The Canadian Initiative on Digital Libraries is not intended to find solutions to these problems. The Initiative will not be developing standards, administering license agreements, or carrying out digitization projects. Rather, the organization is intended to serve as a filter and a means of communication to encourage its members to adopt approaches that have been proven viable or are gaining momentum and support.

The Initiative has determined to focus on nurturing the development of a "national digital collection," that is, the sum of diverse projects to create Canadian content and exploit the resources found in Canadian libraries and related cultural institutions. One or more project frameworks will be proposed to libraries, museums, and archives in the hope that a cohesive collective effort will give a preliminary shape to the "national digital collection."

Since the approaching millennium is perceived as an incentive to effort, it is hoped that libraries will be encouraged to digitize local history resources that document their communities' cultural, economic, natural, and social history.

At this early stage, the Initiative's activities include the following:

- election of a steering committee and formation of three working groups to
- examine creation and production issues, including current digitization standards and best practices to optimize longevity and interoperability;
- address organizational and access issues, with a focus on metadata, user authentication, and rights management; and
- consider awareness, advocacy, and funding;
- a *Web site* describing the Initiative and providing an information resource of useful materials pertaining to digital library topics in a Canadian context. The Web site is found at http://www.nlc-bnc.ca/cidl/index.htm;
- a *discussion list* facilitating communication among members and from the committees and secretariat to members;
- the development of an *information kit* for Canadian libraries that will focus on awareness of the issues, advocacy needs, and potential funding sources for digital library activities. This will be followed by a second tool kit on digital project planning, standards and best practices;
- the formulation of communication strategies to increase awareness of issues and possible solutions, directed toward the alliance's members, the library community, elected officials, and other stakeholders and partners;
- *liaison with complementary organizations* within Canada and internationally.

The Canadian Initiative on Digital Libraries now has a membership of more than 50 Canadian libraries, including large and small institutions that belong to the academic, public, and special sectors. In the short term, the organization is concentrating on activities that will benefit both its members and the library community as a whole. By fostering a cost-efficient growth in digital activity in Canadian libraries, the Initiative will ensure that all Canadians are ultimately better served.

At the same time, there are many libraries engaged in individual or collaborative activities to contribute various forms of content toward our distributed digital library effort.

THE NATIONAL LIBRARY OF CANADA

The National Library is, as befits its mandate, contributing to the effort on a number of fronts. In fact, the National Library of Canada has recently articulated its vision for its digital library program:

The National Library will be a leader in digital library activities within country and will be the richest resource for Canadian information in electronic format now and in the future. To that end, the National Library will actively build its electronic collections and will vigorously promote a diverse digital program that will focus on Canadian information resources of lasting cultural and research value. The program will combine provision of full-texts of Canadian publications with provision of a variety of access tools enabling Canadians and others interested in Canada to find the information they seek.

The Library's large and ever-growing Web site (http://www.nlc-bnc.ca) showcases three forms of digital library content: a collection of Canadian published electronic resources, a set of resources that the Library itself has digitized, and a number of products that organize access to external Canadian information resources.

Electronic Collection

Since the summer of 1994, the National Library has been acquiring, cataloging, archiving, and making available on its Web site a selection of Canadian digital publications. The Library's Electronic Collection now consists of more than nine hundred titles—585 electronic monographs and 316 electronic serials—that are published in Canada or by Canadians. In developing this permanent national digital collection, we have wrestled with many of the fundamental digital library policy and practice issues in the areas of selection, management preservation, and access.

A few of the more relevant policies that we have developed to govern our national electronic collection include the following:

With respect to selection:

- The National Library operates on the basis that anything that is made available to the public on a communications network, such as the Internet, can be considered "published" for the purposes of collection.

- The National Library collects and preserves networked electronic publications according to assigned levels of collecting: archived, served, and linked. The level assigned is determined by the publication's significance in fulfilling the library's mandate and in supporting library services.

- The Library endeavors to collect comprehensively and archive indefinitely original Canadiana networked electronic publications of both Canadian and foreign origin.

- The National Library does not necessarily collect every version/edition or format of all networked electronic publications collected. The frequency of capture will vary from comprehensive to representative and will depend on factors such as publication pattern, scope of changes, and the overall significance of the publication. Priority is given to collecting standard format publications.

With respect to access:

- In principle, all networked electronic publications acquired by the National Library are accessible to both on-site and off-site users.
- The National Library accedes to restrictions on access to certain materials for a negotiated, limited period as required by publishers.
- Networked electronic publications are organized, indexed, and made accessible through the National Library Web service.
- Bibliographic access to networked electronic publications is generally provided through the AMICUS database and associated products. Cataloging levels applied are based on the same criteria as those for other formats.

With respect to preservation:

- The National Library preserves electronic publications electronically.
- The National Library endeavors to preserve both the content and the "look and feel" of all archived networked electronic publications, but when necessary, priority is given to the preservation of content.
- The National Library preserves networked electronic publications in non-standard formats through conversion to a standard format when necessary.

We are still engaged in policy formulation regarding this collection and are studying the need to purchase an electronic document management system to support effective management and access of the collection holdings and our other digital resources.

Digitization Projects

The National Library of Canada does not only collect the publications of others. We have also been creating resources ourselves. The Library has developed more than 30 digital resources of various types since the inception of our Web service in 1994. Early on, we established a policy of creating a virtual exhibit to showcase all physical exhibitions mounted at the Library. There are now some wonderful exhibitions on topics ranging from gardening to science fiction to children's literature illustration. There are also some rich resources for learning about Canada, such as a site featuring the Canadian North and another about Canadian Confederation.

We have a number of in-depth multimedia resources focusing on famous Canadian figures. We are particularly proud of the Glenn Gould Archive (http://www.gouldnlc-bnc.ca/). Along with a wealth of visual and documentary material from the Gould archival *fonds*, the site contains about 3.5 hours of digital audio (using the RealAudio data streaming protocol).

Also in the music sphere, we are about to launch a site of early Canadian 78-RPM recordings that will feature a comprehensive database and the equivalent of compact discs—roughly 340 minutes—of streamed audio of Canadian recorded music produced between 1900 and 1904.

Last, we furnish a range of research tools, such as searchable indexes, lists of Canadian newspapers, subject-specific research guides, and so on. We focus all our digitization efforts on Canadian themes, as befitting our "national" mandate. Our focus tends to be within specific thematic clusters that best support the National Library's mandate: Canadian literature, music in Canada, Canadian history and society, and support and promotion of National Library collections, services, and programs.

We have funded these projects in partnership with a federal program called SchoolNet Digital Collections (described later in this paper) or through a private sector funding partnership with Stentor, Canada's telecommunications companies' alliance. We expect that a growing part of the National Library of Canada's digital library initiatives will be undertaken through such partnerships.

Canadian Information by Subject and Other Resources

The Library has also been building sets of organized links to Canadian Web resources, such as a directory of Canadian libraries and their catalogues, a site dedicated to federal government information, and our flagship Web resources product: Canadian Information by Subject. As one way of imposing order on the vast array of Web resources that any country now has, we have undertaken to list substantive Canadian Web sites by a Dewey Decimal Classification subject arrangement. This product now lists more than 2,600 sites, and the site has proven to be increasingly popular as people begin to seek alternatives to the major Internet search engines.

Virtual Canadian Union Catalogue

The National Library has also been leading an initiative called the virtual Canadian union catalogue (vCuc). This is defined as a series of databases that are accessible via the Z39.50 protocol and the Internet. "Databases" may include existing union catalogs, the databases of individual libraries, or other types of databases such as full-text or government information locator systems. From a user perspective, the catalog can, potentially, be tailored to meet specific needs. For example, a library in western Canada may define its union catalog as the holdings records of other western libraries, the National Library, and the Canada Institute for Scientific and Technical Information (CISTI), while a library in one of the Atlantic provinces might define its union catalog differently. To prepare for such individualized needs and choices, vCuc participants must resolve the issues related to linking complex bibliographic databases. To achieve this goal, the National Library has been leading a controlled project to link databases by using the Z39.50 protocol to search and retrieve information. The objectives for this project are as follows:

- demonstrate the viability of the vCuc using geographically dispersed catalogs accessible via Z39.50 and the Internet;
- propose solutions to technical, service, and policy issues that must be resolved to ensure that Canadians continue to receive high-quality library services based on resource sharing; and
- investigate the costs and advantages of using the standard.

Policies and Standards

The National Library took the lead in identifying and following up on the need for a national body to strengthen Canadian digital library efforts, hence our intimate, ongoing involvement with the Canadian Initiative on Digital Libraries. Internally, we have recently revamped our committee structures to better focus, manage, and coordinate our digital library program. To this end, a strategy has been articulated that incorporates the Library's digital library vision, mentioned above, with tactical plans to accomplish our digital library objectives.

The Library was an early Canadian adopter of Internet technologies, and we continue to expend some effort in the analysis of new and emerging network standards and technologies. We participate in and provide expertise toward many international standards efforts including Z39.50, the Inter-library Loan (ILL) protocol, and metadata standards development.

One of the public fruits of our ongoing analysis of information technologies and standards is the Library's *Network Notes* series, a serial publication that digests a wide variety of digital library and network technology topics into short papers aimed at library professionals (http://www.nlc-bnc.ca/pubs/netnotes/netnotes.htm).

Technical Infrastructure

When the National Library started to look at mounting some of our in-house database resources on the Internet, it became evident that we lacked a scalable and appropriate technical infrastructure to support such projects. To begin to provide the technical infrastructure necessary to support the National Library's mandate in the electronic age, a Digital Library Infrastructure Plan was proposed and approved in follow-up to a Digital Library Needs Study. The Infrastructure Plan uses an incremental, "best of breed" approach, to establish a robust, flexible platform for digital library applications at the National Library of Canada.

The reasoning behind the plan was that an enhanced technical infrastructure would allow the National Library to keep pace with the general trend in libraries of integrating digital collections, systems, and services. With this enhanced technical infrastructure, the National Library will be better positioned to support its growing and evolving digital collections, systems, and services.

Phase One of the plan, now complete, improved the end-user content creation functionality. Additional activity in this area will be driven by the nature and priority of future digital library application development projects.

Phase Two of the Digital Library Infrastructure Plan has established key components of the technical infrastructure, that is, an extended RDBSIS (Oracle), a full-text search component (Oracle ConText), and an application development environment. In addition, it will establish functional requirements and an implementation approach for an electronic document management system.

Phase Three and beyond will look at the consideration and/or implementation of additional components of the technical infrastructure such as electronic document management, enhanced Web site management, storage management systems, additional specific server software, and end-user development tools.

One of our challenges is to marry, to optimal extent, our digital library infrastructure and products with that of our major bibliographic system, AMICUS. The Library has made its online catalog, a subset of the larger union catalog AMICUS database, available free of charge through a Web interface. We are currently engaged in a project to create a similar Web interface to the fee-based AMICUS Search Service. We have successfully mounted other Web products that draw on live AMICUS data such as a Canadian Interlibrary Loan Directory and a cataloging-in-publication product, *Forthcoming Books.*

Our information technology strategy is to ensure that all corporate bibliographic data are or can be incorporated into the AMICUS database. To keep our AMICUS and digital library architectures aligned, we will study the feasibility of moving the large-scale AMICUS database (more than 14 million records and growing rapidly) to the Oracle RDBMS and full-text search engine products in the future.

OTHER CANADIAN LIBRARIES' ACTIVITIES

As a precursor to the establishment of the Canadian Initiative on Digital Libraries, the National Library addressed a survey to about one hundred major Canadian libraries. Findings showed that 66 percent of respondents had engaged in digitization projects involving their print collections, 46 percent were collecting and storing locally digital resources produced by external bodies, and 80 percent were organizing links to external Web resources for the benefit of their clients. Naturally, a range of technologies is used to support these activities. Most libraries have not fully resolved the management and funding issues surrounding digital library resource development.

Much of the activity to that time had been exploratory—discussing issues, planning, and obtaining approvals and funding, and undertaking and evaluating pilot projects. The body of materials, especially of major Canadian research resources, in online digital form had not yet achieved "critical mass." However, there was clearly momentum and a high level of interest and commitment to continuing to build digital library resource collections.

In general, we also found that:

- *Public libraries* tended to be digitizing material of local history or interest. One, North York Public Library, was creating digital audio children's stories.
- *University libraries'* digitization projects tended to be based on special collections, such as the E. Pauline Johnson Archive at McMaster University and loyalist history manuscript materials at the University of New Brunswick; or are based within broad disciplines such as architecture, music, law, education, economics, or history.
- *Legislative libraries* had begun to digitize their province's legislation and sessional document.
- A couple of *provincial libraries* were digitizing their provincial and municipal government documents.
- *Special libraries'* efforts reflect their specialized audiences: for example, the library at the Atlantic Forest Service is digitizing in its areas of forestry, entomology, soil science, and related subjects

The following types of material were starting to be digitized. We hope the Canadian Initiative on Digital Libraries will play a role in encouraging and rationalizing such projects so that more libraries or more provinces come on board with comparable and interoperable projects.

1. *Early Canadiana online.* The Canadian Institute for Historical Microreproduction, in partnership with Laval University, University of Toronto, and the National Library of Canada, will be digitizing 5,000 pre-1900 Canadiana microform titles in the subject areas of native studies, Canadian women's history, and Canadian literature. The project will run from 1997 to 1999.

2. *Electronic theses.* An Electronic Text Center for commercial and public domain texts, using the SGML's Text Encoding Initiative Document Type Definition (TEI DTD), is operational at the University of New Brunswick and a similar center is planned at the University of Waterloo. Electronic theses are part of the plans for both, and the University of British Columbia also plans a project relating to theses.

3. *Archival finding aids*. The University of New Brunswick is planning to head up a project involving several Canadian university libraries and the National Library to encode literary finding aids according to SGML's Encoded Archival Description (EAD) DTD. The University of British Columbia is likewise looking at EAD to make its photographic collection findings aids available.

4. *Legal material* The Nova Scotia Legislative Library plans to digitize the statutes of Nova Scotia from 1758 to 1950, as well as the journals of the Nova Scotia House of Assembly.

5. *Newspapers and newspaper finding aids*. The Manitoba Legislative Library is considering digitizing the Manitoba Newspaper Checklist and the University of Saskatchewan plans to complete the Saskatchewan Newspaper Index. The University of New Brunswick's Electronic Text Center publishes the full text of one of that province's newspapers, the *Telegraph-Journal*. The National Library has produced a major searchable Web listing of its almost comprehensive collection of Canadian newspapers on microform.

6. *Government documents*. As one example, the Indian and Northern Affairs Canada Library plans to digitize white papers and royal commission reports on native affairs.

From this small list, it is clear that digital information resources are emerging from different disciplines and corresponding to a variety of different types of print publications. It is equally clear that Canada has a long way to go before it will have a significant corpus of digital information to constitute a national digital library in the broadest sense.

FEDERAL TASK FORCE ON DIGITIZATION

In April 1997, the federal government initiated a task force to identify issues and propose mechanisms to facilitate electronic access to its own vast stores of Canadian information content. Completing its work by December 1997, the Task Force outlined a vision that advancements in information technology are a means to enhance access to the federally held cultural, economic, and scientific collections, and information holdings. Its report stated:

By strengthening and building upon the existing federal legislative, policy, and operational framework, an enabling environment for expanding access to information in digital form will be possible. The objective is to provide a strategic framework to facilitate effective and efficient creation, development and distribution of, and access to, electronic federal information holdings, and collections. The recommendations promote the concept that the federal government should act as a *model user* and *catalyst* for the creation of, and provision of access to, Canadian content online and off-line.

The Task Force was co-chaired by the National Librarian of Canada, Marianne Scott. Its work was executed within five committees that each studied a specific issue:

- *Issue 1*: Accessibility of Digitized Content
- *Issue 2*: Selection of Materials for Digitization
- *Issue 3*: Common Issues of Intellectual Property
- *Issue 4*: Identification of Standards and Best Practices
- *Issue 5*: Funding Strategies for Digital Conversion

Some of the major recommendations of this Task Force have a broader applicability to improve the coordination and effectiveness of any large-scale digital content creation effort.

With respect to accessibility of digitized content:

- Rationalize information policies into one comprehensive framework.
- Identify and describe types of information, such as "essential," "key," and "customized" information, based on an access and remuneration continuum.
- Continue to publish "essential" and "key" information in conventional and alternative formats for the benefit of Canadians who do not have access to, and the knowledge to use, information technology.
- Seek partnerships with the private sector, where appropriate, to encourage the creation and provision of "key" and "customized" digital information that meets user needs.
- Provide, where appropriate, access points on the premises of federal institutions for citizens to obtain "essential" and "key" information.
- Pursue and enhance partnerships with non-federal organizations to create access points to federal digitized information throughout Canada.
- Promote government-wide initiatives that would identify, locate, and allow for a single-window access to federal information holdings in a digital format (e.g., Government Information Locator Service [GILS]).
- Study the needs of disadvantaged and special-needs segments of the population.
- Develop guidelines for providing digital information that has been adapted to suit different subsets of the intended audience (disadvantaged and special needs).
- Develop a system of authentication for digitized information to ensure that users are accessing authentic information.

With respect to selection of materials for digitization:

- Define the criteria for selection. Federal government policy recommended that the overall concept of "public good" be extended beyond the duty to inform (health, safety, security, consumer protection) to include additional criteria, such as: education and learning, shared national consciousness and informed citizenship, and economic growth and job creation.

- Review existing studies and sponsor additional research into the costs and benefits of providing information through digital means to the general population and target user groups.

- View digitization primarily as a dissemination initiative, rather than a preservation initiative. It was determined that the National Archives of Canada and the National Library of Canada should, according to their respective legislative mandates, continue to develop policies, procedures, and guidelines for the preservation of digital materials and make these available to other federal institutions.

With respect to common issues of intellectual property:

- Continue to resolve outstanding copyright issues related to the Information Highway in consultation with stakeholders.

With respect to standards and best practices:

- Establish a mechanism to facilitate the sharing of technical and product information and emerging technologies, and to assist in product evaluation, benchmarking, and procurement.

- Establish a mechanism to advise government on emerging standards and technologies in the areas of navigation and retrieval of networked information, including but not limited to metadata initiatives, locator naming systems, link maintenance, and retrieval technologies and services. In particular, the mechanism would identify best practices for metadata use, evaluate retrieval technologies as they evolve, and assist in the development of a scalable architecture for the effective retrieval of electronic information, both for government and general public use.

- Seek solutions or best practices to address the problem of the diversity of document formats across contributing agencies. This effort is necessary to ensure the interoperability and long-term preservation of documents. It should be directed toward providing guidance standards and best practices.

- Acquire and use standards-based digitization technologies wherever possible, and ensure that these acquisitions meet specific and well-defined user requirements, which should include interoperability with other government systems.

- Conduct research into preservation practices for digital information.

In the area of standards, in particular, the Federal Task Force on Digitization promulgated a radically different approach to the fast-evolving network context of standards than had been any organization's approach previously. No more would the government be expending enormous technical and human resources in developing and/or adopting standards and then finding applications for them, as we were seen to be doing in the 1980s era of Open Systems Interconnection (OSI).

To promote economies and efficiencies in the global information infrastructure, information technology standards must be based on a strong international consensus and market acceptance. Such global standards increase application interoperability, support the development of cost-effective technical solutions, promote quality of service, and support cultural diversity. The challenge of developing global standards is to provide these benefits in a timely and efficient manner and to build upon existing efforts to develop national and regional information infrastructures. The Task Force acknowledged that the existing organizations and established processes used to develop standards are now being recognized as too slow to be effective. New processes and organizations, mostly within the Internet community and through industry consortia, are providing the framework for developing new networking and digitization standards.

It is clear that the private sector will be largely responsible for the development and deployment of the infrastructure for the Information Highway. It follows that the sector will be the leader in ensuring that the infrastructure is interoperable. The Task Force therefore recommended that appropriate standards be employed expressly and primarily to further organizational goals and to encourage interoperability across government, and between government and the public. The goal of interoperability, it was noted, is more than a standards issue: it is a challenge of communication, organizational coordination, and of understanding user needs.

NETWORK INFRASTRUCTURE AND PROJECT FUNDING SUPPORT

The government of Canada is investing heavily in the development of an information infrastructure for the twenty-first century, with the explicit goal of making Canada the most connected nation in the world by the year 2000.

CANARIE and CA*Net 2

The Canadian Network for the Advancement of Industry and Education (or "CANARIE") was created in 1993 to speed the emergence of Canada's information revolution. CANARIE is an industry-led, not-for-profit consortium with significant support from Industry Canada and some 140 member companies, universities, and organizations in the public and private sectors.

CANARIE's two main program components are: Advanced Networks, which supports the upgrade of CA*Net, Canada's commercial Internet; and Technology and Applications Development, which supports research projects that lead to advanced networking products and applications for the marketplace:

In June 1997, CANARIE launched the CA*Net 2 network. CA*Net 2 is the first "next-generation" national network backbone in the world, and it is intended to support advanced multimedia applications not possible on current networks. This network currently links only the regional research network hubs based at a dozen Canadian universities or research centers.

A new investment of $55 million in the 1998 budget is being provided to CANARIE to build the next-generation Internet (CA*Net 3), the world's first all-optical, broadband network.

This initiative will: (1) equip Canada with a coast-to-coast, high-performance network that is faster than its American counterpart; (2) ensure that Canadian universities have access to the high-speed capacity that they need for collaborative research; (3) provide Canadians with the broadband platform needed to deliver cutting-edge learning and multimedia applications; and (4) make Canada an attractive location for developing next-generation applications in tele-learning and electronic commerce.

Industry Canada's Access Programs

As announced in the 1998 budget, the government will invest $205 million over three years to several programs that aim to ensure that Canadians will benefit from opportunities made possible by today's computer-driven knowledge economy.

The *Community Access Program (CAP)* was developed to help communities in Canada's rural and remote settings obtain affordable public access to the Internet and the skills to use it effectively. Access to the Information Highway will help create new and exciting opportunities for growth and jobs by providing these communities with the ability to communicate with each other, conduct business, enhance job skills, and exchange information and ideas. The Community Access Program will create an additional 5,000 Internet access sites in urban neighborhoods across Canada. Along with the 5,000 rural access sites currently being established, the number of community access sites across Canada will total 10,000, by the year 2000.

Another program, *SchoolNet*, is working with the provinces, learning institutions, and the private sector to:

- connect all Canadian schools to the Internet by the middle of 1999;
- begin to extend broadband connectivity from the school into every classroom;
- support classroom learning projects and online learning products and services that help students to acquire new skills, and teachers and courseware producers to develop new media materials; and
- challenge, through the Computers for Schools program, Canadian businesses and governments to provide 250,000 used or refurbished computers for use in classrooms across the country and enable every young Canadian to experience the full benefit of information technologies for learning.

By the end of the 1998–1999 fiscal year, all of Canada's 16,500 schools will be connected to the Internet. Today, 70 percent of schools have been connected.

VolNet is a recently announced program that will provide Internet access to the thousands of volunteer organizations across the country.

Last, under a program called *LibraryNet*, the government is progressing toward its goal to have all 3,400 Canadian public libraries connected to the Internet by the year 2000. To date, more than half the libraries have been connected.

The results of these programs indicate that we have, in fact, made great strides toward the government's goal of connecting all Canadians by the year 2000.

SchoolNet Digital Collections Program

One program within the broader SchoolNet program marries in an innovative way the goals of youth employment and digital content creation. The program awards contracts to Canadian businesses, cultural institutions, and other organizations to hire young people (ages 15 to 30) to create original Web sites based on significant Canadian material.

There have now been some 230 digital projects completed in all provinces and territories. The collections they have produced range from digital versions of Attestation Papers (enlistment papers) of Canadian Expeditionary Force recruits in the First World War to Canadian Arctic Profiles, a Web site that demonstrates how to minimize environmental damage while navigating Arctic waters.

SchoolNet Virtuoso Electronic Scholarly Publishing Project

As part of its SchoolNet project, Industry Canada has supported research and demonstration projects in online publishing, and has actively promoted Internet-based scholarship within the Canadian academic community. Most recently, SchoolNet has brought together a number of non-profit publishers eager to engage in mutually supportive research and development work exploiting the potential and meeting the challenges of online scholarly publishing. The central purpose of what has been called the "Virtuoso" Group is to develop a sustainable, scholar-centered model of scholarly publishing for the next millennium. A draft background paper on the initiative is being revised and will be forwarded shortly.

"Virtuoso" currently consists of three university presses, a research library, a federal scientific publisher, and a national scholarly association; membership is expected to grow. Each member will be responsible for a major area of research (e.g., archiving, copyright, production, subscription management), and will share the knowledge developed with all other members. There has been one meeting of the group thus far, and another is planned for later this month. SchoolNet is providing interim secretariat assistance.

The "Virtuoso" group recognizes that its members alone cannot provide all of the support necessary to reach its goals, and is currently exploring governance and fund-raising options. It is estimated that $2–3 million would be needed over three years to establish a state-of-the-art, online publication capability. Following that investment, subscription and licensing revenues would sustain operations.

CONCLUSION

We have outlined many initiatives and accomplishments that present an overview of the Canadian approach, and our progress in the development of a national digital information collection or library.

Canada is well advanced in terms of connectivity, and we are proud of the progress we have made in ensuring that the information wealth of the Internet is accessible to all Canadians. The Canadian library community and its partners in government and industry have put in place the building blocks for a coordinated, robust program of digital content creation, preservation, and accessibility. The activities outlined in this paper document that Canada has made a strong beginning toward establishing a substantial body of national digital information resources through an effective, decentralized approach.

REFERENCE

Haigh, Susan. 1998. A Glossary of Digital Library Standards, Protocols and Formats. *Network Notes*, no. 54 (May). Available from http://www.nlc-bnc.ca/pubs/netnotes/notes54.htm.

CHAPTER 17

The Future of Libraries and Library Schools

DANIEL E. ATKINS

THE "CRISIS"

Libraries, archives, and museums are centuries-old institutions committed to physical, intellectual, and long-term access to the artifacts of human endeavor. Degree programs in library science or library studies are more recent inventions of the late nineteenth century, intended to establish librarianship and related archival practice as recognized professions.

Library schools have traditionally prepared graduates for practice in one of four types of libraries: academic, public, school (K–12), or special (e.g., legal, medical, corporate). Some include additional specialization in archives and records management. They prepare people primarily for practice in place-centered libraries of physical objects with rather well-defined organizations, procedures, and customers. They also impart a value system emphasizing service and open and broad access to information for all segments of society.

Beginning in the early 1980s, library education, and, later, libraries, began confronting enormous challenges brought about by the historically instantaneous shift from analog and physical representation of information to increasingly digital and essentially massless representations. The effects of rapid technological change are compounded by a complex array of cultural, economic, demographic, cultural, and legal forces on libraries, library schools, and higher education in general.

It is estimated that more than 90 percent of all new data and information originate in digital form: print-on-paper originates in word processors; pro-

Paper presented at the International Roundtable for Information and Library Science, Kanazawa Institute of Technology, Library Center, Kanazawa, Japan, 1995.

fessional audio is fully digital, and widespread digital video is on the way. Digital information, physically represented by electrons, photons, or magnetic fields, has vastly different properties than information stored on stone, papyrus, paper, or film. Digital information can be moved at nearly the speed of light; it can be stored at atomic scales of density; it can be copied perfectly over and over; and it has the property of "digital coherence."

Digital coherence refers to the fact that traditionally separate media such as text, image, audio, video, citations, and algorithmic information can now all be included in the same "compound document." As we can already see in the crude beginnings of the World Wide Web, we are inventing new genres—new, socially agreed-upon ways to create, disseminate, preserve, and use data-information-knowledge. These new types of documents may contain dynamic objects such as audio, video, or real-time data display, and therefore have no full representation on paper. We are already well into the world of hybrid information—the coexistence of print-on-paper and digital information resources to meet human needs.

As some library schools have died, nearly died, or been forced into marriages of convenience over the past decade, the phrase "crisis in library education" is often heard. Similar phrases are starting to be heard from the library world as public libraries are closed or voted down on requests for new funds, academic libraries are reeling against skyrocketing journal costs, the Library of Congress loses appropriations, and a few mega-companies seem to be amassing control of huge collections of digital content as well as the computer network-based distribution channels. Analogies are being made between libraries and centralized, time-shared computing centers that have been overtaken by distributed, networked computing. Libraries, like computing centers, must move to more distributed but interlinked organizations if they are to remain viable.

What is the future of libraries and library education in the digital age?

THE OPPORTUNITY

To answer this question, we need first to remember that the word *crisis* has its origin in the Greek word meaning *decision*. Similarly, the Chinese representation of the concept of crisis is a composite of two characters: the top one meaning *danger* and the other meaning *opportunity*. Libraries and library schools are at a critical point where they must make bold decisions; they must identify and clearly articulate their opportunities for the future and set out aggressively to seize them. There is grave danger in inaction—in business as usual—and huge opportunity for those with the will and the means to seize it.

Libraries and library schools first need to engage in strategic visioning and planning activities designed to explore a full range of options about how to respond to the huge vector of social and technology forces imping-

Figure 17.1
A Vision Space for New Knowledge and Work Environments

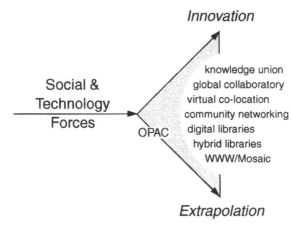

ing on them. They need to define and explore a "vision space." A vision space, as illustrated in Figure 17.1, is defined on the lower side by extrapolation, using technology to do what libraries are doing now, although perhaps faster, cheaper, and better. The upper boundary is the path of innovation—doing new things new ways. The introduction of the online "card" catalog is a beneficial example of extrapolation. Next steps include enriching the catalog with live links to bitmapped facsimiles of printed pages.

Extrapolation is good, but not enough in periods of high rates of change. Those who will lead into the future must stretch higher into the vision space to become hybrid libraries, important nodes of digital library federations, the hubs of community networks, providers of virtual co-location knowledge work environments (collaboratories), and knowledge unions for academia. They need to evolve to new organizational forms that are being enabled by anytime, any-place information, the reduction of barriers of time, and both geographical and organizational distance.

We cannot now fully define this future; we even have problems with what to call it, but we are sure that profound change is under way. The World Wide Web is simultaneously amazing and crude. We are at the horseless carriage stage of creating new knowledge work environments that meet real needs of real people and organizations. Libraries, as traditional centers for knowledge work, have the right, even the responsibility to lead far up into the vision space.

Similarly, library schools have many opportunities to reinvent themselves in broader, multidisciplinary ways. There is intellectual and professional turf to be seized. There are many new needs for future-oriented professional education that are not being addressed by computer science, business information management programs, and information and library studies programs.

THE MICHIGAN RESPONSE: A NEW SCHOOL

Formal education in librarianship at the University of Michigan began about 1926 with the creation of the Department of Library Science under the leadership of Director of Libraries William Warner Bishop. Dr. Bishop was motivated by enlightened self-interest to professionalize librarianship both here and elsewhere. Natural growth and demand for graduates led to the next step in the late 1960s. After a blue ribbon outside review in 1969, the department became the School of Library Science with Russell Bidlack as the first dean.

In 1986, as part of a national trend to examine library education, the faculty acknowledged a broader field of endeavor for the school by voting to change the name to the School of Information and Library Studies (SILS). Other similar schools also adopted broader names, some dropping explicit reference to *library* during this time.

In 1992, President James Duderstadt and Provost Gilbert Whitaker, of the University of Michigan, decided that SILS should take an even bigger step. They offered the school the opportunity to move boldly to educate information professionals for leadership in the new age of knowledge. They perceived both great challenges and opportunities as we move into an era in which quality of life is increasingly dependent upon knowledge, and digital technology is radically changing how this knowledge is created, disseminated, used, and preserved. Although the need for timely access to knowledge and information has never been greater, the institutions, systems, and processes by which humans will meet these needs are rapidly changing. We were given, therefore, the dual challenge to not only re-invent ILS education, but also to help re-invent libraries.

We have subsequently chosen a broader goal—to create a new school to educate professionals who can create and mange knowledge work environments including, but not limited to, what we now think of as libraries. Endurance and vitality for the school of the future requires expansion in size, breadth, synthetic activity, and time horizons for research.

Professional Education

Fortunately, the W. K. Kellogg Foundation also concluded that it must invest in creating new "human resources for information systems management" (HRISM). It decided that SILS would be its flagship for doing so and awarded us a $4.3 million, five-year grant. The Kellogg Foundation has made a series of grants to libraries, schools, and other organizations to pursue, simultaneously, the following coordinated goals: (1) re-inventing both pre-degree and continuing professional education; (2) defining the new services and environments in which professional practice takes place; and (3) strengthening the impact of the library traditions and perspective on inventing the digital information access environments of the future. Kellogg is also encouraging us to pursue very bold change and leadership.

The Kellogg Initiative at Michigan is called the Coalition on Reinventing Information Science, Technology and Library Education (CRISTAL-ED). We aspire to educate a professional with broad competency and a holistic view of information and collaboration ("knowledge work") systems. To accomplish this, the Kellogg CRISTAL-ED project has the following objectives:

- Re-invent the core curriculum;
- Define new specializations;
- Create a distributed community of faculty and practitioners (a collaboratory) to deliver the new professional education;
- Build "living" laboratories in information-intensive organizations to serve citizens, faculty, and students. These pilot projects will provide realistic learning experiences for students, faculty, and practitioners, and will provide the basis for larger-scale digital libraries and collaboration systems.

CRISTAL-ED is investigating both new content and form through greater use of experiential and distance-independent learning formats. A comprehensive and timely Web site about CRISTAL-ED is available at www.siumich.edu/cristaled/. It also includes access to a moderated listserv on the future of ILS education involving hundreds of participants worldwide.

Related Examples of Research

During the past three years, the federal government, industry, and private foundations have also initiated research and development activities aimed at advancing knowledge about how to create and manage digital library systems and services. This has provided significant leverage on the Kellogg investment, particularly toward the goal of defining new services and strengthening the impact of the library and library education world on inventing the future.

A multidisciplinary team of "new school faculty" with roots in SILS, computer science, psychology, economics, and the university libraries won a $4-million award through the Digital Library Initiative funded by the National Science Foundation (NSF), the Advanced Projects Research Agency (ARPA), and the National Aeronautics and Space Administration (NASA). An additional $4.5 million is being provided through industrial contributions and cost-sharing. This project is creating an architecture and working prototype intended to broker access among millions of digital collections, services, and people in ways that are easy, relevant, and timely for humans to use. The testbed is focusing on collections in the areas of earth and space science and supporting users in public libraries, universities, and high school science education.

This work is being further leveraged by grants from other sponsors. The Andrew W. Mellon Foundation is funding the addition of the complete collections of major scholarly journals in the humanities and social science to the collection, under a project called JSTOR (Journal Storage Project).

The U.S. Department of Education is supporting the creation of a prototype of a database of art and architectural images with new interfaces that interleave keyword searching and rapid browsing. Other digital library services are also available through a collaboration between the university libraries, the Information Technology Division, and SILS. Information is available from www.lib.umich.edu/.

CRISTAL-ED is also supporting projects to discover new services and professional education requirements. These include projects to empower public libraries in the Flint, Michigan, area to become the hub of the community information network. CRISTAL-ED also provides partial support for the widely used Internet Public Library, which arose from a recent class project in a master's-level program at SILS. The Cultural Heritage Initiative for Community Outreach Project (CHICO), also supported by the CRISTAL-ED, is creating partnerships between SILS, colleagues in the arts and humanities at the University of Michigan, and local museums and schools to create pilot projects to increase and enhance accessibility to cultural heritage materials. Timely and extensive details on all these projects are available through the SILS Web site, www.sils.umich.edu/.

The Collaboratory

As potentially exciting and useful as they may be, the hybrid library, the digital library, and community information systems are but part of a bigger possibility. One view of the value-adding services we may create on top of distributed, multimedia computing is described by the term "collaboratory"—a term coined at a 1986 invitational workshop sponsored by the National Science Foundation.[1] The basic functions of the collaboratory are shown in Figure 17.2. This concept has been influential in our view of opportunities for the future and led, in part, to the formation of the Collaboratory for Research on Electronic Work (CREW). CREW is a joint activity between SILS, Engineering Business Administration, and the College of Literature, Arts and Sciences.

The focus of CREW is research on the design of organization forms and the technologies of voice, data, and video communication that make them

Figure 17.2
The Collaboratory Concept

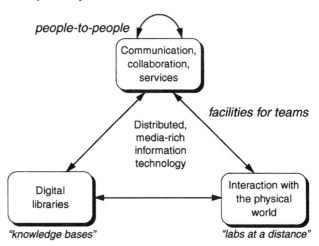

possible. Research on how technologies enable new ways of organizing work is of vital interest to organizations, both as providers and users. CREW has performed large-scale field studies of how people work with technologies in both academic and business environments. CREW is now being intellectually assimilated into the new school and the formation of new professional tracks for students.

Among the projects under way at CREW is the Upper Atmospheric Research Collaboratory (UARC), a joint venture of researchers in upper atmospheric and space physics, computer science, and behavioral science. The UARC project has developed an international networked collaboration laboratory (a collaboratory) in which computing and communication technology are combined to allow geographically distributed scientists to work together. This distributed community of domain scientists has network access to a remote instrument site in Kangerlussuaq, Greenland. In addition to scientific research, communication and collaboration patterns of the scientists are being studied.

A similar collaboration, between the primary health care physicians and health care specialists, is developing a testbed that will support collaboration in using medical images for diagnosis. Other projects are exploring the application of *virtual co-location* technology to support automotive design teams globally, and the feasibility of a global collaboratory to support research in human virology.

The Future

Historically, SILS has educated professionals with American Library Association (ALA) accreditation for practice in libraries: academic, public, school (K–12), or specialized. We will continue to do this at a high level of excellence with special emphasis on leadership for change. We aspire to educate professionals who can lead the changes that libraries of all types must make to continue valuable and appreciated services in the world of hybrid information (print-on-paper and digital multimedia). We need professionals who can not only practice in existing library and information environments, but who can also design, build, and manage new digital library systems and services from a strongly human-centered perspective.

We need professionals who will lead academic libraries into the role of information collectors, preservers, brokers, and publishers in the age of digital library federations; who will lead public libraries into the center of community information networks; who will lead school media centers to become knowledge networks to support learners; and who will lead special libraries into environments of collaboration to serve specific communities of practice.

SILS is and will remain firmly committed to educating people who aspire to continue the traditions and values of librarianship, including service to the information "have nots," in the context of both new and older technologies. We feel however, that it is time to do this as part of an even bigger agenda—as part of a new, larger, and more diverse multidisciplinary school.

We are convinced that there is now the need for an augmented set of professional programs to educate students to create and operate a broad set of "knowledge work environment," including, but not limited to, what we know as libraries. We need people with broad holistic education in technology, behavioral and social sciences; with grounding in specific application domains, and visceral commitment to meeting real human needs. We need librarians but we also need, for example, experts in human computer interaction; in computer-supported cooperative work; in information technology and organizational design; in digital archiving and records management; in the design and production of new information goods; in intellectual property issues; in information economics; and in the architecture of digital libraries, collaboration (collaboratory) environments, and electronic commerce.

We have adopted the "Borromean rings" as a symbol for the unique, multidisciplinary synergy we are hoping to achieve. The symbol is three symmetric, interlocking rings, no two of which are interlinked and in which removing one destroys the synergy. We are now in the process of building such a new school and are considering a new, more encompassing name for it. The faculty and student body are growing in size and intellectual breadth; the research climate is emphasizing larger-scale, multidisciplinary experimental work; the students are doing more hands-on, team projects. All of them will soon have a practical internship experience as part of their educational experience.

SILS at the University of Michigan has evolved over 70 years and must continue to boldly change into a new, broader school if it is to stay the same—a vital and relevant learning environment committed to meeting the real needs of real people in society. We welcome your questions, critique, and participation, whether you want to help create the "new school" here or at your institution, employ our graduates, collaborate on research, or all of the above.

NOTE

1. The report from this workshop, along with three scenarios about the use of the collaboratory in supporting team science, are contained in *National Collaboratories: Applying Information Technology for Scientific Research* (NCR Committee on a National Collaboratory and NRC Telecommunications and Computer Science Board. 1993. Washington, D.C.: National Academies Press).

CHAPTER 18

Redefining the University through Educational and Information Technologies: North Carolina State University, Its Libraries, and Distance Education

SUSAN K. NUTTER

More than one hundred years ago, a hot debate was waged in the state of North Carolina over a proposed college focused on agriculture and the mechanic arts that would complement the existing, public-university education at the University of North Carolina (at Chapel Hill) in classics, law, and medicine. The vision of the upstart proponents was for a school with a more democratic mission that would promote the liberal and practical education of the industrial classes of the state. In 1887, despite opposition from some conservative educators, legislators, and alumni of the existing university, the legislative body of the state approved the founding of the second public university in the state, now known as North Carolina State University, where men, and, since the 1920s, women, could go to study agriculture and engineering in addition to the classics.

Today, the reach of the institution is being debated again. The hot issue now is to what degree NCSU's education should be extended beyond its campus. Long a leader in distance education as well as in technology, the university is exploring its readiness to enter the distance education market in a more meaningful and large-scale way. While distance education has held a position of respect in the university for most of the twentieth century, advances in computing and networking offer the potential to catapult the concept in reach, scope, quality, and, perhaps, quantity of programming.

A confluence of factors has contributed and led to the current, intense debate:

1. The legislative body of the state is encouraging the expanded use of

Paper presented at the International Roundtable for Information and Library Science, Kanazawa Institute of Technology, Library Center, Kanazawa, Japan, 1997.

distance education technologies. In 1993, the legislature, concerned about educational access for adults living in remote regions of the state, called upon the governing body of the University of North Carolina system, of which NCSU is a part, to develop a plan "focusing on the availability of opportunities in underserved areas by means other than the establishment of additional degree programs." The expanded use of distance learning technologies was encouraged, as was avoidance of program duplication among campuses.

2. The university system is facing a projected increase of 30,000 students in the next decade, an increase of almost 25 percent. Not wanting to expand the size or number of the system campuses, state legislators have asked the university system to investigate whether distance education can reduce the need for physical plant expansions.

3. Demand is very high in the state for distance education programs. A needs assessment conducted by the university system in fall 1996 found the following:

- The demand for distance education is expected to increase. The survey results suggest that more than three-quarters of a million North Carolinians who are eligible, but not currently enrolled, are interested in taking courses toward a baccalaureate or master's degree program. Interestingly, more than a half million of them would prefer to take courses through distance education technologies rather than at a central location.

- Most of those interested and eligible have access to a variety of telecommunications delivery systems for the purpose of taking courses. Sixty-nine percent have access to a computer, 45 percent to the Internet, and 11 percent to a satellite dish. Ninety-seven percent have access to a VCR, 98 percent to public television, and 83 percent to cable television.

- About 70 percent want to advance professionally, and their interests are primarily in business, health, education, engineering, and engineering technology (UNC 1996).

4. State funding for distance learning has been promised for the first time in the university's history. The university system has proposed in its budget request for the next biennium that state funding comparable to that provided for on-campus instruction be provided for distance learning instruction. At present and historically, off-campus instruction, whether delivered on-site or by distance learning technologies, does not receive and has never received state-appropriated support. Off-campus courses and programs must be completely receipt-supported, which means that students must pay the full cost of instruction. To keep costs down, each institution is required to set its charges at a level sufficient only to cover direct instructional costs. The result is that any indirect costs, such as information technologies infrastructure, student support services, or the library, are not supported and,

consequently, sometimes not provided. This has greatly limited the scope and size of the university's distance education programming in the past, particularly in terms of adding degree programs as industry has urged us. The prospect of full funding is dramatically changing the climate for distance education.

5. Industry is driving demand upward. There is increasing demand for the types of distance education that NCSU is uniquely qualified to develop and offer. In a field such as engineering, where the demands of the job change rapidly as technology advances, the industry requires state-of-the-art skills, and the practitioners are required to keep pace. In an institution such as ours, which has a long and successful history both of delivering distance education to business and industry, and of partnering in research programs with business and industry, industry needs are compelling.

6. Competition is another compelling factor. Traditional institutions such as NCSU have begun to feel the pressure from online universities that are peddling courses through World Wide Web sites. There are several non–North Carolina institutions, such as the University of Phoenix, Liberty University, National Universities Degree Consortium, and JEC College Connection, offering courses and degree programs to North Carolinians (NCSU 1997: 8). To remain competitive—online, as well as on-campus—NCSU and others must examine their roles and are likely to consider changes.

7. Government—federal and state—support for higher education is declining, both financially and politically, and there is no interest in supporting increased capacity. More than 60 percent of all high school graduates in the United States now go on to some form of post-secondary education, and many state officials see that rate as sufficient or even too high. American higher education is perceived as a mature industry, no longer as a growth industry, and government priorities are, accordingly, changing away from it. Even in states like North Carolina, which expect substantial growth in enrollment during the next decade, universities must find ways to present education more efficiently at lower costs per student than in the past (Levine 1997: A48).

8. NCSU is extremely well positioned to dominate in the growing distance education market. It has become clear that the competitive advantage in the distance education market will belong to providers that effectively use emerging technologies. Success will belong to those providers—whether universities, community colleges, or businesses—that facilitate the fusion of work and learning for employees and that innovate with emerging technologies to provide faster, more effective access to knowledge. NCSU is the primary university in the state providing distance education to the business community and its employees. Recognized nationally as a leader in computing and networking, the campus is currently two to four years ahead of any other higher education institution in the state. Further, NCSU is a charter member of Internet2, a national consortium of universities in part-

nership with government agencies and with corporations from the computing, communications, and information industries, whose mission is to accelerate the next stage of Internet development in academia. Many administrators and some faculty are urging the university to make the most of this strategic advantage now.

9. Successful pilot projects using these new technologies have captured the enthusiasm of students and the imagination of administrators and some faculty. Within the last year, the College of Engineering has begun pilot projects in distance education to develop a scalable, low-cost "virtual classroom" model for distance learning, which makes best use of existing and emerging technologies. To "broadcast" live, real-time NCSU classroom courses to students at remote sites, the project uses the Internet Multicast Backbone (Mbone), that is, video over the Internet, desktop computers, Internet multimedia standards, and the World Wide Web, to support traditional modes of student-teacher interaction, and to allow for sparse distribution of students. The evaluation results of the first year are in, and they are very promising. The enthusiasm of both students and faculty regarding the use of emerging technologies has been widely reported, and has increased interest in distance learning.

10. The application of these emerging information technologies to instruction, in general, is blurring the lines between on-campus and off-campus teaching. Instructional technologies are changing the way we teach, learn, and discover. More and more of our courses are being taught, at least in part, over the Internet. This suggests the potential for making these courses available both on-campus and off-campus without the steep upfront costs of developing distance education courses and enrollment. The research and technical nature of our institution insists that we must not only embrace these changes but that we must lead the way for others.

Now, before I describe our current distance education program and where it is headed in its use of technology, let me put it in context by telling you a little bit about North Carolina State University and its libraries.

The university is fortunate in its geographic location in Raleigh, the capital city, in the east-central part of the state in an area known as the Research Triangle. This region of North Carolina encompasses one of the nation's premier concentrations of academic, corporate, and public research. More than 37,000 people work for the 131 research organizations located there. Within a 15-minute drive of the Park there are three doctoral research universities jointly educating more than 64,500 students: Duke University, the University of North Carolina at Chapel Hill, and NCSU.

NCSU is more than one hundred years old. It was founded on March 7, 1887, by the North Carolina General Assembly under the provisions of the federal Land-Grant College Act of 1882. It was designated the institution in North Carolina whose focus would be "agriculture and mechanic art . . . in order to promote the liberal and practical education of the industrial classes in the several pursuits and professions of life" (Eddy 1958: 1). Its founders sought a "people's college" that would make higher education more widely available to citizens of North Carolina. Also central to its mission was the commitment to making contributions to the state's economic development.

NCSU is now the largest university in the state and one of the largest universities in the Southeast. It has a student body of undergraduate, graduate, and lifelong education students approaching 27,500; a faculty of more than 2,800; an annual budget of more than $640 million; and a research budget exceeding $300 million. It offers baccalaureate degrees in 89 fields, master's degrees in 80 fields, and doctoral degrees in 53 fields. Students come from all 50 states and from 97 other countries. It ranks among the country's top 10 land-grant universities, without medical schools.

The university is one of 16 constituent universities of the University of North Carolina system (UNC system), and one of two research institutions in the system. The UNC system enrolls 138,000 full-time-equivalent (FTE) students (or 154,000 students by head count). The system is governed by the UNC Board of Governors and administered by a president. The chief executive officer of each university is the chancellor.

NCSU is a magnet for business and industry, and ranks seventh nationally in research support from private industry and ninth in the number of patents awarded. Seventeen of the 48 research centers on campus are university-industry partnerships made up of some 251 company members. Three of the country's 41 Industry-University Cooperative Research Centers established by the National Science Foundation are located on the campus of NCSU. The Industrial Extension Service, including the library's Technical Information Center, helps more than 36,000 firms and individuals annually.

The NCSU Libraries system consists of a central library and branch libraries for design, natural resources, textiles, and veterinary medicine. With a staff of three hundred FTEs and a total annual budget in excess of $17 million, the system has more than 2.5 million volumes and more than 4,000 electronic resources in its collection; has a collections budget of more than $7 million; subscribes to more than 22,000 current serials; and adds more than 90,000 volumes annually. Because of a dramatic budget increase of 36 percent in 1996/1997, the library has significantly increased its collections and services, including 24-hour access and services, and aggressively expanded its digital library initiatives.

Although the NCSU Libraries system primarily serves the needs of NCSU's faculty, students, and staff, it also serves the needs of clients from business, industry, extension, and other academic institutions from across the state.

The NCSU Libraries is a member of the Association of Research Libraries (ARL) and ranks 56th among the 109 university research libraries in North

America. The library has assumed a leadership role in researching and applying new information technologies to improve information access for users. In 1994, it was selected as one of six "Research Libraries of the Future" by its peer institutions in the ARL for its work with the World Wide Web and its support for scholarly electronic publishing.

One of the founding principles of NCSU is the belief that education should be offered statewide, beyond the walls and boundaries of its campus. Distance education at NCSU dates to the early 1900s. It began in earnest to fulfill its distance education mission when the Department of Agricultural Extension was established in 1909 "to bridge the gap between the college and the rural citizens" of the state. "Farm schools" and clubs were established in different locations to serve the practical needs of North Carolina's agricultural families.

By the mid-1920s, the university was offering correspondence courses and off-campus credit courses across the state. Substantial course selections were offered in a wide range of disciplines. NCSU was the only college in the world that offered textiles correspondence courses. Many of the courses were taught by the most distinguished faculty. Up until the early 1960s, enrollments remained strong and reached more than 2,500 students annually. However, the introduction of the Community College System to the state, which would eventually assure that there was a state-supported institution of higher education within commuting distance of all of North Carolina's residents, drastically reduced the demand for these courses.

The university has offered off-campus credit courses, as it has correspondence courses, for more than seven decades. Between 1950 and 1970 these ranged from baccalaureate degree–granting "branch campuses," accommodating several thousand students, and at which commuting faculty taught; to professional development programs taught out of state; to master's degree programs taught at several sites across the state; to bachelor's and master's degree programs taught "in-plant" for employees at North Carolina companies.

For a time in the 1950s, the university ventured into the area of electronic delivery and supplemented some of its correspondence courses with televised lectures. Although this first experience in educational television was relatively short-lived, by the 1970s, televised instruction using videocassette technology greatly helped the university respond to persistent demands from North Carolina businesses and industries, especially those in textiles and engineering, for on-site education for their employees. In addition, the College of Engineering expanded its delivery mechanisms to include ITFS (Instructional Television Fixed Service) and NC-REN, the North Carolina Research and Education Network, which operates three analog video and audio channels used for face-to-face communications.

The College of Engineering became a charter member of the National Technological University (NTU) and, through that organization, began offering videotaped courses, transmitted via satellite, at industrial sites throughout the United States.

In the spring of 1987, the College of Humanities and Social Sciences began offering courses by cable television. Building on the success of this program, in 1990 the university established the Office of Instructional Telecommunications (OIT) and charged it to develop this program further. OIT now offers courses from most NCSU colleges through its "Courses via Cable and Video" program.[1]

These historical programs and their strengths of delivery have led to the current environment where virtually all ten of NCSU's colleges are involved in some mode of distance education, and current enrollment remains strong. NCSU is first among colleges and universities in the state in distance education market share, and its College of Engineering leads with 45 percent of NCSU distance enrollment.

Today, NCSU offers distance education credit courses and degree programs to more than 3,000 people throughout North Carolina; in almost every state in the country; as well as in more than fifteen countries, including Japan. I should note that these 3,000 students are not included in the enrollment data of the nearly 27,500 undergraduate, graduate, and lifelong education students on the Raleigh campus, since their education is not supported by state funding. Various modes of delivery and communication are employed, including off-campus sites, independent study, and telecommunications. NCSU is in the vanguard of schools that deliver distance education through telecommunications. These include videocassettes, open broadcast, closed circuit, ITFS, cable television, microwave, satellite, video and audio, the Internet, video over-the-Internet, and computer-based technologies, including the World Wide Web.

NCSU has invested heavily in developing the infrastructure for instructional technology as well. Nearly 75 percent of all classrooms and 50 percent of dormitory rooms are wired for data and video, and the rest will be wired by 1998. All faculty and students have access to the Internet from the university. An estimated 50 percent of all on-campus classes require the use of computers for homework or class projects. Ten to 15 percent of the faculty use multimedia technologies in their classrooms (NCSU 1997). The campus network is a switched FDDI backbone, with an experimental ATM backbone in place, with well over 12,000 nodes. An FDDI concentrator directly on that backbone connects library servers to the outside world. The library network backbone is a redundant, switched, fiber-based Fast Ethernet with switched Ethernet or Fast Ethernet to every workstation with a total of more than 2,500 nodes.

Arguably, the dominant characteristic of the distance education program, both historically and currently, is its focus on programming for business and industry, and their employees. This makes sense for an institution with such strong partnership ties and relationships with business, industry, and state government, and whose mission statement expresses a commitment to making contributions to the economic development of the state.

Distance education at NCSU has a range of objectives. One objective is to provide NCSU's credit courses to non-traditional students, including working adults, evening degree students, and lifelong education students. The program known as "Courses by Cable and Video" works especially well for those students who ordinarily would not be able to enroll in classes because of schedule, distance, location, or time limitations. Instruction consists of regularly scheduled NCSU courses, taken by regularly enrolled students, broadcast by cable television or available by videocassette.

Another objective is to respond to business and industry's need to provide professional development and degree programs on-site for their engineering, computing, science, and management professionals. The long-term strategy of business and industry is to retain valuable employees in whom they have already made a significant investment. As I briefly describe four examples of these on-site programs, you will note that the newer programs are distinguished by the fact that they are delivered entirely by technology:

1. For the past nine years, NCSU has offered courses leading to a bachelor's degree in business management to working adults who are employees of the IBM facility at Research Triangle Park. Courses are taught on-site at IBM by NCSU faculty and consist of sections of regular NCSU courses that are also taught on the Raleigh campus.

2. For a number of years, Northern Telecom (now known as NORTEL) has contracted with NCSU for a program leading to the Certificate in Computer Programming. Faculty from the Department of Computer Sciences provide courses on-site at the company.

3. With sponsorship from the U.S. Environmental Protection Agency, the university is the home of the Air Pollution Distance Learning Network (APDLN), which is a satellite-based video-training network. This program is exploring the use of the World Wide Web for delivery of course materials, and several of the training programs have been broadcast worldwide using the Mbone technology on the Internet.

4. In 1995, a distance education program leading to the Bachelor of Science in Engineering, with emphasis in Nuclear Engineering, was established with sponsorship from Carolina Power and Light, Incorporated (CP&L), one of the two major utility companies in the state. This is a joint program with three community colleges, two in North Carolina and one in South Carolina. Instruction is live at one plant site and is beamed to two other plants over CP&L's corporately owned microwave network.

A third and more recent objective of our distance programs is to provide undergraduate and graduate degrees to students who live a significant distance from the Raleigh campus and for whom a four-year residency is not possible.

In these cases, NCSU is uniquely able to provide the degree in a particular discipline. Most often the university works with another UNC campus or with a community college in coordinating these programs. They are distinguished by having NCSU-appointed program directors at each campus site. Significant resources are invested at each site, including renovation of facilities; upgrading of teleclass, computing, and laboratory equipment; network upgrades; and acquisition of library materials. I'll describe a few of these programs:

- As part of the new, engineering "two plus two" (2+2) program, NCSU offers the first two years of study toward an engineering bachelor's degree at the University of North Carolina at Asheville. Students can take courses approved for transfer to NCSU while in residence at Asheville and then complete their degrees while in residence for two years in Raleigh. The mission of this new program is to provide a measure of engineering education to the population of western North Carolina, the most remote region of the state in relationship to the NCSU campus. Lectures are delivered live via the NC-REN video network, and advanced computer technology, including the Internet and desktop conferencing, are used to facilitate faculty-student communication. The success of this engineering 2+2 program has led to the development of two additional programs, both of which will be delivered using advanced information technologies.

- A Master of Engineering degree, with a concentration in Industrial Engineering, is offered in the western part of the state. The courses originate at NCSU and are taped and shown in the evening at UNC-Asheville.

- As a result of a recommendation from a chamber of commerce in the western part of the state, and based on a needs assessment, the university is developing a pilot program that will lead to a distance Bachelor of Science in Engineering degree program. The student group that is the main target audience is full-time employees of manufacturing industries in western North Carolina. The proposed program will have an emphasis on mechatronics, a combination of mechanical and electrical engineering, and will be delivered using advanced technologies.

- NCSU offers instruction leading to a doctorate in Adult and Community College Education to one cohort of students in western North Carolina. Regular members of the NCSU faculty teach the courses in this program, either by interactive audio-video hookup between the Raleigh campus and UNC-Asheville, or in person on the campus there.

Yet another, and final, objective of NCSU's distance education programs is to provide graduate and professional instruction to individuals who need to enhance their credentials without the constraints of on-campus attendance. In the fields of textiles and engineering, these programs provide for direct interaction between faculty and industry, and enable industries to bring their employees and managers in touch with the newest developments in technology and the applied sciences. All instruction in these programs is offered by regular members of the NCSU faculty, who videotape their current-semester classroom lectures presented on the Raleigh campus for distribution. There are three major programs.

1. The Video-Based Engineering Education program (VBEE), initiated in 1977, is the flagship of the distance education programs in engineering. VBEE offers a number of courses for professional advancement leading to a master's degree in general engineering through telecommunications at various sites, both inside North Carolina and out of state, as well as worldwide. Significant resources have been invested this year to expand the graduate course offerings because of high demand for the VBEE program. VBEE currently enrolls seven hundred course registrants annually—the highest enrollment in any of the distance programs.

2. Since 1976, NCSU's internationally acclaimed TOTE Program (Textile Off-Campus Televised Education) has been providing courses for professional development in textiles as well as master's degrees without a residency requirement. The program offers both undergraduate and graduate instruction leading to post-baccalaureate certificates in seven areas, and master's degrees in textiles and in textile chemistry at remote sites in and out of state, and worldwide.

3. NCSU is a charter member of the National Technological University and, with 46 other universities, broadcasts via satellite graduate courses for professional development leading to a Master of Engineering degree throughout North America.

Special funding from the state legislature is mandating an increase in distance-based offerings of engineering courses. The goal is to provide excellent engineering courses throughout the state without the cost of establishing full-blown engineering programs at almost every UNC system campus. Sites likely to increase their offerings include four-year campuses with 2+2 programs or four-year and community college campuses with pre-engineering programs. An Internet-based technology is the likely delivery mechanism. This program may be extended so that it can provide a distance Bachelor of Science in Engineering statewide.[2]

In all of these distance courses and programs, one-on-one interactions between faculty and students are valued. NCSU has gone to great lengths in designing and administering its programs to provide personal interactions and to ensure that there is no difference in quality between on-campus and distance programs. Further instruction is offered through periodic on-site visits by faculty and exchange by means of e-mail, fax, telephone, teleconference, or meetings. On-campus meetings are welcome and, in some cases, may be required for examinations or laboratory exercises. Textbooks and other classroom materials are available for students by mail through the NCSU bookstore.

Courses and programs are evaluated regularly by the departments and colleges that offer them, with excellence in teaching as the most important goal. NCSU's evaluation results reveal what countless evaluations and studies of distance learning have revealed: distance learning students perform as well or better than their counterparts in traditional, face-to-face instruction settings on the Raleigh campus. There is no significant difference, and there is no significant difference related to method of delivery (Russell 1997).

Until recently, responsibility for provision of library resources and services was distributed and lay with an array of program administrators and faculty and not with the NCSU Libraries. As a result, and due also to the lack of state funding for distance education and distance students' lack of Internet access, I think the library services program of the past could be described as fairly passive and entirely manual.

Students who lived in the Raleigh area and who had registered in telecourses for credit were provided library privileges upon enrollment. Students who registered for off-campus courses or programs were provided with course materials and library resources through mailings from Raleigh, through cooperative arrangements with other UNC libraries or other institutional libraries near them, or, for professional degree programs, through arrangements with companies for whom they work.

However, all students did not always have access to needed library resources. Distance courses could be "taken" anywhere in the world, in Europe, Asia, and South America, where physical access to NCSU's resources was limited or difficult. Although NCSU does limit enrollment to students who have access to resources needed for successful completion of degree work, it was reluctant to do so in the case of library resources, since such courses are intended primarily for professional development by people already in careers, who may find appropriate resources in their workplaces. The rationale was and is that the occasional student in a remote spot should not be denied access to distance learning just because the university cannot provide the student with direct physical access to a library comparable to the NCSU library. In spite of the problems involved in getting access to library materials, people in remote sites may find that instruction delivered electronically is the only viable way to advance their education or enhance their professional credentials.

Those of us in the library feel that we can make dramatic improvements in the provision of library resources through the use of information technologies (and, of course, with state funding for distance services), and are in the process of introducing a much more aggressive program, which includes the following services:

• A free phone number and fax number for library services is issued to every student who registers for a distance course, to provide for on-demand requests.

• A "Federal Express" model of delivery to distance learners speeds library materials to the distance learners wherever in the world they are. We loan them any books they request and send photocopies of any articles they need at no cost to them. Return mailing is free. Turn-around time between request and delivery is between two and three days.

- A library Web site for distance learners will be introduced this fall semester and will provide access to all library resources, basic policies, library staff, electronic reference service via e-mail, course reserves, links to other campuses' libraries, and so on. The Web site will incorporate "CU-See ME" interactive videoconferencing so that distance students may reach and see the reference desk and speak directly with a librarian. The fact that our library now has more than 1,500 full-text, online journals and more than 4,000 online databases should make a significant difference in our ability to provide resources to distance students directly and immediately.

- We plan to negotiate with our sister UNC libraries so that we can all offer direct-to-end-user interlibrary loan from any of our 16 libraries. The current arrangement takes weeks to months. For example, a student requests from us an item in UNC-Chapel Hill's collection. We ask to borrow it from them, they send it to us, and we then send it to the student. The new service will allow the student to request it directly from UNC-Chapel Hill and receive it within a few days.

- An electronic reserves system will be introduced this fall for distance learners. Distance course reserve materials will be scanned and placed on reserve electronically and made available via the Internet.

- All of the library's teaching facilities, auditoriums, and conference rooms are being upgraded for satellite (uplink and downlink), broadcasting, the Internet Multicast Backbone, and videoconferencing so that distance students may take advantage of our teaching and training programs.

- NC LIVE—a North Carolina Electronic Library—will debut in early 1998 and will provide a core of full-text journals, a database aggregator such as OCLC's First Search, and major research and reference materials to libraries across the state. The NCSU Libraries system has been instrumental in developing this project and seeking state funding for it. The libraries of the 16 UNC campuses, of the 58 community colleges, of the 37 private colleges and universities, and all of the public libraries in the state are participating. Any distance learner in the state without a computer simply has to go to the nearest public or academic library to have access to these resources.

NCSU is well positioned to respond to significantly increasing demand and expand both its market and market share. The university already possesses the four essential components—faculty, programs, technology, and library resources—needed to expand and broaden its distance programs quickly.

However, the lack of state funding for distance education has inhibited our assuming this leadership. Despite unusual and distinguished success, historically and recently, NCSU's distance program has not reached its full potential and has, arguably, had to be relegated to secondary status within the university's mission. Because of lack of funding to support the steep, up-front costs of developing new distance programs and degrees, the program has not expanded as it could have. It has remained focused in engineering and textiles; the number and range of degree programs have remained fairly constant despite growing demands for more; and very large-scale implementation of the use of new information technologies has not been possible.

The prospect of a new climate of support for distance education—especially in terms of full funding—has led the university to focus its broad strategic planning efforts over the past year on instructional technology and distance education. Because industry and business have always been key drivers and the major customers of the distance education program, and because they will bear the major responsibility for the kind of education necessary for economic competitiveness in the twenty-first century, the university turned to these communities, through its Board of Visitors, for advice. The Board of Visitors advises the chancellor on broad strategic issues facing the university; it is made up of business and industry leaders from across the state, as well as of higher education leaders from across the country. A committee of the Board was asked to examine developments in instructional technology and distance education, and to evaluate their impact on the university. Committee members spent almost six months studying the issue, including intensive reading; interviewing program administrators, key faculty, and students; and sitting in on distance education courses—both on-site and electronically.

The report that the committee submitted in March of 1997 was insightful, directive, clear, and precise in directions recommended; compelling in its lack of ambiguity; and courageous in its rejection of the current mantra that instructional technology and distance education are economical panaceas for the challenges facing higher education. As a result, the report has been accepted enthusiastically and adopted as a philosophical framework for future directions in instructional technology and distance education. Let me review for you some of the key recommendations.

First, the report supports NCSU's commitment to developing instructional technology for both on-campus and off-campus learners. Further, it affirms that distance education is a natural part of NCSU's land-grant mission to extend access to its programs and services across the state. But the overarching theme of the report is that, as instructional technologies and distance programs based on them are developed, we must ensure that the human dimension of the educational experience is enhanced, not lost. This theme is reflected throughout the following additional recommendations:

- NCSU should strive to utilize technology that enhances human interaction by promoting collaboration, collegiality, and increased one-on-one exchanges between faculty and students.

- The use of sophisticated technology, on- and off-campus, should be viewed as not only central to NCSU's mission but also essential to maintaining its leadership. Innovations and investments in technology-based programs and services should remain a high priority for the institution in all aspects of its mission.

- In developing distance education programs, care should be taken not to threaten NCSU's goodwill, accreditation, or the public's perception of its quality. Further, the university should not undermine the quality of its on-campus programs or erode its investment in its physical plant.

- Consideration should be given to developing a wide range of distance education programs and services. In addition to existing programs, careful thought should be given to executive education programs, to extension and technical assistance programs, to non-credit professional development programs, and to unbundling degree programs into certificate programs or alternative, credit-bearing learning modules.

- The university should review current policies addressing intellectual property and modify or extend them to ensure that the rights and opportunities of its creators and the institution are protected. Further, NCSU should play a leadership role in resolving questions of national policy related to ownership and fair use of intellectual property and copyright.

- The UNC system should take the position and lobby the state legislature that funding must reflect the true capital costs related to distance education. Only in theory are there no capital costs associated with expanding enrollment through distance education. Costs include depreciation of equipment and any plant improvements required to provide student support services and to administer the programs (NCSU 1997a).

Encouraged by this thoughtful and bold report, the university has moved aggressively to respond both by advancing the development of instructional technology-based courses for on- and off-campus learners and by doing so in a manner that ensures the kind of quality and human interaction envisioned by Board members.

A project has been launched to place 25 existing, on-campus courses on the Internet for fall semester 1997. The purpose of "Project 25," as it is now known, is to demonstrate the degree to which the institution is ready to enter the distance education market on the Internet in a meaningful way, pending appropriate funding, while providing support and encouragement for enhancements important to resident instruction. Twenty-eight courses have been selected out of 66, submitted through an interactive and online proposal process that was targeted to faculty who have been using multimedia in instruction. Faculty participating will receive a salary supplement and funding for operational support, which includes teaching assistants, graders, software, minor equipment, and so on.

Project 25 has among its objectives the following:

1. To provide access to approximately 25 courses in a way in which the student may substitute regular lecture attendance for interaction with course materials

presented by the teacher in the World Wide Web. Emphasis will be placed on asynchronous modes, not because there are not synchronous approaches that will work on the Internet, but because capabilities for asynchronous participation are more nearly ubiquitous among those who are users of the Internet.

2. To build upon and foster further development of faculty and staff expertise in developing online course presentations and providing the necessary guidance to students and evaluation of their performance.

3. To gain experience and information for developing the necessary infrastructure and policy changes needed to mount broader delivery of courses and, in the future, programs via the Internet to students, both on- and off-campus.

4. To support active collaboration among faculty and support staff involved in the project, especially on methods of presentation, consultation, testing, and assessment. This will be done through the Educational Technologies Interest Group, a group of more than one hundred NCSU faculty and professional staff who are working on technology enhancements to the education processes.

Because we believe that the success of Project 25 will depend, in large part, on the effectiveness of the support provided to faculty as they transform existing courses through instructional technologies, the library is taking the lead in enhancing the infrastructure and professional support base for faculty engaged in online and multimedia course development. We have already added to the staff permanent positions devoted to educational technologies and multimedia support, and we have established liaisons with related centers of expertise across campus. This spring we put in place, with Information Technology, a *Learning Technologies Center* to provide campus leadership and serve as the focal point for the growing array of educational technology activities and interests. Space for the Learning Technologies Center has been provided in an area of the library that was recently dedicated to supporting learning and research in the digital age. It will benefit from its proximity to an array of related faculty support endeavors also being established and located in the library.

The center will be organized, staffed, and equipped to provide faculty with expert assistance and team-based support in many areas, including instructional design, content enhancement, tools and techniques of production, network delivery, and assessment of learning outcomes. Service will be available with or without an appointment. We are supporting all learning styles and providing consultations in the Center, in the faculty members' offices, or on the Internet. We are offering training sessions in both large and small groups, as well as in a one-on-one setting. In addition, assistance is available over the phone, by e-mail, and over the Internet. Initial staffing will consist of three librarians, two Information Technology staff, and an instructional design professional. Our longer-term goal, based on anticipated demand, is a staff of about 12.

The Learning Technologies Center will:

• Support faculty development of online and multimedia course materials;

• Develop a training program focusing on educational technologies, complemented by individual assistance and support;

• Provide an evaluation and demonstration space, with multi-platform computers, multimedia equipment, software, product literature, and videoconference and projection capabilities;

• Sponsor workshops, seminars, videoconferences, and other events;

• Offer support for distance education courses and projects;

• Act as a campus clearinghouse for current information and expertise on all aspects of educational technologies, including instructional design, computer and software tools, and multimedia production capabilities; and

• Assemble models and resources for assessment of learning experiences and outcomes.

On a larger scale, the NCSU Libraries system is taking the lead in supporting faculty development of instructional technology for both on-campus and off-campus learners. Through a major reallocation of space and resources, it is creating a *Learning and Research Center for the Digital Age* on a 20,000-square-foot, central floor of the main library building. The Center will comprise a state-of-the-art collection of faculty support endeavors that will include a center dedicated to teaching enhancement; a center focused on scholarly communication with an emphasis on intellectual property; the Learning Technologies Center already described; a scanning and digitization laboratory; an information technologies teaching center; a library department for digital library initiatives; and a range of conference and meeting rooms and conversational spaces. By locating these types of services together, we are making available to NCSU faculty and students a range of user assistance and technical expertise in a central campus location with convenient and long hours and professional staffing.

One of the most important elements of this Center is a faculty-driven center for teaching effectiveness and enhancement. Faculty engaged in the Center's recent development sought out the library location because they believe that the library is the most important element in the academic support of faculty. It is initially envisioned that the *NCSU Faculty Center for Teaching and Learning* will promote a culture that values and rewards teaching excellence and enhanced student learning by promoting faculty growth and development in knowledge, techniques, and skills related to teaching and learning. It will provide consultations with individual faculty and teaching assistants on such issues as teaching techniques and learning styles, course and curriculum development, developing teaching technologies, distance education and continuing education activities, formative evaluation of teaching, and the use of teaching portfolios.

The newly established *Scholarly Communication Center* (SCC) is intended to guide both the Libraries and NCSU's faculty and students in matters relating to the dissemination and use of knowledge, particularly in the emerging digital-publishing environment. The SCC will take leadership in safeguarding the role of research libraries in the scholarly communication process as well as those of the creators, disseminators, and users of scholarly information, including promotion of their full rights, under the fair use section of the copyright law. The librarian-lawyer directing the center will offer guidance on university policy in matters such as copyright and fair use, ownership of intellectual property, database licensing, and user privacy issues, and will help faculty make informed decisions relating to copyright and fair use that affect their work, research, and teaching.

The need for the SCC is particularly acute in the digital-publishing environment, where potential changes in U.S. and international legislation may have serious consequences for libraries, universities, and their faculties; as the Libraries system expands its scope to new areas such as an electronic reserves system, exploration of the electronic submission of theses and dissertations, and distance learning issues; and as faculty and students become active "publishers" on the World Wide Web.

The *Information Technologies Teaching Center* (ITTC), a joint project of the Libraries and Information Technology, provides state-of-the-art computing, teaching facilities to help students and faculty learn to use the technical tools available for accessing and managing the enormous amount of information resources available electronically. It includes separate teaching laboratories for each of the principal desktop computing platforms in use at NCSU—DOS/Windows, UNIX, and Macintosh—as well as an instructional center for multimedia teaching tools and techniques.

In the ITTC, faculty, students, and staff are trained in all aspects of information technologies as they relate to the new digital environment. These areas include information access and retrieval; Internet and Web navigation; Web design and electronic text reformatting; Internet course development; scanning and digitization; and instruction in the latest software, hardware, and communications technologies. The skills developed by NCSU faculty and students will be of long-term benefit in helping them to learn new forms of technology and to access a growing information base.

The *Scanning and Digitization Laboratory* is conceived of as a state-of-the-art facility for both production of service and instructional programs such as electronic reserves, faculty Web sites, digitization of unique NCSU collections, and so on; and as a laboratory for research, experimentation, and collaborative projects with faculty and with other libraries and universities.

The goal of the 13-person *Department of Digital Library Initiatives* is to integrate library and Internet resources to create a versatile, unified system, providing an enormous variety of materials in different formats and media so that data, texts, images, video, audio, and other forms of information can be easily accessed by students and faculty alike, and readily manipulated in new ways. The department is staffed by librarians with expertise in development of digital initiatives for client services, cataloging, multimedia, information technology, Web development, and learning technologies. The department is responsible for leading the library in creating advanced World Wide Web–based services, digital collections, new digital services such as electronic reserves and collaborative information laboratories, technologies and programs to integrate digital collections and services in teaching and learning, and emerging, network-based multimedia resources and services.

I cannot begin to describe how excited many of the faculty, library staff, and academic administrators are about the concept of the *Learning and Research Center for the Digital Age*. The excitement is palpable and extends to the architectural team that has designed the new spaces. It is impossible to predict specific outcomes from this new approach to library support for faculty and students, but we do expect that the synergism that we know will be at play will help us to further develop the model for the academic and research librarian and library for the next decade.

We also expect that its impact on the transformed, on-campus and distance education programs will be significant. Many of us at NCSU believe that, strengthened through technology, our on-campus programs will continue to provide students with a foundation for successful careers and satisfying lives. In addition, and through instructional technologies, NCSU, with its mission to serve working adults and others without easy access, can extend its reach farther and with greater effectiveness. Learners formerly constrained by schedules or location can participate in education without always having to interact with faculty in real time or face-to-face. In both cases, the key to success will be effective deployment of technology.

We are in the midst of a culture change, and NCSU is committed to embracing that change and leading the way in the implementation and use of instructional technologies. NCSU's programs will be distinguished from those of other institutions because they will reflect the importance of promoting and enhancing human interactions through technology; not using it as a cost-saving substitute for exchanges between faculty and students. By fostering this preferred use of technology, we will be differentiated from those institutions that fail to do so.

NOTES

1. This historical perspective on distance education programs was derived from the Distance Education Task Force (1995) and Cudd (1996).

2. Description and characteristics of current distance education programs were derived from North Carolina State University (1994), Gilligan (1996), Masnari

(1997), and interviews with NCSU administrators John F. Cudd, Jr., Director of Adult Credit Programs and Summer Sessions; Dr. Thomas K. Miller III, Assistant Dean for Information Technology and Computer Service, College of Engineering; Thomas L. Russell, Director of Instructional Telecommunications; and Dr. Williams E. Willis, Vice Provost for Information Technology.

REFERENCES

Cudd, John F., Jr. 1996. *Distance Education: An Historical Perspective for NC State.* Remarks prepared for the NCSU Chancellor's Retreat, June 26–27.

Distance Education Task Force. 1995. *Reaching the Last Mile: Distance Education at North Carolina State University.* Report of the Distance Education Task Force. Raleigh: North Carolina State University.

Eddy, Edward D. 1958. *The Land-Grant Movement: A Capsule History of the Educational Revolution Which Established Colleges for All the People.* Washington, D.C.: American Association of Land-Grant Colleges and State Universities.

Gilligan, John D. 1996. *College of Engineering, Distance Education.* Remarks prepared for the NCSU Chancellor's Retreat, June 26–27.

Levine, Arthur. 1997. Point of View: Higher Education's New Status as a Mature Industry. *The Chronicle of Higher Education* (January 31): A48.

Masnari, Nino. 1997. *College of Engineering—Priorities for 1996–97.* Report prepared for NCSU Administrative Council, May 28.

North Carolina State University (NCSU). 1994. *North Carolina State University: On the Threshold of a New Century.* Institutional Self-Study Report. Raleigh: North Carolina State University.

———. 1997a. Board of Visitors. Institutional Direction Committee. *Redefining the University through Educational Technology.* Raleigh: North Carolina State University (March 20).

———. 1997b. University Planning and Analysis. *Instructional Technology and Distance Education at NC State.* Raleigh: North Carolina State University.

Russell, Thomas L. 1997. *The "No Significant Difference" Phenomenon as Reported in 248 Research Reports, Summaries, and Papers.* 4th ed. Raleigh: North Carolina State University.

The University of North Carolina (UNC). 1996. Board of Governors. *A Plan for Continued and Expanded Availability of Higher Education in North Carolina.* Final Report. Chapel Hill: The University of North Carolina Board of Governors.

CHAPTER 19

Re-engineering the Undergraduate Curriculum

JACK M. WILSON

From 1993 to the present, Rensselaer Polytechnic Institute has introduced a new model for the undergraduate courses with large enrollment that has become known as the Studio Model. The Comprehensive Unified Physics Learning Environment (CUPLE) Physics Studio, Studio Calculus, and the Laboratory Introduction to Embedded Control (LITEC) were the first courses created, and the model has since been adapted to Chemistry and Computer Science. Plans for future courses span the undergraduate curriculum. This paper will devote most consideration to the Studio Physics and Studio Calculus courses as examples of how the studio model has been (and can be) applied to a variety of courses. Although the discussion will center on mathematics, science, and engineering courses, much of what will be discussed can be addressed to any large lecture courses, including those in the humanities.

The CUPLE Physics Studio is a natural outgrowth of the work of the CUPLE collaboration that was formed in 1989 to develop tools and approaches for innovative undergraduate physics courses and the program at Rensselaer to re-engineer the undergraduate science curriculum for all students. The Studio uses the CUPLE software system in a "theater in the round" classroom that encourages extensive interaction among students and between students, faculty, graduate student assistants, and undergraduate student assistants. Cooperative learning techniques are designed into the structure and content. During the fall 1994 semester, the CUPLE Physics Studio was expanded to full deployment in all Physics I sections and

Paper presented at the International Roundtable for Information and Library Science, Kanazawa Institute of Technology, Library Center, Kanazawa, Japan, 1994.

Physics III sections. There was a one-section pilot deployment in Physics II.

The Studio Calculus program grew out of the Maple Calculus Course, which was first introduced in 1989. Professor Joseph Ecker led the re-engineering program, which combined the studio model with the heavy use of symbolic mathematics introduced by the Maple Calculus program. The classroom model is similar to that described for Physics and relies on group activities known as "Take Time to Think" (T4) and "Paper and Pencil" (p2) sessions.

The courses are particularly designed to meet the needs of the large, research-oriented universities. The traditional large lecture format is replaced by a studio approach that is not only economically competitive but often less expensive. The courses are highly structured and are not self-paced. They use very advanced function computing technology, including computer-based video and video data acquisition, microcomputer-based laboratories, and powerful data analysis and visualization tools. Research faculty who have taught in the pilot courses report that it is a friendly environment in which to teach and reminds them far more of an undergraduate research setting than it does of the large enrollment lecture classes. A faculty member assisted by a graduate student and one or more undergraduates work together in a setting that encourages natural mentoring of the undergraduate and graduate students and promotes a team-oriented approach. The team teaching also allows flexibility to accommodate travel and research schedules that often hamper the teaching programs while putting the introductory students into close personal contact with the faculty and more experienced students.

To some extent, the studio format is designed to transfer some responsibility from the faculty to the student. The focus is on student problem solving and projects and not on presentation of materials. The emphasis is on learning rather than teaching.

RATIONALE FOR CHANGE

The introductory science courses at many of our large universities around the world can be an intimidating experience for the new student. It is not only the difficulty of the material, but also the experience of sitting in the large, non-interactive lectures with a lecturer who is mathematically unapproachable even when personally approachable. Shiela Tobias, in *They're not Dumb, They're Different!* (1990), provides one of the best chronicles of student reactions in the introductory course. This format of large lecture, smaller recitation, and separate laboratory continues to be the dominant method of instruction at larger universities. The recitations are often taught by mixtures of teaching assistants and faculty, with that mix varying widely from university to university. In spite of the uneven quality found in recitations, it is likely that most learning takes place in the recitation and problem sessions. The laboratories are a more dismal case. Taught by teaching assistants with minimal or almost no training, the laboratories are universally panned by the students. Because of this perception of low quality and the resources required to run laboratories, several of the larger universities have abandoned them altogether.

Recognizing the shortcomings of this system, faculty and staff at the major universities have devoted extraordinary attention to the improvement of this system. Each meeting of disciplinary societies such as the American Association of Physics Teachers (AAPT), American Chemical Society (ACS), or Mathematical Association of America (MAA) is filled with ideas for how to improve the lecture. One recurring theme is the use of lecture demonstrations that range from the spectacular to the humorous. Faculty, students, and even the public love and remember the best demonstrations and the best demonstrators. The United States National Science Foundation was even headed by a consummate Chemistry Demonstrator (Bassam Shakhashiri) whose career was best known for his popular lectures. Over the years, we have turned to audio, video, and now computers to make the lectures more interesting and more instructive. Unfortunately, later interviews with the students often reveal that the memory of the demonstration is often not accompanied by an understanding of the physics of that demonstration.

Many efforts to improve the introductory course work come from an assumption that there are "good lecturers" and "bad lecturers," and that students can learn more from the "good lecturers." The strategy then is to improve the "bad" or replace it with the "good." Even many applications of technology are efforts to improve or replace the lecturer with electronic forms of lecture. Many institutions have used videotaped materials to replace the traditional pre-laboratory lecture with videotapes of good lecturers who can articulate in clear English the goals and procedures for the laboratories. Others, including the author, have created computer-based pre-laboratories toward the same ends (Wilson 1980). With the creation of the "Mechanical Universe" this approach of using technology to replace the lecturer may have reached its highest form. Each video opens with a scene of students filing into a large lecture hall and then listening attentively to the opening remarks of a truly outstanding lecturer.

Clearly, these are all worthy efforts toward noble goals, and many have undoubtedly benefited from these efforts, but perhaps it is time to do a more serious re-examination of assumptions and our approaches. Over the last few decades, evidence has been pouring in from those doing research in science education, but it seems to have had little effect on classes in most of our largest universities. There are, of course, some notable exceptions, and I hope to cite some examples.

Those who defend the status quo in the large universities often advance three rationales.

THE THREE RATIONALES FOR THE STATUS QUO

The first is: "Lectures can be an educationally effective method of teaching." Readers of *The Physics Teacher, American Journal of Physics, Journal of College Science Teaching*, or any of the educational research journals know that the evidence is overwhelming against this contention. Unfortunately, few faculty at the large research universities actually read this material, and this misconception is still widely held. As a start, I often provide faculty with a series of four articles that paint a compelling picture of the lack of learning in the lecture. I begin with Halloun and Hestenes' article on "The Initial Knowledge State of Physics Students" (1985), which provides a well-thought-out approach to testing student learning and the dismal results of doing so. The second article, "The Force Concept Inventory" (Hestenes, Wells, and Swackhamer 1992), follows the first and expands the result to many other universities. Ron Thornton's article, "Learning Physical Concepts with Real-Time Laboratory Measurement Tools" (1990), is particularly interesting because it compares interactive methods using microcomputer-based laboratories with traditional lecture approaches, and shows that the interactive methods can reduce student error rates spectacularly. The last article that I cite is from Eric Mazur at Harvard (1996). When confronted with data revealing that students were not learning physics in lectures in other universities, Eric defended the students at Harvard. He felt that they were indeed learning in his lectures. He was challenged to give the Hestenes test to the Harvard students and was chagrined by the results. Eric then developed the pioneering methods of peer teaching that he later chronicled in his book.

This is a small subset of the material that one could read, but it provides a nice conceptual development of the discovery and application of ideas in research in science education, and does so in the context of the large research universities. Others will have their own favorites that could be just as convincing.

The second rationale among those who defend the status quo is that "although the lecture is usually ineffective, outstanding lecturers can turn the lecture into an effective learning environment." The articles cited above and many others provide both statistical and anecdotal evidence to the contrary. Mazur provides an honest personal anecdote illustrating the statistical evidence amassed by Halloun and Hestenes (1985), Laws (1991), Sokoloff and Thornton (1993), and Thornton (1990). Certainly, there are significant differences in the affective domain showing that students enjoy the course more, appreciate the subject, and come away with improved attitudes to the discipline. This can probably be linked to student retention and recruitment of majors, and perhaps even to increased learning through the other areas of the course such as reading, problem solving, and laboratories. Providing good lectures is obviously superior to providing poor lectures, but still does not lead directly to increased learning.

A standard counterargument is that "lectures must work, because students have been learning that way for centuries." The problem with this approach is that it neglects to take into account the many other ways that students learn, such as reading, problem solving, discussion with other students, discussion in the recitations, performing laboratories, and so on. Frequently, it is also based upon a generalization from the speakers' own experiences, which are, by definition, atypical.

The third rationale is often resorted to as the last bastion of defense against change. "The traditional course is the most cost-effective way to educate hundreds or thousands of students per semester." I confess to having believed this myself until I was coerced into doing a detailed cost analysis for the introductory courses. Our introductory courses in Physics, Calculus, Computer Science, Chemistry, and Introduction to Engineering Analysis each educate 600–1,000 students per semester. The traditional approach, until recently, was to divide the courses into two lecture sections of 300–500 students and then subdivide further into about 25–30 recitation sections of less than 30 students, and 30–40 labs of less than 25 each. The lectures are team taught by two or more faculty, the labs are taught by teaching assistants (TAs), and the recitations use a mix of faculty and teaching assistants. The mix varies from discipline to discipline with physics about evenly divided between faculty and TAs. We have two laboratory support staff and one lecture demonstration support person. After compiling the actual cost for this in 1993, I was surprised to see just how expensive this course was. We were able to identify several alternatives that were economically competitive and promised far better educational effectiveness.

DESIGNING AN EDUCATIONAL AND COST-EFFECTIVE ALTERNATIVE

In the spring semester of 1993, we convened a meeting of national experts on course innovation drawn from the three disciplines. Among them were Priscilla Laws, the primary architect for Workshop Physics; Bill Graves, the Director of the Institute for Academic Technology; and Joe Lagowski, editor of the *Journal of Chemical Education*. We invited six architects (including the architect for Bill Gates' house in Seattle) who had gained national attention for their innovative designs for educational facilities. To complete the mix, we added about six industry representatives from Perkin Elmer, AT&T, General Electric, IBM, United Technologies, and Boeing. With such a diverse group, we thought we might be able to elicit a variety of perspectives on the issues but would be unlikely to reach any kind of a consensus. We were wrong.

Indeed, there were a variety of perspectives introduced by the participants, but there were also strong areas of consensus. Among these was the need to reduce the emphasis on the lecture, to improve the relationship between the course and the laboratory, to scale up the amount of doing while scaling back the watching, to include team and cooperative learning experiences, to integrate rather than overlay technology into all of the courses, and, above all, to do so while reducing costs!

COURSE STRUCTURE

The experts' meeting led us to a design for the Studio courses that incorporated integrated use of computing with cooperative group learning techniques (Treisman 1990; Fullilove and Treisman 1990). The Physics course was a natural combination and extension of the CUPLE system (Wilson, Redish, and McDaniel 1992), the M.U.P.P.E.T. materials (Mac-Donald, Redish, and Wilson 1988), the Workshop Physics program (Laws 1991), and the cooperative learning techniques. The approximately seven hundred enrolled in the large semesters would be divided into 12 sections of 50–60 persons. The courses were reduced from six contact hours (two lecture, two recitation, and two lab) to four contact hours and taught either in two periods, each two hours in length, or in two 1.5-hour and one 1-hour period. The reduction from six to four contact hours is an important aspect of stewardship of faculty resources. Each course is led by a team of one faculty member, one graduate student, and one or two undergraduates. The mentoring of graduate students and undergraduate students is an important side effect of the redesigned course structure.

The re-engineering of the course led directly to a redesign of the facilities. In 1993, we completely renovated two classrooms for the first offerings of the Studio Calculus, Studio Chemistry, and Studio Physics courses. One classroom accommodates 64 students and the other is constrained by its size to about 50 students, both in a comfortable workshop facility. There are six-foot-long worktables, each designed for two students, with open workspace and a computer workstation. Often, the tables also contain the equipment for the day's "hands-on" laboratory. The tables form three concentric partial ovals with an opening at the front of the room for the teacher's worktable and for projection. The workstations are arranged so that when students are working together on an assigned problem, they turn away from the center of the room and focus their attention on their own small group workspace. The instructor is able to see all workstation screens from the center of the oval, and thereby receives direct feedback on how things are going for the students.

In the Physics course, the workstations run the CUPLE software system, have full access to networked multimedia, and include a microcomputer-based laboratory system for data acquisition, analysis, and visualization. The Calculus course makes heavy use of the Maple symbolic mathematics program.

In either course, when the instructor wants to conduct a discussion or give a mini-lecture, he or she is able to ask the students to turn back toward the center of the room. This removes the distraction of having a functioning workstation directly in front of the student during the discussion or lecture period, and yields a classroom in which multiple foci are possible. Students can work together as teams of two, or two teams may work together to form a small group of four. Discussion is facilitated by the semicircular arrangement of student chairs. Most students can see one another with a minimum of swiveling of chairs.

This type of classroom is friendly even to those instructors who tend toward the traditional style of classroom, in which most of the activities are teacher-centered rather than student-centered. Projection is easily accomplished, and all students have a clear view of both the instructor and any projected materials.

As a facility in which the instructor acts as a mentor, guide, and advisor, the classroom is unequaled. Rather than separating the functions of lecture, recitation, and laboratory, the instructor can move freely from lecture mode into discussion, and can assign a computer activity, ask the students to discuss their results with their neighbors, and then ask them to describe the result to the class. Laboratory simply becomes another one of the classroom activities that is mixed in with everything else. This course uses the latest in computing tools and incorporates use of cooperative learning approaches. We have created a powerful link between the lecture materials and the problem-solving and hands-on laboratories. This link is tenuous at best in the traditional course.

A TYPICAL COURSE DAY

Usually, students come to class with a homework assignment of three to six problems to turn in. They typically have questions about the assignment, and, since it is collected and graded, most have attempted the problems. The first portion of the class is then most like a recitation. As we go over questions that they have about the problems, we often call on the students to present the solutions. Other students then comment on the problem. This usually consumes about 20 minutes.

Next, we present a topic with a five-minute discussion followed by a laboratory on that topic. For example, we set up a video camera and had a student throw a ball. The video was directly digitized into the computer and available over the network to each work area. Students then analyzed the motion using the CUPLE digital video tool, and created a spreadsheet containing the position-versus-time data. The analysis proceeds in the usual fashion resulting in graphs of position versus time, velocity versus time, and acceleration versus time for each component. The final laboratory report remains in electronic format, although we often have the students record observations on a written worksheet.

Other laboratories are performed entirely at each work area. When we introduced Newton's Second Law, we had the students calibrate a force probe and then hang a spring and mass from the probe with an ultrasonic range finder under the mass to measure the position. The computer terminal displayed a graph of distance versus time, force versus time, and force versus distance. From that, the students were able to calculate the acceleration versus time and compare to the force divided by the mass.

This experiment foreshadowed the introduction of Hookes' Law and the topic of oscillations, both of which come later in the course. There are questions on the worksheet that ask the students to observe and comment upon each of these phenomena, but we do not attempt to name them or introduce theory at this time. We try to do this with most concepts.

In both examples given above, the laboratory data acquisition and analysis tools are embedded into a hypermedia text that introduces the topics, links the students to related materials, and poses questions for the students to answer with the tools. These hypermedia activities are being created by a consortium of schools led by Rensselaer and the University of Maryland. Funding has come from the Annenberg Corporation for Public Broadcasting, the IBM Corporation, and the National Science Foundation. Most of these materials were created by teams of faculty and students. The student involvement has added a fresh approach to much of the material and is appreciated by the students taking the course.

The student has access to the full range of CUPLE facilities during the lab session. She may annotate the book with marginalia by pressing the yellow post-it note button. This allows her to insert typed yellow adhesive notes or freehand scrawls across the pages. The glossary button (GL) brings up a large glossary of physics terms. The Swiss army knife launches the CUPLE toolbox that allows the student to use MAPLE, Excel, the CUPLE mathematical function tools, or any of a variety of references. References include an electronic periodic table, the String and Sticky Tape low-cost experiments, the Lecture Demonstration Handbook, and even access to all of the materials in the Physics InfoMall, assuming you have purchased the InfoMall separately.

The Window on Physics (WinPhys) object-oriented modeling system provides a collection of models and materials for constructing your own models and simulations. The object-oriented nature of the WinPhys system provides for all functions to inherit certain behaviors, among them the ability to differentiate or integrate themselves. The ability to read out, differentiate, integrate, and take the Fourier transform is of great use to the student in both laboratory and problem solving. The early laboratories have the students calculate this explicitly, just to assure that they understand the process.

Hands-on activities are an integral part of the CUPLE Physics Studio. In fact, the number of hands-on laboratories is more than twice that of the traditional course. Each activity is shorter than the traditional laboratory, but it is tightly integrated with both the homework and class discussion. The laboratory portion of the class ranges from 20 to 40 minutes and is often combined with a computational activity.

Lab activities fall into three major categories: microcomputer-based laboratories (MBL) as described above, video laboratories, and modeling and simulation projects. The video laboratories allow the students to take live video of an event (from a handi-cam) directly into their computer and then play that event back as video on their computer screen. Students bring up a graphical overlay on the screen and place points on the graph directly over the object as it moves. Those of us old enough to have done this with spark marks on waxed tape or with a Polaroid camera will recognize that this is conceptually quite similar and leads to the same kinds of data analysis that we performed. On the other hand, the relationship between the marks and the moving object is far more obvious to the student than it was in the earlier cases. Since we use much the same equipment each week, set-up for this lab is limited to bringing in the handi-cam and plugging it into the network. This is also far less cumbersome and less expensive than the specialized equipment that we used to do the spark tapes or strobed Polaroid pictures.

The class ends with a discussion of the material assigned for the next class. At this time we often call attention to the "foreshadowing" that has occurred in the problem solving and the laboratories and pull this together to introduce the next topic.

CONCLUSION

Our experiences thus far with the Studio Courses have been very encouraging. Student response is particularly satisfying. They have been quite enthusiastic about the courses, as measured by responses on the end-of-semester surveys. Nearly twice as many students agree that they enjoyed the Studio Courses as compared with the traditional lecture/recitation/lab format.

The Studio mathematics course was the first of the freshman courses to be conducted and has been through one complete cycle of evaluation. The physics course is one semester behind. One question on an external survey conducted by the dean of the undergraduate school last semester stirred quite a bit of interest in the administration and faculty. When students were asked whether they would cite a particular course as "a positive reason to attend Rensselaer," more than 90 percent agreed! This compares to 63 percent who agreed with this proposition in the other mathematics courses that had been downsized but did not abandon the traditional lecture approach. When student responses were controlled for popularity of the teacher and course, there were significant (actually spectacular) gains in students' satisfaction.

Our initial experiences indicate that faculty are rated far higher in the teaching evaluations in the Studio Courses, but we want to collect data over a longer period of time to be sure that this is not due to a Hawthorn effect.[1] This is a significant issue at institutions like Rensselaer where student evaluations and research results play equal major roles in salary, promotion, and tenure decisions. Increasingly, research universities are revamping these criteria to re-emphasize the teaching aspects of the professor's role; this trend is expected to continue and even accelerate in the next few years.

Students in these courses are performing as well as or better than students in the traditional courses, in spite of the 33.3 percent reduction in class contact time. This was demonstrated by student performance on tests matched in difficulty, length, and content to tests from previous years and those given this year in the traditional course. In both mathematics and physics, more topics were covered in the Studio Courses than in the lecture courses.

During the next year, we intend to use the Hestenes test in both studio and traditional format courses to compare these students with one another and with the results obtained at so many other universities in various instructional situations, including microcomputer-based laboratories and workshop formats. We will also follow the progress of students from the Studio Courses as they enter the upper-level courses in physics and engineering, to determine how successful these students are compared with those from the traditional sections.

We recognize just how difficult it will be to measure and document these changes, and to convince the university community to consider restructuring its courses. The preliminary results are so encouraging that we are beginning to be optimistic.

NOTE

1. The Hawthorn effect refers to the observation that when an innovation is tried, there is often an improvement in performance. Then the performance slowly returns to the original level. When the innovation is reversed, the performance often improves again. This effect implies that change alone can often lead to better performance, but that improvement is transitory. One must observe over a longer period to rule out the Hawthorn effect.

REFERENCES

Fullilove, Robert E., and Phillip P. Treisman. 1990. Mathematics Achievement among African American Undergraduates at the University of California, Berkeley: An Evaluation of the Mathematics Workshop Program. *Journal of Negro Education* 59(3): 463–78.

Halloun, I. A., and D. Hestenes. 1985. The Initial Knowledge State of Physics Students. *American Journal of Physics* 53: 1043–55.

Hestenes, D., M. Wells, and G. Swackhamer. 1992. Force Concept Inventory. *The Physics Teacher* 30 (March): 141–58.

Laws, Priscilla. 1991. Workshop Physics: Learning Introductory Physics by Doing It. *Change Magazine* (July/August): 20–27.

MacDonald, William M., Edward F. Redish, and Jack M. Wilson. 1988. The M.U.P.P.E.T. Manifesto. *Computers in Physics* 2(4): 23–30.

Mazur, E. 1996. Understanding or Memorization: Are We Teaching the Right Thing? In *Proceedings of the Conference on the Introductory Physics Course: The Retirement of Robert Resnick* (1993, Troy, N.Y.), edited by J. M. Wilson. New York: John Wiley and Sons.

Sokoloff, D., and R. Thornton. 1993. *Interactive Lecture Demonstrations*, preprint (May).

Thornton, R. 1990. Learning Physical Concepts with Real-Time Laboratory Measurement Tools. *American Journal of Physics* 58(9): 858.

Tobias, S. 1990. *They're Not Dumb, They're Different: Stalking the Second Tier.* Tucson, Ariz.: Research Corporation.

Treisman, Phillip. 1990. Teaching Mathematics to a Changing Population. Report of the Professional Development Program at the University of California, Berkeley.

Wilson, Jack M. 1980. Experimental Simulation in the Modern Physics Laboratory. *American Journal of Physics* 48: 701.

Wilson, Jack M., Edward F. Redish, and C. K. McDaniel. 1992. The Comprehensive Unified Physics Learning Environment: Part I. Background and System Operation. *Computers in Physics* 6(2): 202–9. Part II. Materials. *Computers in Physics* 6(3): 282–86.

CHAPTER 20

The Internet Public Library: Development and Future

JOSEPH W. JANES

THE ORIGIN

This paper will describe some of the ideas, decisions, and discussions behind the Internet Public Library (IPL); the impact they had, and how they
turned out on the Web (http://www.ipl.org/).

The developmental period of the IPL, roughly from December 1994 to
April 1995, can serve as a useful framework for discussing these ideas and
decisions, but I will also lay out projects and ideas that followed.

THE IDEA

In the fall of 1994, it was becoming increasingly clear that the Internet
was going to have as significant an impact on libraries and librarians as on
the wider world. Lou Rosenfeld, a doctoral student in the School of Information and Library Studies (now School of Information) at the University
of Michigan, and I had taught two successful courses in which we had had
our students build detailed and extensive guides to Internet-based resources
in specific subject areas. We had started to build gophers and learn about
how they would work.

Then the Web happened. I can remember the first time I ever saw Mosaic;
I cannot say that I was thunderstruck by its potential to change the world,
but it did look interesting and I wanted to learn more.

Sometime in September 1994, the phrase "Internet Public Library" entered my consciousness. For several years, I had taught a seminar on the

Paper presented at the International Roundtable for Information and Library Science, Kanazawa Institute of Technology, Library Center, Kanazawa, Japan, 1998.

impact of information technology; each year, the theme had been different. It had been quite some time since I had last taught it, but I was scheduled to do it again in the winter 1996 term. I was planning to repeat the last theme, which was on intellectual property and technology. However, I was not too happy about the idea, because the last one had not been that successful.

It occurred to me that I might use the idea of an "Internet Public Library" as the theme for this course. I talked with several friends and colleagues and asked their opinions. They all said it sounded like a great idea but a lot of work. They were more correct than they knew, but I was encouraged and so went forward. I developed a prospectus for the course, which I circulated to the students in the School of Information and Library Studies. From the beginning, the project was motivated by one central question: What does librarianship have to say to the network environment and vice versa? That question proved (then and now) both provocative and attractive. I asked students to submit statements of interest to join the class; I received more than 50 statements, and selected a group of 35 students.

That group was quite diverse. Their backgrounds ranged from computer scientist and librarian to writer, editor, lexicographer, substitute teacher, IBM marketing representative, medical researcher, art historian, desktop video producer, human factors researcher, and medievalist. That breadth of experience came in handy, and the power of the central idea, which brought them together, focused their collective work.

In December 1994, in an e-mail message to the group, I laid out some thoughts, based on a brief meeting and discussion we had just had:

My current ideas are sketchy, but I think we need to create an entity that people can recognize both as a library and as a "true" Internet institution. That's a tightrope, but one worth walking. More specifically, I think we might publish a journal [with related content], provide a service helping librarians identify really neat Internet sources for use in their daily lives, and other things. The only thing I will insist on is a story hour; but how that might work I have no idea. Other people will probably propose other specific projects.

The big issues that we need to resolve quickly are:

- the mission statement (not carved in stone, but helpful in deciding what we will and will not do);
- structure (of the overall project and of the groups that will do it, both administrative and functional); and
- evaluation methodology (how will you all be graded? A final exam, perhaps?).

Several important ideas are imbedded here. Most of the ideas in the first paragraph don't look much like what goes on in most libraries, but they seemed at the time (and still do) to be important aspects of exploring librarianship in this environment. We never did publish a journal or do collection development/profiling for other libraries, but we have returned to these ideas many times over the years, in thinking not only about services we might provide but also ways in which we might generate revenue. The story hour dictum was, in retrospect, really about making sure that whatever we did, it involved working with children in a meaningful way. In those days, there was almost no presence of children on the Net or resources for them, and this was long before the consuming concern about inappropriate or indecent material.

Those big issues have remained big. The initial mission statement has been revised only once and has helped enormously in guiding work and thinking. Structure also helped, not only administratively but also in doing the work. Evaluation has been difficult and important. Pedagogically, evaluating students doing groundbreaking, original work within the same framework as grading people doing online searches and term papers has been an enormous challenge.

That same message started with the five goals I had outlined for the class: (1) finish the course more excited than when you started; (2) do work of which you and the entire group will be proud; (3) everybody (including me) learn a lot; (4) everybody (including me) have fun doing it; (5) everybody (including me?) get great jobs at the end. This was an attempt to set the tone for the work, to help create an environment where people could explore, apply new technologies, stretch themselves and still have fun, yet work on something that would be meaningful and real. In general, I think we succeeded on all these counts.

THE FIRST DAY

Our first meeting was on Saturday, January 7, 1996. We met then to allow ourselves several hours in which to define precisely what we wanted to do, who wanted to do what, our mission statement, and how to proceed. The mission statement came first. After some discussion, we adopted the following: "The mission of our Internet Public Library is to:

- provide services and information which enhance the value of the Internet to its ever-expanding and varied community of users;
- work to broaden, diversify, and educate that community; and
- communicate its creators' vision of the unique roles of library culture and traditions on the Internet."

This statement conveys our collective notion of what it meant to be a "library" in this chaotic, dynamic, placeless domain. The first clause is fairly standard; the second betrays our desire to help people to understand the value of the Net and get more people on it. The final clause generated much discussion, especially around wording. We wanted people on the Net to know about the value of librarianship, what librarians know, and what they can do in this new environment.

The mission statement has since been changed. The newest statement, as adopted in July 1996, can be seen below. This is clearly a more elaborate and encompassing statement, laying out more precisely and fully our point of view and the perceived reach and scope of our work. It perpetuates the point of view and emphases of the original statement, though, and has served its purpose well.

The Internet is a mess. Since nobody runs it, that's no surprise. There are a lot of interesting, worthwhile, and valuable things out there—and a lot that are a complete waste of time.

Over the last few hundred years, librarians have become skilled at finding the good stuff, organizing it, and making it easier for people to find and use. Librarians also fight for important ideas like freedom of expression and thought, equality of access to information, and literacy.

The Internet Public Library is the first public library of the Internet. As librarians, we are committed to providing valuable services to that world. We do so for many reasons: to provide library services to the Internet community, to learn and teach what librarians have to contribute in a digital environment, to promote librarianship and the importance of libraries, and to share interesting ideas and techniques with other librarians.

Our mission directs us to:

- serve the public by finding, evaluating, selecting, organizing, describing, and creating quality information resources;
- develop and provide services for our community with an awareness of the different needs of young people;
- create a strong, coherent sense of place on the Internet, while ensuring that our library remains a useful and consistently innovative environment as well as fun and easy to use;
- work with others, especially other libraries and librarians, on projects which will help us all learn more about what does and does not work in this environment; uphold the values important to librarians, in particular those expressed in the Library Bill of Rights.

We are committed to providing free services to the Internet community, in the greatest tradition of public libraries. However, we can not sustain our library without a solid financial base. We are continually seeking enterprises that provide both service to our community and funding for our operations. We are always open to new ideas and partnerships.

INITIAL GROUPS

After reaching consensus on the mission statement, small groups brainstormed on what exactly the IPL should be. These groups reported back and the entire class voted on what they thought were the highest priorities. The top six were: (1) reference, (2) architecture/interfaces/design, (3) services for librarians/information professionals/schools, (4) bibliographic instruction/user education/information literacy/outreach/access, (5) youth services, and (6) public relations/development/legacy.

There are some interesting omissions here. Functions that are labeled "technical services" in libraries—collection development, organization of resources—were mentioned but received little support. Although these functions were carried out (under the rubric of reference), this group did not see them as high priorities at the beginning. Possibilities that were mentioned but did not make the list included government resources, real-time interaction with humans, publication, art, community information/bulletin, an "Internet Advisory Conduit," a "900 Library" (fee-for-service research, another recurring idea), and others.

The students organized themselves into groups focusing on specific aspects of the IPL: technology, reference, youth, services to librarians, education and outreach, and public relations. They then met to discuss what they wanted to try to accomplish and how, roles within the group, and logistical matters. Several important decisions were made during those meetings and in the weeks that followed.

Technology

The technology group (led by Nigel Kerr) dealt with architecture, design, and related issues. Their summary of that first meeting captures those decisions well:
Goals include:

- unifying our IPL—technically, intellectually, for users; work closely with other groups;
- acquiring and managing server(s)/infrastructure; and
- providing opportunities for class members to learn about architecture and technical issue (Unix system administration, HTML, interface design, listserv moderating).

    In collaborating with other groups, we want to listen to their needs, use that info as input to our design and decision process, and inform them of what we think is/is not technically possible and feasible.

This group was not going to dictate what was possible or desirable, but, rather, chose to distribute themselves and act as liaisons, consultants, and advisors to the other groups. Those functional groups, such as reference and youth, were told to think first about what they wanted to do, without regard for technological capability or implementation, and the architecture group would see what could be done. This proved vital to the success of the project—it allowed for the free flow of ideas and creativity, which then could be tempered and adjusted as necessary, based on the available technology.

Getting a server was an obvious initial hurdle. When the project began, we neither had one nor knew where we might get one. We were fortunate in this regard. Lee Liming, then the school's technology administrator, met with the architecture group, heard our ideas, and volunteered to donate a spare Sparc 20 server for our use. We are still using this server (with others) to this day; without it there would not have been an IPL at all.

The educational aspect was also important; people in all the groups learned what they needed to know to accomplish their projects. Rather than adopting technological matters as their sole province, the architecture group saw their role as facilitating other people, learning what they needed, and contributing as necessary.

Reference

The reference group, led by David Carter, Nettie Lagace, Sara Ryan, and Schelle Simcox, emerged with the following goals (excerpted from an early report):

1. Create a virtual reference collection (a hotlist, but also a searchable database)
   a. In this regard, collection development will be a big issue. We plan to divide ourselves into subject specialties, although not everyone may be able to specialize in a subject s/he likes (like the real world?).
   b. We are also seriously considering classifying our collection along lines similar to those already used by M-Link.
   c. What kind of format will the reference collection be? Comprehensive or selective?
   d. How will we judge the authority of our sources?
      —identification, dates/updates, contact person, where source is located. . . .
2. Provide online reference service, both via e-mail and in real time.
3. Design the database structure. We want a product that can run on UNIX (so that it can be accessible from the Internet), but cost constraints may hamper this wish. The database must be able to handle big, ever-growing data files, and accommodate Boolean searching as well as field restrictions.
4. Develop a manual for online reference.
5. Collect usage statistics regarding the user community, types of questions asked, and so on.

This list of goals is remarkable in several regards. It pre-dates almost all thinking and discussion in the professional literature about what "reference" means in a networked environment. It identifies a number of crucial issues that have continued to be discussed not only at the IPL, but on the Net in general. Finally, it emerges in almost equal measure from thinking about applying traditional librarianship to the Net (how to do collection

development here) and the other way around (how to use the Net to provide reference service).

The original intent of the ready reference collection was to serve as a
resource for answering reference questions. As it turned out, our collections
(ready reference and beyond) have been our most popular and valued resources, and the actual reference-question-answering service has taken place
on a much smaller scale. This work is, as all librarians know, time-
consuming and labor-intensive, while collections, once built and maintained, are available for use by countless people. Nonetheless, the kind of
personalized service that reference demands is still needed in a world of
"virtual," digital collections—in fact, it is even more necessary in the dis-
tintermediated and incoherent Internet.

Important, collection-oriented questions were and are asked here about
format, selectivity, quality (but not, interestingly, about balance—not all
points of view on issues have always been available in networked resources), access, and so on. Organization is also raised; M-Link, a service
of the University of Michigan Library, had a gopher at this time, which
was among the first organized along library principles. Sue Davidsen, who
designed that gopher and who now heads the Michigan Electronic Library
(http://www.mel.lib.mi.us), saw that opportunity and showed the way for
many projects (including, for example, the Argus Clearinghouse ⟨http://
www.clearinghouse.net/⟩) in applying librarianship to Internet-based resources.

Although the original ready reference collection was encoded in static
HTML pages, it has since been moved to databases, per this original vision.
At present, it and all other IPL collections are stored as FileMaker databases. Some are served out periodically as static pages; others (including
the Online Texts collection) are dynamically drawn directly from the databases on the fly.

The seemingly innocent fourth goal of the reference group, "Develop a
manual for online reference," led to a great deal of experimentation and
exploration of what it means to do reference on the Internet. As our work
has progressed, this has gotten somewhat easier because of the increasing
number and quality of network-based resources, the improved functionality
of search engines and directories, and our growing experience; but the question of how best to integrate the use of the Internet and its resources into
reference librarianship is an ongoing and continually challenging one.

At the beginning, there was no way to know, for example, how many
questions we would receive. There was a continuing, half-joking notion of
the five hundred questions per day that we might get and how we would
deal with them. Discussions followed about how many staff we would need
and how we would solicit participation from librarians and subject experts.

Technological issues were important as well. How would we take questions, and what would happen to them? There was no enthusiasm for re-

ceiving e-mail messages in personal mailboxes, and it was obvious that guidelines would be needed to help people formulate questions so that they could be answered. Despite the desire to do real-time reference, it seemed obvious that using e-mail as the medium made sense, but that meant that reference interviews would be difficult or at least asynchronous and therefore time-consuming. An initial solution was the use of HyperNews, a product of the National Center for Supercomputing Applications, which allowed Web-based conferencing. This was inadequate, and, within a few months, Michael McClennen, a Ph.D. candidate in computer science and member of the first class, wrote a new software package called QRC for handling reference questions; it is still in use at the IPL and several other libraries today.

To date, we still have never actively advertised the question-answering service, fearing the volume of questions we might receive. Without advertising, and with the form buried a few levels down in the IPL site, we typically receive between 20 and 70 questions a day, which is often more than our crew of students and volunteer librarians can handle. As such, we have to reject some questions based on a loose-quota system.

Online Collections. When the IPL opened, ready reference was our only significant collection. Since then, several more collections have been added: a collection designed for teenagers; a reading room for full texts, magazines, and newspapers; and a directory of Web sites of non-profit organizations. The youth division also added a small collection to supplement its offerings.

These collections have separate designs (although all share the overall IPL design dicta, discussed below), collection development procedures, selection policies, and organizational structures. There are areas of similarity, not surprisingly, but all these decisions have been revisited with each new collection.

For example, the original ready reference collection had a fairly simple structure: each resource was represented by its title, URL, a brief description, statement of authorship, and keywords (from an uncontrolled list), and was placed in a category by subject. There was no attempt to create cataloging records, let alone full MARC records; there were too few resources and their nature did not seem to lend themselves to such depth of organization. However, when the online texts collection was organized, David Carter, the IPL head of collections, adopted Dewey classification—most of the resources at issue were from the 1920s and before (since copyright had lapsed and thus they were in the public domain), for which Dewey was intended to be used. As such, we have more comprehensive cataloging and records (though still not full MARC) for those resources. We also use Dewey for the youth collection, since most children use Dewey in schools and it is more likely to be familiar to them.

Original reference resources have also been created: POTUS (Presidents of the United States), on the American presidency; Stately Knowledge, on the U.S. states; Native American Authors; Say Hello to the World (introductions to 30 languages); and A+ Research and Writing (for high school and college students writing papers). These resources owe much to traditional reference publishing, but also take advantage of the hypertextual and multimedia environment, incorporating images and links to other relevant Web sites containing high-quality information.

In all cases, from the beginning, these collections and resources were based on personal or group interest and motivation. Bob Summers, the creator of POTUS, had a lifelong fascination with information about the presidents. He used a summer-long independent study to compile information; organize it; structure, design, and build the site; find good external sites; and make the hundreds of decisions necessary to complete this excellent resource. Lorri Mon, who led the group that built Native American Authors and also compiled Say Hello to the World (while assisting in reference question administration), felt strongly about both topics, which reinforced the IPL's desire to reflect our users both within North America and around the world.

Again, this is librarianship in a new light. The collections work comes from a long and valuable tradition of collection development and maintenance. The original resources look more like publishing, but in all cases, the fact that they are designed to be in a library has strongly flavored their design, intent, and formulation.

Youth

The youth group, led by Josie Parker, focused on these ideas in its initial discussions:

- writing contest,
- FAQs from children to be answered by authors,
- publishing an interactive picture book,
- story hour,
- cool hot list,
- science project guide,
- kids in a MOO [Multi-user Object Oriented Environment],
- book discussion group for older readers.

This group focused on the interests and experiences of younger users (elementary school–aged). Many of the ideas came to fruition: two writing contests drew several dozen entries from the United States and Europe; Ask the Author has children's book authors' answers to questions from kids and parents; several originally illustrated storybooks are available; and an original science project was put up. Projects that would have required continual maintenance (the book discussion group) or more involved development work (interactive picture book) were not possible given the resources. The cool hot list evolved into the youth collection, now cataloged and organized using the Dewey Decimal Classification.

This list is another interesting mix of fairly traditional librarianship and Internet inventiveness and experimentation. The "required" story hour, familiar to most public libraries, is here, as are discussion groups, writing contests, and more; but the author FAQs, interactive book, and MOO participation are still amorphous—in the realm of speculation about serving young people in a networked, interconnected environment.

Services to Librarians

The original mission statement committed us to share our lessons, not only with our patrons and the Internet world, but also with our professional colleagues. The Services to Librarians and Information Professionals group (led by Richard Truxall) worked on this. Their work broke into several large categories: help to librarians in getting connected to and using the Internet, examples of how libraries were using the Net, and professional resources. They wrote original documents on the Internet (how to get connected, use it, and build resources, including telnet, Web, gopher, and Veronica); libraries using networks for their work; and Net resources from professional organizations. They also wanted to create a calendar of meetings, conferences, and events, and foster a mentorship program to help librarians new to the network connect with more experienced colleagues.

In practice, these were successful, but maintenance again became a problem, and most of the ongoing non-Web resources fell away over the years. However, this formed the nucleus for another set of ideas, which was put forth in a proposal in 1996. By simply making the IPL accessible via the World Wide Web, it is possible to reach those people who use the Internet on their own. For the most part, these are people who own their own computers and modems. However, we noted that there is a large segment of the population who cannot afford direct Internet access, whose only connection to the Internet is through schools and public libraries.

To reach this population, the IPL proposed to work closely with public libraries, school libraries, and academic libraries to help them effectively assist their patrons in using Internet resources. Doing this would involve (1) training their staff members to be Internet librarians, (2) providing our expertise to help solve their local problems, and (3) promoting the IPL as the initial place for their patrons to visit. As part of this, we proposed developing a standard method by which each library could present local information resources in conjunction with the IPL as a seamless whole.

Although many libraries have Internet connections, the comments we hear through professional channels and personal contact indicate that many of them have not yet integrated the Internet into their work. Many public libraries are organized into cooperatives or served by regional organizations expressly designed to support their members in dealing with new technology. However, the quality of this support varies and many libraries are on their own. We proposed to work with such agencies to help them help their own members, and with isolated libraries that have few other resources.

Certain realities have evolved from the 1996 proposal—for IPL specifically and librarians generally. We are not in the business of teaching people how to connect to the Internet and use its basic tools. Many other organizations can do better jobs of that than we can. What we can do best is to help librarians build upon their own professional training and apply their skills and experience in new ways. We have found that the techniques and tools of professional librarianship translate well from the world of print to the world of digital information. We can build upon our experience to ease the transition for others, and to help individual libraries solve their own problems in this regard.

The IPL strongly resembles many other initiatives in which libraries and librarians have combined their time and resources to improve or expand the services they can offer to their users. Interlibrary loan, reference referral, and shared cataloging are simple examples; the use of network technologies can enable even more encompassing ideas.

Education and Outreach

Another group, led by Louise Alcorn, was interested in issues of education and user outreach—important functions in any library, and especially in one that would almost never meet its users in person. This group focused on making the Internet easier to use and understand, and increasing general knowledge of it and participation in it. This group worked:

- to provide pathways to access points and equipment for potential Internet users, and to educate current and future users about techniques needed to use the Internet;
- to ensure access to the IPL by a variety of users, employing different platforms;
- to interest non-users in the "beauty" (and value) of the Internet;
- to learn the computing and communication needs of various audiences; and
- to provide navigation tools to the IPL, and, through the IPL, to the Web.

Much of this reflected the thinking of the project as a whole; of particular concern was the use of "different platforms." The rest, though, comes directly from traditional notions of librarianship: equality and ease of access to information and resources, knowledge of those resources, and ability to use them. One aspect of this, navigation, was implemented by building a directory—an alphabetical listing of resources and areas of the IPL. The directory was available when the IPL opened, but became a maintenance problem as the library grew and expanded. The directory, though, was a precursor of similar devices common in large Web sites today, particularly the site map.

In practice, these were (and are) enormous challenges, well beyond our small capacity at the time. The IPL has always remained committed to these ideas, but has not been able to achieve as much as the vision of this group would have required. Much of this invaluable work goes on now in libraries of all kinds, all over the country, and appropriately so. Today, libraries and librarians in direct contact with their users and communities can far more effectively put them in touch with the Net (and help them to use Web resources) than the IPL could ever hope to do.

One other aspect of the IPL grew out of the outreach group. One member of that group, Kendra Frost, wanted to extend the benefits of the project to the Museum of African American History in Detroit. At the time, the museum had no presence or even awareness of the Internet, but she felt this was a chance for them to tell their story, share their resources, and learn about the potential of the Net. With their permission, she built a few pages describing the museum and its work, incorporating images of a few items from its collections. It looked much like the sort of small exhibit one often finds in libraries, and so we built an exhibit hall to house it. Since that time, several exhibits have entered the exhibit hall, each allowing its creators to explore design and work with images, multimedia, sound, or other, more exotic technologies. Exhibits have ranged from photographs of trains and lighthouses to the story of Detroit jazz, ancient Egyptian forgeries, Pueblo pottery, dinosaurs, and the life story of a woman and her family (Grammy Mirk).

Public Relations

Finally, there was the public relations group, led by Maria Bonn and Bradley Taylor. In early 1995, the Web was still a young and comparatively unpopulated place. Students who were interested in or had experience with public relations undertook this responsibility. Their original mandate, which included documentation of our work, fund-raising, and development efforts, was really beyond the scope of what was possible; however, the public relations effort was more successful than any of us could have imagined.

Their priorities, from the first meeting, were to

1. Implement publicity and promotion by
   - Saturating the Internet with ongoing press releases,

- Generating local and national media exposure, and
- Publicizing IPL via ALA, SAA, SLA, etc., newsletters and conferences;

2. Facilitate internal communication by
   - Publishing an in-house newsletter and providing liaison between groups;

3. Develop documentation by
   - Saving EVERYTHING,
   - Producing a video record,
   - Compiling history of process from documentation at end of semester, and
   - Writing a final article; and

4. Implement fund-raising/development by
   - Seeking university support, and
   - Looking for corporate sponsorships.

The first of these was accomplished. (These were still the days when an e-mail message posted to the right newsgroups and listservs could have a large impact.) The press release, sent to the world (but targeted to the library world), was extremely well written, generated great interest and enthusiasm, and raised the stakes dramatically for the work as a whole. The following are excerpts from the text of the release:

Bold Initiative Heralds the Creation of Tomorrow's Library Today

The University of Michigan School of Information and Library Studies proudly announces the advent of the Internet Public Library (IPL), an innovative, online, 24-hour public library designed to revolutionize the way the world thinks about library services. The Internet Public Library will offer an exciting version of the library of tomorrow as envisioned by many of the brightest talents in the field today.

With a stated mission to "provide services and information which enhance the value of the Internet to its ever expanding and varied community of users," IPL is prepared to provide essential library services to a target audience estimated to number ¼ of the entire American population by the end of the century. Among the first services to appear will be an online reference division; a youth services division; a user-education division; and professional services for librarians. A library without windows, walls, or even books, IPL will still provide a user-friendly spot to turn to for questions on how to plan a family budget; learn more about the world of Internet-based resources; or even turn to for a story hour for children. Bringing the best features of the community library forward into a new technological environment, IPL seeks to challenge our thinking about new "communities": that will arise in the future and a broader range of services the library of tomorrow might provide.

The response was overwhelming. So many requests for information were received (going to individuals' e-mail boxes) that we had to set up a listserv to keep people informed on the work. Subsequent messages encouraged people to subscribe to that group. The press release was sent in February; by the time the IPL opened in mid-March, more than 3,000 people from around the world had subscribed.

Now, several thousand people were waiting to see what we would come up with. This marked the transition from a class project that would be up for a few weeks, to a real product, facing a global audience that would want to see it, use it, and perhaps even depend on it. As the number of people on the listserv grew, so did the pressure to produce a high-quality product by the deadline.

LOOK AND FEEL: DESIGN AND DICTA

One of the overarching themes of the early discussion about what the IPL should and would be was making it a "place" where people could explore, relax, read, and so on. The metaphor of a physical library was so strong it was often unspoken; it was taken for granted, and people would talk about the planned IPL in much the same way they would a physical library. Metaphor turned out to be one of our best friends; the more we were able to discuss the IPL in terms of rooms and services and places found in libraries, the easier the work got and the more ideas we generated.

The importance of a sense of place in an inherently placeless environment should not be underestimated. It cuts to the heart of what a "library" is and what it means in a distributed world: a refuge, a stable island in a sea of chaos, an organizing force. It also conveys continuity and durability.

This formed the backdrop for conversations about what the IPL would actually look like. These conversations reflected the desire for stability and place, but also a recognition that many people initially would be coming via slow connectivity, using non-graphical browsers such as Lynx, or would have image-loading turned off to increase navigation speed. We were particularly thinking here of people with low-bandwidth connections, especially internationally. It came as a pleasant surprise, then, when we received many e-mail messages from sight-impaired users praising our text-rich design. Software that vocalizes text on the screen does not work well with images, and so our site was ideal for their use. The recent federal ruling concerning ADA (Americans with Disabilities Act) compliance of Web design confirms our vision in this regard.

There were numerous impassioned discussions about design and consistency during the building period. There was strong sentiment both for basic consistency across the library and for separate divisions to be able to design for specific categories of users and to implement other ideas. The middle ground here was to let all groups experiment for several weeks, trying out different designs, and then combine the best elements to create a single look and feel for the library. This approach worked (though not without

Figure 20.1
Design Template for the Internet Public Library

```
<html>
<head>
<title> IPL the Internet Public Library</title>
</head>
<body>

<h3><a href="/"><img src="/images/ipl.logo.small,gif" alt="To
the lobby of"></a>the Internet Public Library</h3>

<h1>What This Is</h1>

(Your stuff goes here.)



<p><strong>Future Plans</strong></p>

<p><strong>You may also wish to see </strong></p>

<p><strong>Return to <a href="/about">About the Library </a> |
<a href="/">the IPL Main Lobby</a>,</strong>
<hr>

<address>the Internet Public Library - = -
http://www.ipl,org/ - = - ipl@umich.edu</address>


Last updated
</body>
</html>
```

continuing debate), and produced the first set of design dicta and template, shown in Figure 20.1.

The design template is fairly simple, but therein lies its power. The point of the template and the dicta behind it was to provide "wallpaper and carpeting," a basic look for all IPL pages. This freed people from thinking about design to think more about content. The page was designed to be simple, quick and easy-to-load, and unobtrusive, yet provide structure and content.

The logo and name of the library appear at the top of each page, so it is immediately clear that you're in the IPL, and equally clear when you've left. All pages start with a first-level heading and end with a standard footer incorporating the name of the library, its URL, its e-mail address, and the date the page was last updated. Just above that are links back up through the hierarchy of the library sending people, level by level, up to the division home page and the library's home page (called the main lobby, to reinforce the building metaphor). Some pages also had a "You may also wish to see" tag, suggesting related IPL sites.

All IPL pages had to comply with these dicta, with only a few exceptions, including the home page and divisional main pages (reference, services, education), which could incorporate graphics. Each of these, though, had a text-only version in addition to the graphical version. The youth division (and later, exhibits) was granted a blanket exemption; they made a compelling argument that children required larger text, color, more graphics, and big buttons to click on; their designs were based on the dicta when applicable, but also reflected these additional needs.

The main lobby went through several designs. Discussions about design, especially the front page, have often verged on the emotional. There seems to be great depth of feeling about look and feel, which is not surprising. To the world, this conveys who we are—our public face and the first impression people take away. This poses a multiple challenge: we need to be interesting and inviting (which might mean changing designs and using more graphics), but we also need to emphasize consistency (which would argue for few changes). Inertia also plays a role here; but we have incorporated several graphical and design changes while concentrating on adding new resources and enhancing existing ones.

BEYOND THE BEGINNING: WHAT WE HAVE LEARNED

As of this writing, the IPL is more than three years old. We have been visited more than 8 million times by users from more than 130 countries, and answered almost 10,000 reference questions. We presently are averaging more than 20,000 users per day, an average of one about every five seconds, 24 hours a day. Our collections now number more than 19,000 items, including more than 7,000 pointers to online texts, 2,700 reference resources, 2,400 serials, 2,000 newspapers, 1,100 associations, and 1,000 items for young people.

We have learned several important lessons. Three of the more important ones are discussed below.

Librarianship Works . . . Almost All the Time

This can be restated: the IPL performs many functions that almost every other library does, and these are both exactly the same and completely different. We answer reference questions, but we can't see people, read their facial expressions or body languages, or even interview them very well. We tell stories, but to children we never meet. We select, describe, and organize resources, but we don't catalog. Yet in all these instances, traditional librarianship has guided what we do and how we do it. In fact, when faced with a challenge or problem, we almost always explore approaches from the profession, and more often than not, they are helpful.

There also have been instances where that doesn't work. For example, we often have found that when we send e-mail to people who have asked us reference questions, to follow up or ask for more information, we get no response. Whether it's because they don't check e-mail often, don't care about their question that much, have lost interest, or no longer have e-mail, we don't know. There really isn't an analogy to that in the real world— sometimes patrons do drift away, but it's hard to imagine asking someone a question and that person just standing there, making no effort to answer at all. So what do we do? Answer as best we can? What if the patron truly doesn't care any more? Should we use our scarce resources to answer a question for a patron who has evaporated as far as we can tell?

Most libraries attempt to build collections that will endure, and, of course, books and other physical carriers of information will persist, at least until they are stolen, weeded, or replaced by new editions or better resources. It is, in practice, difficult for us to know which "items" in our "collections" are even still there at any given point, whether they have changed, or what's happened to them. It certainly makes collection development (and maintenance) a challenge.

Technology Is Not the Point . . . But This One Is Different

Libraries and librarians have become masterful at incorporating new technologies and storage media into their work. Walk into almost any library, and you'll see not only books but magazines, newspapers, audio CDs, CD-ROMs, videocassettes, pamphlets, posters, art, and so on, as well as connections to digital resources from commercial vendors such as DIALOG and, of course, the Internet. What we always have known is that the medium is less important than the quality of information, and that technology can help provide new and better kinds of access to information.

Of course, those technologies are not the point. Most libraries have microforms of some flavors, but the incorporation of microfilm or fiche didn't fundamentally change librarianship; neither did online resources or CD-ROMs. Frankly, neither will the simple presence of Internet-based resources. They are simply another set of potential aids in helping people find out more about their world and lives. They do raise some new and fascinating questions about the nature of publishing and authority and the value of editing, but just having access to the Net won't change librarianship or libraries.

On the other hand, effective use of the Net might change librarianship and libraries. There is a difference to this technology, as compared to those that have gone before. The Internet is more than just a new storage medium or search facility. The power of the Net, in librarianship as everywhere else, is its ability to make connections to people, organizations, ideas, and information. It could facilitate major change and a quantum leap forward in the quest to allow people to be more fully informed and aware.

The central problem of librarianship is to help get information out of one person's head and into another's. We have been doing this with books and indexes and catalogs and reference books because that's what we've had. When you add the ability to connect directly to people and organizations and communities who know about diverse subjects and can make information directly available, you open a new paradigm.

You can break it open even more widely when you connect librarians. Listservs such as STUMPERS-L and Web4Lib are one thing, but consider the power of thousands of librarians, connected via the Internet, working together on collection development, readers' advisory, reference, storytelling, and all the rest, to serve millions of people on a daily basis. It staggers the imagination, and places librarianship smack in the middle of a revolution in information provision. The Internet won't be the end of libraries, as many have proclaimed—it could be the beginning of the enshrinement of librarianship and what it stands for as one of the most important, valuable, and respected professions.

The Best Way to Learn It Is to Do It

There is simply no way that any of us could have learned the lessons we have over the years if we hadn't been out there developing the Internet Public Library. As we continue to develop new capabilities, we continue to learn both from applications that work well and from implementations that don't.

I said often in the first class that there was no way for that work to fail. I believed it then and still do. Regardless of how many people use the IPL, and what they think of it, the only way for the work to fail is if nobody learns from it.

The IPL always has been a vehicle for learning and trying new technologies. It can be thought of as a teaching and research library in the model of teaching and research hospitals—where people come to learn how to heal more effectively and try out new methods of treatment, all the time interacting with real patients and providing a real service. IPL is much the same; students come to learn about librarianship in the emerging information environment, librarians come to get new perspectives and ideas and continuing education, and thousands of people find the Internet a hospitable source of information.

THE IPL TODAY

And that is how the IPL is proceeding today. We have a small, professional staff to coordinate and provide training and continuity. A class of students and other volunteer professional librarians supports the professional staff. This class is part of the new Practical Engagement Program of the School of Information, which is designed to give students an opportunity to learn by doing through structured workshops engaging communities in the larger world. In our case, that community is not only our users but also professional colleagues who wish to work with us and participate in our projects. That work (maintaining and expanding our collections; answering reference questions; providing stories, exhibits, and original resources) continues the tradition of librarianship: providing a sense of place, resources, and services to help people find information they want or need.

THE IPL TOMORROW

After three years, several million users, and a lot of hard work, what happens next? I'm often asked about how we might do things differently if we were to do it again or start over. In many ways, the IPL is a very traditional library, in terms of the services it provides, and the ideas that motivate it. To be sure, the environment in which it operates is new and exciting, but there are new frontiers, which could be explored. I present here six ideas for the future:

Appropriate Use of New Technologies

Our concern for equality of access to our site means that our pages are quite simple, quick to load, and dominated by text. It also means we don't get a chance to play with new technologies like Java and Shockwave, or explore things like XML. These are important, though, because they form the basis for the technological environment. They also get noticed, and people think they're cool. While I don't think we need lots of animated images and sound files on all our pages, we could try to find ways to investigate and incorporate these new technologies as appropriate, without sacrificing access, and serve as a testbed for a more significant technological development enterprise.

Metadata

The concept of metadata has, of course, been around for quite a while, and librarians are familiar with it through cataloging and indexing. In the Internet world, however, it's becoming increasingly important, in simple ways like using META tags to influence search engine behavior and in more sophisticated approaches such as the work of the Dublin CORE and Warwick Framework groups. This is clearly an area where librarians should participate and the IPL seems a perfect opportunity for experimentation and testing of potentially useful ideas.

Use of Licensed and Proprietary Materials

At present, the IPL collections include pointers only to freely available, Web-based resources. This is of interest and value, but there are so many more and better resources, produced by commercial publishers and available through fee-based licenses. It is intriguing to think about potential arrangements with publishers or vendors or other Web-based services that could combine the best of both worlds, and be of benefit to our users and us.

Scale Up Our Work

We are a small operation with a grand scope and vision. Unfortunately, our resources and size have always limited us. Could the IPL serve more people around the world, answering those five hundred reference questions a day, having a million people a day visiting the site and finding the information they want or need? It would be interesting to think hard about how we could.

Support Our Work More Fully

Obviously, without this, no further ideas can be realized. The School of Information at Michigan has been very good to us, but it is not in their mission to fund a free public library for the world, other than as a limited, educational enterprise for its students. A more entrepreneurial outlook, creating partnerships with other entities that understand what we do and can be of mutual assistance, would move us forward on having broad, stable, and sustainable support for the IPL.

A Closer Connection to the Profession and Our Users

This may be the most important one of all. Reaching out to our colleagues in the library and information professions as well as to our users, understanding what they find of value in the IPL, how we can be better, and how we can take advantage of their talents and help can give to us the power that makes the Internet so strong—the power of distribution and cooperation.

As always, I'm optimistic about our future. The idea of an Internet Public Library has been a powerful one since the beginning, and has attracted interest and support from many quarters. I hope we can now move forward, expanding and improving what we do. These ideas and others can help us to serve our users more effectively, learn more about librarianship in the emerging information environment, and share those lessons with our colleagues.

CHAPTER 21

Public Libraries in the United States: Service to Business and Industry

BEVERLY P. LYNCH

In talking about the services the American public library provides to business and industry, I have been asked to talk particularly about the influence of the Internet and the World Wide Web on these services. After sketching briefly the origins and purposes of the public library in the United States, I will discuss some of the services that public libraries provide to business. I will conclude with comments on current issues and trends.

THE AMERICAN PUBLIC LIBRARY

William Frederick Poole, writing in 1876, defined the public library I am talking about. "The 'Public Library' . . . is established by state laws, is supported by local taxation and voluntary gifts, is managed as a public trust, and every citizen of the city or town which maintains it has an equal share in its privileges of reference and circulation" (476).

In 1790, the population of the country was 4 million people and there were 13 states—the original 13 colonies. By 1850, the population was 23 million people and there were 31 states. Today, the population of the country is more than 260 million people and there are 50 states. In the early years the country was sparsely populated, there was no organized postal system, and the idea of a free public education had not yet been accepted.

Libraries were connected generally with colleges or were organized by private societies. As the country grew, became industrialized and more ur-

Paper presented at the International Roundtable for Information and Library Science, Kanazawa Institute of Technology, Library Center, Kanazawa, Japan, 1997.

ban, the movement toward the establishment of the free public library developed.

There were libraries in the United States almost from the beginning of the colonies. (Harvard College, founded in 1636, had its library by 1638). Libraries were formed in some places by towns assuming to have the power to levy taxes and grant money before the enactment of any state law authorizing them to do so, but there were only a few of these. The American public library really was established in the middle of the 1850s.

Legislation that allowed a free public library to be established and maintained as a part of the regular educational system and supported by taxation was adopted first in New Hampshire in 1849. Other states followed: Massachusetts—1851; Maine—1854; Vermont—1865; Ohio—1868; Wisconsin—1868; Connecticut—1869; Iowa—1870. By 1876, more than 3,500 public libraries had been established and it was estimated that these libraries contained more than 5 million volumes. Today there are more than 15,000 public libraries in the United States (9,165 main libraries without branches, 1,254 libraries with branches, and 6,205 branches) with an estimated total of more than 656 million books and serial volumes in their collections.

The public library was designed as a circulating library available to all citizens, but it was designed especially for those people who were moving from the rural areas into the cities to work as mechanics, apprentices, and laborers. These were people who had no access to libraries or the books, periodicals, and newspapers that libraries were acquiring. Community leaders promoted the development of the public library supported by taxation, for they believed that there was a relationship between reading and the economic well-being of the community. A "List of Principal Books of Reference Important to be Used in Libraries" appeared in *Public Libraries in the United States of America: Their History, Condition, and Management* in 1876. The list includes such titles as *Coal, Iron, and Oil; or the Practical American Miner*, *Annual Record of Science and Industry for 1871–1875*, *Rudimentary Dictionary of Terms Used in Architecture* (688–710). These titles reflect works of interest and importance to the economic development of the community.

The distinguished public libraries of the United States were located in communities prominent in the industrial and trading areas: Boston—1852; Chicago Public Library—1872; Cleveland—1868; Detroit—1865. These libraries enjoyed great support from the community and from the influential industrial leaders. "Their special virtues in distributing economic and technical information were frequently singled out" as reasons for the strong support they received (Ditzion 1947: 110).

By the beginning of the 1900s, public libraries began to extend services more directly to the business community. John Cotton Dana, a president of the American Library Association (1895–1896) and a founder and the first president of the Special Library Association (1909), was the first to establish a business branch. In 1904, he opened the business branch of the Newark, New Jersey, Public Library in a location in the city's commercial center.

Its resources include[d] 13,000 books, maps of more than one thousand cities, towns, states, and countries of all parts of the world, seven hundred directories, which cover[ed] many thousand different towns and countries and scores of occupations; the latest publications of cities, counties and states on subjects of interest to Newark and New Jersey, ninety house organs, sixty trade union papers, ninety business periodicals, sixty municipal and local development journals; many volumes of statistics; a collection of the catalogs of 3,000 Newark manufacturers, very fully indexed; a good collection of modern fiction and of general literature. (1916: 214)

Dana also established services that offered prompt and efficient responses to the information needs of the business community: "A special telephone service which connects [the business branch] in an instant with the lending and reference center of the main library, or with its technical or school or art or fiction or order departments or with the central office; and—a messenger service through which it can get from the main library's collection of 180,000 volumes, in thirty minutes if need be, anything a patron calls for which the branch itself cannot supply" (1916: 214).

In the next several decades, other public libraries established separate collections and services for business. By the early 1950s, nearly 70 public libraries in the United States had specialized business services (Fenner 1953: 224); most were in cities of more than 100,000 population. Two forms of service design developed, the first being the separate business branch as in Newark, the second being a department within the main library building, as in Los Angeles.

In the 1960s and 1970s, strategic planning emerged as an important activity in many public libraries. This was often encouraged by the State Library Agency, which would offer financial assistance for planning activities. Government departments were encouraged to conduct needs assessments before any new service was designed or old service eliminated, and public libraries were encouraged to do this as well. As an example of such planning activities for business services, the California State Library, with monies from the Library Services and Construction Act, sponsored needs assessment studies in various California towns and cities. A needs assessment study was conducted in the cities of Pasadena and Pomona to identify the information needs of the business community, to learn how business people use the public library, and to determine the role the public library played in the development of the business community (Meyer and Rostvold 1969). Some of the recommendations of this study of Pasadena and Pomona are general enough to apply to other libraries seeking to establish services to the business community:

- The public library should be the first point of contact for the business person who needs information and whose company's information resources are inadequate to meet the needs.
- The public library should coordinate the library resources in the community.
- The public library should offer business services that are personalized, flexible, timesaving, and user-oriented.
- The public library should develop and implement an active marketing program to promote its services to the business community.

In the 1970s, led by the program of the Minneapolis Public Library, INFORM (Information for Minnesota), public libraries began to develop more specialized services for business and to do so for a fee. Fee-based information resources were designed in some libraries to meet more specialized information needs of businesses, governmental agencies, and others. In a survey conducted in the mid-1980s, 14 libraries reported that they provided programming to businesses for a fee; 968 libraries reported providing services to businesses at no charge; and 3,233 reported they did not provide organized programming for business groups (Heim and Wallace 1990: 59). The development of fee-based services at the public library, which is established and supported by taxation, has led public libraries to begin to analyze and establish the base level of service they provide without charge and then to set fees for other services that they would not otherwise provide. Each library determines its own approach and its own policies.

PUBLIC LIBRARY BUSINESS SERVICES

The continuing questions for the public library in the United States are whether the business services it provides are contributing value to the economic base of the community, the original purpose of the development of such services; whether these services are important enough to continue the tax support necessary to provide them; and whether there are new approaches to funding which must be considered, that is, attaching fees for service. Another question is whether the commercial information services and the availability of Web access from everyone's desktop will render business services obsolete in the American public library.

The users of the current business departments and business branches of public libraries include job seekers, inventors, entrepreneurs looking for new inventions to build and market, investors, consultants, students, consumers, corporate representatives, and researchers.

While most large corporations have their own corporate libraries, many of these libraries rely upon the comprehensive collections of the public library. Even when full-text materials are found online, they sometimes do not include graphs or charts that can be found only in the print versions. Most of the business users of public libraries, however, are small business owners—people who are seeking information about how to start their own business or who are seeking patents for products that could be marketed. Currently, the business services of the public library support the large corporate library in its need for detailed information, provide the small business person access to information that is not routinely available to the individual, and offer economic data and information to local community development agencies and other governmental departments that seek out new industries and businesses for the community.

Dun & Bradstreet Corporation reported that 170,475 new businesses were created in the United States in 1996, many of these small, entrepreneurial businesses.

Regular users of Seattle Public's business services include the approximately five hundred users daily who call, e-mail, or come in seeking company and industry information, as well as business people being trained in searching the Internet through formal classes or in one-on-one searches as part of the reference transaction. They include the private investor who has made millions in the past half-dozen years, the homeless man who lives in his car and arrives each morning to read the *Wall Street Journal*, the women members of several active investment clubs, the volunteers who use the Aeronautics History and Investments collections to develop programs for school children, and the trade leader who calls on the business librarians' help to research emerging markets worldwide as he prepares trade missions for Seattle's business and government leaders. (Thatcher 1997)

The Los Angeles Public Library's Economics and Business Department (LAPL) is one of the largest of its kind in the country. Business people using the LAPL are seeking information on exports and imports, business plans, investments, sales ideas, and Securities Exchange Commission files. In recent days, the library helped one person who researched companies currently marketing African-American dolls. She has since patented successfully and is marketing a doll of her own. Another wanted information to help him open a tortilla shop. Another wanted to know how to start an incense business; and another asked, "What companies sell sea urchins in Japan?"

The electronic information resources have expanded greatly the library's services. While users must come to the library to conduct their online searches, they can download information to their own disks or can print out information. The expansion of the online services has led the library to add more instruction in how to use these resources and the efficient methods of online searching.

In 1989, the Los Angeles County Public Library (a separate library from the Los Angeles Public Library) established "FYI," which is the library's comprehensive business information research service. Eighty-eight community libraries belong to the Los Angeles County Public Library, and the FYI services and products are available without charge to these libraries. Libraries e-mail, telephone, or fax their requests to the FYI office in Norwalk. These services have been very successful, and the library is planning to extend the program to small business development centers and economic development offices.

The FYI services and products also are available for a fee. People can approach the FYI directly for brief business profiles, which include market data on clients, sources of venture capital, opportunities, and potential employers; the cost of this service is $9.00. Community demographic profiles can be ordered, which include data on population, ethnicity, income, consumer spending habits, crime rates, and many other variables; the cost is $3.00 and up. Standard & Poor's Research Reports include detailed profiles on the largest publicly traded companies in the United States and provide stock information, industry reports, and financial data; the cost is $ 15.00. Trademark search packages are designed to help business people and entrepreneurs evaluate and register trademarks and business names. A variety of search packages are offered to meet all requirements. All FYI trademark searches include interpretative information to help the requester analyze and evaluate trademark search results. The searches come complete with the forms and instructions necessary to file for Federal Trademark Registration. The cost for this service ranges between $45.00 and $410.00. (In 1996, the United States issued 109,700 patents and 80,600 trademarks.)

The FYI service makes its fee-based services available to others around the country. Some of the requests it replied to in one week in December 1996 were:

- The effects of lead exposure on telephone cable workers for an environmental organization in Utah;
- Dun & Bradstreet's data on more than 10,000 company names for an insurance company in Texas;
- Five-year demographic projections at the census-tract level to a city in Wisconsin seeking to identify areas that would be at the greatest risk from juvenile crime in the future;
- Database of more than 2,500 businesses in the metal tubing industry for a manufacturer in Mississippi;
- Consumer spending patterns within a three-mile radius of a particular intersection in Oregon for a shopping center developer;
- Full descriptive trademark searches for companies in Oregon, Kansas, Texas, Nevada, and New York;

• Company profiles for a gaming company in Montana, a financial analyst in Florida, a city councilman in Tennessee, and to people going on job interviews in New York, Ohio, Illinois, Washington, and Missouri (Coffman 1997).

The developments in information technology have had a dramatic impact upon the services that the public library provides. The expansion of the services that the FYI program provides is a good example of the influence that the new technologies have had.

The availability over the Internet of information resources that formerly were only in print has changed the way the public library is providing business services. Many business librarians have identified their own portfolios of useful Web sites. With the growth of international trade, American resources have become more important to people working abroad, and foreign resources have become more important to U.S. business. The Los Angeles Public Library and the Seattle Public Library report that their international business resources are used to support local trade expansion to Asia and Latin America as well as to the emerging countries of Eastern Europe.

A survey of how business libraries in the United Kingdom made use of the Internet revealed that Internet use was expanding rapidly, but respondents commented that the amount of new useful business information was growing more slowly (Kelly and Nicholas 1996). Their concerns about the use of Internet resources in serving the business community mirror the concerns of others:

• Lack of organization and structure. The Internet needs better directories created by people who have knowledge of cataloging and indexing.
• Lack of reliable information. In service to business, the authority and reliability of the data are of chief concern. Tampering with the data would have a serious effect on the user of the data. In business librarianship, the source of the data is as important as the data itself. The need to verify company information will require the use of print resources.
• Too much information.

Connectivity to the Internet has been a priority in all public libraries in the United States, and most of the states and the state library agencies have made it their main objective. Grants and other forms of support have been provided to enable the public libraries to achieve connectivity. All large public libraries are connected to the Internet; it is reasonable to expect that within the next three years Web connectivity will be available to most libraries.

The development of electronic information resources has been phenomenal. As an example, university and public libraries in Georgia have available to them the following databases on Galileo: Georgia's Electronic Library, available to all libraries in Georgia:

- Periodical Abstracts, Research II, a database that offers about 1,600 journals in all fields and provides the full text of about 650;
- ABI Inform, a database that covers about one thousand journals in business and economics and provides the full text for about five hundred journals;
- Periodical Abstracts, which indexes five hundred general interest magazines with full text for 250;
- Business Dateline, a full-text database drawn from regional business magazines and the business sections of a variety of newspapers;
- Newspaper Abstracts, which provides indexing and abstracts for 29 U.S. newspapers.

These databases are not as specialized as the business services. I include them here to illustrate the development of electronic information resources, including full-text materials. Full-text resources, those that are mounted on servers directly available to remote users via the Web, are a new category of information resources; they are already providing a rich source of content. Some of the content, such as the press releases, speeches, and proclamations of the White House, has not been available or at least not easily available to libraries in the past. Other content, including such materials as the back files of the *Christian Science Monitor* and *Time* magazine, have been important print files in libraries. It is the creation of such full-text files, available free of charge on the Web, which raises the questions of whether library services to business will become obsolete.

CURRENT ISSUES AND TRENDS

The response of the American public library to developments in information technology is an amazing success story. Librarians learned the technology and applied it first to library operations, then to resource-sharing activities through shared databases. Many public libraries, through their automated catalogs, were the first public agencies in their communities to offer automated services to users. The quality of the automated services gave government officials in the states and in the communities confidence in assigning to the library other automation responsibilities.

In many communities, the public library was the first governmental agency to have an Internet connection and a home page. In several cities in California, the library has been made the lead agency for Internet-related matters. In Cleveland, which has connected patrons to information resources via the Internet since 1990, the library's electronic library has more than 12 million searches per year and is increasing by about 25 percent per year.

The activities in the United States to bring Internet access to all libraries and to the patrons who use the libraries are many and complex. The efforts in the state of Indiana are indicative of many others.

In 1995, the Indiana legislature appropriated $20 million annually for the 1995–1997 biennium for an Indiana technology fund to help schools and public libraries to use technology. Public libraries could apply for base-level grants up to $5,000 for libraries at the beginning level of technology; grants of $5,001–15,000 were available for libraries that already had some technology; and grants of $15,001–50,000 were available for libraries that could meet criteria for more advanced technology. Indiana libraries also could apply for grants to develop home pages on the Internet. The pages are organized into an Indiana public information database and stored on a server at the Indiana Cooperative Library Services Authority (INCOLSA).

The interests of various states in the development of statewide telecommunications and information networks grow. Some of these developments are public/private partnerships whereby the state government agrees to place all of its communications on the network and a private contractor agrees to build the statewide network. The development of the Kentucky Information Highway is a good example.

The Kentucky network is a statewide digital network providing for high-speed, high-capacity delivery of voice, data, video, image, and, in the future, radio transmissions. BellSouth is the prime contractor, coordinating with Kentucky's 19 other local telephone companies and LCI International, a long-distance carrier.

New York is another state with statewide policies relating to telecommunications capabilities in public libraries and connectivity: The Omnibus Technology in Education Act of 1996 requested a total of more than $900 million over five years to help create a statewide, comprehensive electronic learning community. Libraries are included in this proposal.

State planning in New York has been carried out in three phases. The first statewide library automation plan, issued in 1989, was to develop a virtual bibliographic database for all library materials in the state. The second plan, issued in 1993, emphasized the networking of bibliographic and other databases. Now, the statewide planning effort is concentrating on evaluation and determining content. It will address what content is on the statewide network and what content should be, and then establish guidelines for that (Smith 1996). Business information will be one of the content areas reviewed.

Telecommunications issues are central to the developments of future opportunities for libraries. The federal government, through the recent passage of the Telecommunications Act, has enabled the rate structure to be such that local public and school libraries will be able to use the technologies at lower rates than will be charged others. The rulings of the federal Communications Commission mandates discounts ranging from 20 to 90 percent, with bigger discounts for libraries and schools in rural, high-cost, and low-income communities. Libraries are expected to save up to $2.25 billion annually on telecommunications services beginning January 1, 1998. This regulation will allow public libraries to continue to build the programs essential to make the electronic resources as available to library users as the print resources have been.

Efforts to bring connectivity and Internet access to every public library and every citizen are continuing. There are funding issues that must be addressed, however, particularly if the tax-support base for the library is diminished. Even if the tax base is firm, the costs of electronic resources, in hardware, software, telecommunications charges, and maintenance and support costs, all require an increase in the public library's base budget.

There also are staff costs. A study conducted in public libraries in Florida reported that at least 50 hours of training and hands-on experience are necessary for a staff member to become competent in using the Internet in the service of library users. Most library staff participating in the study found it took a month of practice and use before they felt comfortable serving the public (Wilkins 1996).

Funding issues are the reason some public libraries have established cost-recovery services for business customers in the form of fee-based services and charges for services such as access to meeting rooms and library spaces for special events.

CONCLUDING COMMENT

Services to business identified by John Cotton Dana in 1904 included a special telephone service that connected the branch to the central library and a messenger service for speedy delivery of information. Public libraries now use the technologies of e-mail and fax, in addition to the telephone, to connect the business unit to the central library and to deliver information quickly. The Internet is an extension of early library efforts to serve the local business community.

The public library has continued to develop its collections in order to serve its local business community. Print resources were first. CD-ROM databases followed. Online resources with full-text capabilities now are being added. The next development will be careful consideration of content to be developed for use by the community. Georgia's Business Dateline, a full-text database drawn from regional business magazines and the business sections of a variety of newspapers, is a model.

The study of Pasadena and Pomona in relation to business information needs recommended that the public library do more to market its programs of services to business. This is a recommendation that emerges in many studies. Public libraries generally agree with the recommendation to make their services better known, and they do some publicity. Unlike a for-profit business, however, in which a greater volume of sales produces greater profit, the public library must continue to serve a larger volume of use with little, if any, increase in the human resources, space and technology, or collection resources essential to serve a larger volume. This is an interesting dilemma for the library. It is to the credit of the librarians working in business branches and business and economics departments that they can handle the present volume while bringing up, and thus learning, new online resources and instructing library users in how to use these new materials and technologies.

The continuing expansion of Internet access and the growth of resources available on it will lead libraries to develop new content useful to the local community, and make that content available online. The public library, with its experience and knowledge of the community, the technology, the resources available, and the needs for information will remain an important information center for people seeking business information.

REFERENCES

Coffman, Stephen. 1997. FYI: The County of Los Angeles Public Library Business Service. *Public Libraries* 35 (March): 87–88.

Dana, John Cotton. 1916. *Libraries: Addresses and Essays.* New York: H. W. Wilson Co.

Ditzion, Sidney Herbert. 1947. *Arsenals of a Democratic Culture: A Social History of the American Public Library Movement in New England and the Middle States from 1850 to 1900.* Chicago: American Library Association.

Fenner, Edward H. 1953. Business Services in Public Libraries. *Special Libraries* 44 (July–August): 222–27.

Heim, Kathleen M., and Danny P. Wallace, eds. 1990. *Adult Services: An Enduring Focus for Public Libraries.* Chicago: American Library Association.

Kelly, Sarah, and David Nicholas. 1996. Is the Business Cybrarian a Reality? Internet Use in Business Libraries. *Aslib Proceedings* 48 (May): 136–44.

Meyer, Robert S., and Gerhard N. Rostvold. 1969. *The Library and the Economic Community: A Market Analysis of Information Needs of Business and Industry in the Communities of Pasadena and Pomona, California.* Sacramento: California State Library.

Poole, William F. 1876. The Organization and Management of Public Libraries. In *Public Libraries in the United States of America: Their History, Condition, and Management. Special Report.* Washington, D.C.: Government Printing Office.

Smith, Frederick E. 1996. New York: The Electronic Doorway Library Initiative. *Library Hi Tech* 14: 25.

State of the State Reports Statewide Library Automation, Connectivity, and Resource Access Initiatives. 1996. *Library Hi Tech* 14(2–3): 9–352.

Thatcher, Anne B. 1997. Public Library Business Information Services: Value-added

Services or Superseded Relics? In *Business & Finance Division Bulletin* (a division of the Special Libraries Association), no. 105 (Spring): 39–46.

Wilkins, Barratt. 1996. Florida: Library Networking and Technology Development. *Library Hi Tech* 14: 89.

CHAPTER 22

Prognosis on Becoming Digital: Digital Information, Global Networks, and Business Education

WILLIAM D. WALKER

On May 2, 1996, the New York Public Library (NYPL) opened a major research center dedicated to business and science. During the five years that preceded the opening of the new Science, Industry and Business Library (SIBL), the NYPL staff made site visits to several hundred libraries and information centers worldwide, to gather input into the design of this new $100 million facility and program. Japanese libraries and librarians provided many excellent models for the New York project.

I am especially delighted to have been invited to Kanazawa by Professor Chiku for the 1996 Roundtable for Library and Information Science. I came to the Kanazawa Institute of Technology (KIT) at the outset of our planning process in 1991 to learn from Doctor Sakai and Mr. Moroya. That visit greatly influenced and expanded our thinking. We were excited by KIT's aggressiveness in information technology (IT) that manifested itself in state-of-the-art computer laboratories and classrooms, the use of robotics and advanced media servers, and digital library applications.

Many other Japanese organizations influenced our thinking. As a research library, the New York Public Library is always interested in the policies and practices of its peer institutions. The National Diet Library has been generous in sharing information about the organization of collections, reader services, and security. The digital library and information networking activities at the Toshiba Corporation provided NYPL with an important model for digitizing, filtering, and networking information resources. Also, the staff at JETRO (Japan External Trade Organization), both in

Paper presented at the International Roundtable for Information and Library Science, Kanazawa Institute of Technology, Library Center, Kanazawa, Japan, 1996.

Tokyo and in New York, contributed invaluable advice for the development of the New York Public Library's International Trade Information Service.

One of the primary customer segments served by our new Science, Industry and Business Library (SIBL) is business education, including faculty, students, and administrators. Not only does this Library provide access to a collection of more than 1.2 million volumes, but it also connects clients to many expensive, specialized business files that are often not available outside corporations and elite academic settings.

SIBL provides a dynamic testbed where one can observe the business users' acceptance of digital information systems. In an Electronic Information Center, the Library provides 130 networked workstations from which users can search more than 80 business databases mounted on NYPL servers, access more than seven hundred full-text electronic business journals, search the library's online catalogs, tap into humanities and social sciences files, access OCLC's First-Search databases, and use Internet resources via broad bandwidth (T3) connections. Another one hundred workstations are distributed throughout the Center's reading rooms and other public areas. Furthermore, seats at all reading tables are wired with both power and data to allow users to connect their laptop computers to the Library's Novell network.

The business community expresses a clear and strong preference for, and acceptance of, the digital medium. Of the 2,600 users who come to SIBL each day, 1,700 users come to consult business resources. A staggering 91 percent of these business clients use at least one electronic product or data file—in addition to the online catalogs—providing concrete evidence that electronic information is now a core business tool.

This is not to say print resources have been abandoned. More than 65 percent of SIBL's users also consult at least one print resource. What has emerged is a seamless and integrated use of media—print and electronic. However, the SIBL experience signals the transition toward ubiquitous digital information systems.

OVERVIEW

This paper reports on the distribution of digital information, digital networks, and their impact upon business education and training. For this overview, most examples are drawn from the cutting-edge graduate business education programs in the United States, such as Harvard, Wharton (The University of Pennsylvania), Northwestern, Michigan, Columbia, and the University of California at Berkeley, all institutions with a history of global leadership. It seems highly likely that the information technology and digital distribution strategies adopted by these bellwether schools will be copied and used by the greater global business education community.

To provide a framework from which conclusions can be drawn regarding the impact of the digital revolution upon business education, this paper examines the following areas:

- The cultural differences that have influenced business communication patterns and information use;
- The organization of business education and training; and,
- The evolution of electronic business information resources and networked distribution.

From a review of these three areas and a look at some recent innovations in business education technology, roundtable participants should be able to develop a number of hypotheses regarding the status and future of virtual business systems.

THE GLOBAL CULTURAL CONTEXT

In today's global marketplace, one can send information from one side of the world to the other—instantaneously and in real time. Thanks to satellite links and advanced telecommunications infrastructure, business and financial information can be distributed securely to all parts of the world. Yet, from country to country—and often from one subnational level to another—business communities are behaviorally diverse and heterogeneous. Cultural and political differences can greatly affect the value assigned to business information as a tool for analysis, decision making, and marketing. Cultural values also help to explain why there traditionally has been almost a complete lack of formal business training, business libraries, and business information infrastructures in certain parts of the developed world.

Anthropologist Edward T. Hall has established models based on cultural use and perception of time, space, and communications by dividing society into two groups: low-context cultures and high-context cultures (Hall and Hall 1989). These models can help information scientists understand how much information is enough, information gathering preferences, and favored sources of information, such as friends and colleagues, libraries, or digital pipelines.

Low-context cultures, most of them northern, include North Americans, Germans, Swiss, and Scandinavians. These cultures are explicit, direct, and linear when conducting business. As long as the channels of communication are clear, a business transaction need not involve personal relationships. It's about getting a job done, going forward, and making money. Low-context cultures are generally also achievement cultures.

In a low-context culture, one does not need to know people before conducting business with them. From this, one can conclude that the low-context cultures might be the first to embrace electronic commerce, and current activity in the electronic marketplace validates this thinking.

High-context cultures, which are all the others—Asian, Mediterranean, Central European, Latin American, African, Arab, and American Indian, are affiliation cultures. People are more important than schedules and projects. High-context people get their information from other people with whom they stay in constant touch to absorb news and information. The value-added, personal perspective provided by "human newsfeeds" is important. Furthermore, high-context cultures do not need contracts, except to set a general direction; the details will evolve after the contract is signed. Relationships, honor, and retaining power are more important than business.

Hall provides us with an interesting framework for the consideration of business education, networked information, and information use. Businesses in low-context cultures tend to use published and digital information resources to make business decisions. Facts and data stream from networks to business and commerce where they are used to monitor the competition, to develop models of predictability which determine investment, and to leverage a leading edge in the marketplace.

In contrast, high-context cultures have not usually seen a critical need for business libraries or for business information. In Italy, for example, many domestic business decisions have been based primarily upon relationships with other people, rather than on linear data. Not unexpectedly, in high-context cultures there is a relatively small expenditure on business information resources, and there has not been a priority placed on business training.

As global economies strive to emulate the mega-economies of Germany, the United States, and Japan (by the way, a hybrid of both low- and high-context business [Hall and Hall 1987]), there will be increased migration to the information consumption patterns of low-context business cultures. Migration to information-informed best practices, decision making, and business education will be necessary to successfully participate and compete in the global marketplace.

BUSINESS EDUCATION AND TRAINING

While cultural contexts can influence business behavior, formal education redirects and advances business protocols and behavior through applied learning techniques, internships, and instruction. Career-long ethics, practices, and preferences are grounded in the formal, intensive education experience.

U.S. Business Education in the 1990s

In the United States, business training occurs at the undergraduate, master's, and doctoral levels in more than seven hundred colleges and universities. The premier business program is the two-year, full-time program, which leads to the MBA (Master's in Business Administration) degree. Many schools have also established an Executive MBA Program that enables senior executives from corporations to pursue an intensive, work-related syllabus. In the Executive MBA Program, students typically attend classes only one day per week, while continuing to work full-time for their employers the other four days of the workweek.

In the United States, business training also takes place outside the university, especially when the focus is on small business development and entrepreneurship. Independent learning and mentoring programs thrive in government-sponsored Small Business Development Centers, public libraries, and small business incubators. Often these programs are self-paced, employing self-guided print and multimedia resources to support business start-up and growth.

The Master's Program

The MBA is strictly an American invention, and the course of study has proven to be highly effective in developing top managers, leaders, and visionaries. Corporations from around the world send their best and brightest employees to American MBA programs, making the typical business school class remarkable for its global diversity.

The graduate business school curriculum addresses the *applied* science of business. Most business schools start students with modules of foundation courses in the functional areas of finance, statistics, accounting, management, marketing, and operations. It should be noted that considerable digital content is already available to support each of these core business school disciplines.

There are several aspects of the first year's program that characterize the learning experience:

- Incoming classes are usually divided into sections of approximately 50 students who take classes together, study together, and work together on projects and in teams. Students consider this bonding experience to be an essential part of business school.
- In the business school, much of the learning comes from other students during class discussions.
- Almost all business school assignments include a research component that requires the use of the library or computer center resources. Students are motivated to complete research as quickly as possible, since the first-year curriculum is over-

programmed, stressful, and competitive. Digital information accessed over campus-wide networks is the preferred means of obtaining information, since it offers a convenient and rapid solution.

The second-year curriculum is usually less intense than the first, with a lighter course load. Students select electives in areas of concentration, such as management or marketing. However, the major focus in the second year becomes the job search, with many on-campus interviews and presentations to recruiters. Even the job search process has taken on virtual dimensions, with corporations using teleconferencing facilities and World Wide Web links to brief and interview potential employees. For a country as geographically large as the United States and in the global corporation, virtual recruitment provides obvious benefit for both corporations and job-seeking students.

Business school students have a reputation for being highly motivated— many in search of power and money. As a group, students are also extremely entrepreneurial. The May 6, 1996 *Wall Street Journal* reported that a growing number of students now start successful businesses based on class projects in product development. Many of these projects are IT-related, with increasing use of Internet applications for research and marketing.

THE BUSINESS SCHOOL IT ENVIRONMENT

Dr. Elaine Didier, associate dean of the University of Michigan's Horace Racham Graduate School and the former associate dean for information at the School of Business, recently remarked that only three years ago we still were dreaming of a universal workstation to enhance business instruction, research, and learning. She observed that today, in 1996, we have pretty much realized this objective through online library catalogs, electronic archives of full-text business journals, fully networked campuses, client/server software, and broad connectivity to the World Wide Web.

Didier was one of the first business school information professionals to understand clearly the impact that information technologies can have upon transforming and, in part, displacing the traditional business school library. At Michigan's Business School Library in the early 1990s, she promoted experimentation with full-text digital archives as a surrogate to business journals. Concurrently, she supported that merger of the library with the business school's computer center; Didier anticipated the confluence of information delivery channels, and she focused on an integrated program for the distribution of electronic information, regardless of the source.

Most students entering business school already have corporate work experience, and they are comfortable with high-end electronic information delivery systems and sophisticated corporate library services. Consequently, student expectations also run high, and they assume that the business school infrastructure will be at least equal to the corporate benchmark. Business schools deliver. They have strong motivation to provide state-of-the-art information technologies. As schools compete with one another for the best students, they use high-tech capabilities to demonstrate standards of excellence.

Across the United States, students entering business schools are expected to have advanced personal computer skills, including experience with spreadsheet and financial software, database search engines, statistical packages, and presentation programs. Most schools now require that students own a personal computer or laptop. For example, the Columbia University School of Business has wired classrooms, enabling students to connect their laptops to the campus-wide network from any location in order to participate in interactive electronic presentations and real-time, problem-solving exercises.

Readers of this paper who are interested in greater detail can survey on the Web the levels and types of electronic resources available in many of the business schools' library and computer center facilities.

DIGITAL BUSINESS CONTENT AND APPLICATIONS

The business training community profits from the wealth of digital content generated by the global business community. Global business is a leading producer and consumer of electronic information. For business, information is most often a commodity rather than a public good. When information is relevant to the bottom-line profit, consumers are willing to pay high fees for access, and this, in great part, accounts for the proliferation of high-end, digital information retrieval systems and networks in the business sector.

Given the current explosion of business information products, it is ironic that the development and distribution of electronic business information was slow and unmanaged during the 1970s and 1980s.

The biomedical community was clearly the front-runner in providing significant access to electronic information. By 1980, large numbers of health science libraries in the United States—small hospital libraries as well as large medical school libraries—were routinely accessing the National Library of Medicine's MEDLINE database. Access costs to this U.S. government–supported resource were relatively modest. Furthermore, the National Library of Medicine accepted the responsibility for indexing the world's biomedical literature, and the Library supported programs to train librarians as search analysts.

In contrast, business school libraries in the 1980s showed little evidence of joining the electronic information age. Only the best-funded institutions had access to commercially produced databases through the for-profit, dial-access search systems.

However, during the final years of the 1980s, as the personal computer became a standard desktop and library resource, CD-ROM technology became the major distribution conduit for business information.

THE EVOLUTION OF TRADITIONAL BUSINESS INFORMATION SYSTEMS

Pre-Internet, electronic business resources can be classified within five hierarchical levels: (1) automated databases that evolved from print index products; (2) full-text resources; (3) numeric and statistical data files; (4) real-time business information systems; and (5) hybrid and filtered information services.

Electronic Indexes and Abstracting Services

The electronic indexes and abstracting services were among the first electronic resources to be made available to the business education community. From the outset, distribution was—and continues to be—primarily through libraries. The earliest editions were simply mechanized versions of the print indexes that were made available through second parties, including dial-access bibliographic retrieval systems such as DIALOG and DataStar.

However, database producers quickly realized the economic advantages of direct distribution to a broader audience via CD-ROM subscriptions. The two leading producers of the type of database, University Microfilms, Inc. (UMI) and the Information Access Company (IAC), aggressively marketed *ABI/Inform* and the *General Business File* to the entire range of business libraries in the academic, public, and corporate sectors.

Today, these two vendors continue to be primary suppliers of Western Hemisphere core electronic business information, and each vendor has enhanced its basic product by adding full text. Each also is investing heavily in Web distribution to directly reach audiences of end-users, without the library as an intermediary. Most U.S. business school libraries make these full-text virtual business libraries available at no charge to their clientele because the products deliver high customer satisfaction. Students and faculty embrace the convenience of having the resources on their desktops, and it appears that these files meet a high percent of the literature needs of the business school community.

Full-Text, CD-ROM Databases

Business school libraries and corporate information centers also provide a wide offering of full-text files and reference resources, including electronic versions of newspapers such as the *Wall Street Journal*, the *Financial Times*, and *Commerce Business Daily*. The publication of electronic directories and reference tools has skyrocketed, and certain products now only appear in electronic format, such as the *National Trade Databank*, a file that contains original market research undertaken by U.S. embassies overseas.

Over the past several years, most schools have purchased multiple-site licenses and have mounted these products on CD-ROM servers. Yet, CD-ROM disks are cumbersome to manage and the CD server technology has been unstable and expensive. Consequently, the information industry is aggressively investigating the distribution of these products over secure Internet links.

Numeric and Statistical Data

To support marketing and forecasting projects, many universities have mounted large numeric and demographic magnetic tape files as part of business school and social sciences computer center services. Software packages allow users to retrieve data, which they manipulate to create new information, often in graphical formats, as is the case with Geographic Information Systems (GIS).

Numeric systems also feed students' assignments. Students routinely pull specific data sets and time series down from the campus-wide network; these data provide the content for specific assignments, such as developing models for foreign trade or projecting long-term forecasts of markets.

Real-Time Business Information Systems

"Real" business places high value on real-time information systems, since financial and investment decisions *must* be based on up-to-the-second market activity and business news. In response to this need, a variety of online newsfeeds, real-time investment analysis tools, and specialized information systems have been developed for the business market, including the *Dow Jones News/Retrieval* online research service, LEXIS, and NEXIS.

There is considerable incentive for the information industry to give the business schools special pricing for access to these high-end resources since early use tends to establish a preference for a particular product. For example, Dow Jones makes its online systems available at a substantially reduced "educational" rate to many business schools, and students often favor Dow Jones as their cyberlink-of-choice as they enter the workforce.

During the past five years, many U.S. business schools have emphasized global business. Links to international electronic resources supplement domestic information offerings. For example, Columbia University's Watson Business School Library provides an online connection to NIKKEI Telecom, the Japanese News & Retrieval System, in order to connect faculty and students to Japanese and Asian markets.

Hybrid Business Tools

At the highest end of the hierarchy are resources that are typically marketed only to the corporate and financial communities that need specialized content or digital systems with value-added indexes, access points, or software filters. They are briefly mentioned here because they complete the spectrum of resources, and business education will adapt the best features of these systems.

Traders on every trading floor in the United States have access to "The Bloomberg," an information system for analyst and investor. Proprietary multimedia terminals integrate information sources and mixed media, including the *on-demand* retrieval of multimedia news and reports; 24-hour broadcast news; worldwide shares, options, converts, and warrants; historical trends; and current and projected analysis.

A second hybrid system, which provides selective dissemination of information (SDI), has become popular within the New York banking community. SandPoint's "Hoover" is software that filters electronic data from multiple sources and posts results automatically to users' electronic mail boxes. The value of these passive SDI information search systems has not yet been fully recognized, but as the amount of digital content grows, the potential for filtered information systems is considerable in both the commercial and the educational markets.

TRANSFORMING TECHNOLOGIES

Over the past decade, the five types of electronic resources reviewed above have only supplemented the amount and level of content offered by business libraries, but they have not been insignificant. Many institutions lacked adequate business resources to support the curriculum. Access to digital content has allowed these programs to make large electronic archives available on a just-in-time basis, ensuring a more equitable distribution of information to everyone engaged in business training, regardless of the venue. Nonetheless, these commercially produced business systems have had little impact upon the business school syllabus or curriculum.

Today, the dynamic growth of the World Wide Web is inducing fundamental change in information services and education. The question facing business schools is not whether the Web will play a role, but how the Web will encourage new models of electronic curriculum and distributed online services. Faculty and students have lost no time in developing pioneering applications for business training and development. The leading business schools already have adopted Internet tools (search engines, browsers, and HTML resources) to establish "Intranets"—internal networks which are quasi-proprietary and which emulate Web interfaces and resources.

In this familiar Web shell, faculty members are authoring digital curricula that are interactive; producing digital handouts, media presentations, and reading lists; and programming functions to solicit online polling and student feedback.

In most business schools, students have mounted electronic portfolios on home pages to provide prospective employers with resumes and other presentations of personal and experiential background. Business students are also forming Internet clubs to encourage business development that exploits Internet connectivity to reach target audiences. The impact of the Internet and Web on business education is multifaceted, if unmeasured, but very dynamic.

The following three examples illustrate the types of pioneering Web products that are emerging in the business education environment.

The Harvard Business School Technology and Operations Management Group © Electronic Curriculum

The Harvard Business School's (HBS) Technology and Operations Management Group has developed an electronic curriculum for the course "Designing, Managing, and Improving Operations." Any "Netizen" (a citizen on the Internet) can access the general syllabus for the course, but only members of the registered HBS community can view specific details of the curriculum, the assignment, and class handouts.

Regular classes for this course are held either in the classroom or the computer lab. However, the digital curriculum provides students with electronic versions of the case studies that will be discussed in class, hyperlinked readings, slide presentations via PowerPoint or Acrobat viewers, and interactive student voting modules to determine levels of consensus. Using the latest multimedia applications, cases are offered to students using streamed digital videos and Java presentations. In addition, students are connected to their faculty and to one another via e-mail; they can access working papers as members of an electronic community, and are able to connect to the electronic resources on the campus-wide network, including the resources made available by Harvard's Baker Library.

Within the narrow context of this Harvard pilot, two things stand out: first, digital technology and networked distribution are becoming mainstream resources; second, the role of the library, especially as a physical place, increasingly fades into the background.

The Iowa Electronic Markets

The faculty of the University of Iowa College of Business manages the Iowa Electronic Markets (http://www.biz.uiowa.edu/iem/index.html). This

Internet resource allows actual investors to buy real-money futures where contract payoffs depend upon economic and political events such as elections. Sample U.S. markets currently include the Microsoft Price-Level Market, the 1996 Presidential Election Market, and the 1996 Republican Convention Market. International markets include various political events in Austria, British Columbia, and Russia.

This project is maintained as a teaching and research tool, and investments are open to university and college staff, faculty, and students. Investments are made with real money, ranging from U.S. $5 to $500. The developers believe that by using real money for trading, there is an increased motivation to learn about the underlying fundamentals.

University of California at Berkeley, Haas School of Business Student Projects

The business school marketing curriculum provides exceptional opportunity for the development of prototype digital projects. The third example of IT at work in the business school setting comes from the University of California at Berkeley, Haas School of Business, where students have been leaders in harnessing digital resources to exploit the Internet as a basis for commercial project development. Because the Internet gives direct access to an online audience of customers with no geographic barriers, many Haas students are turning class assignments into actual internal businesses.

The Haas course "Marketing in a Digital Age" has the objective "to enhance students' understanding of the implications of interactivity and convergence in media as well as the impact of the Internet."

The students' marketing projects use Web, broadcast, and other information technologies. For example, one project provides an application that observes Web-user virtual "comings-and-goings" through the tracking and analysis of "click-stream behavior" and user registration. Other projects in this course focus on market research opportunities via kiosks and the global broadcast media in China.

HTML, Java, and Netscape software powerfully enhance traditional business information presented on the Internet. Instructors can make theoretical topics come alive through interactive programming. Students can author and "publish" projects, and then place their work immediately in the hands of the electronic community and marketplace. In this brave new world of the Web, important content comes from many sources, not just the commercial publishing sector.

MIGRATION TO THE WORLD WIDE WEB

Web technology is so seductive that it may well emerge as the dominant distribution media for most commercial and governmental business information files. Two Web files, StockMaster and EDGAR, demonstrate the trend of high-end product migration to the Internet, and since their appearance on the Web, these files have become primary resources for business education.

StockMaster (http://www.stockmaster.com/) provides recent stock market information, including previous day's closing prices and one-year graphs of historical prices, which can be displayed by searching by name of company or the ticker symbol. The Standard & Poor's Comstock service provides the quotes and historical trends. StockMaster also contains an interactive market research module that polls users for an indication of confidence in a stock's performance during the next three months. As recently as three years ago, one could not have anticipated wide and open electronic access to this level of professional resource. EDGAR (http://www.sec.gov/edaux/archivix.htm), the Electronic Data Gathering, Analysis, and Retrieval system, is one of the most successful and important business Web products. All American public companies listed on the stock exchange must file annual reports and financial statements (called 10Ks) with the government agency that regulates business practice, the U.S. Security and Exchange Commission (SEC).

EDGAR has transformed both the collection and distribution of this information. Launched in 1994, it allows for the automated collection, validation, indexing, acceptance, and forwarding of reports by companies. EDGAR filings are posted on the Web site 24 hours after the date of filing.

Pre-EDGAR, the government handled the distribution of and access to the SEC filings poorly. For years, the only logical way to obtain SEC filings was to buy expensive microform or CD-ROM versions from third-party publishers, and the education community often could not afford these services. Now, the Web version provides broad and equitable access to company information for educational communities around the world.

DISTANCE LEARNING AND INFORMATION BUSINESS TRAINING

The convergence of information and broadcast technologies has prompted considerable interest in university-sponsored distance learning initiatives. Focusing on student communities who are off-site and often quite geographically remote, these programs support prototype and Executive MBA programs. At the University of Michigan, a videoconferencing classroom supports the distance learning program from which instructional programs can be broadcast to the off-site student body. In addition to the telecast instruction, students benefit from electronic library and information resources and networked client-server applications such as Oracle and Paradox. Periodically, students travel to a Michigan campus for face-to-face seminars and course work.

Purdue University's Krannert Graduate School of Management also runs a distance learning MBA program that is underpinned by an electronic curriculum. While the University of Michigan distance learning program is domestic, Krannert's "virtual" student body is international. Teamwork continues to be important, even in the context of distance learning. Here students work in virtual teams, communicate and even have arguments using e-mail, and make virtual presentations to other remote members of the class and to the faculty.

At the outset of this paper, there was a brief discussion of business training outside the university setting. Increasingly, there is demand in the United States for self-paced programs of instruction, which provide applied basics for business start-up or for self-education to support re-entry into a downsized job market. Digital and multimedia programs are responsive in this information-training context. Distance learning approaches and networked information resources make an appealing partnership for ensuring that specialized business training can be distributed to all who seek it.

PROGNOSIS FOR THE DIGITAL REVOLUTION IN BUSINESS EDUCATION

The digital revolution in business education and training is already well under way. Colleges and universities have made substantial financial investments to deploy information technology and networked infrastructures, and most sites of business training are very much "electronic places." Faculty and students are beginning to interact with one another dynamically through the technologies of group-ware, electronic collaboratories, and teleconferencing.

Business is accepting, even welcoming, the electronic revolution. As we have seen, abundant and important digital content exists, and large amounts of new electronic knowledge and data are archived every day. Technology and information are indeed primary tools of business.

Early pilots indicate that electronic curricula will become a core component of business education. Yet, a complete instructional revolution in business education is not assured. Shirley Alexander, from the Sydney University of Technology, has explored why new information technologies fail to live up to initially high expectations for their ability to improve learning and teaching. Too frequently, the focus is placed on the features of the new technology. Alexander observes that "these features are then used to provide a learning experience that is often essentially the same as that provided using existing technologies, and (if evaluative studies are carried out at all) there is surprise when the expected learning gains are not realized" (1995).

If networked connectivity and digital content are to become catalysts for changing business education practices and instruction, brand new pedagogic models must be invented and integrated into the curriculum. Barry Diller, multimedia entrepreneur and a trustee of the New York Public Library, has observed that to obtain successful results in the interactive digital universe, one must redefine, not simply repackage. Diller emphasizes that "redefining the mission of your ventures is slow, brain-bending work."

Yet, business and management are themselves the masters of re-invention. In this era of learning organizations and Total Quality Management, businesses are constantly engaged in redefinition. I predict that the business school community will be one of the first groups to make major advances in innovative, interactive, digital instruction. The IT foundation is in place and the climate is ripe for acceptance. Several other trends are emerging:

- The business education community has already embraced digital library resources and they have often displaced the traditional library collection as the primary resource for reference and research. In order to remain viable, the library must exploit roles in training, content development, and the navigation of electronic resources.
- I predict that the distribution of business information on CD-ROMs will be completely overtaken by the World Wide Web within three years. Business and its educational community will embrace interactive, real-time, networked archives.
- There will be an unimagined proliferation of Web resources in business, management, marketing, law, and international trade. Currently, publishers in the financial industries are demonstrating that a relatively secure Web site can be maintained. The allure of interactivity for marketing, presentation, and research will encourage rapid growth.
- Networked resources in business and commerce that are now available on the Web free will migrate to pay-for-access platforms. Both business and business education communities will be willing to pay for access in return for validated, accurate, and edited content.
- Finally, in the next 10 years, distance learning will not, after all, dominate business education. The traditions of case debate, team negotiation, and learning through interaction are intrinsic to the spirit of American business education. Distance learning technology will not provide an acceptable substitute.

Earlier in this paper, it was noted that a chief characteristic of the business school class is the international makeup of the student body. A colleague who recently completed her MBA program observed that perhaps the most important lesson learned in business school was a lesson in global and cultural understanding. In her team, she was required to study with, negotiate with, and debate with students from Asian, European, and African backgrounds. She recognized that only the day-to-day, face-to-face interaction forced by long days and late nights together brought about an understanding of how to manage effectively in the global marketplace. The human intercourse of business, commerce, and management will continue to be a driving force in the marketplace and for business education.

In spite of my prediction that distance learning will not emerge as a replacement for the classroom, I have no doubt that advances in virtual reality will certainly prove me wrong in the near future; and when the technology is at our doorstep, I am certain that business will be first in line to embrace its applications.

Ladies and gentlemen, as information professionals, we are fortunate to be working during a time of immense opportunity and change. It has been a pleasure to speak this afternoon to this distinguished audience. I am deeply appreciative to have had your support for our work at the New York Public Library, and I hope that you will allow your New York colleagues to return your most gracious and professional hospitality.

REFERENCES

Alexander, Shirley. 1995. *Teaching and Learning on the WWW*. Available from http://www.lamp.ac.uk/~alh/alexandr.html.

Hall, Edward T., and Mildred Reed Hall. 1987. *Hidden Differences: Doing Business with the Japanese*. Garden City, N.Y.: Anchor Press/Doubleday.

———. 1989. *Understanding Cultural Differences*. Yarmouth, Maine: Intercultural Press.

Index

Abstracting services, 323
Accessioning, of information, 135
Accuracy, of archival records, 178, 181
Accursius, 46–47
Acland, Glenda, 177, 178
Advanced Projects Research Agency (ARPA), 248
Advisory Committee on the National Information Infrastructure, 27
Air Pollution Distance Learning Network (APDLN), 260
Albert R. Mann Library (Cornell University), 174
Alcorn, Louise, 293
Alexander, Shirley, 329
Alphabet: as three-dimensional space, 44–45; transparency of, 47
American Chemical Society (ACS), CORE study of journals, 70–73
American Library Association Committee on Accreditation, 159
American Memory program. See National Digital Library (NDL) Program
Ameritech Foundation, 220
Amicus database, 235

Anderson, Rachael K., 155–69
Andrew W. Mellon Foundation, The, 63, 65, 101–2, 106, 199–200, 249
Anglo-American Cataloging Rules (AACR), 52, 55
Appraisal, of information, 135
Archives: defined, 176–78; government-sponsored, 173–74; requirements for electronic, 178–82; security of, 61. See also Preservation
Arms, William, 175
Armstrong, Arthur, 137
Association of American Universities, 106
Association of College and Research Libraries, mission statement, 18–19, 24
Association of Research Libraries (ARL), 104, 106, 164; preservation and, 148–49
Atkins, Daniel E., 244–52
Attention-structures, 129–30
Australia, 28
Authority, 3, 6–7
Authors: intellectual property laws and, 111, 114; interactive media and, 119; preservation and, 151–52;

represented in electronic books, 42;
self-publishing of, 199
Avram, Henriette D., 53

Baker, Nicholson, 73
Bancroft Library (University of Califor-
nia at Berkeley), 171, 183–84
Barlow, John Perry, 195
Battin, Patricia, 207
Bear, Greg, 37
Bearman, David, 178, 182
Bellardo, Lewis J., 177
Bellardo, Lynn Lady, 177
Bellcore, 75, 123
Berry, J., 164
Besser, Howard, 149, 150
Biagoli, Bario, 111
Bibliographic Instruction, 19–20
Bibliography. *See* Knowledge, organi-
zation of
Bibliothèque nationale de France, 65
Bidlack, Russell, 247
Bishop, William Warner, 247
Black, Donald V., 50
Bok, Derek, 23
Bonn, Maria, 294
Books, electronic, 40–48; described, 41–
43, 44; implications of, 46–48
Brand identity, of library, 90
Braude, Robert, 161
British Library, 65
Brodman, Estelle, 160
Bronson, Po, 130
Brown University, 189, 202–5
Budgeting, 14
Business, library services to, 304–14;
current, 307–11; historical, 306–7;
real-time information, 324–25
Business Dateline, 313
Business education. *See* Education,
business

CA*Net 2, 240–41
California at Berkeley, University of:
business education, 327; Farm Security Administration photographs at,
171, 183–84

California at San Francisco, University
of, 65
Campbell, Jerry D., 49–62
Campbell, Laura, 213–24
Canada, 225–43; diverse nature of,
225–27; infrastructure/funding in,
240–43; Internet use in, 28; library
issues, 227–29; National Library of
Canada, 230–35; other initiatives,
235–37; Task Force on Digitization,
237–40
Canadian Initiative on Digital Librar-
ies, 229–30
CANARIE (Canadian Network for the
Advancement of Industry and Edu-
cation), 240–41
Carlyle, Thomas, 188
Carnegie-Mellon University, 102–3
Carolina Power and Light, Inc., 260
Carter, David, 288, 290
Castells, Manuel, 116
Catalogs, electronic, 10–11, 143, 144
Catherwood Electronic Archive (Cor-
nell University), 174–75
Catherwood Library (Cornell Univer-
sity), 174–75
CD-ROM databases, 323–24
Chain of custody, 179–80
Chodorow, Stanley, 3–15
Citations, 6, 8
Civic networking, 32
Cleveland, Harlan, 195, 196
Cleveland, Ohio, 311–12
Clinton administration, 27, 125
CLIO Plus, 20–21
Coalition for Networked Information
(CNI), 22
Coalition on Reinventing Information
Science, Technology and Library Ed-
ucation (CRYSTAL-ED), 248–49
Codex Justinianus, 46–47
Collaboratory for Research on Elec-
tronic Work (CREW), 249–50
Collections, 11–12, 200; budgetary re-
strictions on, 21; business, 313; inte-
grating digital resources into, 93–94;
Internet Public Library and, 288–91,
299; of Library of Congress, 221–22;

library's role in development of, 157; of National Library of Canada, 231–32, 238–39

Columbia University: business education, 322, 324–25; *ClioPlus*, 20–21; dual reporting at, 22; instruction at, 24–25; publishers and, 22–23

Commerce, U.S. Department of, 125

Commission on Preservation and Access, 172

Community Access program (CAP), 241

Community service, of higher education: impact of networks on, 30–34, 36–37; network challenges to, 38–39

Completeness, of archival records, 178, 180

Connectivity costs, 228

Content, of information, 133

Content licenses, 140–42

Context, of information, 133, 134–35

Continuous growth model, 194–95

Contract, dependence on, 140–42

Copyright: alternatives to, 199–200; challenges of, 61; commercial control, 87; costs, 79; legal definition, 111; librarians' education and, 163–64; Library of Congress and, 222–23; licenses and, 140–42; National Library of Canada and, 239; print technology and, 109–10. *See also* Intellectual property

Copyright Recordation and Deposit System (CORDS), 215

CORE Project, 70–73

Cornell University: CORE study, 72; government documents published by, 174–75; preservation and, 153; scanning costs at, 64–65

Costs, of resources: book storage, 65, 75–76; digital storage, 63–69; digitizing, 222, 228; public library, 312–13; purchase, 188–89, 198–200; space, 202–3, 205; support, 200–202; undergraduate education and, 32. *See also* Economics; Economics, electronic publishing issues

Council on Library and Information Resources (CLIR), 153

Culbertson, Don S., 50

Cultural Heritage Initiative for Community Outreach Project (CHICO), 249

Culture, business education and, 318–19

Cummings, Anthony, 64, 199–200

CUPLE (Comprehensive Unified Physics Learning Environment) Physics Studio, 272–73, 280–81; structure of, 277–78; typical class, 278–80

Curricula. *See Education entries*

Customization, of digital technology, 123

Dana, John Cotton, 305–6, 313

Database Privacy Directive of the European Union, 117

Databases: full-text, 323–24; structures, 161–62

Data creators. *See* Authors

Davidsen, Sue, 289

Death and Life of Great American Cities (Jacobs), 94

De Gennaro, Richard, 163–64

Dependence on contract, 140–42

Didier, Elaine, 321

Diebold, John, 87–88

Digital Archiving Working Group, 151–53

Digital coherence, 245

Digital Collections: A Strategic Policy Framework for Creating and Preserving Digital Resources (Arts and Humanities Data Service), 151

Digital documents, 111, 117–20. *See also* Information, digital

Digital expressive space, 41–47, 48

Digital information. *See* Information, digital

Digital libraries: advantages of, 69–73; challenges facing, 87–89; marketing techniques applied to, 89–91; as resource providers, 91–92; unfulfilled predictions about, 85–87

Digital Millennium Copyright Act
(DMCA), 117, 120, 124–25
Digital storage: advantages of, 64, 69–
73; economic efficiencies of, 63–69
Digital technology. *See* Information
technology
Diller, Barry, 37, 329–30
Distance education, 166; business in-
formation and, 328–29; North Caro-
lina State University and, 253–56,
258–63; North Carolina State
University libraries and, 263–70
Distributed repositories, 138–40
Ditzion, Sidney Herbert, 305
Doctrine of fair use, 114
*Documents in the Digital Culture:
Shaping the Future*, 117
Doi, Teruo, 113
Dougherty, Richard M., 55
Dow Jones, 324
Drucker, Peter, 77, 128–29
Dual reporting, of librarians, 22
Duderstadt, James, 247
Duranti, Lucianna, 178, 179

Ecker, Joseph, 273
Ecology of information. *See* Resources
Economics: librarians' knowledge of,
163–64; models of, 93–94; of preservation, 128, 136–44
Economics, electronic publishing issues,
95–107; future and, 104–7; in general, 95–96; globalization and, 116–
17; librarians' analysis of, 101–3;
publishers' version of, 96, 100–101;
scientists' version of, 96, 97–99;
value chain and, 120–22. *See also*
Costs, of resources
Eddy, Edward D., 257
EDGAR (Electronic Data Gathering,
Analysis, and Retrieval), 327–28
Edison Project for Communicating
Chemistry (Columbia University), 24–
25
Education, business, 316–31; cultural
context of, 318–19; distance learning
and, 328–31; future of, 329–31; information technology evolution and,
321–25; Internet resources, 325–28;
New York Public Library and, 316–
17; structure of, 319–22
Education, of librarians, 159–65, 244–
52; "crisis" in, 244–45; health science examples, 165–68; opportunity
and, 245–47; specific areas, 161–65;
training and, 57, 59–60; at University of Michigan, 247–52
Education, of library users, 77, 158;
Internet Public Library and, 293–94
Education, public school: Canadian,
241–43; NDL Program, 216–18
Education, undergraduate, 16–20; digital expressive space and, 48; impact
of networks on, 30–38; intellectual
property laws and, 113–14; knowledge economy and, 130; lecture
method, 273–77; as mature industry,
255; networks and, 31–39; new
methods needed, 187–88; research libraries and, 18–25; as role of uni-
versity, 18–25, 131; studio method,
272–73, 277–81. *See also* Distance
education
Education, U.S. Department of, 249
Egan, D., 123
Egan, Dennis, 72
Eisenstein, Elizabeth L., 124
Electronic indexes, 323
Electronic Library, 115–16
Electronic World (Lanham), 129
Eliot, T. S., 107
Elsevier Science Publishers, 102, 103
Encoded Archival Description (EAD),
143, 144
Encryption, 120, 124
England: business libraries in, 310; In-
ternet use in, 28; preservation in,
151–53
Entertainment services, higher educa-
tion and, 37–38
Exhibits: Internet Public Library, 294;
Library of Congress, 215; National
Library of Canada, 232
Expressive space: ancient, 46–47; digi-
tal, 40–48

Fair use doctrine, 114
"Falling through the Net: Defining the Digital Divide" (Department of Commerce), 125
Farber, Evan, 19–20
Farm Security Administration, 170–71; records location, 171–72, 182–84
Febvre, Lucien, 115
Feith, Johan, 176–77
Fenner, Edward H., 306
Field, Francis Bernice, 55
Filling the Pipeline and Paying the Piper (ARL), 106
First Amendment. *See* Freedom of speech
Fisher, Janet, 100–101
Fixity, of information, 133–34
Freedom of speech, 111–12, 113–14
Frost, Kendra, 294
Fruin, Robert, 176–77
Fuller, S. S., 157
Fuller, Steve, 97
Fullilove, Robert D., 277
Full-text databases, 323–24
Funding, 163–64, 247–49
Furlong, Mary S., 121
FYI services, Los Angeles County Public Library, 309–10

Garson, Lorrin, 100
Genre, of digital technology, 123
Georgia: Business Dateline, 313; Electronic Library, 310–11
Germany, 28
Getty Center of Los Angeles, 149–51
Gilder, George, 129–30
Ginsparg, Paul, 64, 98, 105, 139–40
Gladwell, Malcolm, 127
Global economy, 116–17
Global Legal Information Network (GLIN), 215
Gore, Daniel, 202
Gould, John, 73
Government Depository Library program, 173–74
Government records, 170–85; Farm Security Administration photograph locations, 170–72, 182–84; purpose of

locating in libraries, 173–74; records, defined, 176–78; records, requirements of, 178–82; universities and, 174–75
GPO (Government Printing Office) Access, 174, 184
Graham, Peter, 133, 178, 181
Grauer, Neil, 136
Graves, Bill, 276
Gregor, Dorothy, 52
Griffiths, J. M., 75
Growth models, 194–95
Gulia, Milena, 121

Haas, Warren, 162
Haas School of Business (University of California at Berkeley), 327
Hagel, John, 137
Haigh, Susan, 225–43
Hall, Edward T., 318, 319
Hall, Mildred Reed, 318, 319
Halloun, I. A., 275
Harnad, Stevan, 64, 97–98
Harvard Business School Technology and Operations Management Group ©, 326
Harvard University, 65
Havelock, Eric, 47
Hawkins, Brian L., 61, 187–210
Hawthorne effect, 281
Health science libraries/librarians, 165–67, 322
Hedstrom, Margaret, 178
Hegerty, Kevin, 52
Heim, Kathleen M., 307
Hestenes, D., 275
Heterick, Robert, 188
High-context cultures, 318, 319
High-Energy Physics bulletin board, 64
Higher education. *See* Education, undergraduate
Hill, Will, 75
Hillstrom, Kevin, 66
Hire Wire Press, 140
Hirtle, Peter B., 170–86
Hof, Robert, 137
Hoffman, M., 70
Huber, Mary, 77

Hypertext markup language (HTML), 121

IBM, 260
Idea of the University: A Reexamination (Pelikan), 131–32
Ideas, as property, 112–14
Illinois at Chicago, University of, 166
Illinois at Urbana-Champaign, University of, 166
Illustrations: missing, 70; retrieval of, 74–75
Indexes: electronic, 323; of resources, 143, 157–58
Indiana, 312
Indiana University, 166
Information: flow of, 56; growth rate of, 196–97. *See also* Knowledge
Information, digital: created by library, 91; economics of, 63–69; effect on scholarship of, 3–8; integrating into collections, 93–94; integrity of, 133–36; and library organization, 9–13; migratory/living nature of, 5–8, 98; organization of, 157–58; preservation of, 4–5, 7, 12–13; types of, 213–14. *See also* Government records; Information technology; Records
Information Access Company (IAC), 323
Information Infrastructure Task Force, 27
Information retrieval/distribution systems: costs of, 78–80; as free service, 66, 68–69; future of, 158; size of, 66–68
Information technology: applied to libraries, 51–54; growth of, 50–51; Internet Public Library and, 287–88, 299–300; in research libraries, 20–25. *See also* Storage, digital
Innovation, Malthus and, 192
Instruction. *See Education entries*
Integrity: of archival records, 178, 179–80; of information, 133–36
Intellectual property, 109–25; digital document defined, 111, 117–20; economic value and, 120–22; future of,

124–25; intellectual value and, 122–24; and knowledge economy, 115–17; legal/historical context, 109–15. *See also* Copyright
Intellectual value, 122–24
Intellectual virtues, 131
Interface design, 158–59
Internet: business information, 325–28; media coverage of, 27; size of, 28–29, 68–69; value chain of, 120–22. *See also* Networks
Internet Archive, 149
Internet Public Library (IPL), 283–303; concept/mission, 283–86; design, 296–98; evaluation, 298–301; future of, 301–3; organization of, 286–96
Inter-university Consortium for Political and Social Research (ICPSR), 143
Into the Future (film), 153
Iowa Electronic Markets, 326–27

Jacobs, Jane, 94
Jacobson, R. L., 158
Janes, Joseph W., 283–303
Japan: copyright law in, 113, 114; Internet use in, 28
JETRO (Japan External Trade Organization), 316–17
Johns Hopkins University, 17, 22–23, 167
Journals: costs, 63–69; distribution and pricing, 103–4; economic issues, 95–107
JSTOR (Journal Storage Project), 65, 140, 249

Kahle, Brewster, 149, 172
Kellogg Foundation, 217, 247–48
Kelly, Sarah, 310
Kenetics of systems, 192
Kenney, Anne, 64
Kentucky, 312
Kerr, Clark, 17
Kerr, Nigel, 287
Kilgour, Frederick G., 52, 53
King, D., 75
Klein, M., 78

Knowledge: and creation of progress/ wealth, 112, 113; management of, 116; organization of, 161–62; zones of, 34–35. *See also* Information; Information, digital

Knowledge economy: emergence of, 128–31; intellectual property and, 115–17; preservation and, 131–32

Konno, Noboru, 116

Krannert Graduate School of Management (Purdue University), 328–29

Lagowski, Joe, 276

Lange, Dorothea, 171–72

Lanham, Richard A., 40–48, 129, 130

Lave, Jean, 121

Law, librarians' knowledge of, 163–64

Laws, Priscilla, 275, 276, 277

Learning. *See Education entries*

Lecture method of undergraduate instruction, 273–77

Legace, Nettie, 288

Legislative information: Canadian, 236–37; foreign, 215; United States, 214–15

Lehmann, Klaus-Dieter, 133

Leighton, Philip D., 202

Lesk, Michael, 63–81

Letters. *See* Alphabet

Levine, Arthur, 255

Librarians: demographics and, 160; dual reporting of, 22; economics and, 101–3, 105; future role of, 155–57, 164–65, 167–68, 286; Internet Public Library services to, 292–93; professional status of, 18; recruitment of new, 160; as research team members, 12, 13–14; as shapers of body of knowledge, 9–10, 11–12; shared resources and, 11. *See also* Education, of librarians

Libraries: application of digital technology to, 50–54; consortial environment, 13–15; distance education and, 263–70; as function, not place, 156; future of, 75–76; government information in, 173–74; health science, 322; impact of digital technol-

ogy on, 55–61; intellectual property law and, 112, 113, 117, 125; issues facing, 227–29; organization of, 9–13, 55–60, 92; as place, not function, 30–31, 296–98; preservation and, 127–45, 148–53; role of, 178–79; socioeconomic context of, 54; staffing of, 13–14, 157–59, 314; in value chain, 120, 122. *See also* Digital libraries; Public libraries

LibraryNet, 242

Library of Congress: Farm Security Administration photographs in, 171, 183–84; NDL program, 215–24; THOMAS program, 214–15

Library Resources and Technical Services, 50, 52

Library-use instruction movement, 19–20

Life of the mind. *See* Education, undergraduate

Liming, Lee, 288

Lindberg, Donald, 165

Litan, Robert E., 117

Long Now Foundation, 149–51

Los Angeles County Public Library, 309–10

Los Angeles Public Library, 308, 310

Low-context cultures, 318–19

Lowry, Charles, 102

Lyman, Peter, 109–26, 149, 150

Lynch, Beverly P., 304–15

MacDonald, William M., 277

Malthus, Thomas, 187, 188; overshoot concept of, 191–97

Management: librarians' knowledge of, 163–64; technology's impact on, 55–56

Mandel, Carol, 52

Mann Library (Cornell University), 174

Manual for the Arrangement and Description of Archives (Muller, Feith, and Fruin), 176

Maple Calculus Course, 273

MARC (Machine Readable Cataloging), 52, 143

Marcum, Deanna B., 148–54
Marketing techniques, 89–91
Market segments, identifying, 90
Marshall, Joanne, 163
Martin, H-J., 115
Martin P. Catherwood Library (Cornell University), 174–75
Marx, Gary T., 121
Mason, Ellsworth, 53
Mason, Jeff MacKie, 106
Master's in Business Administration (MBA) programs, 320–21
Masys, D. R., 156
Matheson, Nina W., 206
Mayfield, M. K., 160
Mazur, Eric, 275
McClennen, Michael, 290
McClintock, Robert, 23–24
McCoy, Ralph E., 50
McDaniel, C. K., 277
McKemmish, Sue, 178
McKnight, Cliff, 70
Meadows, Donella H., 192, 197, 206
Medical Library Association (MLA), 159–60, 163
MEDLINE database, 322
Mellon Foundation, The, 63, 65, 101–2, 106, 199–200, 249
Meyer, Robert S., 306
Michigan, University of, 247–52; business school library, 321; distance education, 328, 329. *See also* Internet Public Library (IPL)
Microforms, 88–89
Migration, of information: accuracy and, 181; preservation and, 135–36
Miller, Jacquelyn, 175
Miller, James G., 192
Minsky, Marvin, 41, 42
Missouri, University of, 166
Mitchell, Thornton W., 179
M-Link, 289
Mon, Lorrie, 291
Motives of Eloquence, The (Lanham), 43–44
Muller, Samuel, 176–77
Multimedia, 122

Museum of African American History, 294

Naisbitt, John, 52
National Aeronautics and Space Administration (NASA), 248
National Archives and Records Administration, 173; Farm Security Administration photographs and, 171, 182–83; new mission of, 175, 177
National Diet Library, 316
National Digital Library (NDL) Program: American Memory pilot, 215–17; expanded archive, 217–18; funding, 219; future of, 220–23; Learning Page, 218; management of, 219–20; strategy, 218–19
National Library of Canada, 230–35; digitization projects, 232–33; electronic collection, 231–32; infrastructure, 234–35; links, 233; policies/standards, 234; virtual Canadian union catalog (vCuc), 233–34
National Library of Medicine (NLM), 165, 322
National Research Council, 134
National Science Foundation, 144, 248
National Technological University, 262
Natural right philosophy, 114
Naylor, Bernard, 101
Network Notes, 234
Networks: educational missions and, 30–39; historical context, 29–30; status of, 27–29
New Deal Network, 172, 184
Newman, John Henry, 207–8
New York, 312
New York Public Library's Science, Industry and Business Library, 316–17
Niblack, W., 74
Nicholas, David, 310
Nonaka, Ikujiro, 116
Norman, Donald, 130, 145
NORTEL, 260
North Carolina at Chapel Hill, University of, 166
North Carolina State University: about, 256–58; distance education

and libraries, 263–70; distance education history, 253–56, 258–59; distance education objectives, 259–63
Norton, Margaret Cross, 179
Nunberg, Geoffrey, 118, 119
Nutter, Susan K., 253–71

O'Donnell, James, 98, 99, 100, 101
Odlyzko, Andrew, 64, 98–99
Okerson, Ann B., 95–108, 139, 142, 199
Online Computer Library Center (OCLC), 10, 11, 52–53
Open standards, 123–24
Oregon State University Information Sharing Project, 175
Organization, of libraries: changes in structure, 92; technology's impact on, 55–60
Overshoot concept, 191–97

Pack, Theodore P., 60
Parker, Josie, 291
Parker, Ralph, 50
Partnerships: of educational institutions and community, 36–37; strategic, 90–91
Pasadena, California, 306–7, 313
Patent law, 110
Peer review, as cost, 97, 100
Pelikan, Jaroslav, 131–32, 201, 208
Perreault, Jean, 50
Personius, Lynne, 64
Peters, Paul Evan, 26–39
Philosophical self, 44
Pittsburgh, University of, 167, 181, 182
Pixlook interface, 71, 72
Platform for Change (MLA), 159
Pomona, California, 306–7
Poole, William Frederick, 304
Popper, Frank, 119
Post-Capitalist Society (Drucker), 128–29
Powell, Walter W., 111
Preservation, 127–45, 148–53; ARL and, 148–49; as basis of university, 131; CLIR and, 153; of digital infor-

mation, 123; economics of, 128, 136–44; in England, 151–53; Getty Center and, 149–51; knowledge economy and, 128–32; libraries and, 128, 132–36, 159; Library of Congress and, 222; National Library of Canada and, 232; by scanning, 65–66. *See also* Archives
Preserving Digital Information: Report of the Task Force on Archiving of Digital Information, 102, 133, 136, 137, 139, 148, 179–80
Print media, contrasted with digital, 118–19
Private central self, 44
Process patents, 110
Property. *See* Copyright; Intellectual property
Proprietary standards, 123
Protein Science, 100
Provenance, of information, 133, 134
Psycoloquy, 64, 97
Public interest, intellectual property law and, 111, 112, 113
Public library: business services of, 307–11; business service trends, 311–14; history of, 304–7. *See also* Internet Public Library (IPL)
Public ownership, of information, 206
Public relations, of Internet Public Library, 294–96
Public social self, 44
Publishers/publishing: as basis of university, 131; conglomerate, 87; content licenses and, 142; electronic publishing and, 100–101, 138–39; libraries and, 22–23, 54, 92; owning works in perpetuity, 93–94
Purchase costs, 198–200
Purdue University, 328–29

Rand Corporation, 153
Reader, digital technology and, 118–19, 123. *See also* Education, of library users
Real-time business information services, 324–25
Records: accuracy, 178, 181; complete-

ness, 178, 180; defined, 176–78; integrity, 178, 179–80; usability, 178, 181–82. *See also* Government records

Recruitment, of librarians, 160

Redish, Edward F., 277

Reed-Scott, J., 164

Reference services: future of, 158; Internet Public Library and, 288–91

"Regaining the Public Trust" (Bok), 23

Rensselaer Polytechnic Institute, studio model education at, 272–81

Repositories, of information, 138–40

Research: as basis of university, 131; librarians and, 162–63; networks and, 30–35, 38–39. *See also* Scholarship

Research Libraries Group, 172

Research Library Information Network (RLIN), 10, 11

Research university. *See* Universities

Resources, 187–209; availability of, 187–91; new systems needed for, 197, 205–9; overshot concept and, 191–97. *See also* Costs, of resources

Retail services, higher education and, 37–38

Retrieval systems, 142–44

Rhetorical self, 44

Robinson, Peter, 66

Roper, F. W., 160

Rosenfeld, Lou, 283

Rostvold, Gerhard N., 306

Rothenberg, Jeff, 153

Rothstein, Arthur, 171

Rubin, Michael, 77

Rudolph, Frederick, 17

Ryan, Sara, 288

Samuelson, Pamela, 110

Scanning, of literature, 65–66

Scepter interface, 72

Scholarly communication, 94

Scholars, sheltered from economics, 105

Scholarship: effect of new information sources on, 3–8, 10; passive nature of, 24. *See also* Research

SchoolNet, 241–43

School of Information Library Studies (University of Michigan), 247–52

Schultheiss, Louis A., 50

Scientists: and electronic publishing's economic issues, 96, 97–99; sheltered from economics, 105

Scott, Marianne, 238

Searching: CORE Project study of, 70–73; ease of, 64; need for new methods of, 73–75

Seattle Public Library, 310

Self-publishing, 199

Shakhashiri, Bassam, 247

Sigmoid growth model, 194

Simcox, Schelle, 288

Sloan, Elaine, 16–25

Smith, Adam, 115

Smith, Frederick E., 312

Society of Mind, The (Minsky), 41–43, 44

Soete, George, 149

Software, intellectual property rights and, 110

Sokoloff, D., 275

South Carolina, University of, 166

Space costs, 202–3, 205

Springer-Verlag, 103

Staff, 13–14; future skill requirements of, 157–59; of public library, 314

Standards, technical, 123–24

Statistical data, 324

StockMaster, 327–28

Storage, digital: advantages of, 64, 69–73; economic efficiencies of, 63–69

Strong, William S., 113

Studio Calculus program, 272, 273, 278; conclusions about, 280–81

Studio method of undergraduate instruction, 272–73, 277–81

Subject expertise, of librarians, 162

"Subversive Proposal, The" (Harnad), 97–98

Summers, Bob, 291

SuperBook interface, 71–72, 73

Support costs, 200–202

Swackhamer, G., 275

Swain, Leigh, 225–43
Swire, Peter P., 117

Task Force on Archiving of Digital Information. *See Preserving Digital Information*
Taube, G., 64
Taylor, Bradley, 294
Teaching. *See Education entries*
Technical skills, of librarians, 161
Technology, Diebold's stages of, 87–88. *See also* Information technology
Telecommunications and Information Infrastructure Applications Program, 27
Telecommunications services, regulation of, 312–13
Television, educational, 258–59
Text Retrieval Evaluation Conference (TREC) series, 73–74
Thatcher, Anne B., 308
Thesauri, 158–59, 161
They're Not Dumb, They're Different! (Tobias), 273
THOMAS program (Library of Congress), 214–15
Thornton, Ron, 275
Three-dimensional behavioral space, 41–42, 44–45; example of, 45; "fly-through," 45–46
"Time and Bits: Managing Digital Continuity" (Lyman and Besser), 149
Timeliness, of digital technology, 122
Tobias, Sheila, 273
Toshiba Corporation, 316
TOTE Program (Textile Off-Campus Televised Education), 262
Training. *See Education entries*
Treisman, Phillip, 277
Truxall, Richard, 292
Two-dimensional symbolic space, 41–42
Typography, electronic media and, 45

Undergraduate curriculum. *See* Education, undergraduate
United Kingdom. *See* England

United States: business education in, 320–22; Internet use in, 28; legislative information of, 214–15
Universities: government information distributed by, 174–75; growth of, 17–18; library competition in, 207; library role in, 77; purposes of, 131. *See also* Education, undergraduate
University Microfilms International (UMI), 102, 323
University movement, 17–18
Upper Atmospheric Research Collaboratory (UARC), 250
Upward, Frank, 178
Usability, of archival records, 178, 181–82
Usage patterns, identifying, 90

Value, of digital technology: economic, 120–22; intellectual, 122–24; libraries and, 91, 93
Value chain, of information, 120–22
Vanderbilt University, 167
Varian, Hal, 106
Video-Based Engineering Education program (VBEE), 262
Virnoche, Mary E., 121
Virtual Canadian union catalog (vCuc), 233–34
"Virtuoso" Group, 242–43
Vision space, 246
VolNet, 242

W. K. Kellogg Foundation, 217, 247–48
Walker, William D., 316–31
Wallace, Danny P., 307
Washington University, 166
Waters, Donald J., 65, 127–47
Wealth, intellectual capital and, 115–16. *See also* Value chain
Wealth of Nations, The (Smith), 115
Weber, David C., 202
Weingarten, F. W., 159
Wellman, Barry, 121
Wells, M., 275
Welsh Medical Library (Johns Hopkins University), 167

Wenger, Etienne, 121
Wheeler, Joseph L., 60
Whitaker, Gilbert, 247
Wilder, S., 160
Wilkins, Barratt, 313
Wilson, Jack M., 272–82
Window on Physics (WinPhys)
  object-oriented modeling system,
  279–80
Wolpert, Ann J., 85–94

World Intellectual Property Organiza-
  tion (WIPO), 117
World Wide Web. *See* Internet
Wriston, Walter, 115, 116, 120

Yale University, 102
Youth, Internet Public Library and,
  285, 291–92

Zones of knowledge, 34–35
Zuboff, Shoshana, 115–16

About the Contributors

RACHAEL K. ANDERSON has retired as director of the Health Sciences Library at the University of Arizona. She is former president and board member of the Medical Library Association.

DANIEL E. ATKINS was dean of the School of Information and Library Studies at the University of Michigan and remains on the faculty. He is co-author of *Managing Digital Information: Preparing for the Future.*

JERRY D. CAMPBELL is chief information officer and dean of the university libraries at the University of Southern California. He was chair of the USC Presidential Commission on Distance Learning and is the author of "The Case for Creating a Scholar's Portal to the Web: A White Paper."

LAURA CAMPBELL is associate librarian for strategic initiatives at the Library of Congress. She led the National Digital Library program to put the contents of the Library's rare and unique historical collections on the Internet. She has consulted in management, strategic planning, and information technology.

STANLEY CHODOROW is vice president of academic affairs for Questia Media, Inc. He chairs the board of the Council on Library and Information Resources and is a member of the board of the Center for Research Libraries. He is a medieval historian and co-author of *A History of the World.*

SUSAN HAIGH is assistant library network specialist at the National Library of Canada. She has been on the Digital Library of Canada Task Force and is responsible for planning, content development, and partnerships.

BRIAN L. HAWKINS is president of EDUCAUSE. Before that, he was vice president for academic planning and administration at Brown University. He co-authored (with Patricia Battin) *The Mirage of Continuity: Reconfiguring Academic Information Resources for the 21st Century*.

PETER B. HIRTLE is associate editor of *D-Lib* magazine and co-director of the Cornell Institute for Digital Collections. He is the author of "The National Archives and Electronic Access" in *The Record: News from the National Archives and Record Administration*.

JOSEPH W. JANES is an assistant professor in the Information School at the University of Washington. He has lectured on uses of the Internet and information technology, and he is the author of *The Internet Public Library Handbook*.

RICHARD A. LANHAM is president of Rhetorica, Inc. and professor emeritus of English at the University of California, Los Angeles. He is the author of *A Handlist of Rhetorical Terms*.

MICHAEL LESK is division director of the Division of Information and Intelligent Systems at the National Science Foundation and is the author of *Practical Digital Libraries: Books, Bytes and Bucks*.

PETER LYMAN is a former university librarian and current faculty member of the School of Information Management and Systems at the University of California at Berkeley. He is the author of "What Is the Place of Computer Literacy in Liberal Education?" in *Rethinking Liberal Education*.

BEVERLY P. LYNCH is director of the Senior Fellows Program of the School of Education & Information Studies at the University of California, Los Angeles. She is the editor of *The Academic Library in Transition: Planning for the 1990's*.

DEANNA B. MARCUM is president of the Council on Library and Information Resources. She was dean of the School of Library and Information Science at The Catholic University of America, and director of public service and collection management at the Library of Congress. She is the author of *Good Books in a Country Home* (Greenwood Press, 1994).

SUSAN K. NUTTER is vice provost and director of libraries at North Carolina State University. She worked on the M.I.T. Project INTREX and contributed to *Realizing the Information Future: The Internet and Beyond.*

ANN B. OKERSON is associate university librarian of Yale University and has been on the editorial boards of *Serials Review* and *EJournal.* She is co-author of *Gateways, Gatekeepers, and Roles in the Information Omniverse.*

PAUL EVAN PETERS was executive director of the Coalition for Networked Information until his death in 1996.

ELAINE SLOAN is vice president for information services and university librarian at Columbia University. She is a member of the International Federation of Library Associations and Institutions' Section of Information Technology Committee, and a trustee of the Columbia University Press.

LEIGH SWAIN is director of International Dataflow and Telecommunications at the International Federation of Library Associations and Institutions, housed at the National Library of Canada.

WILLIAM D. WALKER is senior vice president and Andrew W. Mellon director of the Research Libraries at the New York Public Library. His research includes medical libraries services, and he is the author of "Physical Access to Library Resources" in the *Handbook of Medical Library Practice*, 4th edition.

DONALD J. WATERS is program officer for scholarly communications at the Andrew W. Mellon Foundation. He was the first director of the Digital Library Federation. He co-chaired the Task Force on Archiving of Digital Information and was the editor and principal author of the Task Force report.

JACK M. WILSON is professor of physics and director of the Anderson Center for Innovation in Undergraduate Education at Rensselaer Polytechnic Institute. He is the author of "CUPLE: The Comprehensive Unified Physics Learning Environment."

ANN J. WOLPERT is director of libraries at the Massachusetts Institute of Technology. Before that she was executive director for library and information services at Harvard University.

DATE DUE